Understanding the Greek Revolution
(1821–1832)

Historical Materialism Book Series

The Historical Materialism Book Series is a major publishing initiative of the radical left. The capitalist crisis of the twenty-first century has been met by a resurgence of interest in critical Marxist theory. At the same time, the publishing institutions committed to Marxism have contracted markedly since the high point of the 1970s. The Historical Materialism Book Series is dedicated to addressing this situation by making available important works of Marxist theory. The aim of the series is to publish important theoretical contributions as the basis for vigorous intellectual debate and exchange on the left.

The peer-reviewed series publishes original monographs, translated texts, and reprints of classics across the bounds of academic disciplinary agendas and across the divisions of the left. The series is particularly concerned to encourage the internationalization of Marxist debate and aims to translate significant studies from beyond the English-speaking world.

For a full list of titles in the Historical Materialism Book Series available in paperback from Haymarket Books, visit: www.haymarketbooks.org/series_collections/1-historical-materialism.

Understanding the Greek Revolution (1821–1832)

New Approaches in Social, Political and Cultural History

Edited by
Elias Kolovos and
Dimitris Kousouris

Haymarket Books
Chicago, IL

First published in 2024 by Brill Academic Publishers, The Netherlands
© 2024 Koninklijke Brill NV, Leiden, The Netherlands

Published in paperback in 2025 by
Haymarket Books
P.O. Box 180165
Chicago, IL 60618
773-583-7884
www.haymarketbooks.org

ISBN: 979-8-88890-509-8

Distributed to the trade in the US through Consortium Book Sales and
Distribution (www.cbsd.com) and internationally through Ingram
Publisher Services International (www.ingramcontent.com).

This book was published with the generous support of Lannan
Foundation, Wallace Action Fund, and the Marguerite Casey Foundation.

Special discounts are available for bulk purchases by organizations and
institutions. Please call 773-583-7884 or email info@haymarketbooks.org
for more information.

Cover art and design by David Mabb. Cover art is a detail from *Construct
83, William Morris, Vine, 1873-4 / Theo van Doesburg, Counter-Composition
VI ,1925*, acrylic on wallpaper mounted on canvas (2024).

Printed in the United States.

Library of Congress Cataloging-in-Publication data is available.

The authors of this volume dedicate the book to
our colleague, scholar, and friend,
Professor Vassilis Kardasis,
in recognition of his profound insights and dedication
to the study of Greek history
and the history of the Greek Revolution

∵

Scene from the Greek War of Independence. Second siege of the Acropolis by the Greeks (November 1821–June 1822). Assault on the Serpentze on November 24, 1821.

PAINTING BY DEMETRIOS AND PANAGIOTIS ZOGRAFOS, UNDER THE GUIDANCE OF YANNIS MAKRIYANNIS. 1839. PUBLIC DOMAIN.

Contents

Preface

In 2021, Greece celebrated the second centenary of the Greek Revolution of 1821. This volume collects new research on the history of the Revolution by researchers who were involved in the project '200 years after the Greek Revolution' of the Hellenic Open University (2018–20), directed by Professors Vassilis Kardasis (2018–19) and Odysseas-Ioannis Zoras (2019–20). Professor Nikos Kotaridis was responsible for the academic supervision and coordination of the research.

The research project was generously funded by the Hellenic Open University, the Hellenic Parliament Foundation for Parliamentarism and Democracy, the Hellenic Petroleum, the Independent Power Transmission Operator in Greece, Alpha Bank and Eurobank.

Chronology

1814: After the surrender of Napoleonic France on 30 May, the Congress of Vienna (September 1814 to June 1815) establishes the Conservative Order against the revolutionary wave of 1789; against the tide, at the end of 1814, in Odessa (in mod. Ukraine), three Greeks of rather humble origins found a secret Friendly Society ('Philike Etaireia') with the aim of working for a revolution of the Greeks against their Ottoman lords.

1818: The secret headquarters of the Friendly Society are transferred to the Ottoman capital of Istanbul and the Society starts a successful campaign to initiate large numbers of new members both in Istanbul and the Greek Lands.

1820: Alexander Hypsilantis, officer of the Russian army of Greek origins, present at the Congress of Vienna as Lieutenant of the Tsar, accepts an offer to secretly lead the Friendly Society.

1820, October: Alexander Hypsilantis and the leaders of the Friendly Society secretly meet in Izmail (in mod. Ukraine) and agree on a plan for launching the Greek Revolution in the Peloponnese.

1821, 26–9 January/7–10 February: Gregorios Dikaios, also known as Papaflessas, emissary of Alexander Hypsilantis, meets with prominent Greek members of the Friendly Society in Vostitsa (mod. Aigio) announcing to them the plan of the Revolution and the imminent arrival of the leader; those Moreot notables present in Vostitsa do not accept the invitation of the Ottoman Governor Deputy to gather in Tripolitsa (mod. Tripoli, Peloponnese) in mid-February.

1821, 22 February/6 March: Alexander Hypsilantis, having changed the revolutionary plan, crosses with a few men the river Prut, the border between the Russian and the Ottoman Empire, and arrives in Iaşi, the capital of the Principality of Moldavia (mod. Romania), announcing the Greek Revolution (24 February/8 March); when the news reaches the Congress of Laibach (mod. Ljiublana, Slovenia), the Tsar repudiates the former Russian officer (14/26 March).

1821, 22 February/6 March: Hurşid Ahmed Pasha, the Ottoman Governor General of Rumelia, having arrived from the Peloponnese in Trikkala, on his way to Ioannina, in order to fight against Tepedelenli Ali Pasha, sends a report with alarming news from the Peloponnese to the Ottoman capital.

1821, 12/24 March: When the news from the rebellion of Alexander Hypsilantis, together with an alarming report from the Peloponnese, reaches the Ottoman capital, a furious Sultan Mahmud II, after the Friday prayers, orders the Janissary Agha to massacre his Greek Orthodox subjects; prominent Greek Orthodox notables of Istanbul (Phanariots) had already escaped the capital in order to save their lives from the Ottoman retaliations and the Greek Orthodox Patriarch had repudiated the rebellion.

1821, 15/27 March: The news of the declaration of the Greek Revolution by Alexander Hypsilantis in the Danubian Principalities arrive in the Morea, giving the signal for a general uprising, culminating on 25 March.

1821, 10/22 April: After a series of executions of Greek Orthodox in Istanbul, Sultan Mahmud II gives the order for the public hanging of the Greek Orthodox Patriarch, Gregorios V, who, being of Peloponnese origin, is charged with alleged participation in the rebellion of the Greeks.

1821, 18/30 April: The islands of Spetses, Hydra, Psara declare that they are willing to fight for the independence of the Greek nation against the Ottoman 'tyrants': the three islands transform some of their merchant vessels to the Greek revolutionary fleet.

1821, 22 or 23 April, 4 or 5 May: After a successful rebellion in the southern part of Rumelia (*sancak* of Evripos), the revolutionary captain Athanasios Diakos is captured in the Battle of the Alamana (mod. Spercheios) Bridge and executed in Zitouni (mod. Lamia). His head and the banners of the revolutionaries are sent to Istanbul to be exhibited outside the Topkapi palace.

1821, 20 May/1 June: A combined effort of the Greek revolutionaries of the Morea and the navy from the islands of Hydra and Spetses to capture Lepanto and Patras is held off; Yusuf Muhlis Pasha saves 20,000 Albanian Muslims of the town of Lalas, escorting them to the fortress of Patras (11–12 June).

1821, 1–3/13–15 June: After an effort of the revolutionary Greek navy to foment rebellion in Ayvalık, the invading Ottomans in the town massacre 2,000 Greek Orthodox residents, capturing 3,000 women and children, while 18,000 Greek Orthodox are drowned during their efforts to escape the massacre.

1821, 7/19 June: Alexander Hypsilantis and his select Retinue (*Hieros Lochos*), having failed to generate popular support in the Danubian Principalities, are defeated by the invading Ottoman army in the Battle of Dragaşani; One day after (8 June), the ship *Fidelissimo* arrives on the island of Hydra, carrying Demetrios Hypsilantis, the younger brother of Alexander, in order to lead the Greek Revolution in the Morea on behalf of the Friendly Society.

1821, 17/29 June: Alexander Mavrokordatos, of Phanariot origins, arrives by sea from Marseilles to Missolonghi carrying a printing press and establishes a local revolutionary administration.

1821, 23 July/4 August: The fortress of Monemvasia, in the Morea, surrenders to the Greek revolutionaries; the Muslims are sent by ships towards the Anatolian coast and are rescued in Kuşadası.

1821, 26 August/7 September: In the Battle of Fontana/Vassilika between Zitouni (Lamia) and Livadeia, the invading army of Hacı Behram Mehmet Pasha is defeated by the Greek revolutionaries. This was a decisive battle, saving the revolution in the south in its critical first year.

1821, 23 September/5 October: The Greek revolutionaries capture Tripolitsa (mod. Tripoli), the Ottoman provincial capital of the Morea; the invading Greeks burn down the Serai and massacre the Muslims and the Jews, with only a few exceptions.

1822, 1/13 January: The first National Assembly of the Greeks, assembled in Piada (mod. Nea Epidavros), announces the Declaration of the Greek Independence and the first Greek democratic Constitution; Alexander Mavrokordatos is elected President of the first Greek national government.

1822, 15/27 January: Haiti, a nation of former slaves who had successfully revolted a few years earlier, is the first nation to acknowledge the Greek Revolution, with a letter from its President Jean-Pierre Boyer.

1822, 20 or 25 January/1 or 6 February: After a long siege, and the desertion of his Greek and Albanian allies, Tepedelenli Ali Pasha is executed by Hurşid Ahmed Pasha on the island of the lake of Ioannina; his head is sent to Istanbul to be exhibited in the courtyard of the Topkapi Palace.

1822, April: The Ottoman fleet and army massacre the Greek island of Chios, provoking a wave of sympathy for the Greek cause in Western Europe; after the massacre, refugees from Chios and elsewhere find refuge on the Catholic island of Syros, where they establish a new port-town, Hermoupolis.

1822, 6–7 June/18–19 June: As a revenge for the Chios massacre, the Greek captain Konstantinos Kanaris, from the island of Psara, blows up during the night the flagship of the Ottoman fleet in the port of Chios, killing the Ottoman Admiral Kara Ali.

1822, 4/16 July: The Philhellenes, young revolutionaries from all around Western Europe who had come to fight for the Greek revolution, are massacred in the Battle of the Village of Peta, Epirus.

1822, 26 July/7 August: The army of Dramalı Mahmud Pasha, invading the Morea, is defeated in the Dervenakia straits by the Greek revolutionaries under Theodoros Kolokotronis.

1822, 3/15 December: After a long siege, the town of Nafplio surrenders to the revolutionaries; Nafplio will become during the next year the first capital of the Greek revolution and the seat of the revolutionary administration.

1823, 28 February/12 March: The London Philhellenic Committee has its first meeting in the Crown and Anchor Tavern on the Strand; the Committee later raised major loans to help the Greek cause.

1823, 8–9 August/20–1 August: Death of Markos Botzaris, an iconic warrior from the mountains of Souli, Epirus, in the Battle of Kefalovryso, on the mountains of central Greece.

1824: Internal strife in the Greek revolution: Alexander Mavrocordatos, the notables of the Morea and the Greek Islands fight against Theodoros Kolokotronis and the military leaders of the revolution and, later, the notables from the islands together with the warriors from southern Rumelia fight against the Moreots.

1824, 7/19 April: Death of the famous English romantic poet Lord Byron in Missolonghi. Lord Byron had joined the Greek Revolution in Missolonghi in 24 December 1823 as a representative of the Greek Philhellenic Committee.

1824, 27 May/8 June: After having suppressed the Greek Revolution in Crete, the Egyptian fleet and army successfully attacks the island of Kassos in the Dodecanese, one of the Greek islands with a strong fleet.

1824, 20 June/2 July: The Ottoman fleet attacks and massacres the island of Psara, one of the headquarters of the Greek fleet.

1824, 29 August/10 September: The Greek fleet under Andreas Miaoulis fights successfully against the Egyptian fleet in the naval Battle of Gerontas Bey, to the east of Leros and Kalymnos in the Dodecanese.

1825, 11 February/23 February: The fleet and army of Ibrahim Pasha, son of Muhammad Ali Pasha of Egypt, arrives in the port of Methoni, invading the Peloponnese in order to suppress the Greek Revolution on behalf of the Ottoman Sultan; on 17 May, the Greek revolutionary Government frees Theodoros Kolokotronis in order to lead the resistance against the invading Egyptians.

1825, June: The Egyptian army of Ibrahim Pasha captures Tripolitsa (mod. Tripoli), the former Ottoman provincial capital in the Morea; the Greeks had already deserted the town and started a fire in order not to leave infrastructure to the invaders.

1825, 10/22 August: Konstantinos Kanaris makes a daring effort to attack the Egyptian fleet in the port of Alexandria.

1825, 21 September/3 October: The former mosque of Ragıb Pasha in Nafplio, after being remodeled, is inaugurated as the Parliament House of revolutionary Greece.

1826, 23 March/4 April: The English agree with the Russians in St Petersburg that Greece would become an autonomous part of the Ottoman Empire, whose government would pay an annual tribute to the Sublime Porte.

1826, 10–11 April/22–3 April: After a long siege, the Greek defenders of the town of Missolonghi attempt a mass breakout, resulting in a heroic defeat; Missolonghi becomes an international symbol of the Greek resistance against the Ottomans.

1827, 24 April/6 May: After the death of the leader of the revolutionary army George Karaiskakis, the Greeks make an unsuccessful effort to break the long Ottoman siege of the Acropolis, Athens. The Greek defenders on the fortress surrender the Acropolis to the Ottoman General Mehmed Reşid Pasha (aka Kioutachis) on 24 May.

1827, 8/20 October: After an agreement in London that England, France and Russia may intervene on behalf of the Greeks, the Allies crush the combined Ottoman-Egyptian fleet at the naval Battle of Navarino Bey; in the next year (1828, 6 August), the Convention of Alexandria requires Ibrahim Pasha to evacuate the Peloponnese, before the arrival of a French expedition force.

1828, 8/20 January: After his election as Governor by the Greek National Assembly and a tour of Western Europe to rally support for the Greek cause, Ioannis Kapodistrias arrives in the island of Aegina, the seat of his government.

1828, 14/26 April: Russia declares war against the Ottoman Empire.

1829, 10/22 March: According to the London Protocol, Greece would become a separate state enjoying complete autonomy under the rule of a hereditary Christian prince to be selected by England, France and Russia; the borders of the new state would run along the line of the Gulf of Arta in the west to the Pagasetic Gulf in the east.

1829, 3/15 May: The Ottomans surrender the town of Missolonghi to Avgoustinos Kapodistrias, brother of the Governor of Greece.

1829, 2/14 September: The Russians, having fought a two-year war against the Ottomans, force the Sublime Porte to accept the autonomy of Greece (Treaty of Adrianople).

1830, 22 January/3 February: The London Protocol recognises Greece as a sovereign and independent monarchy.

1831, 27 September/9 October: Following a movement of opposition against the Governor of Greece, the Maniot warriors Konstantinos and George Mavromichalis assassinate Ioannis Kapodistrias in Nafplio.

1832, 26 April/7 May: England, France and Russia, without consulting the Greeks, offer the throne of Greece to the Bavarian Prince, Otto.

The Greek Revolution in the Age of Revolutions

Historiographical Debates and New Research

Elias Kolovos and Dimitris Kousouris

For long enough, the Greek Revolution of 1821 has been considered a singular event that went against the tide of the Restoration of the old regime in Europe and that finally led to the creation of the modern Greek state. As a revolt of the Greek Orthodox against the Islamic Ottoman Empire, one that took place in the southeastern fringes of the continent in the period between the high tides of the Age of Revolutions, the event has hardly found any place in comparative studies. Most assuredly among the reasons for this was the relative withdrawal of (mostly Greek) scholarly research on the subject after the 1970s. Between 1967–74, the military junta in Greece instrumentalised the commemoration of the 150 years of the Greek Revolution for its internal propaganda: therefore, after 1974, progressive Greek historians moved on to new agendas of research and left the history of the Greek Revolution in neglect.[1] However, recent historical research has not only shed light on the military and political aspects of the Revolution, but has also revisited the social, economic, intellectual and cultural conflicts that composed that seminal event. In this book, we present a series of studies based on new research on the Greek Revolution. At the same time, the bicentenary of the Revolution in 2021 has led to a renewal of the historiographical interest in the event, both in Greece and worldwide.[2]

The history of Modern Greece has been intrinsically connected to some of the major European crises. If 1821 was a by-product of the Age of Revolutions, each and all of the major half-century anniversaries that marked the historiographical debates on the founding event for modern Greece (1871, 1921, 1971) coincided with different sorts of international crises that also determined, in one way or another, the affairs of the Greek state: 1871, in a decade marked by the Franco-Prussian War and the Paris Commune and the Great Eastern Crisis of the 1870s; the celebrations of the centenary, in 1921, were postponed because of the Asia Minor / Anatolia War (1919–22) and its consequences; 1971,

---

1 For an overview of the scholarly literature and research after the 1970s and the gradual decline of research on 1821 until the early 2000s, see Loukos 2004, pp. 579–94.

2 See Kitromiledes and Tsoukalas (eds.) 2021; Mazower 2021.

during the colonels' junta and the international crisis of the 1970s. Likewise, the bicentenary of the 1821 Greek Revolution comes in the midst of an international capitalist crisis, marked by consecutive renegotiations of the country's position within a changing international context that are still far from coming to a halt. In this sense, revisiting the Greek Revolution of 1821 as part of the Age of Revolutions, this short introduction aims to provide the reader with a broad overview of the research and historiographical debates on a topic that has been and will inevitably remain subject to various ideological uses and abuses.

Greece offers a privileged view from the periphery to the transformations that shook the political structures and social hierarchies of the old regimes at the beginning of the long nineteenth century. Reassessing this rather neglected experience,[3] might also count as an attempt to take up the threads of an old debate on the role of revolutions in modern history. As a Marxist response to Winston Churchill's 'The Age of Revolution', the third of his British-centred four-volume *History of the English-Speaking Peoples*, published in 1956–8, Eric Hobsbawm published the first of his trilogy of seminal books, studying the period in Europe between 1789–1848 as a 'twin revolution' (Industrial Revolution, French Revolution).[4] Hobsbawm's approach was the product of the Cold War *Zeitgeist*, in which Jacques Godechot approached revolution as a plural and multifaceted process[5] and in which, on the other side of the Atlantic, R.R. Palmer described an Age of Democratic Revolution.[6]

Since the bicentenary of the French Revolution in 1989, these debates have been marked by a series of revisionist attempts to depoliticise the study of revolution, by which researchers have attempted to distance themselves from the social dimension of modern revolutions.[7] At the same time, the 'global turn' after the 1990s resulted in a gradual conceptual shift to the study of an age

---

3   For a similar emphasis on the so far distorted international significance of the Greek revolution, see Beaton 2021.

4   Cf. Churchill 1956–8 and Hobsbawm 1962.

5   Godechot 1956; see also Godechot 1963. For a historiographical assessment of the aforementioned books, see the Introduction by Paschalis Kitromiledes in Kitromiledes and Tsoukalas 2021.

6   Palmer 1959–64.

7   This is valid also for the left-wing and post-marxist approaches that, based on a criticism of Marxist economism, gradually abandoned or dissolved the concept of class; see Meiksins Wood 1998, pp. 75–89. In the same way political theory and historical sociology substituted material interests with democratic ideas, disconnecting political and economic struggles in the study of revolutions around and after the bicentenary of the French Revolution. The history of mentalities constituted a short-lived but influential trend, mainly in cultural and intellectual history, that marked a withdrawal of class analysis or dissolution of the concept of class into variable cultural, ethnic and ideological components. For a critical overview of dif-

of *revolutions*, plural, that differed from previous comparative approaches of modern revolutions as instances of uneven democratisation, industrialisation and secularisation processes, putting the main emphasis on the globalisation of commercial routes, the forms of imperial governance, the tensions between imperial centres and overseas colonies and/or between central governments and local powerholders.[8] We will discuss this debate after briefly revisiting two centuries of history writing on the founding event of the Modern Greek nation.

1   Histories of the Greek Revolution

The first 100 years. The centrality of the Greek Revolution and War of Independence for European politics of the beginnings of the nineteenth century is demonstrated by the fact that its events were immediately historicised, making the first accounts and histories part and parcel of the revolutionary event itself. British noblemen and officers, American doctors, French officials and diplomats, German-speaking historians and intellectuals of Phanariot origins alike – Philhellene intellectuals of all kinds and tendencies – thematised the Greek Revolution as it was unfolding, mediating the understanding of the events for the learned audiences of European and American metropolises.[9] The influence of those histories was no lesser for the construction of the self-image of the Greeks and of their national ideology thereafter. Early on, the Revolution became a critical link in the narratives based on the romantic pattern of 'fall and rebirth' of the Greek nation, thus providing the blueprint for the establishment of national continuity by the fathers of Greek historicism.[10] Thus, just as Greek pirates could already occupy a place in the revolutionary imaginary of the young Friedrich Engels in the late 1830s,[11] Greece gradually acquired a key position in the international political and ideological landscape of the nineteenth century. To cut a long story short, the first century of Greek historiography was dominated by the effort to bridge the gap between classical antiquity and 1821, reassembling the scattered pieces of Hellenistic and

_____

          ferent revisionist approaches and trends in the history of revolutions, cf. Haynes and
          Wolfreys 2007; Traverso 2005.
8   See, indicatively, Armitage and Subrahmanyam (eds.) 2010.
9   Sheridan 1822; Leake 1826; Gordon 1832; Howe 1828; Dwight 1824; Blaquière 1824; Swan
          1826; Stanhope 1824; Hughes 1823; Pouqueville 1824; Soútsos 1829; Raybaud 1824–5; Gerber
          1821; de Pradt 1822; Münch 1826; Galletti 1826; von Lüdemann 1827; Zinkeisen 1840.
10   Koubourlis 2005; Koubourlis 2012.
11   'A Pirate Tale', Marx and Engels 1975, pp. 557–71.

Roman antiquity, Byzantine Middle Ages and Latin/Frankish and Ottoman rule in order to achieve *completeness and unity* in the national master narrative.[12]

The next 100 years. For the conventional conception of national historiography, 1821 was the result of a common and permanent desire of the Greeks to emancipate themselves from the so-called 'Turkish yoke'. Its difference from the previous revolts would have been its extent and its exemplary organisation of the so-called 'Hellenic' peoples, who finally relied on their own strengths and resources after a long period of economic and moral progress under Ottoman rule. This master narrative was, however, seriously challenged since the turn of the twentieth century, when the labour movement and socialist ideas made their presence felt in the country. The first two major Marxist critiques of the narrative of national re-awakening were published by Georgios Skliros in 1907 and by Yannis Kordatos in 1923. Skliros, a Pontic Greek who never lived in Greece and died in 1919 from tuberculosis, was a representative of late nineteenth-century socialism. Writing at a time when Greece was still a small kingdom at the southern edge of the Balkan Peninsula, Skliros considered the emergence of Greek nationalism as an occurrence of the forces and ideas that brought about the transition from feudalism to capitalism, from the domination of the gentry to that of the bourgeoisie.[13] According to Skliros, the Greek Revolution 'in essence ... was a bourgeois revolution, caused by the unprecedented economic prosperity of the bourgeoisie inside and outside Greece and the awakening of a national spirit, especially among the developed bourgeoisie and the intellectuals of the nation'. At the same time, Skliros goes on to point out that

> ... officially the Revolution did not have a social, class against class, but an ethnic/racial [*fyletiko*], national character aiming to the political emancipation of the entire nation from a foreign race/ethnicity. If you add to this that on the one hand, this nation was the Greek one, i.e. the descendants of the glorious classical Greece, and on the other the tyrants were the barbarians, the heathen Turks, you will see why European nobility did not take a negative stance towards the Greek Revolution.[14]

---

12   Liakos 1994.
13   Skliros 1922, p. 43. For the Marxist narratives concerning the Greek Revolution in the context of the Greek communist movement, see now Karpozilos 2024, esp. p. 106–8 and p. 264–68.
14   Skliros 1922, p. 45 (our translation). See the commentary by Koubourlis 2007, pp. 323–48, on the understanding of the Greek term *fyli* by Skliros, and especially the juxtaposition of the thesis of Skliros to that of his major intellectual opponents, Ion Dragoumis, concerning the understanding of the 'national' interest: for Dragoumis, the national interest

For Skliros, the 'Byzantine-Christian aristocratic ideals' of the Greek Revolution and the various 'semi-feudal elements who took the lead of the movement' were essentially remnants of the past. Skliros kicked off a debate among Marxists and socialists that gravitated around the 'genuine' or 'spurious' bourgeois character of the Revolution, as well as around the extent that had been 'accomplished' or remained 'unachieved'. Yannis Kordatos's *Social Character of the Greek Revolution*[15] was written after the doubling of the country's territory and population in the wars of the previous decade, yet also after (and in the light of) the definitive failure of the irredentist 'Great Idea' and the huge social and political upheavals brought upon the country by the war in Asia Minor (1919–22), which the Socialist Workers' Party (soon to become 'Communist') had stigmatised as 'offensive' and 'imperialist'.[16] In that founding text for twentieth-century Greek Marxist historiography, Kordatos aimed to introduce *historical materialism* to the study of the Greek Revolution as 'the only positive and secure method'. In his view, the Greek Revolution was a national movement led by merchants and shipowners. Discussing the role of feudalist local notables and high-ranking clergy in the Peloponnese, Kordatos attributed it on one side to the influence of Mani region – which enjoyed a status of quasi-autonomy and had strong military forces – and the distance of that southern tip of the Balkan Peninsula from Istanbul and the major administrative centres of the Ottoman Empire on the other. Thus, in another historical conjuncture of change and renegotiation of the country's position in the international context, Kordatos raised the issue of the degree of independence or subordination of the Greek bourgeoisie vis-à-vis European capitalists and the local feudal prelates.

In Kordatos's synthesis, the bourgeois element appears somewhat stunted from early on: 'the bourgeoisie seized political power in 1844, but was forced to capitulate to the *kocabaşıs* [notables] by conceding them privileges of a mainly economic nature at the expense of the workers and the poor masses of the people'.[17] Thus, the erstwhile progressive bourgeois class, which had played the role of 'liberator' in 1821, became 'reactionary' once it gained political power.[18] The pattern of an 'unachieved' or 'spurious' bourgeois revolution was a com-

---

was always superior to that of the class interest; for Skliros the 'national' interest was identified with the interests of the (working) class developing the 'national' forces and even organising the struggle for the liberation of the Greeks from the Ottoman Empire.

15   Kordatos 1924.
16   Carabott 1992.
17   Kordatos 1924, p. 164.
18   Kordatos 1924, p. 166.

mon trope of a debate which got a new political twist after the adoption of the Popular Front line by Comintern parties in 1934–5.

Although in the leadership circle of the party in the early 1920s, Kordatos was gradually estranged and eventually expelled towards the end of the decade. At the beginning of the next decade, he was to be denounced by the party leadership. The attempt to discredit the authority of Kordatos among party and labour union members was not so much about his views on the social character of the Greek 1821 Revolution as, above all, about the character of the social revolution to be carried out by the Greek communists. The new party leadership posited that 'the forthcoming revolution of the workers and peasants in Greece would have a bourgeois-democratic character' which would quickly turn into a proletarian socialist revolution. In an attempt to popularise this theory, Yannis Zevgos – a schoolteacher, war veteran, KUTV alumnus and head of the publishing house of the Greek Communist Party – authored *Why the Revolution in Greece will begin as bourgeois-democratic* (1934). While Kordatos emphasised the conflict of the bourgeoisie against the Turkish and Greek feudal lords, Zevgos argued that the Greek bourgeoisie was from the beginning totally compromised with the feudal lords against the poor peasants and proletarians. Because the bourgeoisie as a whole was in the camp of reaction, the bourgeois-democratic revolution, according to Zevos, should be made without and against the bourgeoisie. According to Zevgos, the driving forces of the Revolution in Greece were 'the working class and the poor and middle masses of the peasantry, in a struggle against the counter-revolutionary bourgeoisie supported by the rich landowners'.

Of course, what was still missing in the debate until the late 1930s was the systematic study of the economic mechanisms and social structures of contemporary Ottoman society based on actual historical evidence.[19] This was due to the fact that those first endeavours to write Marxist historiography were made by non-professional self-taught historians who, in times of upheavals and persecutions by the state, neither had the time nor the practical means to conduct systematic archival research. Thus, if the controversy between Kordatos and Zevgos around the character of the Revolution inaugurated a series of different articulations/versions of the division between workers/peasants on one hand and bourgeois/çiftlik landowners [*astikotsiflikadiki*] on the other, this debate would acquire a considerable historical depth only through the pioneering work of Serafeim Maximos. He was one of the best educated and prominent union and party leaders, twice elected deputy of the Greek Communist Party

---

19   Iliou 2021.

and representative in the Comintern until 1928, when he was to be definitively expelled. A fluent speaker of many languages, Maximos co-published the Greek review *Spartacus*, worked as a journalist and economic analyst for mainstream bourgeois newspapers and journals and had the opportunity to visit the French diplomatic archives in the late 1930s. His articles and two monographs in economic history, the *Dawn of Greek Capitalism* and the *Greek Merchant Navy in the Eighteenth Century*,[20] were the first Greek Marxist historical studies based upon systematic research into archival evidence.

Maximos's study was part of a series thematising the period of Ottoman rule. The end of the irredentist Great Idea, the arrival of the masses of Greek Orthodox refugees from Asia Minor and the economic and social crisis of the interwar period called the national identity (and thus its historiography) into question. By the end of the 1930s, the study of the Ottoman period had also reached the field of academic historiography. Despite the reticence of the academic establishment, three doctoral dissertations prepared at that time on the Ottoman context of the Greek Revolution testify that until the end of the interwar period, the conventional certainty of a nation that was eager to win its freedom had now given way to the question of the historical causes of the revolutionary character of the Greek nation: Michail Sakellariou's history of the 'Second Tourkokratia' (i.e. Ottoman rule) in the Peloponnese (1715–1821); Apostolos Vakalopoulos's history of refugees and population movements during the Greek Revolution; and Nikos Svoronos's study of Ottoman numismatics, which was submitted to the University of Thessaloniki in 1942–3 – however, his doctorate was not awarded due to the circumstances of the Nazi occupation.[21]

The cataclysmic events in Greece during Greek experience of the 1940s – the war, the occupation, the mass movement of anti-fascist resistance, the counter-revolution – shed new light on the revolutionary experience. On one hand, the emergence of the communist left as a mass political space in Greece brought about the discovery of the 'people' as a synonym for the 'nation' and as a revolutionary subject that would first bring the bourgeois-democratic revolution to an end, unleashing a socialist one in its place. Meanwhile, class-struggle analysis gave way to the opposition between 'people' and bourgeois-feudal oligarchy, a reactionary class fighting their final battle against the inevitable victory of socialism. The re-telling of national history through exemplary illustrated biographies of popular heroes – i.e. military chieftains and lower clergy; the discovery of General Makriyannis's *Memoirs*; the time since 1821 recounted in

---

20   Maximos 1976; cf. Asdrachas 2001.
21   Sakellariou 1939; Vakalopoulos 193; for Svoronos's dissertation, see Liata 1996, θ′–ια′.

schoolbooks as a narrative of rise and fall until absolute chaos and regeneration through the National Liberation Front [Gk. *EAM*] of Greece – signalled a passage to the so-called 'populist' period of the official party historians.[22]

In academic historiography, the revolutionary experience of the 1940s and the new interests already introduced in the interwar period led to a paradigm shift after the war. The turn to the 'life of the nation' under Ottoman rule, i.e. to the historical conditions that made the nation revolutionary, led to the establishment of Modern Greek Studies as an autonomous field of study within the post-war university system. Critical contributions came mainly from the history of ideas and the study of Modern Greek Enlightenment by Konstantinos Th. Dimaras as well as from the economic and social history of the period in the research of Nicolas Svoronos, produced first in Greece and then in France, where the former resistance fighter continued his academic career as a political refugee after 1945.[23] According to this new synthesis, the rapid development of a Christian-Orthodox merchant bourgeoisie and its intensive contacts with the ideas of European Enlightenment triggered a similar ideological and educational movement that involved merchants, intellectuals and manufacturers as well as parts of the lower strata of the population who adopted the liberal-nationalist ideals. This led to a 'national reawakening' and the construction of a new political identity that gradually prevailed upon the previously dominant religious and local ones, thus paving the way for the uprising of 1821. The narrative of Dimaras, marked by the liberal modernism of the 1930s, was focusing mainly on the modernist/educated elites as opposed to the inert and illiterate mass of the population; that of Svoronos, shaped by historical materialism and the work of Ernest Labrousse in France, was focusing on the economic developments and the transformations of society and the people as opposed to the state. In both cases, by studying the Greek nation as an active historical subject under Ottoman rule, their work shaped the field of Modern Greek Studies by adding a missing component rather than refuting the national master narrative shaped in the second half of the nineteenth century by K. Paparrigo-poulos.[24]

During the first post-civil war decades, marked by the ban of the Communist Party and the transformation of the country into a frontline state of the so-called Western bloc during the Cold War, both liberal/conservative and Marxist/anti-imperialist approaches of the national past claimed for them-

---

22   Asdrachas 2002; Giannoulopoulos 2003; Theotokas 2012.
23   Dimaras and Svoronos 1995.
24   Liakos 2001, pp. 38–9.

selves the legacies of a 'fighting nation'. If within this framework the position of the revolutionary event in the national continuum remained undisputed, what remained at stake was the question of who the 'real' or 'authentic' subjects of the national revolutionary movement were. General Yannis Makriyannis, a minor chieftain of the Revolution with a political role in the constitutional uprising of 1843, who learned to read and write in order to compose his memoirs, became common reference and, at the same time, a floating signifier for the different ideological approaches to his life and work ('Makriyannisms').[25] Translated into English and French during the late 1960s and early 1970s,[26] Makriyannis became as well an integral part of Western receptions of Modern Greece, either as a 'noble savage', an incarnation of the linguistic and cultural continuity of the Ancient Greeks, or as a 'primitive rebel' and a forefather of the twentieth-century anti-colonial and national liberation fighters.[27] The diverse receptions and interpretations of that long-forgotten hero in the postwar perpetuated the original tension between a social and a political/cultural dimension of the revolutionary event inaugurated by Skliros's and Kordatos's challenge to nationalist historiography. The grotesque nationalist-populist reappropriations of several symbols of 1821 by the colonels' dictatorship (1967–74), such as the use of the mythical bird Phoenix regenerating from its ashes as an emblem of the military regime, discredited in the long term the traditional patriotic narrative celebrating the nation's millennial glory. After 1974, the narrative focusing on the intellectual and material preparation of 1821 by, respectively, the Modern Greek Enlightenment and the rise of an Orthodox merchant bourgeoisie in the long eighteenth century was established and standardised in secondary school and higher education textbooks. Hence, in the following decades of relative political stability and economic growth, the Revolution ceased to be a contentious issue. However, although conducted in the background, research galvanised public debates, not only by providing (physical and – more recently – digital) critical editions of primary sources that broadened the avail-

---

25   Theotokas 2012.
26   Makriyannis 1966; Macriyannis 1986.
27   'I had just been living for years in the same mountains, fighting the same sort of war, with companions who not only seemed the same sort of men but actually often had the same names ... I had only to close my eyes to hear Makriyannis talking – for this is essentially oral Greek – as I heard contemporary pallikaria, arguing, singing, joking around shepherds' fires on Makriyannis's own mountains a century after him. I was also listening, so it seemed, to the language of the Homeric pallikaria, spoken centuries before Homer'; see Woodhouse's foreword in Makriyannis 1966, p. viii; see also the preface by Vidal-Naquet in Macriyannis 1986, pp. 4–5.

able documentation, but also with various original contributions in social and intellectual history as well as new approaches in social anthropology and historical sociology.[28]

Although the absence of a research institution specialising in the study of the Greek Revolution (as, for example, is the case for the Italian Risorgimento or the French Revolution) might have contributed to the considerable slowdown and relative international isolation of academic studies produced on the issue, this lack, on the other hand, has recently ensured a remarkable openness to the various methods and disciplines that meet in the growing field of Modern Greek Studies. In a crossroads of Balkan, Ottoman and Mediterranean Studies, research on the Greek Revolution and on the emergence of the Modern Greek state has also been profiting considerably from recent developments in those fields. Thus, despite the persistence of various 'exceptionalisms', the comparative approach of Gunnar Hering paved the way for various reconsiderations of 1821 within its nineteenth-century Balkan context and the dynamics of the transition from early to high modernity.[29] More recently, the developing field of Ottoman Studies has introduced questions of imperial and global history, addressing issues such as the interaction between international and internal conflicts, the emergence of new political subjects, the relationship between central power and local elites, the dynamics of multi-ethnic societies, governance and legal pluralism.[30] Lastly, research on the Greek Revolution has profited greatly from novel approaches overcoming the boundaries of national historiographies and exploring the role of Mediterranean diasporas and networks in the circulation and dissemination of liberal-national ideas as well as the various ramifications of philhellenism.[31] Such recent developments make visible even more areas and topics for a social history of the Greek Revolution / War of Independence that, despite the fact that they have already been mapped by academic research, have not become object of more systematic approaches and broader interpretations of the event. The political economy of warfare and the role of violence in state-building and social mobility during the war open a window to the mass dimension of the Revolution, beyond the traditional dual pattern of antagonisms between military and political elites,

---

28   Loukos 2004, p. 581.
29   See Hering 1994 and Hering 1999.
30   The topic of the Greek Revolution in its Ottoman and international context is studied masterfully in Ilicak 2011. For recent related studies that also incorporate a comparative imperial history of the early nineteenth century, see Anastasopoulos and Kolovos (eds.) 2007; Philliou 2011; Barkey 2013, pp. 83–108; Yaycioglu 2016; Yildiz 2017; Veinstein 2017.
31   Zanou 2018; Isabella and Zanou (eds.) 2016; Scalora 2018.

integrating the course of action of different social and political actors, their mentalities, ideologies and forms of mobilisation. Accordingly, the study of historical demography opens a window to the various population movements, refugees and subsequent transformations and perceptions of (urban and rural) space and that are only recently being explored.[32]

The dimension of space has been thematised especially by Vassilis Kremmydas (1935–2017), whose work epitomises the pursuits of Marxist historiography on 1821 during the last fifty years. An economic historian of the Ottoman period, Kremmydas bypasses – or rather transcends – the question of continuity between contemporary and previous hellenisms through the concept of ethnogenesis, which describes a process of nation-building marked by the rise of an Orthodox commercial bourgeoisie on the trade routes of the Eastern Mediterranean in the eighteenth century, by means of a broad network of Greek-speaking schools across the Ottoman Empire, but also across maritime and land trade routes. Just as its driving forces, the dominant ideology of the Revolution was, according to Kremmydas, bourgeois liberal. This was also reflected in the ideas of a centralised system and the constitution voted by the National Assembly within the first year of the Revolution. A distinctive feature compared to previous revolts in the Ottoman Empire was that for the first time the insurgents tried to present the Greek question as an international European issue – not a bilateral one between the Russian and Ottoman Empires on the protection of the Orthodox subjects, as was the case since the Treaty of Küçük Kaynarca in 1774. After 1789/91, revolutionary consciousness and action were the product of a secularisation process in a long and gradual transition from feudalism to capitalism. In that sense, the revolutionary event was a breakthrough but not a complete rupture with the Ottoman past.[33] Most importantly, Kremmydas challenged the idea of an alleged unity of the Greeks against Ottoman rule, replacing the previous linear and evolutionary narrative with that of a lasting crisis, due to both the internal conditions of the Ottoman Empire and the external pressures of Napoleonic and post-Napoleonic Europe. In this sense, rather than the culmination of a long national reawakening process, the Revolution was a byproduct of growing tensions and divisions among the Greek Orthodox.[34]

---

32   See, indicatively, Amygdalou and Kolovos 2021, pp. 77–105.
33   Kremmydas 1991, pp. 67–82.
34   Ibid.

2   Modernity, Modernisation, *Sattelzeit*

Re-assessing the post-war historiographical debates on the Greek Revolution, Nikos Theotokas noticed that 1821 has been understood unilaterally as a national (re-)awakening, as the event setting the framework for the nation's 'construction' or as an equivalent of the major bourgeois revolutions that marked the political emancipation of the Western societies.[35] Theotokas suggests that during the Revolution the idea of the 'nation' permeated and gradually replaced the traditional religious conception of the world by the Greek Orthodox Church, a metaphysical chiliastic expectation of an end to the 'evil' Islamic rule of the Ottomans, marking thus a shift from an old, religious *regime of historicity* to a new, modern one in which the future depends on human action rather than divine providence.[36] Studying the Revolution within the historical context of a broader transition means that one has to understand those processes not as mutually exclusive but as instances of the simultaneity of the non-simultaneous, as different aspects of a multidimensional event.

Thus, in what concerns the political and social agents of the Revolution, notwithstanding the diverse aims and goals of the different social, ethnic, confessional and local groups of interests involved, it is generally accepted that the Greek Revolution triggered not only a state-building process but also the making of a new (national) community. Updating an old elite-centred narrative in their recent history of Modern Greece, Giannis Koliopoulos and Thanos Veremis attribute the role of initiator to the elites and that of a catalyst to an impersonal crowd of 'patriots of all descriptions and objectives [who] rubbed shoulders with adventurers and cut-throats ready to cause a rupture by means designed to force the hand of these who had much to lose and were understandably reluctant to cause a break with the Turks'.[37] According to Jack Goldstone, the historical research on revolutions has been 'concerned with explaining twentieth-century revolutions, in which the collisions of international colonial and economic forces with traditional regimes played a major role ... The theory of revolutions has yet to address early modern political crises in their own right'.[38] In this line of thought, Kostas Kostis departs from the social com-

---

35   Theotokas 2006.
36   Hartog 2015, pp. 65–95; Koselleck 2004, pp. 43–57.
37   'Patriots of all descriptions and objectives rubbed shoulders with adventurers and cut-throats ready to cause a rupture by means designed to force the hand of these who had much to lose and were understandably reluctant to cause a break with the Turks, higher clergy and lay notables'; see Koliopoulos and Veremis 2010, p. 20.
38   Goldstone 1991, p. 23.

position of the known members of the Friendly Society [Gk. *Philike Etairia*], highlighting the inability of the state to raise sufficient revenues and, on the other hand, the revolutionary role of disaffected *marginal elites* – who were not the Greek Orthodox ecclesiastical prelates, the Phanariot households in power nor the Enlightenment intellectuals, but rather the marginal groups of local notables, armed bandits and peasants.[39]

150 years later, the concept of 'revolution' is back in style. Nowadays, as in the 150th anniversary, the concept of 'revolution' is back in style, this time with a rather revisionist eye that is turned from the parallels to the divergences, from the West to the periphery and to the plurality of forms of domination, social contest and political sovereignty.[40] Since the definitive formation of the Greek and Turkish republics in the 1920s, Marxists, liberals and nationalists alike debated with concepts and tools forged in the study of the French and Russian revolutions or of anti-colonial national liberation movements to stress the importance of the national or the social aspect of the Revolution and to explore the antagonist ideologies and social forces involved. This book aims to present how, during recent decades, academic research on the subject has tuned itself with the debates on a global Age of Revolutions. Such research thus paves the way for the study of the Greek Revolution, to follow the standard Skopcol rationale, within an imperial power system and a changing international context that put pressure on the existing state structures and social hierarchies of the territory under question, which lead to rapid social and political transformation, driven by the elites but also involving a sort of popular/peasant revolt, and to the creation of a new state that became a political arena for competing factions, clans, groups and classes.[41]

The debate on the character of the Revolution in the light of the most recent conceptual and methodological paradigms was rekindled on the occasion of its bicentenary. Based on recent scholarly research on economy, society, mentalities, ideology and political ideas, the work of Petros Pizanias (2021) integrates the revolutionary upheaval in the longue durée of modern Hellenism and provides an account of the political ideology, international entanglements and the social forces involved in the Greek Revolution.[42] Implementing concep-

---

39   Kostis 2018.
40   For a glimpse of this debate, especially in conjunction with developments in the historiography of the French Revolution, cf. the reviews of Armitage and Subrahmanyam (eds.) 2010 by Annie Jourdan (2013) in *Annales historiques de la Révolution française*, 373: 209–21 and Frédéric Regent (2011) in *Annales HSS*, 66, 2: 600–1.
41   Skocpol 1979, pp. 24–36.
42   Pizanias 2021.

tual tools forged by research in historical sociology and political theory for the study of revolutions and mass movements, Dimitris Papanikolopoulos (2021) provides an account of the 1821 Greek Revolution through the grid of resource-mobilisation theory.[43] For his part, revisiting the historiographical and theoretical debates around the Greek nation, Yannis Milios (2020) picks up the threads of Svoronos's and Kremmydas's analyses of the bourgeois character of the Revolution, according to which linguistic Hellenisation went hand in hand with the proliferation of capitalist relations within Ottoman society at the end of the eighteenth century and the beginning of the nineteenth century. According to this view, despite the diverging aims of the social forces involved, the revolutionary process accelerated the consolidation of the capitalist relations of production, constituting a point of no return; bourgeois hegemony conditioned both the liberal republicanism of the first period and its subsequent renunciation in favour of a monarchical regime after 1826.[44] The good old tension around the social/popular and bourgeois/national elements of the Revolution becomes all the more noticeable in a relative return to the concept of class, especially through approaches focusing on the role of the working classes in the revolutionary process – particularly sailors and poor peasants .[45] On the other hand, recent research on the social history of the Greek Revolution by Vaso Seirinidou focuses on the interaction between interpersonal violence, crime and the administration of penal justice in revolutionary Greece, suggesting a new political history of the Greek Revolution 'from below'.[46] The comparative evolution of the political vocabulary of the Greek Revolution in Greek and Turkish is being studied by Elias Kolovos and Leonidas Moiras, based on the Ottoman translation of the Greek Declaration of Indepedence.[47] Meanwhile, comparative and transnational approaches that highlight the involvement of multiple forces and actors in the different stages and places of the Revolution invite the consideration of different temporalities and spatial perspectives that challenge the persistent western-centred perspective of Modern Greek Studies.[48]

∙ ∙ ∙

---

43   Papanikolopoulos 2021.

44   Milios 2020.

45   Katsoridas 2021; Alexiou 2021; Margaritis 2020; for women and the Revolution through a gendered approach, see Lazou 2021.

46   Seirinidou 2022, pp. 203–227.

47   Kolovos and Moiras 2022.

48   See, indicatively, Stamatopoulos (ed.) 2019.

Fruit of a two-year-long research initiative of the Hellenic Open University that brought together specialists in social, intellectual and cultural history, the contributions included in this volume adopt a broader temporal perspective and juxtapose the view from without against the view from within the Ottoman Empire in an attempt to reconsider the dialectics of social transformation and revolution. The volume thus points towards a new synthesis that is able to overcome simplistic dichotomies between structural continuities and conjectural ruptures, international context and internal conflicts, social and political components, and central state and local powerholders.[49]

One of the three revolutions that broke out in the early 1820s in the Mediterranean – with a close parallel with the fourth 'Knight of the Apocalypse' in post-Restoration Europe,[50] the Decembrist revolt of 1825 in Russia – the Greek Revolution offers a panorama of the conflicts and contradictions that accumulated across the periphery of the continent during the three decades since the outbreak of the French Revolution and the ensuing wars that deeply shook imperial political structures and social hierarchies. Seen as the magnetic field of the struggles between revolution and counterrevolution, *ancien régime* and liberalism, empires and nations, the Greek Revolution occurred after a decade of an 'ongoing civil war between the Ottoman central state and provincial power-brokers across religion and ethnicity'.[51]

Born under the influence of Romanticism, conventional Greek national historiography had initially focused on the agency of an ahistorical Greek nation through the ages, ignoring both the contemporary revolutionary aspect of the formation of the Greek nation and the historicity of the Ottoman rule against which the Greeks revolted.[52] With roots in traditional, orientalist, anti-Turkish European stereotypes, the depiction of the Ottomans as an alien and despotic *other* served the narrative of a 'march towards the West' and contributed in the de-Ottomanisation of the history of the Greek Revolution, inaugurating a long tradition of national constructions of Balkan *intimate otherness*.[53] Des-

---

49   Cf. the remarks of Faroqhi 2002, pp. 351–82.

50   Stites 2014. The unfolding of the events in the decade after 1821 offers a panorama of those processes in pace or at a variance with the events in Western Europe and in the Iberian and Italian peninsulas. Cf. Isabella and Zanou (eds.) 2015.

51   As the reaction to an Ottoman project of *de-ayanization*, according to the pioneer research by Ilıcak especially focused on the years immediately before the Revolution's outbreak (1812–21); see Ilıcak 2011, pp. 16–17.

52   For an overview of these debates, see Diamantouros 1976, pp. 193–230; Kitromilides 2004, pp. 37–52; Panagiotopoulos 2004, pp. 567–77.

53   Todorova 1997; cf. Faroqhi and Adanir 2002 with the other Balkan and Arab historiographies.

pite the fact that the archives contain thousands of documents related to the Greek Revolution and the Ottoman reaction,[54] Turkish historiography made no exception, neglecting almost totally a topic that did not quite fit the modernist or the heroic national narrative. Making use of the most recent developments in Ottoman studies, contemporary researchers have only begun to understand the necessity of a comparative approach to the Greek Revolution, relying heavily on the Ottoman sources as well.[55] In order to study the Revolution, it is indispensable to consider the realities of the Ottoman peasant societies and economies.[56] The leaders of the Greek Revolution in situ were Christian Orthodox notables and military leaders, who were affected by the Ottoman *de-ayanisation* project of the 1810s and aspired to retain their traditional autonomies. At the same time, the revolutionaries were Greek Orthodox peasants, *reaya*, who also aspired to release themselves from tax oppression. Both social groups of the Orthodox Christian society under the Ottomans were inspired, in times of crisis, by the traditional 'primitive rebellion' against Islamic rule; the modern national ideology was inscribed exactly upon the traditional cultural codes. This is how the idea of the 'nation' made its way through the traditional society and gradually transformed it.[57]

In order to provide the reader with a sense of the historicity of the debates around a popular/democratic or a bourgeois/national revolution, in a special Theoretical Debate chapter in this volume, **Panagiotis Sotiris traces the development of the key concept of bourgeois revolution within the Greek** Marxist intellectual tradition. Starting from the writings of Marx and Engels, Sotiris insists on the importance of popular participation as a hegemonic practice in Gramsci's approach of the Italian Risorgimento, in order to introduce the debates and controversies around the social or national character of the Revolution within the Greek Left since the publication of Kordatos' history.

Focusing on primary-source research, the first part of this volume approaches the Greek Revolution as an Ottoman revolt **Chapter One, by Elias Kolovos, H. Şükrü Ilıcak and M. Shariat-Panahi,** is based on a series of documents revealing the central administration's understanding of and reactions to the outbreak of the revolt in 1821.[58] From the viewpoint of the imperial capital, one can follow how Sultan Mahmud II's project of *de-ayanisation* after

---

54   On the almost totally unexplored Ottoman archives, see Ilıcak 2011, p. 9, fn. 17.
55   Loukos 2007, pp. 195–204; Laiou-Sarigiannis 2019; Moiras 2020; Kolovos, Ilicak and Panahi 2021.
56   Kolovos (ed.) 2015.
57   Theotokas 2006; see also Asdrachas 2019.
58   See also Kolovos, Ilıcak and Panahi 2021.

1812 transformed relations between the Ottoman government and the Phanari-ots[59] on one hand and between the various local power-brokers – Muslims or Christians – on the other. This resulted in a 'civil war between the Ottoman central state and a myriad of provincial magnates-*cum*-warlords of varying cal-ibres, religions, ethnicities and levels of popular support'.[60]

If the first chapter describes the view from Istanbul, the headquarters of the Ottoman power, and its various representatives across the Danubian princip-alities, Continental Greece and the Peloponnese, the two chapters that follow focus on one of the major Ottoman cities on the European side of the Empire (Rumelia), Salonica, and offer new insights in the study of the Ottoman military and its role in restoring and maintaining social order in times of war and revolu-tion. The chapter by **Phokion Kotzagiorgis**, focuses on the revolt in Halkidiki, near Salonica, and the military conscription of Muslims in order to suppress it between 1821 and 1828. Archival evidence sheds light on the Ottoman percep-tions of the military action of the rebels in land and sea as well as on the social and political dynamics of military mobilisation of Muslim subjects. In the third and last chapter of this part, **Dimitris Papastamatiou** draws from material of the Ottoman judicial archives to interrogate legal prosecutions of Greek Ortho-dox notables in Salonica until shortly after Greek independence, giving new insight into the purpose and character of trials that often led to executions and confiscations of property.

The **second part** deals with the broader transformations in the Ottoman Empire in the *Age of the Ayans*[61] and with the impact of the international con-text after the French Revolution. The emphasis is put on the internal dynam-ics of Ottoman society and more concretely on the Greek Orthodox of the Empire – who called themselves (and were called by the Ottomans) 'Romans' [Ott. Turk. *Rum*; Gk. *Romioi*][62] and who had their own powerbrokers, both in the imperial capital and in the provinces.

Rhigas Velestinlis (also known as Rhigas Feraios) – who was born in Thessaly in central Greece and studied in Istanbul and (then under Phanariot rule) the Danubian Principalities – was an emblematic figure of the way in which the

---

59   On the Phanariots, see Philliou 2011.
60   Ilıcak 2011, pp. 27–8.
61   McGowan 1992, pp. 637–758; Yaycioglu 2016.
62   The Greek Orthodox of the Ottoman Empire – who were often called 'Romans' [Ott. Turk. *Rum*; Gk. *Romioi*] – had their own powerbrokers, both in Istanbul, the imperial capital, and in the provinces. In Istanbul, the leading Greek Orthodox had their own political house-holds, which were called Phanariots [Ott. Turk. *Fenerli takımı*], since they were based on the neighbourhood of Fener around the Patriarchate. For the *Romioi*, see Katsiardi-Hering et al. (eds.) 2018.

ideas of Radical Enlightenment[63] and modern revolution spread in the Ottoman Empire after the catalytic event of the French Revolution. After publishing a monumental *Chart of Greece* – including the entire Balkan peninsula and Asia Minor (1797) – inviting all ethnic groups to rise up against Ottoman 'despotism', and making an effort to coordinate his activity with Napoleonic France and thus put his vision into practice, he was arrested with a small group of comrades by the Austrian police in December 1797. The Austrian interrogation concluded that Rhigas had a plan to organise a rebellion within the Empire and handed him over to the Ottoman authorities in Belgrade, where he and his comrades were finally strangled.[64] However, his revolutionary legacies survived to inspire the generation of 1821, who considered him, the main precursor of the Revolution.[65]

Nikos Rotzokos follows this revolutionary tradition through a study of Christophoros Perraivos, the only one of Rhigas's group to survive after their arrest. Having escaped execution, Perraivos moved to the Ionian Islands, where he was a military officer at the service of Russia and France consecutively until 1815, when he was initiated in the Friendly Society. His mission was to maintain contacts with the Russian networks in Eastern Mediterranean and across the Ottoman Empire. In this case study of the *interstitial emergence* of revolutionary conspiracy through manifold political and ideological networks,[66] Perraivos's actions demonstrate the transition from the expectation for an enlightened ruler to redeem the enslaved nation to the idea of liberation as a political project, relying on the nation itself, as well as on the role of the Filiki and other secret societies of the Jacobin tradition in the politicisation of Greek ethnicity in the early nineteenth century.

The perpetuation of the tradition of radical enlightenment, in the action of secret societies, depicts the *temporalisation* of the political community together with the politicisation and ideologisation of preexisting concepts – in other words, what Reinhart Koselleck described as a *Sattelzeit*, a *saddle time of transition from early* to *high* modernity.[67] The rest of part two deals with the

---

63 As used by Israel 2010.

64 See Botzaris 1962; Kitromilides 2013, pp. 200–29; Guiomar and Lorain 2000, pp. 101–25.

65 At the same time, as studied meticulously by Arvanitakis 2020, the ideas of the French Revolution made their way into practice on the Ionian Islands under Napoleonic-French rule (1797), in a revolutionary experiment which also contributed to the gradual evolution of the Orthodox into a 'Greek' nation.

66 Rotzokos uses the concept developed by Mann 1986, vol. 1, p. 16.

67 Koselleck described *Sattelzeit* as a transitional period roughly between 1750 and 1850, in which the society, lifestyle and mentality of the Europeans developed towards 'modernity' and took the form that it has had up until our days. See his Einleitung in Koselleck, Conze

main components of this period, in what concerns the distribution of power among the central state representatives and local notables, and the new and upcoming local elites amongst the Rum population in the heartland of the Revolution, the Peloponnese. Adopting a view from the top of the local social hierarchy, chapters five and six investigate the Moreote notables, called, in distinction to the Muslim *ayans*, *kocabaşıs* [elders] in Ottoman Turkish. Those lesser notables were, however, no less notables than their Muslim counterparts, controlling the local economies through contracts of tax farming, loans to the communes and the people, landowning, investments in industry and trade.[68] Adopting a longer perspective, **Aliki Fakoura** explores the political and economic activity and family strategies of some of the most powerful Moreote households in the half century before the outbreak of the revolution (1770–1820). In tune with recent research on the subject, Fakoura's approach highlights a drastic change of demographic situation in the region, the consecutive realignments and alliances between the various religious and secular Christian Orthodox powerholders and a generational change of guard that brought up a new entrepreneurial and revolutionary spirit. Following this thread through the revolutionary upheavals of the 1820s, **Dimitris Bacharas** provides a case study of political, military and family alliances of a group of three families of landed aristocracy in the Peloponnese. From this viewpoint, the perpetuation of the preexisting sophisticated and wide-ranging alliances highlights the ways in which those networks adapted themselves in the emergence of new players and powers.

The **third part** deals with the dynamics of modernisation in what concerns military groups and warfare, central state, distribution of powers, economic, social and cultural transformation that have been at the centre of scholarly interests, for good and for bad, for decades. A singular aspect of the *Sattelzeit*, according to Koselleck, was the process of *secularisation* of traditional concepts and forms of social action and political engagement. In the Greek case, among the veterans of the Napoleonic Wars who organised the Greek insurrection were many former warlords [*klephts*], like Theodoros Kolokotronis,[69]

---

68   Asdrachas 1986, pp. 45–62; Kostis 2018; Papastamatiou 2009.

69   Kolokotronis had to leave the Peloponnese in 1806, during the Ottoman persecution of the klephts, and arrived in the peninsula of Mani in January 1821 to start preparations for the Revolution. According to the plan of the Friendly Society, he was to become one of the leading figures of the Greek War of Independence.

and Brunner (eds.) 1972, pp. xiii–xxvii. For a general introduction to the discussions and uses of the concept thereafter, see Koselleck 1996, pp. 59–70; Décultot and Fulda (eds.) 2016; Escudier 2009. For an approach to Greek historiography during the Greek Revolution from a Koselleckian perspective, see Stassinopoulou 1992.

who had fled to the Ionian Islands and elsewhere. Since the seminal book by Eric Hobsbawm on *Primitive Rebels*, Greek historiography has researched these armed groups and their roles in the Greek societies under the Ottomans.[70] Adopting a Schmittian approach, **Dionysis Tzakis** describes the transformation during the Greek Revolution of these combatants into modern partisans or guerillas, who became, like the Spanish guerillas in the Napoleonic wars, precursors of the later national liberation armies of the nineteenth and twentieth centuries.[71] In his chapter on the emergence of military medicine in the Greek revolutionary groups, **Thanasis Barlayannis** further explores the transformations of warfare during the 1820s. The requirements of a long-term war in terms of public and military hygiene was met by European military doctors who introduced military medicine amongst the Greek troops, thus contributing to a process of transformation of the traditional irregular bands of 1821 into a modern regular army. **Simos Bozikis** follows the emergence of the central state within the limits of the revolutionary territories between 1822–32, inquiring into the state's finance apparatus and its function. Tracing the continuity of the state finance sector and its impact on political spheres, Bozikis describes state finance as the main arena of concurrence between rival groups and parties. Public finance operations describe the effort to form a national political centre, interwoven not only with the struggle for political power but also with the organisation of the military and the conduct of war. Finally, especially after the foreign loans from London in 1824–5, the management of public finance was intimately connected with the effort to acquire international recognition.[72]

From this viewpoint, the Revolution is described as a struggle for the control of the new political centre over the national territory against an imperial system of domination with significant historical depth. In order to achieve control of the centre, the new state dignitaries were to be conscripted at a local level, thus undermining or sometimes even drastically shaking the traditional hierarchies.[73] In the last chapter of this part, **Zacharias Antonakis** looks into the emblematic case of the Commune of Athens in order to explore how this local administrative institution was gradually integrated into a modern centralised

---

70   Hobsbawm 1971. For the *armatoloi* and *klepht*s as *primitive rebels* in the Greek lands, see Asdrachas 2019.
71   See also Tzakis 2021.
72   See also Bozikis 2020.
73   Cf. the work by Dimitris Dimitropoulos on the role of the central administration of the revolution, represented in the studied case of the island of Andros by three members of the Friendly Society, vis-a-vis the local notables of the islands. Dimitropoulos 2020.

state apparatus and how this process transformed the property, political relations and influence of the older and the new notables of the city. The conflict
between the old notables and the rising group of local 'heads of households', a
new local elite that rapidly accumulated land property, and the final prevalence
of the latter, also conveys a process of democratisation of political institutions
that culminated in the Revolution of the 1820s. Antonakis eventually deals with
the exercise of the state sovereign over a region and its territory and with the
local agents available to implement and sustain the new form of national sovereignty. The question of the transition from the supra- or extra-territoriality of
imperial sovereignty to a new type of national territorial sovereignty has been
at the centre of scholarly research in imperial and international legal studies
since the final phase of the decolonisation process in the 1970s.[74] Attica, the
region of Athens – then a small town – was on the border zone between the
centre of the revolutionary activities in Peloponnese and the territories controlled until 1820 by Ali Pasha of Ioannina, who since the 1780s had built an
almost autonomous and hereditary-to-be principality around Janina, expanding into Albania, northern and southern Greece.[75]

In the first chapter of the **final part** of this book, **Panagiotis Stathis** intro-
duces us to the broader borderlands of the so-called Continental Greece, long
disputed between different forces and sovereigns, in the transitional period
after the collapse of Tepedelenli Ali Pasha in late 1820, and the beginning of
the efforts of the revolutionary government to hire and/or contain the power of
various local warlords, *armatoloi* and *klephts*.[76] The view from this gap between
what no longer existed and what had not yet emerged provides a panorama of
the various actors involved in the revolutionary preparations on the southern
tip of the Ottoman Balkans: local *beys* and warlords, Christian and Muslim notables, members of the Friendly Society, agents of the Great Powers and many
others.

Since the years of Thucydides, the southern tip of the Greek peninsula could
easily transform itself into an island in order to survive in times of war. The
last two chapters of this part and the volume introduce the reader to the maritime space *par excellence* of shared sovereignty in early modern Europe and
beyond.[77] The maritime space between the Cyclades, the northern Dodecan-
nese, the Saronic Gulf and the islands near the East coast of the Peloponnese

---

74   For the involvement of the Ottoman Empire and the comparative analysis of forms of
      extraterritoriality, cf. Kayaoglu 2010, pp. 104–48.
75   Skiotis 1971, pp. 219–44; Panagiotopoulos 2009, pp. 13–128; Fleming 1999.
76   See: Asdrachas 2019; cf. Theotokas and Kotaridis 2006.
77   Benton 2009, pp. 279–300.

(Hydra, Spetses, Poros) – and its ability to continuously supply the government and fortresses of the Moreote coast with money, food and ammunition through trade, taxation, pirate or privateer booties – assured the survival of the Greek Revolution. During the grim years between the conquest of the quasi-totality of Morea by Ibrahim, the son of Mehmet Ali of Egypt, in 1825 and the destruction of the Egyptian-Ottoman Fleet by the joint forces of the British, French and Russian navy at Navarino Bay in October 1827, the revolutionaries persisted.[78] **Dimitris Kousouris** focuses on the centre of the Greek archipelago, exploring the encounter between an ethno-religious minority, the Catholics of Syros and the new nation-state that would first set foot on the 'Pope's island', later taking it over as a mass wave of Greek Orthodox refugees settled and, through a combined use of military and paramilitary violence, forced the local population to pay the tithe and to comply with the laws of the national revolutionary government. The emergence of a new city, built on the neutral and thus safe territory of the Syros Catholic community, would become a hub of piracy, casting its shadow on the experience of the local Catholics who saw their lands usurped or confiscated and who were forced to rebrand themselves from 'Latines' to 'Greeks of the Western Church'. By exploring the viewpoint of an ethno-religious community, as well as of its representatives and advocates in Istanbul, Smyrna, Paris and the Vatican, this chapter opens a window onto the legal pluralism and the forms of overlapping and conflicting ecclesiastical, local, and seigneurial jurisdictions in the Ottoman Empire.[79] This theme is further explored in the last chapter of the volume, in which **Eleftheria Zei** investigates the archipelago as a 'maritime city' and as a space of shared sovereignty, focusing on the agents of conflicting jurisdictions and sovereignties, the vice-consuls of the European powers on the islands.[80] Usually members of the local elites, consular agents acted often as intermediaries between the local communities and Istanbul or the imperial courts, and were often also members of secret societies and servants of two (or more) masters. The mapping of this new territory for scholarly research points towards the exploration of the multiple threads that linked the Ottoman Eastern Mediterranean with European imperialist and revolutionary politics.

---

78   See on the subject Schulz 2011; St. Clair 2008, pp. 314–33.
79   For example, cf., Barkey 2013, pp. 83–108.
80   Cf. Lucien Frary 2013 and Massé 2019.

Bibliography

Alexiou, Spyros 2021, *21 ρωγμές στην επίσημη ιστορία για το 1821* [*21 cracks on the official history of 1821*], Athens: Τόπος.

Amygdalou, Kalliopi and Elias Kolovos 2021, 'Το τζαμί του Ναυπλίου που μετασκευάστηκε στο «πρώτον εν Ελλάδι Βουλευτήριον»' ['The mosque in Nafplio that became the first Parliament House in Greece'], *Πώς προσεγγίζουμε το Εικοσιένα; Πολιτική, κοινωνία, ιδεολογία στην Ελληνική Επανάσταση* [*How do we approach the 1821? Politics, society, ideology in the Greek Revolution*], edited by Elias Kolovos and Dimitris Dimitropoulos, Athens: Έκδοση της «Εφημερίδας των Συντακτών».

Anastasopoulos, Antonis and Elias Kolovos (eds.) 2007, *Ottoman Rule and the Balkans, 1760–1850: Conflict, Transformation, Adaptation*, Rethymno: University of Crete, Department of History and Archaeology.

Armitage, David and S. Subrahmanyam (eds.) 2010, *The Age of Revolutions in Global Context, c. 1760–1840*, New York: Palgrave MacMillan.

Arvanitakis, Dimitris D. 2020, *Η αγωγή του πολίτη. Η γαλλική παρουσία στο Ιόνιο (1797–1799) και το έθνος των Ελλήνων* [*Citizen's education: The French presence in the Ionian Sea (1797–1799) and the nation of the Greeks*], Herakleio: Crete University Press.

Asdrachas, Spyros I. 1986, 'Φορολογικές και περιοριστικές λειτουργίες των κοινοτήτων στην Τουρκοκρατία' [Fiscal and regulatory functions of the communes during the Tourkokratia], *Τα Ιστορικά* 3,5: 45–62.

Asdrachas, Spyros I. 2001, 'Ο Σεραφείμ Μάξιμος ως ιστορικός της γενεαλογίας της ελληνικής κεφαλαιοκρατίας' [Serafeim Maximos as a historian of the Greek capitalism], *Αρχειοτάξιο* 3, pp. 60–64.

Asdrachas, Spyros I. 2002, 'Ο "γνήσιος λαϊκισμός" του Γ. Λαμπρινού' [The "genuine populism" of G. Lambrinos], *Τα Ιστορικά*, 36: 201–204.

Asdrachas, Spyros I. 2019, *Πρωτόγονη επανάσταση. Αρματολοί και κλέφτες (18ος–19ος αι.)* [*Primitive Revolution: armatoloi and klephts (eighteenth-nineteenth c.)*], Athens: Hellenic Open University Press.

Barkey, Karen 2013, 'Aspects of Legal Pluralism in the Ottoman Empire', in *Legal Pluralism and Empires, 1500–1850*, edited by L. Benton and R. Ross, New York: NYU Press.

Beaton, Roderick 2021, *The Greek Revolution of 1821 and its Global Significance*, Athens: Aiora Press.

Benton, Lauren 2009, *A Search for Sovereignty. Law and Geography in European Empires, 1400–1900*, Cambridge: Cambridge University Press.

Blaquière, Edward 1824, *The Greek Revolution; its origin and progress*, London: G. & W.B. Whittaker.

Botzaris, Notis 1962, *Visions balkaniques dans la revolution de la evolution grecque (1789–1821)*, Geneva and Paris: Libraire E. Droz, Genève and Libraire Minard.

Bozikis, Simos 2020, *Ελληνική Επανάσταση & Δημόσια Οικονομία: Η συγκρότηση του ελληνικού εθνικού κράτους 1821–1832* [*The Greek Revolution and Public Finances: The formation of the Greek nation state 1821–1832*], Athens: Ασίνη.

Carabott, Philip 1992. 'Οι Έλληνες «κομμουνιστές» και η μικρασιατική εκστρατεία' ['The Greek 'communists' and the Greek expedition to Asia Minor'], *Δελτίο Κέντρου Μικρασιατικών Σπουδών*, 9: 99–118.

Churchill, Winston, *History of the English-Speaking Peoples*, 4 volumes, London: Cassel and Company Ltd.

De Pradt, Dominique Georges Frédéric de R. 1822, *Griechenland in seinem Verhältnisse zu Europa*, Stuttgart.

Décultot, Elisabeth and Daniel Fulda (eds.) 2016, *Sattelzeit. Historiographiegeschichtliche Revisionen*, Berlin: Oldenbourg Verlag.

Diamantouros, Nikiforos 1976, 'Bibliographical Essay', *Hellenism and the First Greek War of Liberation (1821–1830): Continuity and Change*, edited by J. Petropoulos, N. Diamantouros, J. Anton, P. Topping, Thessaloniki: Institute for Balkan Studies

Diamantouros, Nikiforos, and J. Anton, J. Petropoulos, P. Topping (eds.) 1976, *Hellenism and the First War of Liberation. 1821–1830: Continuity and Change*, Institute for Balkan Studies: Thessaloniki.

Dimaras, Konstantinos Th. and Nikos Svoronos 1995, *Η μέθοδος της ιστορίας: Ιστοριογραφικά και αυτοβιογραφικά σχόλια – συνεντεύξεις με τους Στέφανο Πεσμαζόγλου και Νίκο Αλιβιζάτο* [*The method in history: historiographical and autobiographican comments – interviewed by Stefanos Pesmazoglou and Nikos Alivization*], Athens: Άγρα.

Dimitropoulos, Dimitris 2020, *Τρεις Φιλικοί, έπαρχοι στην Άνδρο. Από το επαναστατικό σχέδιο στην κρατική διοίκηση* [*Three Members of the Friendly Society Governors of Andros: From the Revolutionary Plan to the Administation of a State*], Athens: National Hellenic Research Foundation.

Dwight, Sereno Edwards 1824, *The Greek Revolution*, Boston: Crocker & Brewster.

Escudier, Alexandre 2009, '«Temporalisation» et modernité politique : penser avec Koselleck', *Annales HSS* 6: 1269–1301.

Faroqhi, Suraiya 2002, 'Coping with the Central State, Coping with Local Power: Ottoman Regions and Notables from the Sixteenth to the Early Nineteenth Century' in *The Ottomans and the Balkans: A Discussion of Historiography*, edited by Suraiya Faroqhi and Fikret Adanir, Leiden: Brill.

Faroqhi, Suraiya and Fikret Adanir (eds.) 2002, *The Ottomans and the Balkans: A Discussion of Historiography*, Leiden: Brill.

Fleming, Katherine E. 1999, *The Muslim Bonaparte. Diplomacy and Orientalism in Ali Pasha's Greece*, Princeton: Princeton University Press.

Frary Lucien 2013, 'Russian consuls and the Greek war of independence (1821–31)', *Mediterranean Historical Review*, 28 (1), pp. 46–65.

Galletti, Johann Georg August 1826, *Geschichte von Griechenland*, Gotha: Hennings.

Gerber, Carl 1821, *Griechenland und dessen zeitiger Kampf in seinem Ausgang und seinen Folgen betrachtet*, Schmalkalden: Varnhagen.

Giannoulopoulos, Giorgos 2003, *Διαβάζοντας τον Μακρυγιάννη: η κατασκευή ενός μύθου από τον Βλαχογιάννη, τον Θεοτοκά, τον Σεφέρη και τον Λορεντζάτο* [*Reading Makrygiannis: the construction of a myth by Vlachogiannis, Theotokas, Seferis and Lorentzatos*], Athens: Πόλις.

Godechot, Jacques 1956, *La Grande Nation: L'expansion de la France révolutionnaire dans le monde (1789–1799)*, 2 Volumes, Paris: Aubier.

Godechot, Jacques 1963, *Les Révolutions (1770–1799)*, Paris: Presses Universitaires de France.

Goldstone, Jack A. 1991, *Revolution and Rebellion in the Early Modern World*, Berkeley: University of California Press.

Gordon, Thomas 1832, *History of the Greek Revolution*, Edinburgh: William Blackwood.

Guiomar, Jean-Yves and Marie-Thérèsse Lorain 2000, 'La Carte historique de Rhigas et le nom de la Grèce', *Annales de la Révolution Française*, 319, 1: 101–25.

Hartog, François 2015, *Regimes of Historicity. Presentism and Experiences of Time*, New York: Columbia University Press.

Haynes, Mike and Wolfreys, Jim (eds.) 2007, *History and Revolution. Refuting revisionism*, London-New York: Verso.

Hering, Gunnar 1994, *Der griechische Unabhängigkeitskrieg und der Philhellenismus*, Amsterdam: Rodopi.

Hering, Gunnar 1999, *Das Kanzleiwesen Serbiens und Griechenlands in der ersten Hälfte des 19. Jahrhunderts*, Köln: Weimar and Wien: Böhlau Verlag.

Hobsbawm, Eric 1962, *The Age of Revolution: 1789–1848*, London: Weidenfeld & Nicolson.

Hobsbawm, Eric J. 1971 [1959], *Primitive Rebels: Studies in Archaic Forms of Social Movement in the 19th and 20th Centuries*, Manchester: Manchester University Press.

Howe, Samuel Gridley 1828, *An historical Sketch of the Greek Revolution*, New York: White, Gallaher & White.

Hughes, T.S. 1823, *Considerations upon the Greek Revolution*, London: G. and W.B. Whittaker.

Ilıcak, H. Şükrü 2011, *A Radical Rethinking of Empire: Ottoman State and Society during the Greek War of Independence (1821–1826)*, Ph.D. Dissertation, Harvard University.

Iliou, Philippos 2021 [1976], 'Η ιδεολογική χρήση της ιστορίας' ['The ideological use of history'], in *Πολεμική για τον χαρακτήρα της επανάστασης του 1821*, Athens: Εφημερίδα των Συντακτών.

Isabella, Mauricio and Konstantina Zanou (eds.) 2016, *Mediterranean Diasporas. Politic and Ideas in the Long Nineteenth Century*, London: Bloomsbury.

Israel, Jonathan 2010, *Revolution of the Mind: Radical Enlightenment and the Intellectual Origins of Modern Democracy*, Princeton: Princeton University Press.

Karpozilos, Kostis 2024, *Ελληνικός Κομμουνισμός. Μια διεθνική ιστορία (1912–1974)* [*Greek Communism. A Transnational History (1912–1974)*], Athens: Antipodes.

Katsiardi-Hering, Olga et al. (eds.) 2018, *Έλλην, Ρωμηός, Γραικός: συλλογικοί προσδιορισμοί και ταυτότητες* [*Hellene, Romios, Greek: Collective identifications and identities*], Athens: Ευρασία.

Katsoridas, Dimitris 2021, *Πρώιμη εργατική τάξη κατά την επανάσταση του 1821* [*Primitive working class during the revolution of 1821*], Athens: Ινστιτούτο Εργασίας Γ.Σ.Ε.Ε.

Kayaoglu, Turan 2010, *Legal Imperialism. Sovereignty and Extraterritoriality in Japan, the Ottoman Empire, and China*, New York: Cambridge University Press.

Kitromiledes, Paschalis and Triantafyllos Sklavenitis (eds.) 2004, *Πρακτικά του Δ'Διεθνούς Συνεδρίου Ιστορίας Ιστοριογραφία της νεότερης και σύγχρονης Ελλάδας 1833–2002* [*Historiograpy of modern and contemporary Greece 1833–2002*], 2 vol., Athens: National Hellenic Research Foundation.

Kitromiledes, Paschalis M. and Constantinos Tsoukalas (eds.) 2021, *The Greek Revolution: A Critical Dictionary*, Cambridge, MA and London: Harvard University Press.

Kitromilides, Paschalis 2004, 'Η ιδέα του έθνους και της εθνικής κοινότητας στην ελληνική ιστοριογραφία' ['The idea of the nation and of the national community in Greek historiography'], in *Πρακτικά του Δ'Διεθνούς Συνεδρίου Ιστορίας Ιστοριογραφία της νεότερης και σύγχρονης Ελλάδας 1833–2002*, edited by Paschalis Kitromiledes and Triantafyllos Sklavenitis, vol. 1, Athens: National Hellenic Research Foundation.

Kitromilides, Paschalis 2013, *Enlightenment and Revolution: The Making of Modern Greece*, Cambridge, MA and London: Harvard University Press.

Koliopoulos, John and Veremis Thanos (eds.) 2010, *Modern Greece: A History since 1821*, Hoboken, NJ: Wiley-Blackwell.

Kolovos, Elias (ed.) 2015, *Ottoman Rural Societies and Economies*, Rethymno: Crete University Press.

Kolovos, Elias, Şükrü Ilıcak, Mohammad Shariat-Panahi 2021, *Η οργή του σουλτάνου. Αυτόγραφα διατάγματα του Μαχμούτ Β' το 1821* [*An angry Sultan: Imperial rescripts of Mahmud II in 1821*], Athens: Hellenic Open University Press.

Kolovos, Elias and Leonidas Moiras, *Παραδοσιακά λεξιλόγια, νεωτερικά περιεχόμενα: η οθωμανική μετάφραση της Διακήρυξης της Ελληνικής Ανεξαρτησίας* [Traditional vocabularies, modern meanings: the Ottoman translation of the Declaration of the Greek Indepedence], in *Κατανοώντας τον Πόλεμο της Ανεξαρτησίας* [Understanding the Greek War of Indepedence], edited by Elias Kolovos and Kostas Kostis, Athens: Patakis.

Kordatos, Gianis 1924, *Η κοινωνική σημασία της Ελληνικής Επαναστάσεως του 1821* [The social significance of the Greek Revolution of 1821], Athens: Vasileiou.

Koselleck, Reinhart 1996, 'A response to comments on the Geschichtliche Grundbegriffe', in *The meaning of historical terms and concepts: New studies on Begriffsgeschichte*, edited by H. Lehmann and M. Richter, Washington: German Historical Institute.

Koselleck, Reinhart 2004, *Futures past: on the semantics of historical time*, New York: Columbia University Press.

Koselleck, Reinhart, Conze, Werner, Brunner, Otto (eds.) 1972, *Geschichtliche Grundbegriffe. Historisches Lexikon zur politisch-sozialen Sprache in Deutschland*. v. 1, Stuttgart: Klett-Cotta.

Kostis, Kostas 2018, *History's Spoiled Children: The Formation of the Modern Greek State*, London: Hurst.

Koubourlis, Ioannis 2005, *La formation de l'histoire nationale grecque. L'apport de Spyridon Zambélios (1815–1881)*, Athens: National Hellenic Research Foundation.

Koubourlis, Ioannis 2007, 'G. Skliros et la première critique marxiste du discours nationaliste grec', in *Byzantina et Moderna. Mélanges en l'honneur d'Hélène Antoniadis-Bibicou*, edited by Gilles Grivaud and Socrate Petmezas, Athens: Alexandreia.

Koubourlis, Ioannis 2012, *Οι ιστοριογραφικές οφειλές των Σπ. Ζαμπέλιου και Κ. Παπαρρηγόπουλου. Η συμβολή Ελλήνων και ξένων λογίων στη διαμόρφωση του τρίσημου σχήματος του ελληνικού ιστορισμού (1782–1846)* [*The historiographical debts of Sp. Zambelios and K. Paparrigopoulos. The contribution of Greek and foreign intellectuals on the formation of Greek historicism*], Athens: National Hellenic Research Foundation.

Kremmydas, Vassilis 1991, ' «Μάχου υπέρ πίστεως και πατρίδος». Μεθοδολογικές προτάσεις για τη μελέτη του Εικοσιένα' [*Fight for faith and homeland*: Methodological propositions for the study of 1821'], *Θεωρία και Κοινωνία*, 5: 67–82.

Laiou, Sophia and Marinos Sarigiannis 2019, *Οθωμανικές αφηγήσεις για την Ελληνική Επανάσταση: από τον Γιουσούφ Μπέη στον Αχμέτ Τζεβντέτ Πασά* [*Ottoman narratives on the Greek Revolution: From Yusuf Bey to Ahmed Cevdet Pasha*], Athens: National Hellenic Research Foundation.

Lazou, Vassiliki 2021, *Γυναίκες και επανάσταση: από τον οθωμανικό κόσμο στο ελεύθερο ελληνικό κράτος* [*Women and revolution: from the Ottoman world to the free Greek state*], Athens: Διόπτρα.

Leake, William Martin 1826, *An historical outline of the Greek Revolution*, London: John Murray.

Liakos, Antonis 1994, 'Προς επισκευήν ολομέλειας και ενότητος. Η δόμηση του εθνικού χρόνου' [The Construction of National Time], *Επιστημονική συνάντηση στη μνήμη του Κ. Θ. Δημαρά*, Athens: KNE/EIE, 171–199.

Liakos, Antonis 2001, 'The Construction of National Time: The Making of the Modern Greek Historical Imagination', *Mediterranean Historical Review*, 16:1, 27–42.

Liata, Eftychia 1996, *Φλωρία δεκατέσσερα στένουν γρόσια σαράντα. Η κυκλοφορία των νομισμάτων στον βενετοκρατούμενο και τουρκοκρατούμενο ελληνικό χώρο, 15°–19° αι.* [*The circulation of coins in the Greek lands under Venetian and Ottoman rule, fifteenth-nineteenth c.*], Athens: KNE/EIE.

Loukos, Christos 2004, 'Η Επανάσταση του 1821: από κυρίαρχο αντικείμενο έρευνας και διδασκαλίας, στην υποβάθμιση και σιωπή' ['The Revolution of 1821: a dominant subject of research and teaching has been neglected], in *Πρακτικά του Δ'Διεθνούς Συνεδρίου Ιστορίας Ιστοριογραφία της νεότερης και σύγχρονης Ελλάδας 1833–2002*, edited by Paschalis Kitromiledes and Triantafyllos Sklavenitis, vol. 1, Athens: National Hellenic Research Foundation.

Loukos, Christos 2007, 'Some Suggestions for a bolder Incorporation of Studies of the Greek Revolution of 1821 into their Ottoman context', in *Ottoman Rule and the Balkans, 1760–1850: Conflict, Transformation, Adaptation*, edited by A. Anastasopoulos and E. Kolovos, Rethymno: University of Crete, Department of History and Archaeology.

Makriyannis, Yannis 1966, *The Memoirs of General Makriyannis*, New York-Toronto: Oxford University Press.

Macriyannis, Yannis 1986, *Mémoires*, Paris: Albin Michel.

Mann, Michael 1986, *The Sources of Social Power*, 4 Volumes, New York: Cambridge University Press.

Margaritis, Giorgos 2020, *Ενάντια σε φρούρια και τείχη: Μια μικρή εισαγωγή για την Ελληνική Επανάσταση* [*Against fortresses and walls: A short introduction to the Greek Revolution*], Athens: Διόπτρα.

Marx, Karl & Engels, Friedrich 1975, *Marx & Engels Collected Works, Vol. 02: Engels: 1838–1842*, London: Lawrence & Wishart.

Massé, Alexandre 2019, *Un empire informel en Méditerranée. Les consuls de France en Grèce et dans l'Empire ottoman : images, ingérences, colonisation (1815–1856)*

Maximos, Serapheim 1976 [1940], *Το ελληνικό εμπορικό ναυτικό κατά τον XVIII αιώνα* [The Greek Merchant Fleet during the eighteenth century], Athens: Στοχαστής.

Mazower, Mark 2021, *The Greek Revolution: 1821 and the Making of Modern Europe*, New York: Penguin Press.

McGowan, Bruce 1992, 'The Age of the *Ayan*s, 1699–1812', in *An Economic and Social History of the Ottoman Empire*, edited by Halil İnalcık with Donald Quataert, Cambridge: Cambridge University Press.

Meiksins Wood, Ellen 1998, *The Retreat from Class. A New 'True' Socialism*, New York: Verso.

Milios, Yannis John 20202023, *1821. Ιχνηλατώντας το Έθνος, το Κράτος και τη Μεγάλη Ιδέα* [*1821. Tracing the Nations, the State and the 'Megali Idea'] Nationalism as a Claim to a State: The Greek Revolution of 1821 and the Formation of Modern Greece*, AthensBrill: Leiden – Boston.

Moiras, Leonidas 2021, *Η Ελληνική Επανάσταση μέσα από τα μάτια των Οθωμανών*, Athens: Τόπος.

Münch, Ernst Hermann Joseph 1826, *Geschichte des Aufstandes der hellenischen Nation: von der Ermordung des Patriarchen und Erklärung des Kongresses von Kalamata bis auf unsere Tage*, Basel: Schweighause.

Palmer, R.R. 1959–64, *The Age of the Democratic Revolution: A Political History of Europe and America, 1760–1800*, 2 Volumes, Princeton: Princeton University Press.

Panagiotopoulos, Vassilis 2004, 'Η αριστερή ιστοριογραφία για την Ελληνική Επανάσταση' ['The leftist historiography on the Greek Revolution'], in *Πρακτικά του Δ΄ Διεθνούς Συνεδρίου Ιστορίας Ιστοριογραφία της νεότερης και σύγχρονης Ελλάδας 1833–2002*, edited by Paschalis Kitromilides and Triantafyllos Sklavenitis, vol. 1, Athens: National Hellenic Research Foundation.

Panagiotopoulos, Vassilis 2009, 'Ένα δοκίμιο για τον Αλή Πασά', in *Αρχείο Αλή Πασά Γενναδείου Βιβλιοθήκης*, vol. IV, Athens: Hellenic National Research Foundation.

Papanikolopoulos, Dimitris 2021, *Το 1821 ως επανάσταση. Γιατί ξέσπασε και γιατί πέτυχε* [*1821 as a revolution. Why it erupted and why it succeeded*], Athens: ENA.

Papastamatiou, Dimitrios 2009, *Οικονομικοκοινωνικοί μηχανισμοί και το προυχοντικό φαινόμενο στην οθωμανική Πελοπόννησο του 18ου αιώνα. Η περίπτωση του Παναγιώτη Μπενάκη* [*Economic and social mechanisms and the notables in the Ottoman Morea during the eighteenth century: the case of Panagiotis Benakis*], Ph.D. dissertation, Aristotle University of Thessaloniki.

Philliou, Christine 2011. *Biography of an Empire: Governing Ottomans in an Age of Revolution*, Berkeley: University of California Press.

Pizanias, Petros Th. 2021, *Η Ελληνική Επανάσταση 1821–1830* [*The Greek Revolution 1821–1830*], Athens: Estia.

Pouqueville, François 1824, *Histoire de la régénération de la Grèce*, Paris: Firmin Didot Pere et fils.

Raybaud, Jean-François-Maxime 1824–5, *Mémoires sur la Grèce pour servir à l'histoire de la guerre de l'Indépendance, accompagnés de plans topographiques*, Paris: Tournachon-Molin, Libraire.

Sakellariou, Michail 1939, *Η Πελοπόννησος κατά την δευτέραν Τουρκοκρατίαν (1715–1821)* [*The Peloponnese during the second Tourkokratia (1715–1821)*], Athens: Verlag der byzantinisch-neugriechischen Jahrbucher.

Scalora, Francesco 2018, *Sicilia e Grecia. La presenza della Grecia moderna nella cultura siciliana del XIX secolo*, Palermo: Istituto Siciliano di Studi Bizantini e Neoellenici "B. Lavagnini".

Schulz, Oliver 2011, *Ein Sieg der zivilisierten Welt?: die Intervention der europäischen Grossmächte im griechischen Unabhängigkeitskrieg (1826–1832)*, Münster: Lit.

Seirinidou, Vaso 2022, 'Βία, έγκλημα και ποινική δικαιοσύνη στην επαναστατημένη Ελλάδα' [Violence, Crime and Penal Administration in Revolutionary Greece], in *Κατανοώντας τον Πόλεμο της Ανεξαρτησίας* [Understanding the Greek War of Indepedence], edited by Elias Kolovos and Kostas Kostis, Athens: Patakis.

Sheridan, Richard Brinsley 1822, *Thoughts on the Greek Revolution*, London: John Murray.

Skiotis, Dennis N. 1971, 'From Bandit to Pasha: First Steps in the Rise to Power of Ali of Tepelen, 1750–1784', *International Journal of Middle East Studies* 2,3: 219–44.

Skliros, Giorgos 1922, *Το κοινωνικό μας ζήτημα*, Athens: Εκδόσεις Σοσιαλιστικού Κέντρου [first edition 1907].

Skocpol, Theda 1979, *States and Social Revolutions. A Comparative Analysis of France, Russia and China*, New York: Cambridge University Press.

Soútsos, Aléxandros 1829, *Histoire de la révolution grecque*, Paris: Firmin Didot.

St. Clair, William 2008, *That Greece Might Still Be Free. The Philhellenes in the War of Independence*, Cambridge: Open Book.

Stamatopoulos, Dimitris (ed.) 2019, *European Revolutions and the Ottoman Balkans, Nationalism, Violence and Empire in the Long Nineteenth Century*, London: I.B. Tauris.

Stanhope, Leicester 1824, *Greece in 1823 and 1824; being a series of letters and other documents on the Greek Revolution, written during a visit to that country*, London: Sherwood, Jones & Co.

Stassinopoulou, Maria 1992, *Weltgeschichte im Denken eines griechischen Aufklärers. Konstantinos Michail Koumas als Historiograph*, Frankfurt am Main: Lang.

Stites, Richard 2014, *The Four Horsemen: Riding to Liberty in Post-Napoleonic Europe*, Oxford: Oxford University Press.

Swan, Charles 1826, *Journal of a Voyage up the Mediterranean; principally among the Islands of the Archipelago, and in Asia Minor: including particulars relative to the Greek Revolution*, London: C. and J. Rivington.

Theotokas, Nikos 2006, 'Η επανάσταση του έθνους και το ορθόδοξο γένος. Σχόλια για τις ιδεολογίες στο. Εικοσιένα' [The revolution of the nation and the Orthodox community. Comments on the ideologies of 1821], in *Η οικονομία της βίας. Παραδοσιακές και νεωτερικές εξουσίες στην Ελλάδα του 19ου αιώνα* [*The economy of violence. Traditional and modern powers in nineteenth-century Greece*], edited by Nikos Theotokas and Nikos Kotaridis, Athens: Βιβλιόραμα.

Theotokas, Nikos 2012. *Ο Βίος του στρατηγού Μακρυγιάννη. Απομνημόνευμα και ιστορία* [*The Life of General Makrygiannis: Memoirs and history*], Athens: Βιβλιόραμα.

Todorova, Maria 1997, *Imagining the Balkans*, New York: Oxford University Press.

Traverso, Enzo 2005, *Le passé: modes d'emploi histoire, mémoire, politique*, Paris: La fabrique.

Tsoukalas, Constantine 2021. 'On National Anniversaries: Greece, 1821–2021', *Journal of Balkan and Near Eastern Studies*, 23:2, 181–198.

Tzakis, Dionysis 2021, *Η μεταστροφή του Καραϊσκάκη. Από τον κλεφταρματολό στον επαναστάτη* [*The transformation of Georgios Karaiskakis: from klephtarmatolos to revolutionary*], Athens: Hellenic Open University Press.

Vakalopoulos, Apostolos 1939, *Πρόσφυγες και προσφυγικόν ζήτημα κατά την επανάστασιν του 1821: ιστορική μελέτη* [*Refugees and the issue of refugees during the revolution of 1821: historical study*], Thessaloniki.

Veinstein, Gilles 2017, *Les Ottomans. Variations sur une société d'Empire*, Paris: EHESS.

von Lüdemann, Wilhelm 1827, *Geschichte Griechenlands und der Türkei / 4: Geschichte der Osmanen und Griechen, vom Frieden von Kainardgé bis auf unsere Tage : von 1774–1827*, Dresden: Hilscher.

Yaycioglu, Ali 2016, *Partners of the Empire. The Crisis of the Ottoman Order in the Age of Revolutions*, Stanford: Stanford University Press.

Yildiz, Aysel 2017, *Crisis and rebellion in the Ottoman Empire. The Downfall of a Sultan in the Age of Revolution*, London: I.B. Tauris.

Zanou, Konstantina 2018, *Transnational Patriotism in the Mediterranean, 1800–1850: Stammering the Nation*, Oxford: Oxford University Press.

Zinkeisen, Johann Wilhelm 1840, *Geschichte Griechenlands vom Anfange geschichtlicher Kunde bis auf unsere Tage*, Leipzig: J.A. Barth.

Revisiting a 'Bourgeois Revolution'

The Greek Left and the Challenge of Theorising '1821'

Panagiotis Sotiris

The notion of the 'bourgeois revolution' is one of the most debated in the history of Marxism, in terms of both its definition and its applicability to specific historic conjunctures. As Perry Anderson has stressed, '[a]mong the concepts traditionally associated with historical materialism, few have been so problematic and contested as that of bourgeois revolution'.[1] Part of this has to do with the very way it emerged in the texts of Marx and Engels.

It is interesting that Marx does not refer to the notion of a bourgeois revolution in his early writings. Instead, in the 1843–4 period, he refers to the revolutions led by the bourgeoisie as forms of 'political revolution' aiming at a purely political emancipation, a historical process opposed to the 'radical revolution' that would be led by the proletariat. In the words of Marx, *'political* emancipation itself is not *human* emancipation'.[2] This opposition between the merely political and the social revolution aiming at total social emancipation forms the basis of Marx's early critique of bourgeois politics as inverted and alienated, with Marx suggesting that in a certain way it is political emancipation that liberates the forces that lead to social alienation.

> But the completion of the idealism of the state was at the same time the completion of the materialism of civil society. Throwing off the political yoke meant at the same time throwing off the bonds which restrained the egoistic spirit of civil society. Political emancipation was at the same time the emancipation of civil society from politics, from having even the *semblance* of a universal content.[3]

Here is one of the first formulations of this opposition, in the 'Introduction' to the *Critique of Hegel's Philosophy of Right*:

---

1   Anderson 1992, p. 105.
2   *MECW*, vol. 3, p. 160. Emphases in the original.
3   *MECW*, vol. 3, p. 166. Emphases in the original.

It is not the *radical* revolution, not the *general human* emancipation which is a Utopian dream for Germany, but rather the partial, the *merely* political revolution, the revolution which leaves the pillars of the house standing. On what is a partial, a merely political revolution based? On the fact that *part of civil society* emancipates itself and attains *general* domination; on the fact that a definite class, proceeding from its *particular situation*, undertakes the general emancipation of society. This class emancipates the whole of society but only provided the whole of society is in the same situation as this class, e.g., possesses money and education or can acquire them at will.[4]

In contrast, the proletariat emerges as the class that can actually induce this kind of radical social emancipation.

Where, then, is the *positive* possibility of a German emancipation?

Answer: In the formation of a class with *radical chains*, a class of civil society which is not a class of civil society, an estate which is the dissolution of all estates, a sphere which has a universal character by its universal suffering and claims no *particular right* because no *particular wrong* but *wrong generally* is perpetrated against it; which can no longer invoke a *historical* but only a *human* title; which does not stand in any one-sided antithesis to the consequences but in an all-round antithesis to the premises of the German state; a sphere, finally, which cannot emancipate itself without emancipating itself from all other spheres of society and thereby emancipating all other spheres of society, which, in a word, is the *complete loss* of man and hence can win itself only through the *complete rewinning of man*. This dissolution of society as a particular estate is the *proletariat*.[5]

However, what Althusser has described as Marx's 'epistemological break',[6] namely the emergence of a new theoretical problematic around 1845, articulated in the new theoretical vocabulary of historical materialism, also brought along a new notion of the 'bourgeois revolution'. Although the references to it are relatively few in the texts by Marx and Engels, this notion will acquire a sort of canonical status in the history of Marxism.

---

4   *MECW*, vol. 3, p. 184. Emphases in the original.
5   *MECW*, vol. 3, p. 186. Emphases in the original.
6   Althusser 1969.

The crucial aspect in this new problematic is that we are not dealing simply with political revolutions that were inspired or led by the bourgeoisie but with revolutions that were crucial and necessary for the very emergence of capitalism. In this new emerging narrative, a 'bourgeois revolution' is a prerequisite of any full transition to capitalism; at the same time, a bourgeois revolution is not possible if capitalism is not already developed to a certain extent.

> Incidentally, if the bourgeoisie is politically, that is, by its state power, 'maintaining injustice in property relations', it is not *creating* it. The 'injustice in property relations' which is determined by the modern division of labour, the modern form of exchange, competition, concentration, etc., by no means arises from the political rule of the bourgeois class, but vice versa, the political rule of the bourgeois class arises from these modern relations of production which bourgeois economists proclaim to be necessary and eternal laws. If therefore the proletariat overthrows the political rule of the bourgeoisie, its victory will only be temporary, only an element in the service of the *bourgeois revolution* itself, as in the year 1794, as long as in the course of history, in its 'movement', the material conditions have not yet been created which make necessary the abolition of the bourgeois mode of production and therefore also the definitive overthrow of the political rule of the bourgeoisie. The terror in France could thus by its mighty hammer-blows only serve to spirit away, as it were, the ruins of feudalism from French soil. The timidly considerate bourgeoisie would not have accomplished this task in decades. The bloody action of the people thus only prepared the way for it. In the same way, the overthrow of the absolute monarchy would be merely temporary if the economic conditions for the rule of the bourgeois class had not yet become ripe. Men build a new world for themselves, not from the 'treasures of this earth', as grobian superstition imagines, but from the historical achievements of their declining world. In the course of their development they first have to *produce* the *material conditions* of a new society itself, and no exertion of mind or will can free them from this fate.[7]

This is accompanied, especially in the *Communist Manifesto*, by an insistence on the initially revolutionary character of the bourgeoisie and the way that it dissolved feudal relations, thus helping the full expansion of capitalist social relations and the forms of class struggle they entail.

---

7   *MECW*, vol. 6, pp. 319–20.

The bourgeoisie, historically, has played a most revolutionary part.

The bourgeoisie, wherever it has got the upper hand, has put an end to all feudal, patriarchal, idyllic relations. It has pitilessly torn asunder the motley feudal ties that bound man to his 'natural superiors', and has left remaining no other nexus between man and man than naked self-interest, than callous 'cash payment'. It has drowned the most heavenly ecstasies of religious fervour, of chivalrous enthusiasm, of philistine sentimentalism, in the icy water of egotistical calculation. It has resolved personal worth into exchange value, and in place of the numberless indefeasible chartered freedoms, has set up that single, unconscionable freedom – Free Trade. In one word, for exploitation, veiled by religious and political illusions, it has substituted naked, shameless, direct, brutal exploitation.[8]

The canonical description of this general notion of *social revolution* seen as a necessary aspect of any transition process can be found in the preface to the 1859 *Critique of Political Economy*. Here, social revolution is presented as a notion applicable to all forms of modes of production.

The mode of production of material life conditions the general process of social, political and intellectual life. It is not the consciousness of men that determines their existence, but their social existence that determines their consciousness. At a certain stage of development, the material productive forces of society come into conflict with the existing relations of production or – this merely expresses the same thing in legal terms – with the property relations within the framework of which they have operated hitherto. From forms of development of the productive forces these relations turn into their fetters. Then begins an era of social revolution. The changes in the economic foundation lead sooner or later to the transformation of the whole immense superstructure.[9]

Here it seems as if Marx is offering a general theory of social revolution as a necessary aspect of any transition from one mode of production to the other. However, this general theory remains very abstract in its formulation, and there is also the problem of the possible economistic reading of the productive forces / relations of production contradiction. Moreover, this emerging narrative was

---

8 *MECW*, vol. 6, pp. 486–7.
9 *MECW*, vol. 29, p. 263.

tested mainly retroactively to the English, American and French revolutions, the last one always being the main 'case study'. It was also projected upon the insurrectionary upheaval of 1848, which marked the end of a certain era of revolutions, exemplified in the brutal suppression of the Paris workers' rebellion of June 1848. Other major processes of social upheaval and social transformation – such as the Risorgimento in Italy, the Meiji restoration in Japan or even German unification – did not receive a similar treatment. As Perry Anderson notes,

> There is nothing surprising, of course, in their ignorance of events in the secluded empire of Japan, of which few Europeans of any kind were aware. Their relative indifference to, and incomprehension of, the Italian Risorgimento ... are much more curious. Equally, if not yet more, disconcerting is the blackness with which they met the unexpected process of unification in their own country, Germany: about which Marx left us no significant text at all.[10]

One possible way to see this conceptualisation of the social revolution is to consider that such a modelling of a 'bourgeois revolution' was also necessary to support the idea and necessity of a 'socialist revolution'. If a revolution is at the heart of any process of transition from one mode of production to the other, then, in order to strengthen the idea of the historical necessity and inevitability of socialist revolution, we also need a similar conception of the historically necessary and inevitable socialist proletarian revolution.

The notion of the bourgeois revolution would re-emerge as part of the discussions on strategy in the Russian and international social democracy at the beginning of the twentieth century. Here, the stakes of the debate are not only analytical but also political and strategic. The crucial question was whether social democracy must aim first at enhancing a 'bourgeois revolution', and gain the democratic freedoms it entailed, before proceeding with a 'socialist revolution'. Here is Lenin's position on this:

> A bourgeois revolution is a revolution which does not depart from the framework of the bourgeois, i.e., capitalist, socio-economic system. A bourgeois revolution expresses the needs of capitalist development, and, far from destroying the foundations of capitalism, it effects the contrary – it broadens and deepens them. This revolution, therefore, expresses the

---

10   Anderson 1992, p. 106.

interests not only of the working class but of the entire bourgeoisie as well. Since the rule of the bourgeoisie over the working class is inevitable under capitalism, it can well be said that a bourgeois revolution expresses the interests not so much of the proletariat as of the bourgeoisie. But it is quite absurd to think that a bourgeois revolution does not at all express proletarian interests. This absurd idea boils down either to the hoary Narodnik theory that a bourgeois revolution runs counter to the interests of the proletariat, and that, therefore, we do not need bourgeois political liberty; or to anarchism which denies any participation of the proletariat in bourgeois politics, in a bourgeois revolution and in bourgeois parliamentarianism. From the standpoint of theory this idea disregards the elementary propositions of Marxism concerning the inevitability of capitalist development on the basis of commodity production. Marxism teaches us that at a certain stage of its development a society which is based on commodity production and has commercial intercourse with civilised capitalist nations must inevitably take the road of capitalism. Marxism has irrevocably broken with the Narodnik and anarchist gibberish that Russia, for instance, can bypass capitalist development, escape from capitalism, or skip it in some way other than that of the class struggle, on the basis and within the framework of this same capitalism.[11]

However, it is interesting that Lenin's main preoccupation is not the historical inevitability of 'bourgeois revolution', but the need for the proletariat to take advantage of any such conjuncture and use the political freedoms thus acquired to promote its political goals and, in particular, to help achieve proletarian hegemony in regards to other subaltern strata.[12] It is also important to stress how Lenin eventually moves on to a thinking of the possibility of a revolution that goes beyond the framework of 'bourgeois democratic revolution'.

The problems with such a theorisation of history going through stages, with bourgeois revolution being presented as a necessary phase, are important. This was stressed by the fact that a 'bourgeois revolution' did not fully materialise in certain cases – the German unification was more of a process and compromise from above – and also that the cases under consideration were not all led by the bourgeoisie. As Perry Anderson stresses,

---

11   *LCW*, vol. 9, p. 49.

12   On Lenin's conceptualisation of hegemony in the context of the democratic revolution, see Shandro 2014.

For in effect the English, North American, Italian, German and Japanese revolutions were all in different ways dominated by different landowning classes. The hegemonic force in the English Civil War were gentry; the leaders of the American War of Independence were mostly planters and farmers; German Unification was steered by junkers; the Meiji Restoration was led by samurai … Secondly, these upheavals were characteristically marked by an objective interference of lower classes in the overall interplay of forces. In France, it was the spontaneous peasant rising of 1789 that unexpectedly heaved the whole revolution forward, and the support of the peasantry that provided the mass basis for Napoleon's stabilization; in Japan, village tumults and widespread unrest accelerated the downfall of the Shogunate. In the Low Countries, the unemployed driven by hunger who smashed icons in Flanders set off the train of violence that engulfed Spanish rule. It was the laboring poor in the sanscullote crowds who gave force to the *enragés*, and demanded the Law of the Maximum. The independent organization of the German proletariat in the 1860s critically influenced the option of the industrial bourgeoisie for a bloc with the junker class. In the American Civil War, abolition was finally adopted because of the need to rally to war-weary working class.[13]

To these questions a more extensive challenge emerged, coming from those Marxists that questioned the dominant narrative. The current that came to be known as 'political Marxism' centred upon a conception of the emergence of capitalist social relations that had less to do with political upheavals and more to do with structural transformations of social property relations. In such a perspective, the actual 'revolution' in England was the emergence of agrarian capitalism as a new form of production based on new social property relations and aiming at agricultural production for the market.[14] Consequently, the English Civil War, or the Glorious Revolution, did not signify a 'bourgeois revolution' that enabled the establishment of capitalist economy. Moreover, the social forces that participated in these conflicts cannot easily be presented as those in favour of capitalism and those against. In contrast, we can see the gentry supporting the Revolution and the London merchants siding with the King.[15] Ellen Meiksins Wood summarised in the following manner Robert Brenner's position:

---

13   Anderson 1992, pp. 113–14.
14   Ashton and Philpin (eds.) 1985; Wood 2002.
15   Brenner 2003.

The traditional conception of bourgeois revolution, he argued, belongs to a phase of Marx's work still heavily dependent upon the mechanical materialism of the eighteenth-century Enlightenment and contrasts sharply with his mature critique of political economy. The earlier theory of history simply begs the central question: productive forces develop almost naturally via the division of labour which evolves in response to expanding markets, so that the pre-existence of capitalism is invoked in order to explain its coming into being. The traditional conception of bourgeois revolution as an account of the transition to capitalism is, then, self-contradictory and self-defeating.[16]

In a different context and based on his theory of the 'aleatory' and non-teleological nature of the transition to capitalism, John Milios has challenged the idea that 'bourgeois revolutions' are a necessary aspect of any transition to capitalism. Milios points to both the example of Venice as a transition to capitalism that occurred without a 'bourgeois revolution' and to the fact that the French Revolution 'broke out at least two centuries after capitalism had prevailed in (non-agrarian sectors of) the French and other European economies and societies'.[17] Milios does not deny the importance of 'bourgeois revolutions' in regards to consolidating bourgeois rule and helping the emergence of new forms of cohesion of capitalist societies, especially around nationalism, but refuses the idea that they signify the transition from feudalism to capitalism. Instead, he insists that

> So-called bourgeois revolutions, like the English of the seventeenth, or the French of the eighteenth centuries, were first and foremost mass movements that shook the relation of forces between the ruling and the ruled classes, and in this manner, by definition, also reshuffled the balance of power between the different fractions comprising the ruling class, and also created new balances of power between state apparatuses ... The American or French Revolutions in the late eighteenth century did not signify the 'transition from feudalism to capitalism', but a major reshuffling of class relations of forces within a capitalist social formation and a relevant restructuring of capitalist state apparatuses, bringing to the fore new forms of oppression, governance and consensus ... The transformations of capitalist power brought about by the French Revolution

---

16   Wood 1996, p. 221.
17   Milios 2018, p. 210.

established and subsequently disseminated across the rest of Europe a new form of cohesion of existing capitalist social formations: nationalism![18]

Historically, it was the case of more conservative theorists that provided the greater challenge to the very usefulness of 'bourgeois revolutions'. From Edmund Burke – who at the same time opposed the Revolution yet supported a political and constitutional arrangement suitable for the safeguarding of capitalist accumulation, thus offering the first reference point of subsequent conservative critiques of the French Revolution[19] – to the 'revisionist' reading of François Furet in his polemics[20] against the Marxist histories of the French Revolution,[21] the common thread is that the 'bourgeois revolution' did not represent a 'necessary historical stage.' Moreover, such positions insist that the processes of establishing capitalism as a dominant mode of production and of modernising institutions and setting the foundations of a modern State were already in progress and to a certain extent jeopardised by the social and political upheaval and violence that the Revolution brought along. This was also, to an extent, the position of Alexis de Tocqueville, who would dedicate the last phase of his work to the attempt to explain why in fact the emergence of what we can define as a bourgeois capitalist state was already in progress when the Revolution erupted. De Tocqueville did not deny the importance of the Revolution or, as he had already done in his book *Democracy in America*,[22] the inevitability of a certain democratic and egalitarian impetus, yet he insisted upon the elements of continuity between the *Ancien Régime* and the post-Revolutionary institutional forms.

As I progressed in my study, I was astonished to find again and again in the France of that time any number of the features that would strike an observer of France today. I discovered a host of sentiments that I thought had been born with the Revolution, a host of ideas that I believed to have been revolutionary ideas, and a myriad of habits purportedly bequeathed to us by that great event alone. Everywhere I found the roots of today's society firmly implanted in the soil of the old. The closer I came to 1789,

---

18   Ibid.
19   Burke 1910.
20   Furet 1978.
21   Lefebvre 2005; Soboul 1988.
22   de Tocqueville 2010.

the more distinctly I perceived the inception, birth, and development of the spirit that made the Revolution. The entire physiognomy of that Revolution revealed itself to me little by little. Its temperament, its genius, could already be divined; it was already itself. I discovered not only the logic that would guide its first steps but, perhaps more important, early hints of its long-term aftereffects.[23]

The debates in the nineteenth century and those during the twentieth century were not simply analytical or theoretical. What has been at stake is the very notion of the Revolution. One might say that there has been a constant and persistent attempt to imply that revolutions are just unhappy historical accidents and that thus we are not entitled to refer to an 'Age of Revolutions'.[24] In this respect, Domenico Losurdo has argued that there has been an entire reactionary current that has actually attempted to erase the importance of the revolutionary traditions associated with modernity.[25]

At the same time, the analytical and theoretical questions remain open, because these revolutions did occur and were to a large extent experienced as revolutions, as major social and political upheavals, as moments of historical rupture by those that took part in them. Furthermore, these revolutions seem to be a crucial and defining moment in the establishment of both bourgeois hegemony and those state forms that facilitate, guarantee and expand capitalist accumulation. One way to avoid the problems is to think beyond the 'necessity' question. In such a perspective, bourgeois revolutions do occur, but this does not mean that there must be a revolution in all cases of a transition to capitalism. As Neil Davidson has stressed:

> [T]he bourgeois revolution is not the embodiment of a structured relationship, like those of wage labor to capital or of peasants to the tax collector; it is the enactment of a process. Consequently, to treat the characteristics of the French case as the highest level of bourgeois revolutionary development is to imply that countries that do not display these characteristics have either undergone an incomplete experience or failed to undergo the experience at all, with all the political and theoretical confusions that follow.[26]

---

23   de Tocqueville 2011.
24   Hobsbawm 1996.
25   Losurdo 2020.
26   Davidson 2012, p. 489.

If we leave aside the notion of necessity, with all its teleological connotations, then we can think of the possibility and contingency of bourgeois revolutions (necessarily in the plural). Consequently, we are talking about specific con-junctures where the emergence and reproduction of capitalist social relations also entails an accumulation of contradictions that might lead to a revolution-ary process that will ensure the dominant political role of the bourgeoisie and its potential hegemony. Revolutions might have sometimes been the result of bourgeois/capitalist ascendancy to power, sometimes the preconditions and in other cases the way to deal with the contradictions accumulated. As Davidson notes:

> In fact, there are no examples where a perfect equilibrium between feud-alism and capitalism existed prior to the bourgeois revolution taking place. Bourgeois revolutions are the only types of social revolution that have occurred *during* the transition from the dominance of one mode of production to another; consequently, they were neither the culmination of a socioeconomic process like the feudal 'revolution' nor a moment of politico-social transformation like the socialist revolution. The extent to which individual bourgeois revolutions tended toward either the former or the latter varied depended on the stage in the transition to capitalism during which they took place. In some cases, bourgeois revolution was primarily a means of facilitating the further development of capitalism in conditions where key aspects of the transition had taken place before the revolutions began: these cases resemble the transition to feudalism. In other, later cases, bourgeois revolution was primarily a precondition for the emergence of capitalism in conditions where key aspects of the transition had still to take place after the revolutions ended: these cases resemble the socialist revolution.[27]

1   Gramsci, Jacobinism and Hegemony

Antonio Gramsci was not a historian of bourgeois revolutions. Moreover, he focused on the contradictions of a process, that of the Italian Risorgimento, that was more contradictory and rather far from the 'ideal type' of a 'bourgeois revolution'. However, Gramsci reads the French Revolution as an example of a

---

27   Davidson 2012, pp. 507–8.

new hegemonic political practice, the political practice of an emerging bourgeois hegemony.

> On the subject of Jacobinism and the Action Party, an element to be highlighted is the following: that the Jacobins won their function of 'leading' [*dirigente*] party by a struggle to the death; they literally 'imposed' themselves on the French bourgeoisie, leading it into a far more advanced position than the originally strongest bourgeois nuclei would have spontaneously wished to take up, and even far more advanced than that which the historical premises should have permitted – hence the various forms of backlash and the function of Napoleon I. This feature, characteristic of Jacobinism (but before that, also of Cromwell and the 'Roundheads') and hence of the entire French Revolution, which consists in (apparently) forcing the situation, in creating irreversible *faits accomplis*, and in a group of extremely energetic and determined men driving the bourgeois forward with kicks in the backside, may be schematized in the following way. The Third Estate was the least homogeneous; it had a very disparate intellectual elite, and a group which was very advanced economically but politically moderate. Events developed along highly interesting lines. The representatives of the Third Estate initially only posed those questions which interested the actual physical members of the social group, their immediate 'corporate' interests (corporate in the traditional sense, of the immediate and narrowly selfish interests of a particular category). The precursors of the Revolution were in fact moderate reformers, who shouted very loud but actually demanded very little. Gradually a new elite was selected out which did not concern itself solely with 'corporate' reforms, but tended to conceive of the bourgeoisie as the hegemonic group of all the popular forces. This selection occurred through the action of two factors: the resistance of the old social forces, and the international threat.[28]

However, what is important is how Gramsci stresses that the revolutionary legacy is a crucial aspect of the emergence of the new politicity of modernity that incorporates the element of recognition of the subaltern classes and the formation of the national popular elements. This is expressed in this emphasis on the 'Jacobin' aspect as part of the formation of a 'national-popular collective

---

28   Gramsci 1971, p. 77; Gramsci 1975, pp. 2027–8 (Q19, §24).

will', which is one of the aspects of a hegemonic political practice. Referring to the limitations of the Italian sequence, he stresses that:

> An effective Jacobin force was always missing, and could not be consti-
> tuted; and it was precisely such a Jacobin force which in other nations
> awakened and organised the national-popular collective will, and foun-
> ded the modern States.[29]

At the same time, he stressed that the Jacobins in fact always remained within the contours of a bourgeois capitalist perspective: 'That the Jacobins, des-pite everything, always remained on bourgeois ground is demonstrated by the events which marked their end, as a party cast in too specific and inflexible a mould, and by the death of Robespierre. Maintaining the Le Chapelier law, they were not willing to concede to the workers the right of combination; as a consequence they had to pass the law of the *maximum*'.[30]

All these references to Jacobinism point to this conceptualisation of a revo-lutionary political practice that manages to mobilise the subaltern classes as well – in a certain way enhancing the hegemony of the bourgeoisie, but in a hegemonic relation that is based on active consent and recognition of the subaltern. In contrast, in the post-1848 period, Gramsci discerns a period of 'passive revolution', where the crucial aspect is emphasis on the fragmentation and disaggregation of the subaltern classes. 'Passive revolution' is a concept that Gramsci takes from Vicenzo Cuoco, who in his classic history of the Naples Revolution of 1799 suggested that it was a 'passive' revolution led by a revolu-tionary elite unable to mobilise the people.[31] For Gramsci, 'passive revolution' acquires a broader meaning, pointing to processes of political transformation and the establishment of bourgeois political forms where no 'Jacobin' revolu-tionary appeal is involved.

I think that Gramsci is important not because of an answer to the ques-tion of whether 'bourgeois revolutions' represent a necessary historical stage, since he was far from any variety of teleology, but as an answer to the signi-ficance of popular participation as a part of the emergence of a hegemonic practice. Moreover, Gramsci's conceptualisation of Jacobinism, although to a certain extent a 'metonymic' reference rather than an actual historical analysis, is important in order to understand the importance of intellectuals and those

---

29   Gramsci 1971, p. 131; Gramsci 1975, pp. 1559–60 (Q13, §1).
30   Gramsci 1971, p. 79; Gramsci 1975, pp. 2020–30 (Q19, §24).
31   Cuoco 1913.

strata that take over the task of bringing forward that revolutionary enthusiasm that is instrumental in enabling the hegemonic relation with subaltern groups.

2   The Debate inside the Greek Communist Movement

In the case of the Greek Revolution of 1821, on the one hand we have all the elements suggesting an association between the revolutionary process and dynamic and the emergence of capitalist social forms and the fact that the main demand of the Revolution was the formation of a bourgeois state. We also have the fact that it actually took the form of an armed uprising, from the first moment using the rhetoric and symbolism of a revolution.

However, at the same time the Greek Revolution offered the cornerstone of a national narrative that also included territorial expansion in the form of the 'Megali Idea'. The idea of an entire nation united in struggle remained for a long time not only a basic source of legitimacy for the new state but also a form of recognition and, at the same time, a mystification of the role of the subaltern classes. This can explain why it was important for the socialist and communist movement to counter this narrative and offer an alternative explanation. At the same time, the narratives that the Marxist left attempted to present varied according to the different ways the left, and in particular the Communist Party, defined its political strategy, thus making the historiography of the Greek Revolution the terrain par excellence of what Philippos Iliou in 1976 called 'the ideological use of history'.[32]

What is more important is how these questions coincided with the different readings offered by the Marxist left. Historically, the first reading stressed the element that it was a bourgeois revolution, and one might say that this was an attempt to 'deconstruct' the dominant nationalist narrative. However, a big debate would erupt that centred on the extent of subaltern-class participation in a 'popular' or 'national' revolution.

The first reading of the Greek Revolution by a Greek Marxist was offered by Georgios Skliros. Coming from the Black Sea, Skliros was a student in Moscow during the 1905 Revolution and a follower of Plekhanov, and he would later study in Germany and end up as a doctor in Cairo. Skliros's 1907 book the *Social Question* perhaps represented the first attempt to offer a Marxist reading of modern Greek history. It is here that we find the first reference to the Greek Revolution as a 'bourgeois revolution, caused by the outstanding eco-

---

32   Iliou 1976, pp. 197–207.

nomic well-being of the bourgeois elements, both inside and outside Greece, and the awaking of national sentiment, especially in the advanced bourgeois classes and the scholars of the nation'.[33] In his 1919 *Contemporary Problems of Hellenism,* one can find an apprehension of the complexities of the social, political and ideological dynamics of the Greek Revolution. For Skliros, even in Rigas Feraios one can find references to, at the same time, the nation, religion, Ancient Greece and the coming together of all peoples of the Ottoman Empire against the Sultan. Skliros also conveys how the complexity of the situation of the Greek nation at that particular conjuncture could explain choices such as starting the Revolution in the Danube hegemonies. This can also account, according to Skliros, for the co-existence of both a bourgeois element and a more 'aristocratic' one coming from the Byzantine traditions. For Skliros, the Revolution was the result of the alliance of social forces coming from the Greek islands, the Morea and Roumeli. He attributed particular importance to the islands because among the merchants and ship-owners one could find the more advanced bourgeois elements and the clear demand for a 'united central Government, with a liberal constitutional bourgeois polity'.[34] Skliros also referred to the other social forces, such as the landowners of Moreas or the leaders of armed groups from Roumeli, but it is interesting that he treated them as the 'one big *bourgeois class* of the Greek people, with its different *varieties,* depending on each one's labour: sailor, merchant, farmer, warrior, man of letters and politics'.[35]

The main argument in favour of treating the Greek Revolution as a bourgeois revolution was offered by Giannis Kordatos in his 1924 book *The Social Significance of the Greek Revolution.*[36] Kordatos was at the time a member of the leadership of the Greek Communist Party. For him, it was the economic growth of the Greek bourgeoisie that led to the Revolution:

> [T]he newly formed social class, the *bourgeoisie,* had reached *significant material development.* Because of this reason (the objective condition of a revolution) and the prevailing Pan-European upheaval because of the appeal and fanaticism caused by the French revolutionary (democratic) ideas (the subjective condition), the Greek *bourgeois* class was pushed towards the idea of the Revolution against the Turkish yoke. And if the recently emerged Greek bourgeois class were not as materially advanced

---

33   Skliros 1976, p. 114.
34   Skliros 1976, p. 234.
35   Skliros 1976, p. 241.
36   Kordatos 1924.

as it was, with the huge growth of commerce and shipping both inside and outside of Greece, it would not have been psychologically prepared to receive the French revolutionary ideas and to be fanatically inspired by the doctrines of the French Revolution.[37]

For Kordatos, in Rhigas Feraios we can find the 'prevailing *bourgeois spirit* of the Greek Revolution'.[38] The contradictory ideological elements that Skliros stressed in the *Contemporary Problems of Hellenism* were for Kordatos something to be expected, since 'in no national revolution, even in *social* revolutions, is it possible to have a full eradication of old prejudices'.[39] In regards to the civil wars within the Greek Revolution, Kordatos insisted that they should be explained on the basis of the conflicting class strategies of the bourgeoisie and the landowners of the Peloponnese and not on the basis of personal ambitions. For Kordatos, the bourgeoisie was the leading force of the revolution, even if it 'needed the cooperation of the kodjabashis and the clergy'.[40] However, both Kapodistrias's rule and the arrival of King Otto represented a 'defeat of the bourgeoisie and the prevalence of feudal (royalist) elements'.[41] However, Kordatos insisted that after the end of the crisis of trade and shipping the bourgeoisie managed to regain power in 1844, and that by 1863 the *kocabaşıs* had lost their social and political primacy and chose to ally with the petty bourgeois and backward elements of the bourgeoisie. Moreover, in regards to the stance of the Great Powers, Kordatos insisted that it had nothing to do with philhellenism but simply with their specific interests in the regions. Kordatos believes that after 1880 'the old bourgeoisie is transformed into *a capitalist class*'.[42] Consequently, the main form of class conflict was not between the bourgeoisie and feudal remnants but between capital and labour. And this is the period, in particular 1912–22, when the bourgeoisie 'plays the role of imperialism by actively taking part in the European war'.[43] Ergo, the progressive role of the bourgeoisie 'has long bygone',[44] and only the 'organized working class is a *progressive* class'.[45]

---

37   Kordatos 1924, p. 47.
38   Kordatos 1924, p. 61.
39   Kordatos 1924, p. 64.
40   Kordatos 1924, p. 134.
41   Kordatos 1924, p. 135.
42   Kordatos 1924, p. 166.
43   Ibid.
44   Kordatos 1924, p. 167.
45   Kordatos 1924, p. 168.

Kordatos tended to underestimate the role of the kodjabashis and the clergy as part of the alliance around the Revolution in order to stress its bourgeois character. However, in a certain manner such an approach was necessary in a period where the Communist Party attempted to draw a line of demarcation with all varieties of bourgeois politics, both royalist and democratic. This is particularly apparent if we take account of the Party's attempt to fight the influence of varieties of 'Venizelism', some of them even reclaiming a social democratic reference. Consequently, it was imperative for communist intellectuals like Kordatos to distance themselves from the 'democratic nationalist' reading of the Greek Revolution in order exactly to suggest the need for radical political and ideological independence of the proletariat against all forms of bourgeois politics.

Kordatos's reading of the Greek Revolution in 1924 coincides with the line of SEKE/KKE at that period, namely the insistence on a socialist revolution led by the proletariat and a clear anti-capitalist program. As John Milios has stressed:

> We can see that until the mid-1920s, G. Kordatos appears as the main representative of the official Marxism of that period, as this was expressed by the main Marxist political organization, SEKE / KKE, in a direction similar to the analysis and theoretical conclusions of the Third International. This Marxism arrives at different conclusions than the Soviet Marxism that will become dominant some years later: it considers social relations in Greece as capitalist and on the basis of this analysis it grounds the necessity and pertinence of socialist revolution as the political strategy of the working class and its allies (mainly poor peasants).[46]

Kordatos disagreed with some of the key decisions of the third extraordinary congress of the KKE at the end of 1924, and he would distance himself from the party as a result.[47] Gradually, the party's analysis would change both in regards to the nature of Greek capitalism and the degree of its advancement. It was no longer a question of Greek capitalism on the rise, aggressive and imperialist; the emphasis shifted to the backward, underdeveloped and semifeudal country, in line with the changing positions of the Communist International.[48] At the same time, the factional divisions in the Communist Party and the fight against the varieties of Left Opposition added extra fuel to the heat of the debates. It is in this context that in 1933 Kordatos would be the target of a harsh attack by

---

46   Milios 2017, p. 51.
47   On Kordatos's overall theoretical and political trajectory, see Milios 2017.
48   Milios 2017, pp. 56–60.

Giannis Zevgos, at that time a member of the Party leadership, an attack that would focus exactly on the question of the character of the Greek Revolution.

This attack coincided with a major change in the line of the KKE, a change that would be made official on January 1934, at the Sixth Plenary of the Central Committee, the party body that would mark the solidification of the new leadership. The change of the party line in regards to the character of Greek society, and consequently the struggle for socialist revolution, is presented simply as an application of the general line of the 1928 Sixth Congress of the Communist International. There we can find the following reference to countries like Greece and the character of the Revolution. Greece was considered one of the

> [c]ountries with a medium development of capitalism (Spain, Portugal, Poland, Hungary, the Balkan countries, etc.), having numerous survivals of semi-feudal relationships in agriculture, possessing, to a certain extent, the material pre-requisites for socialist construction, and in which the bourgeois-democratic reforms have not yet been completed. In some of these countries a process of more or less rapid development from bourgeois democratic revolution to socialist revolution is possible. In others, there may be types of proletarian revolution which will have a large number of bourgeois-democratic tasks to fulfil. Hence, in these countries, the dictatorship of the proletariat may not come about at once, but in the process of transition from the democratic dictatorship of the proletariat and peasantry to the socialist dictatorship of the proletariat. Where the revolution develops directly as a proletarian revolution it is presumed that the proletariat exercises leadership over a broad agrarian peasant movement. In general, the agrarian revolution plays a most important part in these countries, and in some cases a decisive role: in the process of expropriating large landed property a considerable portion of the confiscated land is placed at the disposal of the peasantry; the volume of market relations prevailing after the victory of the proletariat is considerable; the task of organising the peasantry along co-operative lines and later, of combining them in production, occupies an important place among the tasks of socialist construction. The rate of this construction is relatively slow.[49]

In the Greek case, this was translated into a repudiation of previous positions, both supposedly 'right-wing' and sectarian and into a new emphasis on

---

49   Communist International 1929.

Greece's 'significant dependency on foreign capital' and the survival of 'semi-feudal elements'.[50] According to the new line, these characteristics were combined with a relatively low degree of development of the productive forces and an emphasis on the importance of the peasantry as an ally to the proletariat. Consequently '*the imminent revolution of the proletariat and the peasantry in Greece will have a bourgeois-democratic character with a tendency towards quick transformation into a proletarian revolution*'.[51] In this context, the challenge for the proletariat was to be the 'hegemon of the revolution',[52] in a phrasing that echoes again the theses of the Sixth Congress of the International.

This was translated into a different approach to the historiography of the Greek Revolution. It was Giannis Zevgos, one of the leading cadres of the KKE, who took up the task of this 'translation' by means of an outright attack against Kordatos and his conceptualisation of the Revolution. Firstly, Kordatos was accused of 'developing an eonomistic, mechanical, social-democratic theory that has nothing to do with Marxism',[53] because he stressed the role of the economy and not of class struggle and because he 'identifies the productive forces with tools'.[54] Secondly, Kordatos was accused of offering a 'fatalistic' conception,[55] because he treated the bourgeoisie as the only progressive class in the bourgeois revolution, thus underestimating the importance of the class struggle waged by the proletariat. In contrast, Zevgos insisted that it was possible that the proletariat

> ... realizing its historical role within favourable historical conditions, can achieve hegemony within the bourgeois-democratic revolution, smashing the united feudal-bourgeois reaction and offering a revolutionary solution to the problems of the bourgeois-democratic revolution makes it develop into a socialist revolution and begins constructing socialism.[56]

Zevgos's main point of disagreement with Kordatos refers to the leading role played by the bourgeoisie in the Greek Revolution. He accused Kordatos of presenting a simplified opposition between the bourgeoisie and the *kocabaşıs*

---

50   KKE 1975, p. 19.
51   KKE 1975, p. 23.
52   KKE 1975, p. 25.
53   Zevgos 1933a, p. 13.
54   Zevgos 1933a, p. 16.
55   Zevgos 1933b, p. 24.
56   Ibid.

and of underestimating the role of the popular masses. For Zevgos, the sailors were more instrumental than the island merchants and ship-owners in the Revolution, and he criticises Kordatos for not paying enough attention to the class struggle between the poor peasants and the *kocabaşıs*. In contrast, Zevgos insisted that the Revolution was marked by intense class struggle that even took the form of civil war, a 'struggle for hegemony of the revolution'.[57]

Zevgos presented an image of the Greek Revolution where in the end a 'left-wing, popular, democratic bloc' was formed 'by the insurgent peasantry, the artisans, the sailors and petty intellectuals'.[58] The bourgeoisie fought against both this democratic bloc and against the military leaders that wanted a form of absolutism and to impose their own oligarchic version of a constitutional monarchy. For Zevgos, the bourgeoisie was in the end the main enemy of all the popular masses. Its conservatism, oscillations and 'at certain points betrayal' ran contrary to the 'sacrifices of the Greek people, offered a half-baked solution to the national question and did not offer solutions to the peasant question, the constitutional question and the language question'.[59]

Zevgos would continue the polemic with two more articles[60] which dealt with how Kordatos viewed the history of the Greek working-class movement and the economics of Greek capitalism. In these texts, which are full of polemics articulated in the 'Third Period' language of that time (Kordatos as 'Trotskyist' and apologist of social-fascism, etc.), again the main point is that Kordatos did not understand the 'parasitic' character of Greek capital and the importance of its dependency on foreign capital, and that he used the same arguments about an inability of economic development that was due to the lack of natural resources that the Greek bourgeoisie used to justify its imperialist endeavours. Kordatos in his responses[61] would accuse Zevgos of misrepresenting his positions (and also of misquoting him), and he would insist that the bourgeoisie played a progressive role in the Revolution, such as in its confrontations with the *kocabaşıs*.

Obvious in Zevgos's critique of Kordatos is the attempt to offer an alternative narrative of the bourgeois revolution, one in which the class struggle of the subaltern strata against both the bourgeoisie and the *kocabaşıs* was the driving force of the Revolution and in which the bourgeoisie was credited with not

---

57   Zevgos 1933b, p. 29.
58   Zevgos 1933b, p. 30.
59   Zevgos 1933b, p. 35.
60   Zevgos 1933c and Zevgos 1933d.
61   Kordatos 1933a and Kordatos 1933b.

being able to fulfil the tasks of the bourgeois-democratic revolution. This new narrative was closer to the changed line in regards to the Revolution in Greece. If there was not going to be a 'proletarian revolution' in Greece, but instead a bourgeois-democratic revolution that would transform into a socialist one, then two premises were necessary: (a) an analysis of the War of Independence that would insist on the unfinished character of the 'bourgeois-democratic revolution', and (b) an emphasis on the role that the poor peasantry could play in such an alliance with the proletariat.

Moreover, in Kordatos's 1924 analysis one can find the attempt to draw a sharp line of demarcation between the dominant narrative of the Revolution as the moment of the resurrection of the nation and to present the proletariat as offering an antagonistic historical project (i.e. socialism against all the competing bourgeois strategies expressed in the 'Great Divide'). As Philippos Iliou noted in 1976,[62] Kordatos's positions corresponded to a period in which it seemed imperative to the communist movement in Greece to insist on an accomplished bourgeois-democratic revolution in nineteenth-century Greece in order to support the position that only a proletarian-socialist revolution was now possible. In contrast, in Zevgos's new narrative we can find the attempt to reclaim for the proletariat and its allies parts of the legacy and dynamics of the Greek Revolution and to present the strategy of the Communist Party as both a road to socialism and an answer to open questions and historical dilemmas of Greek society in a period of crisis. Such a strategic shift coincided with the incorporation of the economism of the Comintern's characterisation of Greek society, which tended to underestimate the actual dynamism of Greek capital.[63] At the same time, as Iliou noted, the new strategy pointed towards a 'revolution of bourgeois-democratic character that will take place without the participation of any segment of the bourgeoisie, and against it, because the latter is fully positioned within the reactionary front'.[64] Iliou's assessment of this dialogue is that both positions lacked an actual analysis of the contradictory dynamics of the Greek Revolution and 'of the actual economic mechanisms, social structures and collective stances', the result being that 'prescription substituted for historical analysis'.[65] Moreover, Iliou thinks that Zevgos's attempt to offer an image of a strong popular bloc in the Revolution led to a form of 'populist' historiography in the Greek left, where the references to class and

---

62   Iliou 1976.
63   On the political line of the KKE during the 1930s, see Elefantis 1979.
64   Iliou 1976, p. 203.
65   Iliou 1976, p. 205.

class struggle were replaced by the dichotomy between 'popular' and 'anti-popular',[66] thus leading to an 'ideological conception of history'.[67]

As the Communist Party moved more towards a 'popular front' strategy in the second half of the 1930s, the emphasis on alliances within the antifascist front became stronger, and this also had an impact on the line of the party in regards to the Greek Revolution.[68] As the general secretary of KKE Nikos Zahariadis noted, the sequence of popular insurrections, internal strife, military coups and national tragedies that form the history of the modern Greek state had its roots in the way dominant social groups imposed a form of 'quasi-colonial exploitation' that 'strangled the internal productive capabilities and condemned the people to deep poverty'.[69]

During the period of the German Occupation and the antifascist resistance, the analogies between the national liberation struggle against the Nazi occupation and the Greek Revolution became part of the rhetoric of communist intellectuals and also of the imagery of the resistance movement. The general feeling that the Greek bourgeoisie had opted for capitulation and collaboration with the forces of the occupation meant that it was up to the popular bloc to take up the historical task of national liberation. This made even stronger the importance of presenting a history of the Greek Revolution as one in which the bourgeoisie in its collaboration with the *kocabaşıs* was responsible for its unfulfilled character.[70] This new attempt to present the Greek Revolution as above all a 'People's Revolution' is exemplified in the popularity of books such as Giorgis Lambrinos's *Figures of Twenty One*, which was first published in 1942. The full uncensored version that appeared in 1945 makes the analogies between the antifascist resistance and the Greek Revolution even more obvious.[71] It is also interesting to note that during this period Kordatos moved towards a reading of the Greek Revolution that was closer to the new line expressed by both KKE and EAM. In 1946, Kordatos presented an updated edition of his *Social Significance of the Greek Revolution of 1821*, which included substantial changes that stressed the importance of 'Great Powers' and insisted that 'foreign capital ... robbed the people and kept the country underdeveloped, in order to treat us like colonial subjects'.[72]

---

66   Iliou 1976, p. 206.
67   Iliou 1976, p. 207.
68   Mailis 2020.
69   Zachariadis 1953, p. 10.
70   Mailis 2020.
71   Lambrinos 2002. On the even greater emphasis given during the 1940s to the role of the 'people' in the Greek Revolution, see Stathis 2014.
72   Kordatos 1972, p. 273.

In the 1950s a more 'balanced' approach gradually appeared. The Revolution was again presented as a national liberation movement, yet this time the role of the Greek bourgeoisie was not negated; at the same time, however, the bourgeoisie's inability to fully take up the task of national liberation was stressed as the root of the subsequent crisis.[73] This coincided with a period in which the Greek left, facing repression after defeat in the Civil War – with the dominant state rhetoric being that the communists were 'anti-national elements' – attempted to present itself as the more consistent 'national' political force, one that struggled for the interests of the Greek people (and nation) much more than a bourgeoisie that was servile to imperialism. However, it is interesting that there was a debate on the 1954 draft programme of the KKE, particularly on the question of whether the Party should adopt a view of Greek history that stressed the continuity of the Greek nation as the programme seemed to suggest.[74]

A notable exception to the emerging consensus within the KKE during the 1940s was Serafeim Maximos. A former leading figure of the KKE who later aligned himself with the 'Left Opposition' – yet eventually returning to positions closer to the KKE – Maximos offered significant studies of the emergence of Greek capital under Ottoman Rule from the late seventeenth century to the eighteenth century and hence of the formation of the Greek bourgeoisie.[75]

Subsequent historiography has offered valuable insights into the social and political dynamics of the Revolution, leaving aside the 'prescriptive' attempts to justify a conception of a 'People's Revolution'. In these readings, both the relation between the emergence of a Greek national movement and the gradual expansion of capitalist social relations, in the form of commercial capital, and the particular and complex power relations and subaltern dynamics, all contributed to the contradictory articulation of social forces behind the Revolu-

---

73   See for example Strigkos 1966. This attempt for a more 'balanced' approach is also evident in Vournas's *Short History of the Greek Revolution* (1966) where the positions that 'overlooked the role of the bourgeoisie in Greece as a vanguard revolutionary force' (p. 5) are treated as erroneous and 'populist' (p. 6).

74   See the critique in Hadjis 1954. Curiously enough, the strategy part of the Draft insisted on the socialist and not bourgeois character of the Revolution for which the Communist Party was struggling. The Draft Programme would eventually be abandoned (see KKE 2012). However, a certain reference to some form of continuity could still be found in the work of left-wing historians. See for example Svoronos 2004 and Svoronos 1995.

75   See for example Maximos 1973 and Maximos 1974. On Maximos as a Marxist, see Milios 2017.

tion. Beginning with the work of Svoronos in the 1950s[76] – and his subsequent work,[77] despite its limitations–[78] there have been important contributions to the study of the social and economic dynamics that led to the Greek Revolution,[79] the political conflicts[80] and the subaltern currents in action in the Revolution.[81] There have also been more recent attempts[82] to read the Greek Revolution in light of Charles Tilly's conceptualisation of social movements and revolution.[83]

Recently, there have been new contributions to the study of the social and economic dynamics of the Greek Revolution as a bourgeois revolution or as one conditioned by the aspirations of the Greek bourgeoisie.

One came in the form of a collective volume by the history section of the Communist Party,[84] a volume which concludes a certain shift in the positions of the KKE towards a rethinking of the Greek Revolution as a bourgeois revolution. This is most evident in the essay by the late Makis Mailis, the head of the Party's history section, which stresses that a large part of the previous interpretations of the Greek Revolution – and in particular the conception of a 'popular-democratic' or 'national' revolution – had more to do with political exigencies in the 1930s and 1940s, and the Party's turn towards a 'popular front' line and choices made during the resistance, than with actual historical research.[85] Moreover, the contributions to the volume return to the conception of the Greek Revolution as a bourgeois revolution, one that

> ... necessarily expressed the interests of the rising bourgeoisie and consequently could only lead to the formation of a bourgeois state. The bourgeois nation-state represented the truly revolutionary answer in that era to the impasse of feudal power, but it could not lead to the elimination of class exploitation. Consequently, the Revolution was not the product

76 Svoronos 1992.
77 Svoronos 1995.
78 On this, see Stathis 2014.
79 See inter alia Asdrachas (ed.) 2003; Katsiardi-Herring 2003; Kremmydas 2016; Pizanias 2021.
80 Petropoulos 1985; Herring 2004.
81 On this, it important to stress the work of Asdrachas (2019), Theotokas and Kotaridis (2006), Theotokas (2013) and also the way that the 'primitive revolution' thematic (Hobsbawm 1959) has been used.
82 Papanikolopoulos 2021.
83 Tilly 1978.
84 KKE – History Section (ed.) 2020.
85 Mailis 2020.

of national unity, but in contrast the result of unresolved class struggle, which continued both during the revolution and after the recognition of Independence.[86]

It is obvious that we are here dealing with a return to a 'classical' Marxist conception of the bourgeois revolution as a solution to the contradictions between the rising bourgeoisie and the existing feudal social relations, with a stronger emphasis on the element of the persistence of class struggles during the revolution, in comparison to approaches such as the ones offered by earlier theorists such as Kordatos.

Another important contribution to a Marxist reading of the Greek Revolution came from John Milios in a book that first appeared in Greek[87] and more recently, in an updated version, in English.[88] His approach is based on a conception of the emergence of the capitalist mode of production[89] that stresses its non-teleological character and the importance of the gradual emergence of both merchant capitalists and a 'free' labour force (as well as their 'encounter'), a process that precedes 'bourgeois revolutions' (which cannot be considered to represent some form of necessary 'historical stage'). For Milios, the Greek Revolution aimed at creating bourgeois-representative institutions and establishing a bourgeois-constitutional state. In particular the revolution was the 'result of the dominance of nationalism and thus also of the demand of a large segment of the population for a representative-constitutional state'.[90] As such, it was this 'national politicization of the masses, and their demand for institutions of representation (and therefore for a national-constitutional bourgeois state of 'citizens'), which formed a historically new way of integrating the populations into the state, subsuming them under the already prevailing capitalist relations of domination and exploitation'[91] by means of imposing 'national unity' over class antagonism. What is important about Milios's contribution is that it is not limited to bringing to the fore the importance of the emergence of capitalist social relations as historical context of the Revolution, for it also stresses the emergence of nationalism as at the same time a potential consolidation of bourgeois rule and a form of recognition of the subaltern classes, which

---

86   KKE – History Section (ed.) 2020, p. 15.
87   Milios 2020.
88   Milios 2023.
89   Outlined in Milios 2018.
90   Milios 2023, p. 15.
91   Milios 2020, p. 3.

can also account for the more radical and democratic aspects of the dynamics of such revolutionary processes.

Consequently, the emphasis is not on the Revolution as a facilitation of the transition to capitalism (the classical idea of 'bourgeois revolution' as the 'social revolution' necessary for the transition to capitalism) but on the 'national revolution' as contradictory historical process. This process emerged as the result of acute social and political antagonisms. These aimed at consolidating the rule of capital (and the extended and expansive reproduction of capitalist accumulation) within constitutional forms that recognise the demands and aspirations of the subaltern classes. This, however, also worked to mystify class antagonisms, attaching them to the dominant capitalist strategy (and imperialist aspiration), which was itself presented as a 'national project'.

3   Conclusion

The Greek Revolution posed both an analytical/theoretical and a political challenge. On the one hand it called for the 'application' of Marxism as alternative historical interpretation. But on the other it tested its ability to offer an alternative historical narrative that could justify strategic positions of the Greek left. In this sense, it was an inherently contradictory process and confrontation overdetermined by specific conjunctures and the political projects articulated within them. Of particular importance was the attempt on the part of the Communist Party, especially during a Resistance movement that also took part in a prolonged Civil War, to present the proletariat as a leading national force. This had to with an anti-fascist resistance – one that also represented an original form of a potentially socialist revolutionary process, even though it was conceived within the limits of the 'Popular Front strategy'. This retrospective projection of the realities of the antifascist resistance can account for the attempt of the left to reappropriate the Greek Revolution as part of its own narrative. Moreover, the continuous appeal of such an interpretation is explained by the viewpoint that this historical phase marked the most extensive ability of the left to represent the subaltern classes (thus in a certain way representing the closest example of the emergence of an antagonistic 'historical bloc').

At the same time, the Greek Revolution brings to the fore the open question of a Marxist interpretation of the historical phenomena traditionally defined as 'bourgeois revolutions'. The preceding presentation made evident that this is still a contested theoretical terrain, and it is beyond the scope of this chapter to attempt to offer an answer to questions that remain so stubbornly open. However, I think that it is possible to sketch at least some starting points.

Even if 'bourgeois revolutions' were not indispensable for the emergence and becoming-dominant of the capitalist mode of production, and thus do not represent a necessary historical stage – an interpretation that would have brought us back to the impasse of such a combination between economism and a certain version of historical teleology – actual historical 'bourgeois revolutions' were more than crucial in the articulation of forms of bourgeois hegemony. Not only were they the outcome of historically specific and over-determined dynamics within particular historical conjunctures of social and political antagonisms – induced by the extended reproduction of capitalist social relations and forms – but such revolutions also enabled the emergence of new hegemonic practices by means of uneven and complex forms of recognition and subsumption of the subaltern classes and of new forms of mass politicity within 'national' or 'national-democratic' interpellations. In this sense, they were indeed crucial historical nodes in the formation of the 'national-popular' element that for Gramsci sets the terrain for both the articulation of bourgeois hegemony (and the new forms of mass politicisation associated with modernity and all the 'molecular' foundations of hegemony) and its potential challenge by an antagonistic subaltern hegemony. The way Gramsci moved from the discussion of Jacobinism to the discussion of the potential hegemonic practice of the 'modern Prince', the political form of a potential subaltern 'hegemonic project' and a profound process of social transformation by means of the elaboration of an antagonistic 'national-popular collective will', is instructive of the dynamics and historical potentialities associated with what are usually defined as 'bourgeois revolutions'.

> The modern Prince must be and cannot but be the proclaimer and organiser of an intellectual and moral reform, which also means creating the terrain for a subsequent development of the national-popular collective will towards the realisation of a superior, total form of modern civilisation.
>
> These two basic points – the formation of a national-popular collective will, of which the modern Prince is at one and the same time the organiser and the active, operative expression; and intellectual and moral reform – should structure the entire work. The concrete, programmatic points must be incorporated in the first part, that is they should result from the line of discussion 'dramatically', and not be a cold and pedantic exposition of arguments.[92]

---

92   Gramsci 1971, pp. 133–134; Gramsi 1975, pp. 1560–1561 (Q13, § 1).

In such a perspective, one might say that the question is not about a choice to be made between stressing the bourgeois / national or popular / democratic character of the Greek Revolution. In fact, both dynamics are present from the first moment in a contradictory yet 'necessary' co-existence, a contradiction that in a certain manner is constitutive of such 'bourgeois revolutions'. Such contradictions can explain both the specific importance of nationalism as bourgeois hegemonic practice in the formation of the modern Greek capitalist state and the importance of the persisting democratic expectations and demands around which the subaltern classes rallied during the nineteenth century. They can also account for the conflicting attempts to incorporate '1821' into both the dominant national narrative as well as antagonistic social forms and projects, in various forms of 'ideological uses of history', that also marked the context of the celebration of the bi-centenary of the Greek Revolution. Finally, these contradictions point towards the need to 'deconstruct' historical constructions (and even 'mythologies') and, at the same time, to defend the political pertinence of revolution as historical rupture.

Bibliography

Anderson, Perry 1992, *English Questions*, London: Verso.

Asdrachas, Spyros 2019, *Πρωτόγονη επανάσταση. Αρματολοί και κλέφτες (18ᵒˢ–19ᵒˢ αιώνας)* [*Primitive Revolution. Armatoloi and Klephts [18th–19th centuries]*], Athens: Hellenic Open University Press.

Asdrachas, Spyros (ed.) 2003, *Ελληνική οικονομική ιστορία ΙΕ΄– ΙΘ΄ αιώνας* [*Greek economic history 15th–19th century*], Athens: Piraeus Bank Cultural Foundation.

Ashton T.H and C.H.E. Philpin (eds.) 1985, *The Brenner Debate. Agrarian Class Structure and Economic Development in Pre-Industrial Europe*, Cambridge: Cambridge University Press.

Brenner, Robert 2003, *Merchants and Revolution. Commercial Change, Political Conflict, and London's Overseas Traders, 1550–1653*, London: Verso.

Burke, Edmund 1910, *Reflections on the Greek Revolution*, London: J.M. Dent & Sons Ltd.

Communist International 1929, *The Programme of the Communist International. Together with the Statutes of the Communist International*, https://www.marxists.org/history/international/comintern/6th-congress/index.htm.

Cuoco, Vincenzo 1913, *Saggio storico sulla rivoluzione napoletana del 1799 seguito dal Rapporto as Cittadino Carnot di Francesco Lomonaco*, Bari: Gius. Laterza & Figli.

Davidson, Neil 2012, *How Bourgeois Were the Bourgeois Revolutions?*, Chicago: Haymarket.

Dimitropoulos, Dimitris and Vangelis Karamanolakis 2014 (eds.), *Οι αναγνώσεις του 1821 και η Αριστερά* [*Readings of 1821 and the Left*], Athens: Αυγή.

Elefantis, Aggelos 1979, *Η εξαγγελία της αδύνατης επανάστασης. Κ.Κ.Ε. και αστισμός στον μεσοπόλεμο* [*The declaration of an impossible revolution. The* KKE *and the bourgeoisie between the two wars*], Athens: Θεμέλιο.

Furet, François 1978, *Penser la Révolution française*, Paris : Gallimard.

Gramsci, Antonio 1971, *Selections from the Prison Notebooks*, edited and translated by Quentin Hoare and Geoffrey Nowell Smith, London: Lawrence and Wishart.

Gramsci, Antonio 1975, *Quaderni del carcere*, edited by Valention Gerratana, Torino: Einaudi.

Hadjis, Dimitris 1954, 'Τύρω από τα προβλήματα της «συνέχειας»' ['On the questions of "continuity"'], in Dimitris Hadjis, *Το πρόσωπο του νέου ελληνισμού. Διαλέξεις και δοκίμια* [*The face of the new Hellenism. Lectures and essays*], Athens, Ροδακιό, 2005.

Hering, Gunar 2004, *Τα πολιτικά κόμματα στην Ελλάδα 1821–1936* [*Political Parties in Greece 1821–1936*], translated by Th. Paraskevopoulos, Athens: ΜΙΕΤ.

Hobsbawm, Eric 1959, *Primitive Rebels*, Manchester: Manchester University Press.

Hobsbawm, Eric 1996, *The Age of Revolution 1789–1848*, New York: Vintage Books.

Iliou, Filippos 1976, 'Η ιδεολογική χρήση της ιστορίας. Σχόλιο στη συζήτηση Κορδάτου – Ζεύγου' [The ideological use of history. A comment on the Kordatos-Zevgos debate], in Iliou 2007.

Iliou, Filippos 1989, *Ιδεολογικές χρήσεις του Κοραϊσμού στον 20° αιώνα* [*ideological uses of Coraism in the Twentieth Century*], Athens: Πολίτης.

Iliou, Filippos 2007, *Ψηφίδες ιστορίας και πολιτικής του εικοστού αιώνα* [*Tesserae of twentieth century history and politics*], Athens: Πόλις.

Katsiardi-Herring, Olga 2003, *Η ελληνική διασπορά. Το εμπόριο ως εθνική εξειδίκευση* [*The Greek diaspora. Trade as national specialization*], in Vassilis Panagiotopoulos (ed.), *Ιστορία του νέου ελληνισμού 1700–2000*, [*History of Modern Hellenism 1700–2000*], Athens: ΝΕΑ.

ΚΚΕ 1975, *Επίσημα κείμενα. Τόμος τέταρτος 1934–40* [*Party texts Volume 4, 1934–40*], Athens: Σύγχρονη Εποχή.

ΚΚΕ 2012, *Δοκίμιο ιστορίας του* ΚΚΕ. *Β΄ Τόμος 1949–68* [*Essay of history of the* ΚΚΕ. *Volume 2 1949–68*], Athens: Σύγχρονη Εποχή.

ΚΚΕ – History Section (ed.) 2020, *1821. Η επανάσταση και οι απαρχές του ελληνικού αστικού κράτους* [*The revolution and the origins of the Greek bourgeois state*], Athens: Σύγχρονη Εποχή.

Kordatos, Gianis 1924, *Η κοινωνική σημασία της Ελλην. Επαναστάσεως του 1821* [*The social significance of the Greek Revolution of 1821*], Athens: Βασιλείου.

Kordatos, Gianis 1933a, 'Παραχαράκτες κειμένων και κομπογιαννίτες του μαρξισμού' ['Forgers of texts and charlatans of Marxism'], in Petropoulos and Psaras (eds.) 2021, pp. 71–93.

Kordatos, Gianis 1933b, 'Πάλι οι παραχαράκτες!' ['The forgers again!'], in Petropoulos and Psaras (eds.) pp. 109–10.

Kordatos, Gianis 1972, *Η κοινωνική σημασία της Ελληνικής Επαναστάσεως του 1821* [*The social significance of the Greek Revolution of 1821*], Athens: Εκδόσεις Διεθνούς Επικαιρότητας.

Kremmydas, Vasilis 2016, *Η ελληνική επανάσταση του 1821. Τεκμήρια, αναψηλαφήσεις, ερμηνείες* [*The Greek Revolution of 1821. Documents, new research and interpretations*], Athens: Gutenberg.

Lambrionos, Giorgis, [1945] 2002, *Μορφές του Εικοσιένα. Ιστορικές μονογραφίες* [*Figures of Twenty-One. Historical Monographs*], Athens: Καστανιώτης.

Lefebvre, Georges 2005, *The French Revolution. From its origins to 1793*, translated by Elizabeth Moss Evanson, London: Routledge.

Lenin, V.I. 1962, *Collected Works*, Moscow: Progress Publishers.

Losurdo, Domenico 2020, *War and Revolution. Rethinking the 20th Century*, translated by David Broder, London: Verso.

Mailis, Makis 2020, 'Η κομματική ιστοριογραφία για το χαρακτήρα και τις κινητήριες δυνάμεις της επανάστασης του 1821 και η στρατηγική του ΚΚΕ' ['Party historiography on the nature and the driving forces of the 1821 revolution and the strategy ΚΚΕ'], in ΚΚΕ – History Section (ed.) 2020, pp. 17–42.

Marx, Karl and Friedrich Engels 1975–2005, *Collected Works*, London: Lawrence and Wishart (MECW).

Maximos, Serafeim 1973, *Η αυγή του ελληνικού καπιταλισμού. Τουρκοκρατία 1685–1789* [*The dawn of Greek capitalism. The Tourkokratia 1685–1789*], Athens: Στοχαστής.

Maximos, Serafeim 1974, *Το ελληνικό εμπορικό ναυτικό κατά τον XVIII αιώνα* [*The Greek Merchant Navy during the 18th Century*], Athens: Στοχαστής.

Milios, John 2017, *Ο «σοβιετικός μαρξισμός» και οι έλληνες στοχαστές* [*'Soviet Marxism' and Greek Thinkers*], Athens: Εφημερίδα των Συντακτών.

Milios, John 2018, *The Origins of Capitalism as a Social System. The Prevalence of an Aleatory Encounter*, London: Routledge.

Milios, John 2020, *1821. Ιχνηλατώντας το Έθνος, το Κράτος και τη Μεγάλη Ιδέα* [*1821. Tracing the Nations, the State and the 'Megali Idea'*], Athens: Αλεξάνδρεια.

Milios, John 2023, *Nationalism as a Claim to a State The Greek Revolution of 1821 and the Formation of Modern Greece*, Leiden: Brill/Historical Materialism Book Series.

Papanikolopoulos, Dimitris 2021, *Το 1821 ως επανάσταση. Γιατί ξέσπασε και γιατί πέτυχε* [*1821 as a revolution. Why it erupted and why it succeeded*], Athens: ΕΝΑ.

Petropoulos Giorgos and Dimitris Psaras (eds.) 2021, *Πολεμική για τον χαρακτήρα της επανάστασης του 1821* [*Polemics around the nature of the 1821 revolution*], Athens: Εφημερίδα των Συντακτών.

Petropoulos, John A. 1985, *Πολιτική και συγκρότηση κράτους στο Ελληνικό Βασίλειο (1833–1843)* [*Politics and Statecraft in the Kingdom of Greece (1833–1843)*], Athens: ΜΙΕΤ.

Pizanias, Petros Th. 2021, *Η Ελληνική Επανάσταση 1821–1830* [*The Greek Revolution 1821–1830*], Athens: Εστία.

Shandro, Alan 2014, *Lenin and the Logic of Hegemony. Political Practice and Theory in the Class Struggle*, Leiden: Brill.

Skliros, G. 1976, *Έργα* [*Works*], edited by Loukas Axelos, Athens: Επικαιρότητα.

Soboul, Albert 1988, *Understanding the French Revolution*, translated by April Ane Knutson, New York: International Publishers.

Stathis. Panagiotis 2014, 'Το Εικοσιένα στην αριστερή ιστοριογραφία του 20ού αιώνα ['1821 in 20th century Greek historiography']', in Dimitropoulos and Karamanolakis (eds.) 2014, pp. 29–44

Strigkos, Leonidas [1959] 1966, *Η επανάσταση του 21* [*The revolution of 21*], Athens: Θεμέλιο.

Svoronos, Nikos 1992, *Επισκόπηση της νεοελληνικής ιστορίας* [*An overview of Modern Greek History*], Athens: Θεμέλιο.

Svoronos, Nikos 1995, *Ανάλεκτα νεοελληνικής ιστορίας και ιστοριογραφία* [*Analects of Modern Greek History and Historiography*], Athens: Θεμέλιο.

Svoronos, Nikos 2004, *Το ελληνικό έθνος. Γένεση και διαμόρφωση του νέου ελληνισμού* [*The Greek nation. Genesis and formation of the new Hellenism*], Athens: Πόλις.

Theotokas, Nikos 2013, *Ο βίος του στρατηγού Μακρυγιάννη. Απομνημονεύματα και ιστορία* [*The life of general Makrygiannis. Memoir and history*], Athens: Βιβλιόραμα.

Theotokas. Nikos and Nikos Kotaridis 2006, *Η οικονομία της βίας. Παραδοσιακές και νεωτερικές εξουσίες στην Ελλάδα του 19ού αιώνα* [*The economy of violence. Traditional and modern powers in 19th century Greece*], Athens: Βιβλιόραμα.

Tilly, Charles 1978, *From Mobilization to Revolution*, New York: Random House.

Tocqueville, Alexis de 2010, *Democracy in America. Historical Critical Edition of De le démocratie en Amérique*, translated by James T. Schleifer, Indianapolis: Liberty Fund.

Tocqueville, Alexis de 2011, *The Ancient Regime and the French Revolution*, translated by Arthur Goldhammer, Cambridge: Cambridge University Press.

Vournas, Tasos 1966, *Σύντομη ιστορία της Ελληνικής Επανάστασης* [*A short history of the Greek Revolution*], Athens: Δρακόπουλος.

Wood, Ellen Meiksins 1996, 'Capitalists, Merchants and Bourgeois Revolution: Reflections on the Brenner Debate and its Sequel', *International Review of Social History* 41: 209–32.

Wood, Ellen Meiksins 2002, *The Origin of Capitalism. A Longer View*, London: Verso.

Zahariadis, Nikos 1953, *Συλλογή Έργων* [*Collection of works*], Bucharest: Central Committee of the KKE.

Zevgos, Giannis 1933a, 'Ο «μαρξιστής» Γ. Κορδάτος, ιστορικός της μπουρζουαζίας' ['The "Marxist" G. Kordatos, an historian of the bourgeoisie'], in Petropoulos and Psaras (eds.) 2021, pp. 11–21.

Zevgos, Giannis 1933b, 'Ο Γ. Κορδάτος σαν ιστορικός της επανάστασης του 1821' ['G. Kordatos as an historian of the 1821 Revolution'], in Petropoulos and Psaras (eds.) 2021, pp. 23–36.

Zevgos, Giannis 1933c, 'Ο Γ. Κορδάτος σαν ιστορικός του εργατικού μας νικήματος' ['G. Kordatos as an historian of our labour movement'], in Petropoulos and Psaras (eds.) 2021, pp. 37–55.

Zevgos, Giannis 1933d, 'Ο Γ. Κορδάτος σαν οικονομολόγος στις πρώτες γραμμές της αντεπανάστασης' ['G. Kordatos as an economist, at the front line of the counter-revolution'], in Petropoulos and Psaras (eds.) 2021, pp. 57–70.

PART 1

The Ottoman Context of the Greek Revolution

∵

CHAPTER 1

'Inciting the *Rum Milleti* to Rise Up'

The Outbreak of the Greek Revolution of 1821 according to the Ottoman Sources

Elias Kolovos, H. Şükrü Ilıcak and Mohamet Shariat-Panahi

Every year, the 25th of March is celebrated as Greek Independence Day, even by Google.[1] This date, which coincides with the Feast of Annunciation, was very probably (but not conclusively) set by the secret Friendly Society [Gk. *Philiki Hetaireia*], as the date to take up arms for the revolution against the Ottoman Empire.[2] The decision made in an important meeting of the Friendly Society in Izmail, Bessarabia, at the beginning of October 1820, was that Alexander Hypsilantis, the leader of the Society,[3] would travel through Trieste to the peninsula of Mani in the Peloponnese and start the Revolution there.[4] Hypsilantis, however, changed the original plan, deciding to start the Revolution in the Danubian Principalities, where he had, as a Phanariot, allies and friends.

---

1 Google Doodle celebrates Greek Independence Day, 25 March 2020. The celebration was established in 1838, with a Royal Decree by the Government of King Otto. Later, in the second half of the nineteenth century, a legend was also popularised that the Bishop Germanos of Palaiai Patrai raised, on 25 March 1821, the flag of the Monastery of Hagia Lavra with an image of the Dormition of the Holy Virgin, as the revolutionary flag, and administered an oath to the revolutionaries before calling them to attack the neighbouring town of Kalavryta. However, Germanos of Palaiai Patrai had already left the Monastery of Hagia Lavra before the 25 March with the other leaders who had been there before. See Despotopoulos (ed.) 1975, pp. 83–4; Kremmydas 1996; Koulouri 2020, pp. 64–6.

2 See the hypotheses by Panagiotopoulos 2001–2. For the Friendly Society, see Frangos 1973; Panagiotopoulos 2011.

3 Alexandros Hypsilantis was the son of the Phanariot Voivode of Wallachia Konstantinos Hypsilantis (1760–1816), who had abandoned his post during the Ottoman-Russian War of 1806–12 and resorted to Russia. For his biography, see Giannopoulos 2010. In the Ottoman documents, Alexandros Hypsilantis is mentioned as 'the son of Hypsilantis the fugitive [*firari*]'. Alexandros served as an officer in the Russian army and, on 12 April 1820, accepted leadership of the Friendly Society. For the Phanariots in Ottoman governance, see Philliou 2009; cf. Sfyroeras 1974. The document assigning Alexandros to the leadership of the Friendly Society has been published by Philimon 1859–61, vol. 1, p. 33.

4 For the decisive meeting in Izmail and the plan(s) discussed there, see Panagiotopoulos 2015, pp. 65–71.

This change of plan might have been made according to his Phanariot vision of a Balkan and/or an 'Ottoman' revolution against the Sultan in Istanbul itself.[5]

1   A Failed Balkan and 'Ottoman' Start for the Revolution

On 24 February 1821,[6] Alexander Hypsilantis, wearing his Russian military uniform, crossed the river Prut in a small retinue. Three days later, on 24 February, in the town of Iaşi – where he had been welcomed by the Mikhail Soutsos, the Voivode of Moldavia (a leading Phanariot and recent member of the Friendly Society) – Hypsilantis issued a revolutionary pamphlet, calling the Greeks [Gk. *Hellenes*] to take up arms and 'Fight for Religion and Motherland' [Gk. *Machou hyper pisteos kai patridos*]. One day before, on February 23, Hypsilantis had issued another pamphlet addressing the 'nation of Moldowallachia' and announcing the Greek Revolution.[7]

According to an Ottoman imperial order reproduced in a later memorandum, dated Receb 1236 (23 March–22 April 1821), Hypsilantis, after 'inciting the *Rum milleti* to rise up, had the evil intention of crossing the Danube and trampling upon the Muslim *millet*, provided that he had the chance to do so' [*Rum milletini ayaklandırub elinden gelür ise berü tarafa geçmek ve millet-i İslâmiyye'yi ayaklar altına almak dâ'iyye-ifâsidesinde idüği*].[8] According to the deputies [*Kaimmakam*] Konstantinos Negris and Stephanos Vogoridis[9] hast-

---

5   Panagiotopoulos 2015, pp. 142–71. The origins of the idea of a 'Balkan' and/or 'Ottoman' revolution against the Empire goes back to Rhigas Velestinlis, who was propagating the idea of a French-Greek Republic. See Botzaris 1962.

6   All dates follow the Julian calendar (OS). We would like to thank Nikola Rakovski for helping us with some of the English translations of the Ottoman Turkish documents.

7   For a reproduction of the Greek pamphlet, written by Georgios Kozakis-Typaldos, see Despotopoulos (ed.) 1975, p. 23. For the English translation of the text, see Clogg 1976, p. 202. For the Ottoman Turkish translation of the same text, see former Başbakanlık Osmanlı Arşivi, now T.C. Cumhurbaşkanlığı Devlet Arşivleri [Istanbul, Ottoman Archives], HAT 40280-D. For the pamphlet addressing the 'nation of Moldowallachia', see Photeinos 2020, pp. 89–90; cf. his pamphlet to the 'Dacians' [Wallachians] on 3 March 1821, published by Photeinos 2020, pp. 92–94; Philimon 1859–61, vol. 2, pp. 119–21. For Hypsilantis's revolt according to the Ottoman sources, see Ilıcak 2011b, pp. 225–39.

8   Istanbul, Ottoman Archives, HAT 38748 (Kolovos et al. 2021, 152–4). For the importance of the Ottoman sources concerning the Greek Revolution, see Ilıcak 2011a, pp. 9–11. For the polysemy of the term *millet*, see in detail Ursinus 1993. For the *Rum milleti*, the Greek Orthodox, in particular, see Konortas 1999, pp. 169–80. For the introduction of a modern notion of *millet* as 'nation' in Ottoman political language, see Karabıçak 2020, pp. 68–106.

9   For the Kallimachis family and Skarlatos Kallimachis, see Philliou 2009. For Stephanos Vogoridis see in detail Philliou 2011.

ily sent to Bucharest by the newly appointed Voivode of Wallachia Skarlatos Kallimachis in a memorandum they sent to Mehmed Selim Pasha of Silistre on 4 March 1821, 'this sedition did not look like a depredation caused by brigandage, but was certainly a massive plot devised in advance [*bu fesâd eşkıyâ fesâdına benzemeyüb evvelce kurulmuş cesîm bir dest-gâh olmak gerekdir*]'.[10] In the same memorandum, the deputies referred to the peasant rebellion led by Tudor Vladimirescu and initially supported 'by purpose' by the Friendly Society in Black Wallachia (Oltenia), targeting the Wallachian landowners and the Phanariot Voivodes as mere bandits [*eşkıyâ*] – without, however, questioning the Sultanic authority.[11] The critical difference, according to the deputies, was the rumour spread from Iaşi that the Russian forces would follow Hypsilantis, a perspective indirectly expressed (but without any real basis) in his second revolutionary pamphlet.

After mustering a peasant and Pandur army,[12] Tudor Vladimirescu entered Bucharest on 18 March 1821. According to a message sent to the Porte by Ismail Hakkı Pasha, Castellan [*Muhafız*] of Yergöği [mod. Giurgiu] on March 25, 'the bandit named Tudor' [*Tudor nâm şakî*] had sent two letters in Romanian to the *Kaimmakam*s to justify his movement with the cause: 'to fight off the pernicious innovations and oppression [*bida'ü mezâlim*] that had befallen the poor'. He claimed, however, that he had nothing to do with the 'sedition' [*fesâd*] of Hypsilantis, who was about to enter Bucharest, and declared that he was 'ready to fight against' him and 'drive him away from Bucharest if the everlasting Sublime State granted its support'. That was a crucial defeat for the revolutionary plan of the Friendly Society, which counted on his cooperation.[13] However, Sultan Mahmud II was extremely mistrustful and considered Vladimirescu's offer 'another trick of the infidels and unworthy of contemplation'.[14] Vladimirescu, eventually, was executed in Goleşti on 23 May 1821 after an order of Hypsilantis.

---

10   Istanbul, Ottoman Archives, HAT 45963-K (Kolovos et al. 2021, 108–110).

11   Tudor Vladimirescu, who had fought on the Russian side during the Russian-Ottoman war of 1806–12, left Bucharest on 17 January 1821 for Black Wallachia, calling the peasants to arms against the aristocracy. In his pamphlet, he promised the confiscation of aristocratic properties 'for the common good'. See the Greek translation of his pamphlet published by Photeinos 2020, pp. 63–4, 68–71, and Philimon 1859–61, vol. 2, pp. 297–301, 306–8, as well as the petition [*arz-ı mahzar*] he sent to the Ottoman authorities on behalf of the people. Philimon suggests that Giorgakis Olympios from the Friendly Society had incited Vladimirescu 'in purpose' [ἐπιτηδείως] to revolt and occupy the Principalities.

12   The Pandurs were a light cavalry force organised initially by the Habsburgs. They could be compared to the *armatoloi* in the southern Balkans.

13   For his mention in the revolutionary plan decided in Izmail, see Philimon 1859–61, vol. 1, p. 53.

14   Istanbul, Ottoman Archives, HAT 38413 (Kolovos et al. 2021, 147–9).

Another memorandum by Ismail Hakkı Pasha, dated April 16,[15] refers to an offer from *binbaşı* Savvas Phokianos – a former attendant of the court of Skarlatos Kallimachis who was based in Bucharest and who was a key member of the Friendly Society and its revolutionary plan[16] – of loyal service to demonstrate his allegiance to the Exalted State. It looks like Savvas had finally opted to be faithful to his patron, Skarlatos Kallimachis.[17]

Without local support, even from key members of the Society like Phokianos, Hypsilantis was bound to fail. On March 30, he left the outskirts of Bucharest, moving up north to Tirgovişte [mod. Târgovişte]. On May 29, the town was captured by the Ottoman army of the Kahya Bey (Lieutenant) of Mehmed Selim Pasha of Silistra. Savvas, along with his seven or eight hundred men, was granted amnesty by the Kahya Bey; he subsequently volunteered to chase Hypsilantis.[18] However, according to Sultan Mahmud II in one of his imperial rescripts,[19] Savvas was not to be trusted, nor was Stephanos Vogoridis, Konstantinos Negris or the consuls of the Christian powers. Actually, Savvas was later, in 7 August 1821, invited to Bucharest under the pretext of obtaining compensation for his services to the Kahya Bey, and was executed.[20]

When he had learned the news of the revolution in the Morea as well (see below), the Sultan declared the rebellion of the Rum *millet* in its entirety [*umûm milletin isyânı*]:[21] 'The Rum infidels had united, from first to last, to perpetrate all sorts of villainy and abominable deeds against religion and the Exalted state' [*Rum gâvurlarının dîn ve Devlet-i Aliyye aleyhine mürtekib oldukları envâ'-ı habâset ü mel'anetinde büyüği ve küçüği müttefik oldığı*]. This was a very new situation for the Ottomans, who had never before defended the

---

15   Istanbul, Ottoman Archives, HAT 45833 (Kolovos et al. 2021, 189–92).

16   In contrast to Tudor Vladimirescu, Savvas Phokianos, originally from the island of Patmos, had fought on the Ottoman side during the Russian-Ottoman war of 1806–12, gaining the rank of *binbaşı*. He is also mentioned in the revolutionary plan of Izmail; see Philimon 1859–61, vol. 1, p. 53. See also Panagiotopoulos 2015, pp. 160–3.

17   See Photeinos 2020, p. 201; Philimon 1859–61, vol. 2, p. 125.

18   Photeinos 2020, pp. 201–2; Philimon 1859–61, vol. 2, p. 178. On 30 May 1821, *binbaşı* Savvas, leading his men and 2,000 Muslim mounted soldiers, chased Hypsilantis and took 20 prisoners, who he beheaded and presented to the Kahya Bey. On 10 June, Selim Mehmed Pasha of Silistre sent to Istanbul 37 heads of the executed revolutionaries, 50 pairs of ears together with eight prisoners, four flags, two military headscarfs, one dagger and three bayonets. See Istanbul, Ottoman Archives, HAT 38428 (Kolovos et al. 2021, 219–21).

19   Istanbul, Ottoman Archives, HAT 16269 (Kolovos et al. 2021, 217–8).

20   Despotopoulos (ed.) 1975, pp. 65–6.

21   Cf. Karabıçak 2020, p. 70, for the similar use of the word *milletçe* [*millet*-wide] in another contemporary Sultanic order, and for his commentary on the non-territorialised use of the word.

Empire against a non-territorialised internal enemy, like a modern nation in the making. This explains the fury of Sultan Mahmud II, who, according to the court chronicler Şanizade, gave the order for the massacre of all his *Rum* subjects [*Rum re'âyâsına katl-ı âmm olunmak*] in Istanbul.[22]

2   The 'Sedition' in the Morea

In the Morea (i.e. the Peloponnese), the members of the Friendly Society, including the leading Christian notables and prelates[23] were, according to the original plan of Izmail, scheduling to begin the Revolution in March. Gregorios Dikaios, also known as Papaflessas, arrived in the Morea in December 1820 as the emissary of Hypsilantis. Between 26–9 January, Dikaios secretly met with prominent Moreot members of the Society in Vostitsa [mod. Aigio].[24] However, even in late February, he had no idea that Hypsilantis had changed the plan.[25]

The Moreots were preparing for the Revolution. In sharp contrast to the Danubian Principalities, 'the entire Peloponnese was trembling under the earth' [η Πελοπόννησος όλη υπόκωφα εσείετο].[26] The Muslims of the Morea had amassed information that something was under way. According to a message sent to the Sublime Porte by Hurşid Ahmed Pasha dated 22 February 1821, the former Vali [governor] of the Morea, who had been appointed Governor of Rumelia and Serasker [commander in chief] with the task of suppressing Tepedelenli Ali Pasha[27] while he was in Tırhala [mod. Trikala], – on his way to Yanya [Janina, mod. Ioannina] he had already been sent alarming letters from the Morea:[28] his *Kaimmakam* [deputy] Mehmed Salih Agha[29] and the notables of the capital town of the Morea, Tripoliça [Tripolitsa, mod. Tripoli], had writ-

---

22 Şânî-zâde Mehmed 'Atâ'ullah Efendi 2008, pp. 1072–3. For the Ottoman reaction to the Greek Revolution, and especially for the public violence against the *Rum*s, see in detail Ilıcak 2011a.

23 For the mass participation of the notables and prelates of the Morea in the Friendly Society, see Rotzokos 2020, pp. 65–73.

24 For the participants in the assembly, see Gritsopoulos 1972–4, pp. 3–60. Cf. the new interpretation of the decisions taken there, despite the disputes, by Tzakis 2018a, pp. 125–48.

25 See Panagiotopoulos 2001–2, pp. 452–4.

26 Chrysanthopoulos 1858, p. 14, cited by Sarafis 2017, p. 47.

27 For Tepedelenli Ali Paşa, see Panagiotopoulos 2009, pp. 13–128; cf. Ilıcak 2022.

28 Istanbul, Ottoman Archives, HAT 38866 (Kolovos et al. 2021, 103–7).

29 For *kapıcıbaşı* Mehmed Salih Agha, see Sahhâflar Şeyhi-Zâde Seyyid Mehmed Es'ad Efendi 2000, pp. 144–6, where he is called a 'pompous naïve' [*Ka'immakam-ı mağrûr-i sâde-zamîre*]. According to Trikoupis (1860, vol. 1, p. 50), Mehmed Salih Agha 'was neither capable, nor inspired fear'.

ten to inform him that 'some seditious persons, sent by [Tepedelenli] Ali Pasha, the invoker of His Majesty's wrath, have come to the Morea and incited the *reaya* with many false rumors; and that in consequence thereof, the Moreot *reaya* have been observed to perpetrate acts of defiance' [*magzûb-ı pâdişâhî olan Alî Paşa tarafından Mora'ya birkaç nefer müfsid gelüb nice nice erâcîf neş-riyle re'âyâyı tahrîk itmiş ve binâ'en'aleyh Mora re'âyâsından dahi ba'zı harekât-ı reddiyye hiss olunmuş*]. Moreover, Mehmed Salih Agha and the Moreot Muslim notables, in other letters they sent to Hurşid Ahmed Pasha, reported that 'the Bey of Mani [Petro Bey Mavromichali] was given one thousand purses of aspers (i.e., half a million *kuruş*) in order to get military equipment from the Russians, and also that the chief-captain has won the Maniot infidels' confidence and thereby the majority of the *reaya* in the peninsula took up arms' [*Rusyalu tarafından asker techîz ve âmâde eylemesi-çün Manya beğine bin kîse akçe irsâl olunmuş ve ol dahi Manya keferesini kendüsüne i'timâd itdirmiş ve bu vesîle ile cezîre re'âyâsının ekserîsi silâhlanmış*]. They suspected that the financial supporter of the Maniots was Tepedelenli Ali Pasha.[30]

The idea that Tepedelenli Ali Pasha was behind the events was a particular revolutionary strategy of spreading false information devised by Gregorios Dikaios. In the assembly of Vostitsa, Dikaios had consulted the notables of the Morea to start the Revolution there and in Mani in order to make the Ottomans believe that it 'was incited by Ali Pasha'. In this way, in case of a failure, the notables would resort to Mani, or the Aegean islands, and later apply to the Sublime Porte that they had revolted against for its heavy taxation and tyranny. The plan aimed to make time for Hypsilantis to cross from Bulgaria to Macedonia and to force Russia into a war against the Porte.[31]

It is interesting to note that Hurşid Ahmed Pasha commented in his memorandum that 'considering the Maniots' temperament, it is not unlikely that they will commit improper acts' [*Manyalunun dahi merkûz-ı cibilliyyetleri oldığı üzere bir gûne harekât-ı nâ-becâya cesâret idecekleri*].[32] We should also note

---

30   According to the court chronicler Sahhâflar Şeyhi-Zâde Seyyid Mehmed Es'ad Efendi (2000, pp. 145–6), the *kocabaşı* of Karytaina Papalexis, who was in Tripoliça, blamed Tepedelenli Ali Paşa for the incitement of the *reaya* in the Morea. Cf. Despotopoulos (ed.) 1975, pp. 80–1; it was after this meeting that Mehmed Salih Agha decided to invite the Moreot notables in Tripoliça for the customary distribution of the taxation.

31   See Deligiannis 1957, vol. 1, p. 110.

32   For the Maniot society in general, see Saitas 2009, pp. 133–52. According to a letter sent by Petrobey Mavromichalis to the Grigorakis family on 11 March 1821, their son, Tzanet-akis, 'was making an assembly' [of people in arms] and not waiting for the proper time for the revolutionary movement; see Anonymous 1858, p. 56. Perhaps, as a response to the mistrust against him, Petrobey Mavromichalis had already by 28 February sent his son,

that Theodoros Kolokotronis, a former brigand [*klepht*] and one of the future prestigious military leaders of the Greek Revolution, had already arrived in Mani on 6 January 1821, secretly preparing for the insurgency.[33]

As an answer to the petition by Mehmed Salih Agha and the Moreot notables, Hurşid Ahmed Pasha reported that he had already dispatched 1,500 men to the Peloponnese.[34] Moreover, Hurşid Ahmed Pasha requested from the Sublime Porte to send three or four imperial ships under the Vice-Admiral [*Kapudane*] Ali Bey[35] to Mani so that the Maniots 'would somehow be overawed [*Manyalunun bir gûne tahzîrleri lâzım geldikde*]'. However, the Pasha noted, if the Exalted State concluded that Russia was behind the rebellion, they should send immediately the Governor of the Morea with a big army in order to supress it. In the addendum to the same document, Hurşid Ahmed Pasha reported that he was 'strongly convinced that the actions of defiance of the Moreot *reaya* in this manner were a result of Ali Pasha's incitement'.

In Istanbul, the Grand Vizier Seyyid Ali Pasha wrote a summary for the Sultan upon receiving the memorandum of Hurşid Ahmed Pasha: he looked convinced that the 'spread of some false rumors in Boğdan (Moldavia) and Mani' was not entirely because of 'the foreign powers', but should be attributed to 'the traitor Ali Pasha', 'who is a betrayer of religion and state' [*erâcîf-i mezkûrenin hudûsı her ne kadar düvel-i ecnebiyyeden alâ-külli-hâl emniyyet câ'iz değil ise de bu sûret hâ'in-i dîn ü devlet olan Alî Paşa'nın ifsâdından nâşî olması akreb-i melhûz olub*].

Anastasis, and one of his nephews to Tripoliça; see Trikoupis 1860, vol. 1, p. 53 and Ottoman Archives, HAT 38276-D-1 (the letter in Greek that Petrobey Mavromichalis wrote as a reference for his son to go from Kalamata to Tripoliça).

33   For his personal account on his activity in Mani, see Kolokotronis 1846, pp. 50–1. Kolokotronis relates that the Ottomans from Arkadia [mod. Kyparrissia] and Mystras had come to Mani to see if he had an army with him and that they found him 'playing games' [ἔπαιζα ταῖς ἀμάδαις]. They thus returned home. However, Kolokotronis had sent letters to all the Western Peloponnese to prepare people for 25 March (though he, with the Maniots, finally attacked Kalamata on 23 March). It should also be noted that Kolokotronis relayed that, 'even he was a *Bey*', i.e. an Ottoman official, Petrobey Mavromichalis did not gave him away to the Ottomans. Cf. Trikoupis 1860, vol. 1, p. 151; Deligiannis 1957, vol. 1, p. 124; Spiliadis 1851–7, vol. 1, pp. 21–4.

34   He had sent only 300 men under the command of Mustafa Agha, Register Keeper [*Defter Kethüdası*] of the Morea and others; cf. Sahhâflar Şeyhi-Zâde Seyyid Mehmed Es'ad Efendi 2000, p. 146.

35   Nasuhzade Ali Bey, of Albanian origin and known in the Greek sources as Kara Ali, was on November 1821 to become the Grand Admiral. He was killed when his flagship was blown up by Konstantinos Kanaris from the island of Psara in early June 1822. Mani belonged to the administration of the Ottoman Grand Admiral.

The imperial rescript of Sultan Mahmud II upon the same document is very telling: already from the beginning of March 1821, when the memorandum of Hurşid Ahmed Pasha arrived in Istanbul, Mahmud II had good knowledge of the events which escalated to the Greek Revolution, both in Moldavia and the Morea:

> I have seen the Commander-in-chief's [Hurşid Ahmed Pasha] letter and the documents he received from the Morea. [Tepedelenli] Ali Pasha's sedition is apparent everywhere. In light of the news from the Castellan of Brăila, however, it is clear that there is sedition in that other place [i.e. Moldowallachia] too. Four or five ships will not suffice for this matter. Instruct the Grand Admiral [*Kapudan Paşa*][36] to equip as many ships as needed by spreading the rumor that he will set off for the White Sea [Mediterranean] in the spring. He shall announce 'I will go to the White Sea this spring' and begin equipping the fleet. In a couple of days, the issue will become clearer. It can be discussed afterwards whether the Grand Admiral should go in person or whether [another] commander should be sent. Let the soldiers who were arranged to join the Commander-in-chief be reminded to make haste. Let close attention be paid to guard the son of the Bey of Mani, who is being kept as pawn in Istanbul;[37] the *zimmi* scribe of Veli Pasha,[38] and the Serbian prelates [*knez*] and priests.[39] Let also the Grand Admiral increase the number of his officers who patrol in Galata, Beyoğlu and other neighbourhoods, and make them observe secretly the actions of the *reaya* who dwell in the outskirts [of Istanbul]. And do not put these instructions in writing, you shall declare them to the Grand Admiral orally.

---

36   The Grand Admiral was then Abdullah Hamdullah Paşa, later to become Grand Vizier on 1 November 1822.

37   However, the son of Petro Bey Mavromichali, named George, managed to escape from Istanbul with the help of members of the Friendly Society and arrived in Mani. See Despotopoulos (ed.) 1975, pp. 33, 38.

38   Veli Pasha was the son of Tepedelenli Ali Pasha. He had surrendered to the Imperial Fleet on 2 September 1820 and was exiled to Kütahya. He and his two brothers, Muhtar and Salih, were ordered to be executed in July 1821; see Sezer 1995. His scribe was Dimitraki Moraitis or Apostolopoulos; see Ilıcak 2011a, p. 197; Kasomoulis 1940, vol. 2, p. 408.

39   Right before the outbreak of the Greek Revolution, a committee of Serbian prelates [*knez*] and priests came to Istanbul to negotiate with the Sublime Porte over several issues regarding the autonomy of the Serbian administration. When the Revolution broke out, they were kept hostage for several years to prevent possible Serbian support to the Greek Revolution.

Mahmud II was reluctant to send the Imperial Fleet far away from the Golden Horn in Istanbul, being afraid that Russia could declare war. At the same time, the Sultan was concerned that the Revolution would break out in the imperial capital as well; actually, that was one of the secret plans of the Friendly Society.[40] Thus, all the Greeks of Istanbul and its environs were to be monitored by the police very carefully.

Back in the Morea, the alarmed *Kaimmakam* had already from mid-February called the Greek notables of the vicinity to gather in Tripoliça.[41] In the meantime, news of the declaration of the Revolution by Hypsilantis in the Danubian Principalities arrived in the Morea on 15 March.[42] This must have been the signal for a general uprising.

In Tripoliça, Mehmed Salih Agha, the *kaimmakam* [deputy] of Hurşid Ahmed Pasha, reacted immediately. On 19 March, he reported to Hurşid Ahmed Pasha what was happening in the Morea. We publish here, in English translation (see below, 3.1, Facsimile and Transliteration), this important letter:[43]

> My Most Benevolent, Illustrious and Merciful Master,
> For some time, I have been working hard to ascertain the source of the false rumours that circulate in the peninsula [of the Morea], disprove the rumours and suppress them with well-judged measures. The news we heard that is claimed to be accurate, as well as the pieces of information reported by some people whom we expect to be faithful and upright, may prove true or false. I also wrote in one of my previous letters to Your Excellency that the *kocabaşıs* of Kalavryta started to recruit and employ *bolukbaşıs* and *sekbans* [i.e. mercenaries] from among the *reaya* they call *kapo* [It. *capo*] whose employment had been previously banned by an imperial firman. Earlier, I received orders from the Grand Vizier and Your Excellency commanding me to summon all the *kocabaşıs*, metropolitans and bishops of the *kaza*s in order to suppress the said rumours. In compliance therewith, I drew up and sent mandates to all *kocabaşıs*, as customary, so that they come in the forthcoming month of Receb [starting on 23 March] and prepare a register of the distribution of taxation in the pen-

---

40   See Panagiotopoulos 2015, pp. 154–9.
41   For the prelates and clerics who had accepted to go to Tripoliça in mid-February 1821, see Sarafis 2017, p. 48, and Zafeiropoulos 1852. According to Germanos of Palaia Patra, not all of those who accepted to go to Tripoliça were aware of the decisions made in the meeting in Vostiça in January; see Germanos, Metropolitan of Palaias Patras 1900, p. 26.
42   See Panagiotopoulos 2001–2, pp. 457–8.
43   Istanbul, Ottoman Archives, HAT 38453 (Kolovos et al. 2021, 121–5).

insula for the past six months, and to the metropolitans and bishops so
that they come and explain the causes of the rumours. Most of the *kocabaşıs* and around ten metropolitans came. Three *kocabaşıs* and the bishop
of Kalavryta, the metropolitan of Patras and the *kocabaşı* of the *kaza* of
Vostitsa gathered in Kalavryta, after which they departed for Tripoliça but
diverted from their course and went into a monastery in an inaccessible
place near the said *kaza* [of Kalavryta].[44] They sent [us] a letter full of
false statements, saying that a man from Tripoliça whom they trusted had
written in a letter to them, 'The [Muslim] notables of the Morea united
to slaughter all *kocabaşıs*, metropolitans and bishops when they come
together. Beware! Do not come! If you are on your way, turn back!', and
that having been thus warned, they had gotten back in a state of distress.[45]
We, the *kocabaşıs* and other men present [in Tripoliça] wrote separate
letters of assurances and dispatched them by one of their compatriots,
whereafter they sent him back with another fabricated response showing
that our letters had produced no effect on them.[46] Moreover, they started instigating the *reaya* of the surrounding *kaza*s and villages by sending
them letters containing misrepresentations and encapsulating all sorts
of fraud and intrigues. Their coreligionists and metropolitans wrote and
sent again letters of assurances, exhorting them to present themselves.
While we were waiting for their response, they instigated – true to their
perfidy and roguery and defiant character, which were hinted at by their
very nature – about four to five hundred despicable infidels from the *reaya*
of the said *kaza* [Kalavryta] to revolt. The doomed infidels robbed a merchant named Tabakopoulos, a money changer [*sarraf*] who was returning
home after he had collected a debt of around fifty thousand *kuruş*, which
Ibrahim Agha, Voivode of Kalavryta, had owed him; and one of Tabakopoulos's men escaped and the other was wounded.[47] Apart from that, it

---

44   Germanos of Palaia Patra and the other notables and clerics hid in the Monastery of Hagia
     Lavra on 10 or 13 March. See in detail Despotopoulos (ed.) 1975, pp. 81–2. According to
     Germanos of Palaia Patra, this was a decision made in Kalavryta with Andreas Londos of
     Vostiça on 27 February; see Germanos 1900, p. 26.
45   A summary of this letter in Ottoman Turkish, claiming that the notables were told by their
     Muslim friends not to go to Tripoliça, because they would be executed, is to be found also
     in Sahhâflar Şeyhi-Zâde Seyyid Mehmed Es'ad Efendi 2000, p. 148; cf. Germanos 1900, p. 27;
     Spiliadis 1851–7, pp. 24–8; Phrantzis 1839, vol. 1, pp. 139, 141.
46   From the Greek sources, we know that the notable Andreas Kalamogdartis was sent to
     the Monastery of Hagia Lavra to persuade all those gathered there to return with him to
     Tripoliça; see Germanos 1900, pp. 39–40; Phrantzis 1839, vol. 1, p. 141.
47   For the attack against Nikolaos Tabakopoulos and his Muslim guard, Seydi Chamoutsas,

was reported on the date of my letter that the infidels assaulted a traveler and seized his arms, stole ten *kuruşes* from a messenger who was passing thereabouts and now roam the *kaza* in great numbers and disrupt the traffic. Hence, it is now certain that the fugitive *kocabaşıs*, metropolitan and bishop are the source of the false rumours and news which has been circulating for some time. Soldiers should be sent against them, but even though there are three to four hundred infidels now, they may increase their numbers when soldiers are sent. Be that as it may, I have no soldiers at my disposal. Although Bekir Agha and Mehmed Bey have come with five hundred soldiers, these troops will avail us nothing in this situation. Therefore, I gave up on the idea of sending soldiers against the infidels for now and wrote and sent out mandates in Greek to gain the goodwill of the *reaya* in the surrounding *kaza*s and villages. Their metropolitans also sent out anathemas according to their vain rite. Your Excellency will acquaint yourself with the condition of the *reaya* and the state of affairs in the Morea from the documents enclosed herewith which were received from other *kaza*s. There is a great need of at least two thousand robust soldiers to be dispatched as soon as possible in order to bring this issue to an end. Hence, I beg Your Excellency to grant your succour and detach this number of soldiers, or perhaps a little more, from your retinue and swiftly send them on caiques from Salaora [the port of Arta]. The final command rests with Your Excellency.
Your servant [Seal of Mehmed Salih]

Ioannis Philimon, in his 'Historical Essay Concerning the Greek Revolution', has published the Greek translation of the order [*buyuruldu*] Mehmed Salih Agha sent the next day, on 20 March, to the notables and the *reaya* of the villages of the *kaza* [district] of Karytaina,[48] concerning the same series of alarming

---

from Lalas, see Germanos 1900, pp. 40–41; Deligiannis 1959, vol. I, p. 142, which attrib-utes the attack to an order by Asimakis Zaimis; cf. Photakos [Photios Chrysanthopoulos] 1858, pp. 14–16, which explains that there was not an attack against the two travellers, who had been warned before, but an attack against their servant, Nikolaos Giannako-poulos, and a looting for their things; Phrantzis 1839, vol. I, pp. 146–7, and Oikonomou 1873, p. 86, date the attack to 16 March 1821. Nikolaos Tabakopoulos was a well-known moneylender in the Morea, and Asimakis Zaimis had a lot of debts to him; see Kremmydas 2013.

48   The notable of the district of Karytaina was Kanellos Deligiannis, whose brother Theodo-rakis had arrived in Tripoliça and dispelled the fears of the *kaimmakam* that a revolution-ary plan was under way; see Deligiannis 1959, vol. I, p. 122.

events and asking for their good behaviour and even help in their suppression.[49] We publish here this letter in English translation (for the original letter, as published by Philimon, see below, 3.2., transcription):

Mehmed Salih, by divine right *Kapιcιbaşι* and *Kaimmakam* of the Morea. We announce to you, elders and the rest of the *reaya* of the villages in the *kaza* of Karytaina, that in the *kaza* of Kalavryta, on the road of Katzanais [River Aroanius],[50] some bandits appeared and attacked some travelers, as well as Nikolis Tabakopoulos, who was on his way to [Tripoliça]. This action is very much against the general order [νιζάμι, Ott. Turk. *nizam*] of the province, the high royal decrees and the stipulations [σουρούτι, Ott. Turk. şurut] for all the districts [*kazas*] of the Morea which had been written down in judicial contracts [νέζρι χοτζέτια, Ott. Turk. *nezir hüccetleri*].[51] Because of that, and being highly alerted, we have sent for the present some of our people to the *kaza* of Kalavryta to attack and chase those criminal bandits. However, it is possible that those evildoers will cross to your *kaza* as well, or other criminals will appear there. Thus, we wrote the present order [μπουγιουρδί, Ott. Turk. *buyuruldu*] ordering you strictly: being faithful and obedient *reaya*, do not take those bandits; do not host any of them in any way, neither secretly nor in plain light; do not give them bread, nor any other provisions [ζαχιρέ, Ott. Turk. *zahire*]. According to the standing law and contracts, when those bandits appear in your area, you should inform the Voivode of your *kaza*. Yourselves and together with your men, when they appear, you should honour your subjecthood [ρεαγιαλίκι, Ott. Turk. *raiyyetlik*] and loyalty [σαδδακάτι, Ott. Turk. *sadakat*] and chase those villains, in whatever manner you can; kill them and send their filthy heads here, to the Diwan of the Morea. However, in case those villains try to fool you, saying that they are appointed captains [κάποι, It. *capo*] of certain *kazas*,[52] or even if they show you appointment documents [μουρασελέδες, Ott. Turk. *mürasele*], do not pay any attention: those captains are not appointed with a royal decree, nor have they our consent. Outside our people and the guards [σεϊμένηδες, Ott. Turk. *sekban*] of the

---

49   Philimon 1859–61, vol. 3, pp. 14–15.

50   See Leake 1830, vol. 2, p. 264.

51   For these contracts [*nezir*] of collective responsibility in Ottoman practice, see Tamdoğan 2005, pp. 259–69.

52   This is perhaps a reference to an undated incident in the village of Alonistaina, where *kapobaşı* Dimitris Koliopoulos or Plapoutas exchanged shootings with some Muslims; see Oikonomou 1873, pp. 85–6.

bölükbaşı of your kaza, whom you should recognise as your police [ζαμ-πίτηδες, Ott. Turk. *zabıt*], all others are bandits, and they pretend to be captains and assassins. You should not host them at all; on the contrary, you should chase them, in whatever manner you can, and try to annihilate them without any shortage in the fulfilment of your loyal duties. In case you succeed to annihilate those evildoers, you will be rewarded properly. In case – God forbid! – you do not succeed in that, you will also be punished. We will call more soldiers and you will have to feed them at a heavy price ...

20 March 1821, Diwan of the Morea.

Ioannis Philimon published the letter of Mehmed Salih Agha as 'the first official document which certifies the date of the first [revolutionary] incidents in Kalavryta, showing the spirit and the reactions of the Turkish autorities of the time'.[53] This should actually be corrected now, after the publication of his letter one day before, on March 19.

We also publish below, in English translation (see below, 3.3., Facsimile and Transliteration), the letter Mehmed Salih Agha sent two days later, on March 22, adding some more information about the escalation of the events:[54]

> My Most Benevolent, Illustrious and Merciful Master,
> I have sent a petition to Your Excellency through a courier [*tatar*], in which I reported that the *kocabaşıs* and the bishop of the *kaza* of Kalavryta, the metropolitan of Patras and the *kocabaşı* of the *kaza* of Vostiça [Vostitsa, mod. Aigio] entered into agreement and turned back while en route to Tripoliça. They shut themselves into a monastery located in an inaccessible place in the said *kaza* [Kalavryta] and sent letters [around] containing obvious lies. Although I and even people of their own *millet* and compatriots separately sent them letters promising them safety and accommodation, they remained unaffected and obdurate. Apart from the *reaya* soldiers whom they had previously recruited despite the ban thereon, they even instigated many of the riffraff and dissolute *reaya* in Kalavryta to revolt, roamed around carrying arms and military equipment and abused the travelers and merchants going to Tripoliça, thus demonstrating wicked and sinful behavior contrary to the principles of *raiyyet*

---

53   Philimon 1859–61, p. 43.
54   Istanbul, Ottoman Archives, HAT 38445 (Kolovos et al. 2021, 126–8).

[i.e. subjecthood] and engaging in rebellion and sedition. On the following day of my petition, the number of the said *reaya* in Kalavryta that were intent on perpetrating sedition and perdition had increased. Rumour has it that they have laid ambush in several places and attacked and caused harm to the passers-by, killing some of them and robbing others. It seems that the road from Kalavryta to Tripoliça has thus been blocked. Moreover, I was told that İbrahim Agha, Voivode of Kalavryta, departed with his *bölükbaşı* from the said *kaza* in order to come to Tripoliça. The *bölükbaşı* turned back when they reached a place one hour from Kalavryta. As İbrahim Agha proceeded to his destination with five to ten of his servants, the brigands ambushed them and slaughtered them all. However, this is yet to be confirmed, so obviously this item of news may prove true or false.[55] Since my petition was urgent and it was inexpedient to delay it, I could not find time [to confirm] the news about İbrahim Agha. At this present moment, there has been no action in the other *kaza*s [of the Morea], but it is very probable that the sedition of these brigands will spread among the *reaya* of the other *kaza*s and settlements in the vicinity. Hence, I beg and beseech Your Excellency to take pity on the people and the poor and grant your favour and succour by dispatching a great number of soldiers from the ones under your command as soon as possible so that the fire of sedition can be extinguished, the rebellion suppressed, order restored in the towns and peace brought to all servants of God. As reported in my petition, which I previously submitted to Your Excellency, efforts are being made to keep in custody the *kocabaşı*s and metropolitans who are present here [in Tripoliça]. Your Excellency will acquaint yourself with the state of affairs from the round robins that I now submit to you. The final command rests with Your Excellency.

---

55   From the Greek sources, we know that İbrahim Agha Arnavutoğlu left Kalavryta on 17 or 20 March with his retinue for Tripoliça. His Black slave and coffee servant [*kahveci*] went ahead to prepare his accommodation to his estate [*çiftlik*] in the village of Dara. On the road from Kalavryta to Dara, the servant was attacked and killed after an order from the elder Asimakis Zaimis, and İbrahim Agha Arnavutoğlu was forced to turn back and fortify himself in the three towers in the town of Kalavryta with the Muslim families of the town. They were sieged there and surrendered after five days. For this incident, see Despotopoulos (ed.) 1975, pp. 82–3; Philimon 1859–61, vol. 3, p. 11; Oikonomou 1873, pp. 85–6; Deligiannis 1959, vol. 1, pp. 148–9; Phrantzis 1839, vol. 1, pp. 147–9; Photakos [Photios Chrysanthopoulos] 1858, pp. 16–17; Trikoupis 1860, vol. 1, p. 59; Spiliadis 1851–7, vol. 1, p. 29; for the Arnabutzade İbrahim Agha incident, cf. Sahhâflar Şeyhi-Zâde Seyyid Mehmed Es'ad Efendi 2000, pp. 148–9.

Hurşid Ahmed Pasha forwarded to the Sublime Porte the letters of the *Kaim-makam* of the Morea, and the Deputy Grand Vizier since 17 March, Hacı Salih Pasha, wrote the following summary and recommendation to the Sultan upon the letter of 19 March:

> Letter from Salih Agha, *Kaimmakam* of the Morea, to Hurşid Pasha. The information contained herein regarding the acts of defiance of the *koca-başıs* and bishops of Kalavryta and the disgraceful villainies of the *reaya* whom they incited to rebellion will be excerpted in a separate letter. The Reis Efendi will then give this letter to the Rum Patriarch and speak to him in the following manner: 'You stated in a report that you had drawn up and sent out stern anathemas to instruct the *Rum millet* from submitting to the bandits and doing anything contrary to the customs of subject-hood [*raiyyet*]. Now, this misconduct has appeared among the *reaya* in the Morea. The Sublime State makes an effort to punish them; however, we do not trust that they act out of dissent and defiance inspired by lack of esteem for your anathemas or the leaders of their *millet*. It is feared that His Imperial Majesty's burning wrath may be invoked and that He may give orders for a wholesale execution of the *Rum millet* if this *mil-let* does nothing to stop them [the rebels] and the Rum *reaya* continue to engage in such disgraceful acts and sedition here and there. In this respect, you should immediately undertake whatever plans and measures you have as millet and give any assurances the Sublime State may need. The *Rum millet* should be quick to express a unanimous opinion about the measures necessary for both the suppression of this sedition at any cost and the actual and full prevention of inappropriate actions on the part of the *reaya* at any time hereafter.' [Furthermore] Salih Agha reques-ted soldiers from Hurşid Pasha. The latter wrote that he had dispatched some soldiers by sea[56] and would send the Governor of the Morea with additional soldiers. In light of that, these documents and other related dispatches will be read and some other necessary measures regarding the Morea will be discussed in the Imperial Council that is to convene at the

---

56 As a reply to the letters of Mehmed Salih Agha, Hurşid Ahmed Pasha has sent to the Peloponnese 3,500 Albanian soldiers under the command of Kapucıbaşı Mustafa Bey, the Kethüda of Köse Mehmed Pasha. They crossed to the Peloponnese from Antirrio-Rio in mid-April and advanced towards Tripoliça. See Sahhâflar Şeyhi-Zâde Seyyid Mehmed Es'ad Efendi 2000, pp. 95–6; Philimon 1859–61, vol. 3, pp. 180–90.

Şeyhülislam's residence. Whatever Your Imperial Majesty may order with regard to those matters, it will be done, for the final command rests with Your Imperial Majesty.

Sultan Mahmud II wrote in his imperial rescript upon the recommendation of Hacı Salih Pasha:

> These actions of the *Rum millet* are incomprehensible. So many of them were slaughtered and many more are being slaughtered, and yet they do not show even a trace of alarm or change. All these documents shall be read in the Imperial Council that will convene at the Şeyhülislam's residence on Thursday. A thorough discussion shall be held as to how to address the patriarch and what other measures should be taken in this respect. When the decisions are made, they shall be presented to me and their implementation shall begin.

Sultan Mahmud II wrote in his imperial rescript upon the second letter of Mehmed Salih Agha:

> I have considered this note and the other documents. You [i.e. the Grand Vizier] shall present the matter to the Rum [Greek Orthodox] Patriarch and instruct him to find the Moreot representatives who hide here [in Istanbul] or, should they have sought refuge in one of the [foreign] Powers, to report their whereabouts.[57]

Together with the letter of Mehmed Salih Agha of 20 March in Greek, these three Ottoman documents – in Ottoman Turkish and Greek respectively – report the outbreak of the Greek Revolution, starting in the days just before 19 March and culminating towards the 25 March, primarily around the Peloponnese but also in Rumelia and the Aegean islands.[58] The Ottoman authorities in the Peloponnese, who were fearing that a revolt was under way already from mid-February or even earlier, tried to raise an alarm. According to M. Oikonomou,

> Many actions, one after the other, were dared in the Peloponnese. Some of these actions happened after a secret agitation; some others happened

---

57   The Moreot *vekil*s, Thanos Kanakaris and D. Peroukas, had already escaped and were wanted by the Ottoman authorities. See Deligiannis 1959, vol. I, pp. 128–32.

58   See Panagiotopoulos 2001–2, p. 458.

by chance; and some, even irregular, were inspired by the spirit of the Revolution, caused by anarchy and impatience. The Turks were thinking that maybe the apostate Ali Pasha was behind them, or that the *reaya* had the spirit of revolution, or both. Those incidents, however, one after the other, disrupted their peace and their sleep, and boosted their suspicions and fears.[59]

In this chapter, we focused on the outbreak of the Greek Revolution, as seen from the other side, the side of the Ottomans. From the Ottoman point of view, and especially for Sultan Mahmud II and the Ottoman state apparatus in Istanbul, as evident from the documents discussed above and many others, it was unthinkable that the 'riff-raff and dissolute *reaya*' would take up arms on their own: it should have been the Russians[60] or Tepedelenli Ali Pasha, who was behind the rebellion. However, at the end of the same year, 1821, the Ottoman generals Viziers and Pashas, who 'kept dragging their feet, reluctant to execute their mission, although the besieged Muslims have been expecting help with bated breath night and day', had to acknowledge that those 'dissolute infidel rebels in the Morea', 'having renounced submission and obedience and embarked upon the path of sin and rebellion [abandoned] their malignant souls with the intention of – God forbid! – seizing complete control over the Morea from the Muslims by committing overt acts of violence in their sin and rebellion and coercing our brothers in religion that are besieged in fortresses in the Morea' [*Mora cezîresinde ribka-i itâ'at ü inkıyâddan rû-gerdân ve zirve-i şekâ ve isyâna urûca şitâbân olan usât-ı kefere-i fecere mütecâsir oldukları şekâ ve isyânlarında izhâr-ı şiddet ve Mora kılâ'ında mahsûr olan dîn karındaşlarımızı tazyîkle ma'âzallâhü Te'âlâ Mora'yı külliyyen eyâdîi İslâmiyye'den çıkarmak dâ'iye-i kâsidesiyle cân-ı habîslerinden geçmiş oldukları*].[61] To 'abandon their malignant souls' voluntarily was actually the motto of the Greek Revolution: 'Freedom or Death'. This was a political motto the Ottomans could not easily understand, not because they were Ottomans but because they were Sultans and Viziers without a modern nation in the making.[62]

---

59   Oikonomou 1873, p. 85.

60   For the 'Russian Hand' behind the Greek Revolution, see in detail Ilıcak 2011a, pp. 171–9.

61   Istanbul, Ottoman Archives, HAT 38579-A, Memorandum of Ali Şefik Pasha, former Castellan [*muhafız*] of the Dardanelles, 22 November 1821 (Kolovos et al. 2021, 303–4).

62   For the Ottoman understandings of the Greek Revolution, see also Theotokas and Kotaridis 2011 and Moiras 2020. For the Greek nation as political subject, see Rotzokos 2011.

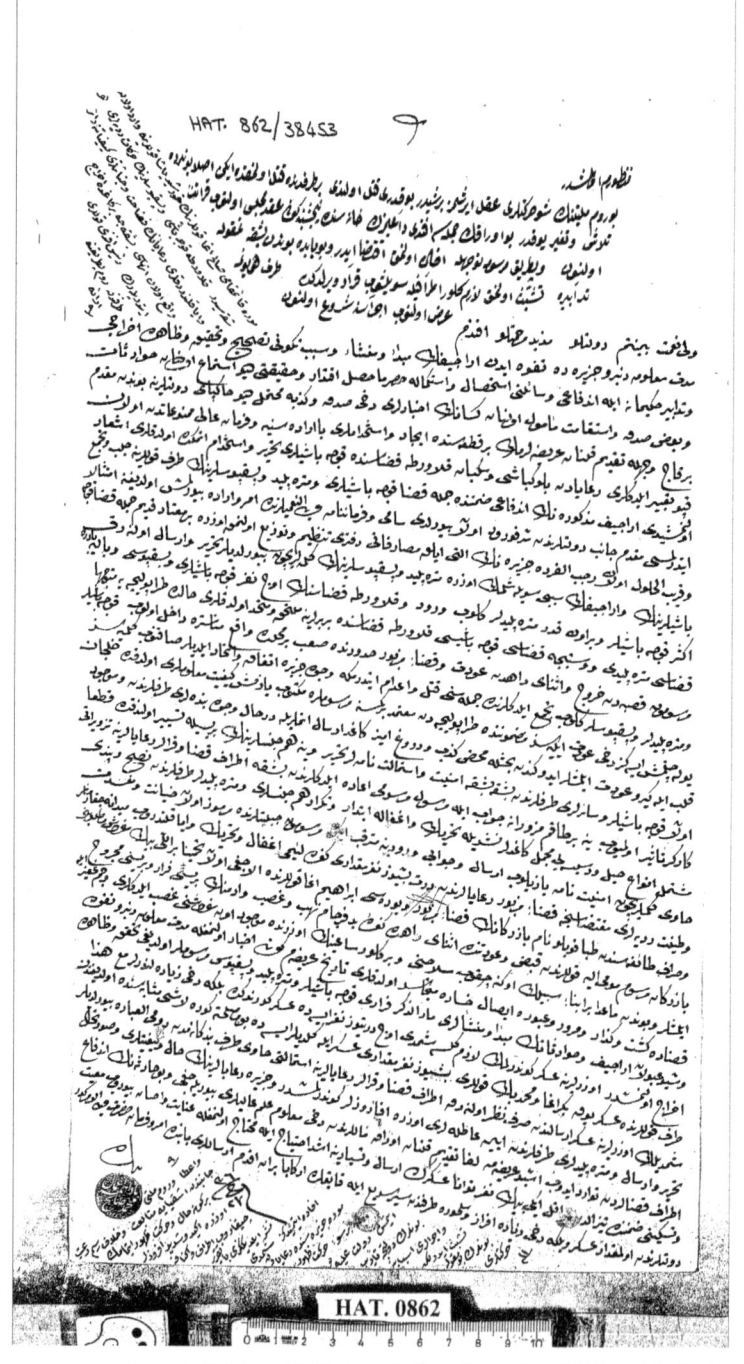

FIGURE 1.1   Report of Mehmed Salih Agha in Tripoliça to Hurşid Ahmed Pasha in Ioannina (19 March 1821)

3   Appendix: Facsimiles and Transliterations

3.1   *Report of Mehmed Salih Agha, 19 March 1821, Facsimile and Transliteration*

SALIH AĞA: *Velîni'met-i bî-minnetim devletlü, mezîd merhametlü efendim; müddet-i ma'lûmeden berü cezîrede tefevvüh iden erâcîfin mebde' ü menşe' ve sebeb-i tekevvüni tashîh ü tahkîk ve zâhire ihrâcı ve tedâbîr-i hakîmâne ile indifâ'ı vesâ'ilini istihsâl ve istikmâle hasr-ı mâ-hasal-i iktidâr ve hakîkati deyu istimâ' olunan havâdisât ve ba'zı sıdk ü istikâmet me'mûl olunan kesânın ihbârları dahi sıdk ve kizbe muhtemel deyu hâk-pâ-yı devletlerine bundan mukaddem birkaç vechile takdîm kılınan arîzalarımın bir kıt'asında îcâd ve istihdâmları bâ-irâde-i seniyye ve fermân-ı âlî memnû'âtdan olan kapu ta'bîr eyledikleri re'âyâdan bölükbaşı ve sekbân Kalavrita kazâsında kocabaşıları tahrîr ve istihdâm itmekde oldukları iş'âr olunmuş idi. Erâcîf-i mezkûrenin indifâ'ı zımnında cümle kazâ kocabaşıları ve metropolid ve piskoposlarının taraf-ı kullarına celb ve tecemmu' itdirilmesi mukaddem cânib-i devletlerinden şeref-vürûd olan buyuruldı-i sâmî ve fermân-nâme-i veliyyü'n-ni'amîlerinde emr ü irâde buyurulmuş olduğuna imtisâlen ve karîbü'l-hulûl olan Recebü'l-Ferd'[d]e cezîrenin altı aylık masârifâtı defteri tanzîm ü tevzî' olunmak üzere ber-mu'tâd-ı kadîm cümle kazâ kocabaşılarının ve erâcîfin sebebi söyleşilmek üzere metropolid ve piskoposlarının gelmeleri-çün buyuruldılar tahrîr ve irsâl olunarak ekser kocabaşılar ve bir on kadar metropolidler gelüb vürûd ve Kalavrita kazâsının üç nefer kocabaşıları ve piskoposı ve Balyabadra kazâsı metropolidi ve Vostice kazâsı kocabaşısı Kalavrita kazâsında birbirlerine mültehik ve müttehid oldukları hâlde Trapoliçe'ye müteveccihen mersûmûn kasabadan hurûc ve esnâ-yı râhdan avdet ve kazâ'-i mezbûr hudûdunda sa'b bir mahalde vâki' manastıra dâhil olub "kocabaşılar ve metropolidler ve piskoposlar gelüb tecemmu' eylediklerinde cümlesini katl ve i'dâm itdirmeğe vücûh-ı cezîre ittifâk ü ittihâd eylediler. Sakınub gelmeyesiz, yola çıkmış iseniz dahi avdet eyleyesiz" mazmûnunda Trapoliçe'den mu'temed bir kimesne mersûmlara mektûb yazmış. Keyfiyyet ma'lûmları oldukda halecân-ı kalb ile girü avdet eylemişler idüğünden bahisle mahz-ı kizb ve dürûğ-âmîz kağıd irsal itmeleriyle derhâl vücûh bendeleri taraflarından ve mevcûd olan kocabaşılar ve sâ'irleri taraflarından başka başka emniyyet ve istimâlet-nâmeler tahrîr ve yine hem-cinslerinin birisiyle tesyîr olundukda kat'an kâr-ger-i te'sîr olmayub yine birtakım müzevvirane cevâb ile mersûl-ı mersûmu i'âde eylediklerinden başka etrâf kazâ ve kurâlar re'âyâlarına tezvîrâtı müştemil envâ' hiyel ü desîseyi mücmel kâğıdlar neşriyle tahrîk ü iğfâle ibtidâr ve tekrâr hem-cinsleri ve metropolidler taraflarından nush ü pendi hâvî gelmeleri-çün emniyyet-nâme yazılub irsal ve cevâbı vürûdına müterakkıb iken mersûmûn cibilliyyetlerinde mermûz olan hıyânet ü mefsedet ve tıynet-i reddiyeleri muktezâsınca kazâ'-i mezbûr re'âyâların-*

dan dört-beş yüz nefer mikdârı kefere-i le'îmi iğfâl ü tahrîk ve ayaklandırub
meydana çıkarmışlar ve sarrâf tâ'ifesinden Tabakopulo nâm bâzergânın kazâ'-
i mezbûr voyvodası İbrâhîm Ağa kullarında alacağı olan tahmînen bir elli bin
guruş matlûbını bâzergân-ı mersûm mûmâ-ileyh kullarından kabz ve avdetinde
esnâ-yı râhda kefere-i bed-fercâm nehb ü gasb ve adamının birisi firâr ve birisini
mecrûh eylemişler ve bundan mâ'adâ bir ebnâ'-i sebîlin önüne çıkub silâhını ve
bir gelür sâ'înin üzerinde mevcûd on guruşını gasb eyledikleri ve cemm-i gafîr ile
kazâda geşt ü güzâr ve mürûr ü ubûra îsâl-i hasâra mütecâsir oldukları târîh-
i arîzam güni ihbâr olunmağla müddet-i ma'lûmeden berü tefevvüh ve şüyû'
bulan erâcîf ü havâdisâtın mebde' ü menşe'leri mârrü'z-zikr firârî kocabaşılar ve
metrepolid ve piskopos mersûmlar oldığı tahakkuk ve zâhire ihrâc olunmuşdur.
Üzerlerine asker gönderilmek lâzım gelse şimdi üç-dört yüz nefer ise de asker
gönderdikde belki dahi ziyâdelenürler. Ma'a-hâzâ taraf-ı kullarında asker yok;
Bekir Ağa ve Mehmed Beğ kulları beş yüz nefer mikdârı asker ile geldiler ise
de bu maslahata göre lâ-şey mesâbesinde oldığından şimdilik üzerlerine asker
irsâline sarf-ı nazar olunarak etrâf-ı kazâ ve kurâlar re'âyâlarına istimâleti hâvî
taraf-ı bendegânemden Rûmiyyü'l-'ibâre buyuruldılar tahrîr ve irsâl ve metre-
polidleri taraflarından âyîn-i âtılaları üzere afarozlar gönderilmişdir ve cezîre
re'âyâlarının hâl ü keyfiyyetleri ve sûret-i hâl etrâf kazâlardan tevârüd idüb işbu
arîzama leffen takdîm kılınan evrâk me'âllerinden dahi ma'lûm-ı ilm-i âlîleri buy-
urılacağı ve bu hâdisenin indifâ' ü teskîni zımnında tîz elden ekal iki bin nefer
tüvânâ askerin irsâl ü tesyârına eşedd-i ihtiyâc ile muhtâc olunmağla inâyet ü
ihsân buyurub ma'iyyet-i devletlerinden ol mikdâr asker ve belki dahi ziyâde ifrâz
ve Salahora tarafından seyr-i serî' ile kayıklara irkâben bir ân akdem irsâlleri
bâbında emr ü fermân hazret-i veliyyü'l-emrindir.
Fi 27 C(emaziyülahır) sene (12)36
Bende [**Seal:**] *Mehmed Sâlih 1231*

GRAND VIZIER: *Mora Kâ'im-makâmı Sâlih Ağa kullarının Hûrşîd Paşa kullarına*
vârid olan şukkasıdır. Kalavrita kocabaşı ve piskoposlarının harekât-ı reddiyeleri
ve ayaklandırdıkları re'âyânın fezâhat ü habâsetleri keyfiyyâtına dâ'ir vâki' olan
inhâsı başkaca bir kâğıda ihrâc itdirilerek Re'îs efendi kulları tarafından Rum pat-
rikine irâ'e ve i'tâ ve "Rum milleti cânibinden eşkıyâya mütâba'at ve hilâf-ı resm-i
ra'iyyet bir gûne hâl ü hareket zuhûr itmamek üzere ekîd ü şedîd afarozlar çıkarub
etrâf ü eknâfa neşr eylediğinizi bâ-takrîr ifâde itmişdiniz. Şimdi Mora cezîresinde
re'âyâdan bir sû'-i hareket zuhûr itmiş. Devlet-i Aliyye bunların devletçe te'dîb ve
icrâları esbâbına teşebbüs ider. Lakin bunların bu makûle hareketleri afarozları-
nıza ve milletlerinin rü'esâsına adem-i i'tibâr ile muhâlefet ve isyân sûreti oldığına
Devlet-i Aliyye i'timâd idemiyor. Eğer bunların milletçe ıtfâsına bakılmaz ve mil-
letiniz re'âyâsından orada burada bu makûle fezâhat ve fesâd zuhûr idecek ise

bunun netîcesi kânûn-ı gazab-ı pâdişâhîyi tehyîc ile Rum milleti hakkında ale'l-
'umûm sell-i seyf-i siyâset misillü bir irâde-i seniyye sudûrına bâ'is olmasından
havf olunur. Bu bâbda milletçe re'y ü tedbîriniz ne vechile ise bir ân akdem
teşebbüs iderek ve Devlet-i Aliyye'ye ne suretle iktizâ ider ise emniyet-i tâmme
virerek gerek işbu fesâdın bi-eyyi-vechin ke-enne indifâ'ı çâresine dâ'ir ve gerek
min-ba'd bir tarafda re'âyâdan harekât-ı nâ-mülâyime vukû'a gelmamesinin
fi'ilen ve kâmilen icrasına mütedâ'ir tedâbîr-i mukteziyenin serî'an milletçe mütâ-
la'a ve beyân olunması" su'âli zemîninde patrik-i mersûma îrâd ve isticvâb olun-
ması ve Mora Kâ'im-makâmı, Hûrşîd Paşa kulları tarafından asker matlûb itmiş
ve müşârun-ileyh dahi bahren biraz asker irsâl idüb Mora vâlîsini dahi asâkir
ile göndereceğini yazmış oldığına nazaran işbu evrâk ve sâ'ir buna dâ'ir tahrî-
rât bundan sonra bâb-ı fetvâ-penâhîde meclis akdiyle kırâ'at ve Mora'ya dâ'ir
bu bâbda sâ'ir icrâsı lâzım gelan tedâbîrin müzâkeresine mübâderet kılınması
husûslarında ne veçhile irâde-i seniyye-yi şâhâneleri müte'allik olur ise emr ü fer-
mân hazret-i men-lehü'l-emrindir.

MAHMUD II: *Bu Rum milletinin şu hareketleri akl irişmez bir şeydir. Bu kadarı*
katl olundı, bir tarafdan da katl olunmakda iken aslâ bunlarda telâş ve tagayyür
yokdur. Bu evrakın cümlesi efendi dâ'îmizin hanesinde pençşenbe güni akd-i
meclis olunub kırâ'at olunub ve patrik-i mersûma ne vechile ifade olunmak ikt-
iza ider ve bu babda bundan başka ne makûle tedâbîre teşebbüs olunmak lâzım
gelür, etrâfıyla söyleşüb karâr virildikde taraf-ı hümâyûnuma arz olunub icrâsına
şürû' olunsun.

3.2 *Greek translation of an order of Mehmed Salih Agha, 20 March 1821*

Μεχμὲτ Σαλὴχ ἐλέῳ Θεοῦ Καπιτζήμπασης καὶ Μόρα Καϊμακάμης

Πρὸς ἔσᾶς, γέροντες καὶ λοιποὶ ῥαγιάδες τῶν χωρίων καζᾶ Καρύταινας, φανερόνομεν, ὅτι
εἰς τὸν καζᾶ Καλαβρύτων ἐπάνω εἰς τὸν δρόμον Κατζάναις εὐγῆκαν μερικοὶ κλέπται, ὡς
ἐπληροφορήθημαν, καὶ ἐβάρεσαν μερικοὺς περαστικοὺς καὶ τὸν Νικολῆν Ταμπακόπου-
λον, ἐδῶ ἐρχόμενον· καὶ ἐπειδὴ τοῦτο τὸ κάμωμα εἶναι πολλὰ ἐναντίον καὶ εἰς τὸ γενικὸν
νιζάμι τοῦ τόπου καὶ εἰς τὰς ὑψηλὰς βασιλικὰς προσταγὰς καὶ εἰς τὸ σουροῦτι, ὅπου μὲ
νέζρι χοτζέτια εἶναι δεμένον εἰς ὅλους τοὺς καζάδες τοῦ Μορέως, διὰ τοῦτο ἔχοντες ἄγρυ-
πνον πρόνοιαν εἰς ὅλα αὐτά, ἐστείλαμεν κατὰ τὸ παρὸν μερικοὺς ἐδικούς μας ἀνθρώπους
εἰς τὸν καζᾶν Καλαβρύτων, διὰ νὰ κτυπήσουν καὶ κυνηγήσουν αὐτοὺς τοὺς κακούργους
κλέπτας. Ἐπειδὴ ὅμως ἐνδέχεται αὐτοὶ οἱ κακότροποι νὰ καταντήσωσι καὶ εἰς τὸν ἐδικόν
σας καζᾶν, ἢ νὰ φανῶσιν αὐτοῦ ἄλλοι τοιοῦτοι κακοῦργοι, διὰ τοῦτο γράφοντες τὸ παρὸν
μας μπουγιουρδὶ σᾶς προστάζομεν σφοδρῶς, ὅπου ὡς πιστοὶ καὶ εὐπειθεῖς ῥαγιάδες, νὰ
μὴν ὑποφέρετε τοὺς τοιούτους, μήτε να δεχθῆτε τελείως κανένα ἀπὸ αὐτούς, μήτε κρυφά,
μήτε φανερά, μήτε νὰ τοὺς δώσετε ψωμὶ ἢ ἄλλον τίποτε ζαχιρὲ, ἀλλὰ ἀμέσως κατὰ τὸ
κοινὸν σουροῦτι καὶ νιζάμι, ἅμα ὅπου φανῶσιν εἰς τὰ μέρη σας, καὶ εἰς τὸν Βοεβόδα τοῦ

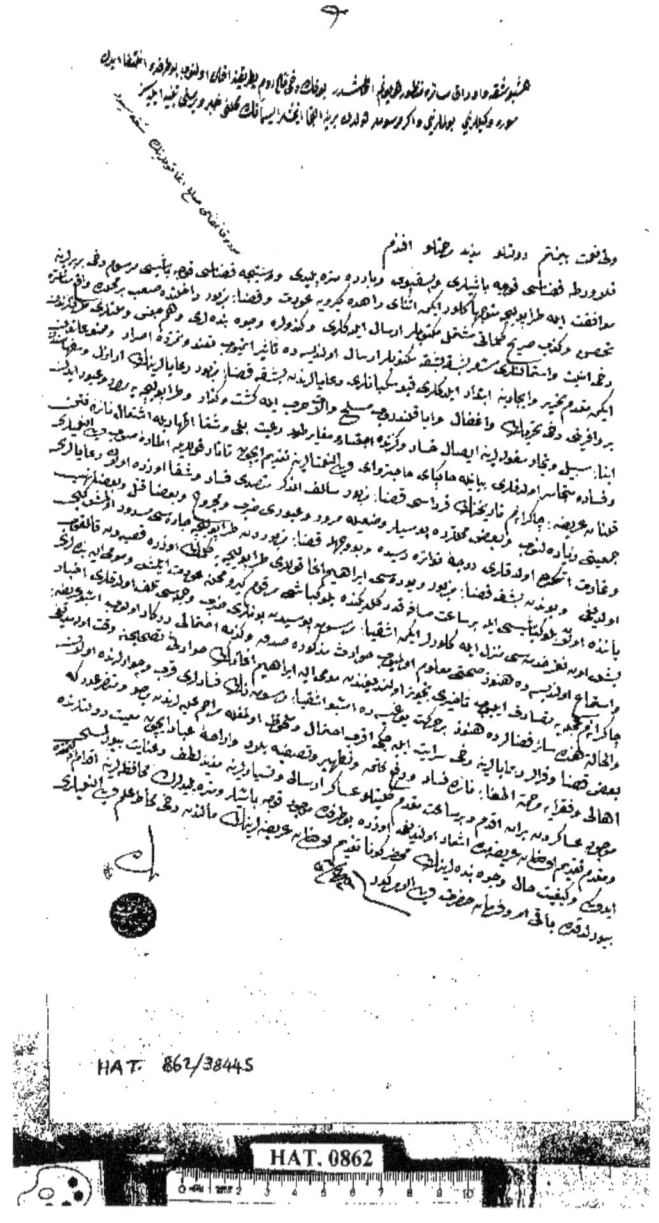

FIGURE 1.2   Report of Mehmed Salih Agha from Tripoliça to Hurşid
Ahmed Pasha in Ioannina (22 March 1821).

καζᾶ σας νὰ δίδητε εἴδησιν, καὶ ἐσεῖς οἱ ἴδιοι ἢ μαζὴ μὲ τοὺς ἐδικούς μας ἀνθρώπους, ἄν ἔλθωσιν αὐτοῦ, ἢ καὶ μόνοι σας, νὰ φιλοτιμηθῆτε νὰ ἀποδείξητε τὸ ῥεαγιαλίκι καὶ τὸ σαδ-δακάτι σας, καὶ νὰ τοὺς κυνηγήσετε αὐτοὺς τοὺς ἀχρείους, ἢ νὰ τοὺς βαρέσετε, μὲ ὅποιον τρόπον ἠμπορεῖτε, νὰ τοὺς σκοτώσετε καὶ νὰ στείλετε τὰ μιαρὰ κεφάλια τους ἐδῶ εἰς τὸ Διβάνι τοῦ Μορέως. Ἄν ὅμως αὐτοὶ οἱ ἀχρεῖοι θελήσωσι νὰ σᾶς γελάσουν καὶ σᾶς εἰποῦν, ὅτι εἶναι κάποι διωρισμένοι ἀπὸ κανέναν καζᾶν, ἢ ἤθελαν σᾶς δείξουν καὶ μουρασελέδες, νὰ μὴ τοὺς ἀκούσητε τελείως· ἐπειδὴ αὐτοὶ οἱ κάποι καὶ βασιλικῶς εἶναι διόλου ἐμποδι-σμένοι, καὶ ἀπὸ τὸ μέρος μας δὲν εἶναι τελείως ῥιτζᾶς ἢ μεσολάβησις δι' αὐτούς. Ὅθεν ἔξω ἀπὸ τοὺς ἐδικούς μας ἀνθρώπους καὶ ἀπὸ τοὺς σεϊμένιδες τοῦ μπολούκπαση τοῦ καζᾶ σας, ὁποῦ πρέπει νὰ γνωρίζητε διὰ ζαμπίτας, τοὺς ἐπιλοίπους, εἴτε φανεροὶ κλέπται εἶναι, εἴτε ὡς κάποι καὶ πράβοι περιφέρονται, νὰ μὴ τοὺς δέχεσθε τελείως, ἀλλὰ μὲ κάθε προθυμίαν νὰ τοὺς κυνηγήσετε, μὲ ὅ,τι τρόπον ἠμπορεῖτε, καὶ νὰ πασχίσητε διόλου νὰ τοὺς ἐξολοθρεύ-σετε, χωρὶς νὰ κάμετε παραμικρὸν κουσοῦρι εἰς τὸ χρέος τοῦ σαδδακατίου σας. Καὶ ἄν μὲ τὸ κυνήγημα καὶ τὴν προθυμίαν σας ἐξολοθρευσῶσιν αὐτοὶ οἱ κακότροποι, θέλετε εὐεργε-τηθῆ μὲ τὴν πρέπουσαν ἀνταμοιβήν· ἄν ὅμως (ὅ μὴ γένοιτο!) δὲν κατορθωθῆ τοῦτο, καὶ ἐσεῖς θέλετε ὑποπέσει εἰς ὀργήν, καὶ ἄλλα περισσότερα ἀσκέρια εἶναι ἀνάγκη νὰ κάμω-μεν ταῖνι, καὶ θέλουν σᾶς προξενηθοῦν βαρειὰ ἔξοδα καὶ ζημίαι ... 1821 μαρτίου 20 Διβάνι Μορέως.[63]

3.3 *Report of Mehmed Salih Agha, 22 March 1821. Facsimile and Transliteration*

SALIH AĞA: *Velîni'met-i bî-minnetim devletlü, mezîd merhametlü efendim;*

Kalavrita kazâsı kocabaşıları ve piskopos[ı] ve Badra metropolidi ve Vostiça kazâsı kocabaşısı mersûm dahı birbirlerine muvâfakat ile Trapoliçe['ye] müteveccihen gelür iken esnâ-yı râhda girüye avdet ve kazâ-i mezbûr dâhilinde sa'ab bir mahalde vâki' manastıra tahassun ve kizb[i] sarîh kelimâtı müştemil mektûblar irsâl eyledikleri ve kendülere vücûh bendeleri ve hem-cins ve milletleri taraflarından dahı emniyyet ve istimâletleri müş'ir başka başka mektûblar irsâl olundıysa da te'sîr itmeyüb ta'annüd ü temerrüdde ısrâr ve memnû'âtdan iken mukaddem tahrîr ve îcâdına ibtidâr eyledikleri kapu sekbânları re'âyâlarından başka kazâ-i mezbûr re'âyâlarının erâzil ve süfehâsından bir vâfirini dahı tahrîk ü iğfâl ve ayaklandırub müsellah ve âlât-ı harb ile geşt ü güzâr ve Trapoliçe'ye mürûr ü ubûr iden ebnâ-i sebîl ve tüccâr makûlelerine îsâl-i hasâr ü gezende ictisâr

---

63   Philimon 1859–61, vol. 3, pp. 14–15. Philimon notes that all the documents of the Ottoman authorities in the Greek provinces were written in such a 'mixed Greek-barbarian [lege: Greek with Turkish words] language, in Greek letters', making the Ottomans, 'more just than the previous Venetian rulers, due to the fact that at least they respected the languages of their occupied people'.

ve mugâyir-i tavr-ı ra'iyyet bağy ü şekâ izhârıyla iştigâl-i nâ'ire-i fiten ü fesâda
mütecâsir oldukları beyânıyla hâk-pâ-yı hâcet-revâ-yı veliyyü'n-ni'metâ[ne]lerine
takdîm içün tatar kullarıyla itâre-i savb-ı veliyyü'n-ni'amîleri kılınan arîza-i çâker-
ânem târîhinin ferdâsı kazâ'-i mezbûr sâlifü'z-zikr mütesaddî-i fesâd ü şekâ üzere
olan re'âyâları cem'iyyeti ziyâdelenüb ve ba'zı mahallerde pusılar vaz'ıyla mürûr
ü ubûrı darb ve merzûh ve ba'zan katl ve ba'zan nehb ü gâret itmekde olduk-
ları derece-i tevâtüre resîde ve bu vechile kazâ'-i mezbûrdan Trapoliçe câddesi
mesdûd olmuş gibi oldığı ve bundan başka kazâ'-i mezbûr voyvodası İbrâhîm
Ağa kulları Trapoliçe'ye gelmek üzere kasabadan kalkub yanında olan bölük-
başısı ile bir sâ'at mesâfe kadar geldiğinde bölükbaşı-i merkûm girü mahalline
avdet eylemiş ve mûmâ-ileyh bendeleri beş-on nefer hademesi menzil ile gelürler
iken eşkıyâ-i mersûme pusıdan bunları darb ve cümlesi telef oldukları ihbâr ü
istimâ' olundıysa da henüz sıhhati ma'lûm olmayub havâdis-i mezkûre sıdk ü
kizbe ihtimâli der-kâr olub işbu arîza-i çâkerânem aceleye tesâdüf eyleyüb te'hîri
tecvîz olunmadığından mûmâ-ileyh İbrâhîm Ağa'nın havâdisi vakt olamadığı ve
el-hâletü hâzihî sâ'ir kazâlarda henüz bir hareket yoğ ise de işbu eşkıyâ-i mer-
sûmenin fesâdları kurb ü civârlarında olan ba'zı kazâ ve kurâlar re'âyâlarına
dahı sirâyet eyleyeceği akreb-i ihtimâl ve melhûz olmağla merâhim-i aliyyeler-
inden mercû ve mutazarra'dır ki ahâlî ve fukarâya merhameten ıtfâ'-i nâ'ire-i
fesâd ve def'-i fiten ve tathîr ü tasfiye-i bilâd ve irâha-i ibâd için ma'iyyet-i dev-
letlerinde mevcûd asâkirden bir ân akdem ve bir sâ'at mukaddem külliyyetlü
asâkir irsâl ü tesyârlarına mezîd-i lutf ü inâyet buyurulması ve mukaddem tak-
dîm olunan arîzamda iş'âr olundığı üzere bu tarafda mevcûd kocabaşılar ve
metrepolidlerin muhâfazalarına ikdâm olunmakda idüği ve keyfiyyet-i hâl vücûh
bendelerinin mahzar-gûnâ takdîm olunan arîzalarının me'âlinden dahı muhât-
ı ilm-i veliyyü'n-ni'amîleri buyuruldukda bâkî emr ü fermân hazret-i veliyyü'l-
emrindir. Fî 29 C(emaziyülahır) sene [12]36.

Bende [**Seal**] *Mehmed Sâlih 1231*

GRAND VIZIER: *Mora Kâ'im-makâmı Sâlih Ağa kullarının şukkasıdır.*

MAHMUD II: *İşbu şukka ve evrâk-ı sâ'ire manzûr-ı hümâyûnum olmuşdur.*
Bunun dahı me'âli Rum patrikine ifâde olunub bu tarafda ihtifâ iden Mora vekîl-
lerini bulmalarını ve eğer mersûmlar düvelden birine iltic⠠itmişler ise anın
mahallini haber virmesini tenbîh eyleyesiz.

Bibliography

Anonymous 1858, *Ιστορικαί αλήθειαι συμβάντων τινών της Μάνης. Από του 1769 και εντεύθεν. Ο Τζανέτμπεης Καπετανάκης Γρηγοράκης και η οικογένειά του* [*Historical truths on the events in Mani from 1769 until today: Tzanetbey Kapetanakis Grigorakis and his family*], Athens: Φ. Καραμπίνης και Κ. Βαφάς.

Botzaris, Notis 1962, *Visions balkaniques dans la préparation de la révolution grecque (1789–1821)*, Geneva and Paris: Librarie E. Droz, Genève and Librarie Minard.

Clogg, Richard 1976, *The Movement for Greek Independence 1770–1821*, London: Barnes & Noble.

Deligiannis, Kanellos 1957, *Απομνημονεύματα* [*Memoirs*], 3 Volumes, Athens: Γ. Τσουκαλάς και Υιός.

Despotopoulos, Alexandros (ed.) 1975, *Ιστορία του Ελληνικού Έθνους* [*History of the Greek Nation*], Volume 12, Athens: Εκδοτική Αθηνών.

Frangos, George D. 1973, 'The Philiki Etairia. A Premature National Coalition', in *The Struggle for Greece Independence: Essays to mark the 150th Anniversary of the Greek War of Independence*, edited by Richard Clogg, London: MacMillan.

Germanos, Metropolitan of Palaias Patras 1900, *Απομνημονεύματα* [*Memoirs*], 3rd edition, Athens: Σπύρος Τσαγγάρης.

Giannopoulos, Giannis 2010, *Αλέξανδρος και Δημήτριος Υψηλάντης* [Alexandros and Demetris Hypsilantis], Athens: Τα Νέα.

Gritsopoulos, Tasos 1972–1974, 'Η εις Βοστίτζαν μυστική συνέλευσις των Πελοποννησίων ηγετών (26–29 Ιαν. 1821)' ['The secret meeting of the Peloponnesian leaders in Vostitsa (26–29 Jan. 1821)'], *Μνημοσύνη*, 4: 3–60.

Ilıcak, H. Şükrü 2011a, *A Radical Rethinking of Empire: Ottoman State and Society during the Greek War of Independence (1821–1826)*, Ph.D. Dissertation, Harvard University.

Ilıcak, Şükrü 2011b, 'The Revolt of Alexandros Ipsilantis and the Fate of Fanariots in Ottoman Documents', in *The Greek Revolution of 1821. A European Event*, edited by Petros Pizanias, Istanbul: The Isis Press.

Ilıcak, H. Şükrü, 2022, *Μια διερεύνηση της πολιτικής των Αλβανών κατά τον ελληνικό Αγώνα της Ανεξαρτησίας (1821–1825)* [*An Examination of Muslim Albanian Politics during the Greek Revolution (1821–1825)*], Digital Library RCH (Athens: Research Centre for the Humanities and National Documentation Centre, 2021) https://doi.org/10.12681/rch .70.

Karabıçak, Yusuf Ziya 2020, 'Ottoman Attempts to Define the Rebels during the Greek War of Independence', *Studia Islamica*, 115: 68–106.

Kasomoulis, Nikolaos K. 1940, *Ενθυμήματα στρατιωτικά της επαναστάσεως των Ελλήνων, 1821–1833* [*Military memoirs on the revolution of the Greeks, 1821–1833*], introduction and commentary by Giannis Vlachogiannis, 3 Volumes, Athens.

Kolokotronis, Theodoros K. 1846, *Διήγησις συμβάντων της ελληνικής φυλής από τα 1770 έως τα 1836* [*Account of events concerning the Greek people from 1770 until 1836*], Athens: Χ. Νικολαΐδης Φιλαδελφεύς.

Kolovos Elias, Şükrü Ilıcak, Mohammad Shariat-Panahi 2021, *Η οργή του σουλτάνου. Αυτόγραφα διατάγματα του Μαχμούτ Β΄ το 1821* [*An angry Sultan: Imperial rescripts of Mahmud II in 1821*], Athens: Hellenic Open University Press.

Konortas, Paraskevas 1999, 'From Tâ'ife to Millet: Ottoman Terms for the Ottoman Greek Orthodox Community', in *Ottoman Greeks in the Age of Nationalism: Politics, Economy, and Society in the Nineteenth Century*, edited by Dimitris Gondicas and Charles Issawi (eds.), Princeton: Darwin Press.

Koulouri, Christina 2020, *Φουστανέλες και χλαμύδες: Ιστορική μνήμη και εθνική ταυτότητα 1821–1930* [*Foustanellas and togas: Historical memory and national identity 1821–1930*], Athens: Αλεξάνδρεια.

Kremmydas, Vassilis 1996, 'Μηχανισμοί παραγωγής ιστορικών μύθων. Σχετικά με μια ομιλία του Παλαιών Πατρών Γερμανού' [Mechanism for the production of historical myths. On a speech by Germanos of Palaia Patras], *Μνήμων*, 18: 9–21.

Kremmydas, Vassilis 2013, *Εταιρεία τοκογλυφίας Ν. Ταμπακόπουλος και Σία, 1816–1820* [*Usury Society N. Tampakopoulos and Co., 1816–1820*, Athens: Gutenberg.

Leake, William Martin 1830, *Travels in the Morea*, 3 Volumes, London: John Murray.

Moiras, Leonidas 2020, *Η Ελληνική Επανάσταση μέσα από τα μάτια των Οθωμανών* [*The Greek Revolution as seen through Ottoman eyes*], Athens: Τόπος.

Oikonomou, Mikhail. 1873, *Ιστορικά της Ελληνικής Παλιγγενεσίας ή ο ιερός των Ελλήνων αγών* [*History of the Greek Ressurection, or the holy struggle of the Greeks*, Athens: Θ. Παπαλεξανδρής.

Panagiotopoulos, Vassilis 2001–2002, 'Η έναρξη του αγώνα της ανεξαρτησίας στην Πελοπόννησο. Μία ημερολογιακή προσέγγιση' ['The outbreak of the War for Indepedence in the Peloponnese'], in *Πρακτικά του ΣΤ΄ Διεθνούς Συνεδρίου Πελοποννησιακών Σπουδών (Τρίπολις 24–29 Σεπτεμβρίου 2000)*, vol. 3, Athens.

Panagiotopoulos, Vassilis 2009, 'Ένα δοκίμιο για τον Αλή Πασά', in *Αρχείο Αλή Πασά Γενναδείου Βιβλιοθήκης*, vol. IV, Athens: Hellenic National Research Foundation.

Panagiotopoulos, Vassilis 2011, 'The Filiki Etaireia (Society of Friends). Organizational Preconditions of the National War of Independence', in *The Greek Revolution of 1821. A European Event*, edited by Petros Pizanias, Istanbul: The Isis Press.

Panagiotopoulos, Vassilis 2015, 'Οι ελληνομολδαβοί αδελφοί Αλέξ. και Γεώργ. Καντακουζηνός στην Ελληνική Επανάσταση' ['The Greek-Moldavian brothers Alex. and Georg. Kantakouzinos in the Greek Revolution'], in *Δύο πρίγκιπες στην Ελληνική Επανάσταση. Επιστολές αυτόπτη μάρτυρα και ένα υπόμνημα του πρίγκιπα Γεώργιου Καντακουζηνού* [*Two princes in the Greek Revolution*], Athens: Ασίνη.

Philimon, Ioannis 1859–61, *Δοκίμιον Ιστορικόν περί της Ελληνικής Επαναστάσεως* [*Historical Essay on the Greek Revolution*], 4 Volumes, Athens: Π. Σούτσας και Α. Κτενάς.

Philliou, Christine 2009, 'Communities on the Verge: Unraveling the Phanariot Ascendancy in Ottoman Governance', *Comparative Studies in Society and History*, 51,1: 151–81.

Philliou, Christine M. 2011, *Biography of an Empire: Governing Ottomans in an Age of Revolution*, Berkeley, Los Angeles, London: University of California Press.

Photakos [Photios Chrysanthopoulos] 1858, *Απομνημονεύματα περί της Ελληνικής Επαναστάσεως* [*Memoirs concerning the Greek Revolution*], Athens: Π.Δ. Σακελλαρίου.

Photeinos, Elias 2020 [1846], *Οι άθλοι της εν Βλαχία Ελληνικής Επαναστάσεως το 1821 έτος* [*The efforts of the Greek Revolution in Wallachia in 1821*], Athens: Η Καθημερινή.

Phrantzis, Amvrosios 1839, *Επιτομή της ιστορίας της αναγεννηθείσης Ελλάδος* [*Compendium of the history of resurrected Greece*], 4 Volumes, Athens: Βιτώρια.

Rotzokos, Nikos 2011, 'The Nation as a Political Subject. Comments on the Greek National Movement', in *The Greek Revolution of 1821. A European Event*, edited by Petros Pizanias, Istanbul: The Isis Press.

Rotzokos, Nikos 2020, 'Τοπική και εθνική ταυτότητα στα απομνημονεύματα των Πελοποννήσιων αγωνιστών της Επανάστασης του 1821' [Local and national identity in the memoirs of the Peloponnesian fighters in the Revolution of 1821], in *1821 και απομνημόνευμα. Ιστορική χρήση και ιστοριογραφική γνώση* [*1821 and memoirs: history and historiography*], edited by Dimitris Dimitropoulos, Vangelis Karamanolakis, Niki Maroniti, Pantelis Boukalas, Athens: Hellenic Parliament Foundation.

Sahhâflar Şeyhi-Zâde Seyyid Mehmed Es'ad Efendi 2000, *Vak'a-nüvîs Es'ad Efendi Tarihi 1237–1241/1821–1826* [*History 1821–1826*], edited by Ziya Yılmazer, Istanbul: Osmanlı Araştırmaları Vakfı.

Saitas, Yannis 2009, 'Social and Spatial Organisation in the Peninsula of the Mani (Southern Peloponnese): Medieval, Post-Medieval and Modern Times', in *Medieval and Post-Medieval Greece: The Corfu Papers*, edited by J. Bintliff and Hanna Stöger, England: British Archaeological Reports.

Şânî-zâde Mehmed 'Atâ'ullah Efendi 2008, *Şânî-zâde Târîhî 1223–1237/1808–1821* [*History 1808–1821*], edited by Ziya Yılmazer, 2 Volumes, Istanbul: Çamlıca.

Sarafis, Vangelis 2017, '[...] να νομίζωμεν εμαυτούς απηλπισμένους, χωρίς να βλέπωμεν διόρθωσιν τινά προς οικονομίαν. Φόβος για την αναπότρεπτη εξέγερση, Φεβρουάριος 1821' [February 1821, fear before the outbreak of the revolution], in *Φόβοι και ελπίδες στα νεότερα χρόνια*, edited by Katerina Dede, Dimitris Dimitropoulos, Tassos Sakellaropoulos, Athens: National Hellenic Research Foundation.

Sezer, Hamit 1995, 'Tepedelenli Ali Paşa'nın Oğulları' ['The sons of Tepedelenli Ali Pasha'], *Tarih Araştırmaları Dergisi*, 29: 155–64.

Sfyroeras, Vassilis 1974, 'Ο Κανουνναμές του 1819 για την εκλογή Φαναριωτών στις Ηγεμονίες και στη Δραγομανία' ['The Kanunname of 1819 for the appointment of Phanariots in the Danubian Principalities and the Office of the Chief Dragoman'], *Ο Ερανιστής*, 11: 568–79.

Spiliadis, Nikolaos 1851–1857, *Απομνημονεύματα* [*Memoirs*], 3 Volumes, vols, Athens: X. Νικολαΐδης Φιλαδελφεύς.

Sürreya, Mehmed 1996 [1890/91–1893/94], *Sicill-i Osmanî*, edited by Nuri Akbayar, Istanbul: Tarih Vakfı Yurt Yayınları.

Tamdoğan, Işık 2005, 'Le *nezir* ou les relations des bandits et des nomads avec l'État dans la Çukurova du XVIIIe siècle', in *Sociétés rurales ottomanes/Ottoman Rural Societies*, edited by Mohammad Afifi, Rachida Chih, et al., Cairo: Institut français d'archéologie orientale.

Theotokas, Nikos and Nikos Kotaridis 2011, 'Ottoman Perceptions of the Greek Revolution', in *The Greek Revolution of 1821. A European Event*, edited by Petros Pizanias, Istanbul: The Isis Press.

Trikoupis, Spyridon 1860, *Ιστορία της Ελληνικής Επαναστάσεως* [*History of the Greek Revolution*], 4 Volumes, London: Taylor and Francis.

Tzakis, Dionysis 2018, 'Από την Οδησσό στη Βοστίτσα: η πολιτική ενσωμάτωση των τοπικών ηγετικών ομάδων στη Φιλική Εταιρεία' ['From Odessa to Vostitsa: the incorporation of the local notables into the Friendly Society'], in *Οι πόλεις των Φιλικών: οι αστικές διαδρομές ενός επαναστατικού φαινομένου. Πρακτικά Ημερίδας* [*The towns of the Friendly Society: the urban itineraries of a revolutionary phenomenon*], edited by Olga Katsiardi-Hering, Athens: Hellenic Parliament Foundation.

Ursinus, Michael O.H. 1993, 'Millet', in *Encyclopaedia of Islam*, 2nd edition, edited by P. Bearman, Th. Bianquis, et al., Leiden: Brill.

Zafeiropoulos, Iosif 1852, *Οι αρχιερείς και οι προύχοντες εντός της εν Τριπόλει φυλακής εν έτει 1821* [*The prelates and the notables in the Tripolitza prison in 1821*], Athens: Νικόλαος Αγγελίδης.

CHAPTER 2

Salonica in the Revolutionary Conjuncture of 1821

Phokion P. Kotzageorgis

Salonica, or Thessaloniki, the important economic and administrative centre of the Ottoman Balkans, was involved in the revolutionary conjuncture of 1821 in two ways. Firstly, Salonica was the closest city to the centre of the revolutionary initiative in Macedonia (i.e. the Halkidiki peninsula) and at the same time the target of the Greek insurgents. In fact, it was the Ottoman authorities of this city who coordinated any policy to suppress the Rebellion. Secondly, Salonica, as an important military and economic hub of the Ottoman Empire, was naturally the centre of administration of the Ottoman repression measures for the south of the Greek peninsula, being an intermediary station for dispatching munitions, food and troops to the war front. The Ottoman interest in shielding the city or the unimpeded flow – from Salonica to Istanbul or from Salonica's hinterland to the city itself – of taxable material (either in money or in kind) explains the considerable amount of information we have in the court registers [*şer'iyye sicilleri*] of Salonica. The local Ottoman court was the addressee of the state orders, and its preserved archive provides a unique example of how the Ottoman administration handled the revolutionary conjuncture at its birth. This paper attempts to view a Balkan national rebellion through the 'eyes' of the local Ottoman court.

The outbreak of the Greek Revolution in Halkidiki in the spring of 1821 is one of the central topics in the Ottoman court's archival material. The first document on the subject is a sultanic order [*ferman*], dated at the beginning of Şaban 1236 / 4–13 May 1821.[1] According to this order, the Deputy Governor [*mütesellim*] of the city, Yusuf Bey, had sent a report to the Porte informing it of the arrest of some Christian Ottoman subjects by state spies. In particular, the priest Ananias, son of Markopoulos, was arrested possessing documents with

---

1   Thessaloniki, Historical Archive of Macedonia (*Ιστορικά Αρχεία Μακεδονίας*), Judicial registers (*Ιεροδικαστικοί κώδικες*), n. 205, p. 127. See the Greek translation in Vasdravellis 1950, pp. 191–2, and Stamboulis 2000, pp. 261–2. In the latter, the last two lines of the ferman have not been translated. For the incident, see Vacalopoulos 1988, p. 546. For the revolution in Halkidiki, see the article, which is mainly based on the material from the former Başbakanlık Osmanlı Arşivi, now T.C. Cumhurbaşkanlığı Devlet Arşivleri: Aydın 2018, pp. 303–4.

a revolutionary content [*fitne-i amiz evrak*]. According to the confiscated documents, other persons were also involved into the Revolution's preparations
[*Rum taife şeriresinin mütecasir oldukları hıyanet ve mel'anetinde medhal ve itti-
fakları*]: a man named Vassilikos from the village of Galarinos in Halkidiki with
his sons Dimitris and Stamos, who, however, had in the meantime moved to
Larissa; a Tzamtzakos[2] from the miners of Sidirokafsia/Sidrekapsi (in north-
eastern Halkidiki); another Vassilikos on Mount Athos; a Joseph from the district [*kaza*] of Tikveş (today in Northern Macedonia); and a grocer from Salonica.[3] Of these, Vassilikos of Galarinos, the priest Ananias and the grocer were
imprisoned, while the local authorities were ordered to arrest the men from
Mount Athos and Tikveş. There was information that Vassilikos from Mount
Athos had escaped, while for the man from Tikveş, no answer had been received
yet. The rest were arrested and imprisoned, Dimitris and Stamos by the *mütesellim* of Tırhala [Gk. *Trikala*] and Tzamtzakos by the inspector [*emin*] of the
mines of Sidirokafsia. The Porte ordered that all prisoners be executed, while
the two who were not already detained had to be arrested immediately. In addition, it was ordered that the priest Ananias, Vassilikos, Tzamtzakos and the
grocer had to be executed in Salonica.

The document and the information it contains are extremely valuable as a
primary report from just a few days before the outbreak of the revolutionary
activity in Halkidiki. The document shows that there was a conspiracy network of revolutionaries in Macedonia. We are not aware of the contents of the
'revolutionary documents' that were confiscated, but it is likely to be evidence
of a broader revolutionary planning.

In addition to the arrest of some conspirators, the first revolutionary movements in the Halkidiki peninsula had already begun. Salonica's *mütesellim*,
Yusuf Bey and the judge [*kadı*] informed the Governor General of Rumelia
[*Rumeli valisi*] that they intend to proceed in recruitment of forces in order to
protect the peninsulas of Kassandra and Mount Athos from the rebels. The Governor General gave his approval by a decree dated 22 Ramadan 1236 / 23 June
1821, informed that a firman had also been issued on the matter, and drew the
attention of the addressees of the decree in this regard: if they saw rebellious
movements, they must take immediate action by capturing women and children, seizing the fortunes of the rebels and burning their houses. Regarding

---

2   In the first instance, the name is written as *Cam cano*.
3   According to Vasdravellis, he is probably identified with the grocer Anagnostis. See Vasdrav-
    ellis 1950, p. 69.

the payroll of the conscripts, it was ordered not to worry about it at this time, as it will burden the taxation of the two peninsulas.[4]

At the same time, the first revolutionary movements in Halkidiki are mentioned in the Ottoman court registers.[5] Firstly, the Porte informs local authorities that the rebellion and betrayal of the Rum *millet* against the Muslim state became apparent [*Rum millet habisesinin devlet-i vala-i muhammediye hakkında icrasına mütecasir oldukları fesad ü hıyanet her tarafına sirayet ile*]. In particular, in the Salonica area, the Porte became aware of the uprising of the Christians of Polygyros, the killing of the local state tax collector [*voyvoda*] and fourteen of his men as well as the wounding of three others, while three others were killed and three were injured near the village of Kayacık (today Palaiokastro) by bands of rebels. The news had already spread, and by the time the firman was issued five or ten villages of Sidrekapsi and the whole Kassandra peninsula had already joined the rebellion. According to the legal opinion [*fetva*] issued by the Chief of religious-judicial personnel [*şeyhülislam*] regarding the Greek Revolution, insurgents should be killed, women and children captured and arrested and property distributed among the soldiers.[6] The Porte indicated that the Governor of the provinces of Aydın and Saruhan, Hacı Behram Pasha, who was on a march to Salonica, was coming to the aid of the Ottoman troops. Kavala and Drama were also requested to dispatch troops, as was the supervisor of the Sidrekapsi mines. The Porte's orders are strict and speak of an immediate and complete overthrow of the rebels, the captivity of women and children and the seizure of property; however, the officers were expected to protect those Christians who did not participate in the revolt. An expression at the end of the text is of special importance. There, the Porte stresses that the present issue is a matter of faith and that it was sin for those Muslims to sit idle rather than mobilise [*imdi bu madde mevad-ı saireye bir vechle üzere kıyas kabul etmeyüb din gavgası olarak müslüman olanlara durub oturmak haram olmağla*].

At the same time, and at the request of the Governor of Salonica, the first munitions were sent to the city to suppress the rebellion. At the end of June, two decrees were issued, to send 10,000 rounds of ammunition, a machine gun [*süra't topu*] and twelve horsemen of artillery for the defence of the fortress of

---

4 Historical Archive of Macedonia, Judicial Registers, 205, pp. 132–1. See the Greek translation in Vasdravellis 1950, p. 198, and Stamboulis 2000, pp. 263–4.

5 Historical Archive of Macedonia, Judicial registers, 205, p. 133 (111 Ramazan 1236 / 22 June–1 July 1821). See the Greek translation in Vasdravellis 1950, pp. 200–2, and Stamboulis 2000, pp. 264–6. For the incidents in Polygyros, see Vacalopoulos 1988, pp. 551–2.

6 The text of the *fetva* is reproduced in Ilıcak 2011, p. 148, n. 163.

Salonica.[7] The problem of supplying the city's defence forces during this crucial period was not easily resolved. Thus, on 28 September, a register was sent to
Istanbul for the quantities of shells, lead and gunpowder required to equip the
five forts of the city [*Selanik, Vardar, Kelemerye, Tophane* and *Bala*]. Moreover,
it is noted in the accompanying text that the rebellion lasted for three and a
half months and that the need for ammunition was high.[8]

Appointed as head of the Ottoman troops to suppress the rebellion in Halkidiki, Behram Pasha ordered the killing of the Christians of the villages in the
sub-districts [*nahiye*] of Langada and *Maden* [i.e. Sidrekapsi] and required
from the soldiers their total devotion and submission. He urged Muslim sympathy and mobilisation, referring to the sacred struggle and religious duty of
every faithful Muslim to take up arms and abandon apathy.[9] Behram Pasha also
referred to the difficulty that the Ottoman troops had at that time in suppressing the rebellion. In particular, he claimed that by that time people had been
recruited from neighbouring *kaza*s – who were interested in plundering the
*reaya*s, rebellious or not, and not killing them – something unacceptable to
religion. Therefore, he called on the Muslims to join the army, to comply with
the orders and not to do anything on their own initiative.

Almost at the same time, a firman informs that at his request and because
of the needs in the Peloponnese, Behram Pasha was relocated to the south and
that, as he had reported to the Porte, he had almost suppressed the rebellion in
Halkidiki and confined the rebels to the peninsula of Kassandra and Mount
Athos.[10] According to the *fetva* issued on it, the Porte designated the city's
Mütesellim, Yusuf Bey, as head of an army of Muslims recruited from Salonica
and its district to capture and kill the rebels in those areas.[11] The order under-

---

7   The first ferman is Historical Archive of Macedonia, Judicial registers, 205, p. 139 (24
         Ramazan / 25 June 1821). See the Greek translation in Vasdravellis 1950, pp. 198–9, n. 9. The
         second is in Historical Archive of Macedonia, Judicial registers, 205, pp. 140–1 (28 Ramazan
         1236 / 29 June 1821).

8   Historical Archive of Macedonia, Judicial registers, 205, pp. 150–1 (29 Zilhicce 1236 /
         28 September 1821). See the Greek translation in Vasdravellis 1950, p. 213, and Stamboulis
         2000, pp. 278–9.

9   Historical Archive of Macedonia, Judicial registers, 205, p. 134 (5 Şevval 1236 / 6 July 1821):
         *bu da'va din da'vası oldığından ashab-ı din ve ehl-i iman olanlara bu babda hab ü rahatı terk
         birle cansiparane-i gayret ve ittibat-i mera'yı hamiyet ve diyanet eylemek farz-ı a'yin oldığı.*

10   Historical Archive of Macedonia, Judicial registers, 205, pp. 138–9 (I Şevval 1236 / 2–11 July
         1821). See the Greek translation in Vasdravellis 1950, pp. 202–4, and Stamboulis 2000,
         pp. 269–70.

11   In its content, the order does not differ from the previous one. It lists the districts from
         which troops were to be sent to Salonica for the suppression of the rebellion (Prav-
         işta, Dırama, Nevrekob, Razlok, Siroz, Demirhisar, Avrethisar, Melnik and Zihne). It is

lines that confiscated property would be distributed among the soldiers. The Porte, along with its orders and exhortations to set up an army, did not fail to invoke religious sentiment and emphasise that the present conditions could not compare with any previous ones: to participate in the war was seen as a matter of faith [*imdi bu vakt-ı evkat-i saireye bir vechle mekıs olmayub uğur-i din mübeyyinde bezl-i can ve sarf-ı tab ve tüvan-i namus şevketmanus islamiyeyi vikayeye-i gayret edecek günler olmağla*].

After a few pages in the same register – and without mentioning details of the battles and movements of the rebellion – a decree of the then head of the Ottoman troops, Salonica's new Governor Mehmed Emin Pasha, is addressed to the city's authorities, dated 17 Safer 1237 / 14 November 1821.[12] In a text full of religious symbolism and a propagandistic language for the victory of Islam, Mehmed Emin Pasha announces that, on the morning of the same day that the decree was issued, the Ottoman forces attacked and, without a second opera-tion, the rebels' resistance was bended. Almost one thousand rebels were killed, the wagons around their fortifications were set ablaze and about six or seven hundred women and men were captured. This was the final Ottoman victory in Kassandra, which also saw the end of the Revolution in the Halkidiki.[13]

Despite the repression of the rebellion, security measures in the city of Salonica did not relax; instead, they were intensified. Thus, at his behest, the Governor Mehmed Emin Pasha drew attention to the city's protection and defence, calling for thirty or forty well-armed soldiers to guard the towers under the responsibility of the city's authorities. Salonica, it was stressed, was a very large city and on the border of the empire and therefore had to be constantly and carefully guarded.[14] The same warnings are found in two other decrees, simultaneously issued by the same person. The first was an order to transport

---

worth mentioning the text's reference to the exceptional circumstances that the state encountered [*imdi bu vakt-ı evkat-i saireye bir vechle kıyas kabul etmeyüb uğur-ı din ü dev-letimde ... can-i bezl-i tab ü tüvan edecek ve faiza-ı cihad ve gazayı icra ile dünya ve ahırın saadetini tahsil edecek günler olmağla*]. The formula 'religion and state' [*din ü devlet*] had been known in the Ottoman political vocabulary since the seventeenth century, and it was used 'to denote an inseparable entity uniting religious authority to maintain the *Shari'a* with the sultan's personal rule'. See Sariyannis 2013, p. 101 n. 32, and p. 113.

12   Historical Archive of Macedonia, Judicial registers, 205, pp. 160–1. See the Greek transla-tion in Vasdravellis 1950, pp. 225–6, and Stamboulis 2000, pp. 288–9.

13   For this battle, see Vakalopoulos 1988, p. 572.

14   Historical Archive of Macedonia, Judicial registers, 207, p. 69/1 (15 Şevval 1237 / 5 July 1822). See the Greek translation in Vasdravellis 1950, pp. 270–71, without mention of the date; and Stamboulis 2000, pp. 316–7. See the passage: *serhadat-i hakaniyeden Selanik bir şehir-i mu'azam olub ala 'l-devam muhafazasına takayyüd ve ikdam-i müham lazim ül-ihtimamdan oldığı ecilden.*

grain, supplied by the farms [*çiftlik*s], since there was fear of it being damaged in the city by the insurgents. The second was an order that the city ought to be patrolled by thirty men from the Governor's sequence and thirty from among the city's Janissary corps, divided into three patrols, in order to counteract the oppression of shopkeepers which had recently been observed.[15] Increased food needs due to the war, in fact, led the city's elites to offer money for wheat supply, and a list of people offering money was drawn up in the court register.[16]

The concern for the recruitment of men for the Ottoman army due to the Revolution, not only in Halkidiki but also in the south of the Greek peninsula, was ongoing. One aspect of the state's policy was the registration of military forces in the fortresses of the city.[17] In addition, Salonica's authorities were also the addressees of munitions sent from the Ottoman capital for reinforcement of its fortresses; or, the city was an intermediate station for their final dispatch to the war front in the south of the Greek peninsula. We learn from a firman that, on the basis of registers, black powder and other necessary ammunition for the Acropolis [*kala-ı bala*] of Salonica were sent from Istanbul. The short list of ammunition delivered also notes the quantity of shells for the fortress of Vardar.[18]

The registration of soldiers and weapons in the various fortresses of the city, which took place at regular intervals, became more frequent during the war period. Such a detailed register was compiled on 15 Şaban 1239 / 15 April 1824, at a crucial phase for the outcome of the war in the south.[19] The danger for Salonica apparently had not disappeared, according to the state authorities, so the full manning of the city's forts and their equipment was seen as an urgent

---

15   Historical Archive of Macedonia, Judicial registers, 207, p. 69/2–3 (13 Şevval 1237 / 3 July 1822). See the Greek translation in Vasdravellis 1950, pp. 269–70.

16   Historical Archive of Macedonia, Judicial registers, 207, p. 8 (15 Cemaziyülevvel 1237 / 7 February 1822). It follows a list of sixteen persons from the Muslim elite of the city along with the quantities of wheat they had offered for the provisioning of the city.

17   Historical Archive of Macedonia, Judicial registers, 208, p. 31/2, where undated order [*buyuruldu*] of the governor Mehmed Pasha for the registration; 210, p. 104 (111 Muharrem 1239 / 27 September–6 October 1823); and 213, p. 4/3 (Muharrem 1239 / 7 September–6 October 1823), fermans with a similar content.

18   Historical Archive of Macedonia, Judicial registers, 213, p. 106 (17 Zilkade 1239 / 14 July 1824). In another ferman, the dispatch of cannons for the Fort of Vardar is mentioned; see Historical Archive of Macedonia, Judicial registers, 213, p. 140/1 (15 Zilhicce 1239 / 11 August 1824). The text of the ferman does not contain the addressees, while at the beginning it contains the small list of cannons delivered to Salonica on 20 Rebiyülahır 1240 / 12 December 1824.

19   Historical Archive of Macedonia, Judicial registers, 213, pp. 38–47. See a short summary in Stamboulis 2000, p. 327.

need. However, it is clear from the content of the registers that Salonica was a centre for dispatching munitions to the south. There are many notes concerning the shipment of certain types and quantities from the forts of Salonica to those in the Peloponnese (e.g. in Patras).

At the beginning of 1826, Salonica continued to be equipped, as it is evidenced by the receipt and registration of war material in various records in the registers.[20] In a report for armament receipt from the Ottoman capital, it is clearly stated that the munitions were intended to defend Salonica [*Selanik kala'sında hıfz olunmak üzere*].[21] Frequent robberies were observed in the city at night. The situation was so particularly serious that the Porte issued a decree to the city's authorities with strict orders for arrests and subsequent punishments.[22]

After the suppression of the Revolution in Halkidiki, the court of Salonica was the centre of assistance for the Peloponnese and the central Greek peninsula. From a *firman*, dated from early 1822, it appears that the Porte asked Governor of Salonica Mehmed Emin Pasha to equip a ship [*bir kıtaa bırik sefinesi*] with twenty-four[23] cannons [*gemi topları*], which the commander-in-chief of the Morea, Yusuf Pasha, had just bought from English captains.[24] The order was triggered at the request of Yusuf Pasha, while the Admiral of the Fleet was also asked; he not only accepted the proposal but suggested that the English flag be hanged on the ship in order not to be harassed by the rebels.

Sending Ottoman troops to the south was another parameter of the war that involved Salonica. The port of Salonica was a station for the preparation, concentration and transport of food supplies to the war front. For example, on 16 of Muharrem 1240 / 10 September 1824, the city's authorities were ordered to arrange and dispatch 3,000 *kantar*s of biscuit for the needs of the fleet's personnel.[25]

---

20   Historical Archive of Macedonia, Judicial registers, 216, p. 31/1 (13 Cemaziyülahır 1241 / 23 January 1826). See a summary in Stamboulis 2000, p. 349.

21   Historical Archive of Macedonia, Judicial registers, 216, p. 32/3 (28 Rebiyülevvel 1241 / 10 November 1825). See also 216, p. 33/1 (10 Muharrem 1241 / 25 August 1825), where a transportation of shells to the city's *Tophane* is mentioned.

22   Historical Archive of Macedonia, Judicial registers, 216, p. 32/2 (9 Cemaziyülahır 1241 / 19 January 1826). See the Greek translation in Vasdravellis (ed.) 1952, pp. 494–5, and Stamboulis 2000, p. 349.

23   The translation writes twenty.

24   Historical Archive of Macedonia, Judicial registers, 207, p. 7/2 (17 Rebiyülahır 1237 / 11 January 1822). See the Greek translation in Vasdravellis (ed.) 1952, pp. 451–3.

25   Historical Archive of Macedonia, Judicial registers, 213, p. 112. See a similar order to Salonica's governor Salih Pasha in Historical Archive of Macedonia, Judicial registers, 220, p. 39/1 (19 Cemaziyülevvel 1243 / 8 December 1827).

The difficulties faced by the Ottoman army in recruiting are clear in the content of decree sent by the Porte in January 1823.[26] In this decree, the sultan orders that a certain number of sailors and marines [*kalyoncu*] ought to be registered, gathered and dispatched from the district [*kaza*] of Salonica to the Imperial Fleet. The recruits would be distinguished for zeal [*hamiyeti cihetiyle*], being of appropriate conscription age and fully armed. At the end of the decree, the number of soldiers due to the Fleet are recorded. The decree states that there were consripted soldiers who were less than they should have been and now the Porte is coming back and calling for their gathering until the day of *Nevruz* (i.e. on 22 March). In order to mobilise Muslims, the Sultan invoked religion, arguing that it was a sacred obligation and a religious duty [*bu husus cümle ehl-i islama aid hıdmet-i diniyeden oldığı*] to join the army and participate in the campaign against the infidels, while he threatened punishment for those who would not join in.[27]

Continuing operations in the south led to a new recruitment order. In March 1823,[28] after stressing again the obligation of all faithful Muslims to participate in the war and in the destruction of the infidels, and following the request of the Commander-in-chief Mehmed Reşid Pasha (or Kioutahis in the Greek historiography),[29] the Porte ordered the dispatchment of 3,000 fully armed troops from the *Yürük* population [*evlad-ı fatihan*]. Recruitment concerned a wide geographical area, including Macedonia and Thessaly, while Salonica was the centre for the deployment and dispatchment of troops to the south. Three years later, in 1826, at a crucial stage of the war, the situation on the front and the Ottoman army's needs for human resources had not disappeared. The Porte thus still required additional troops.[30] At the request of the commander in chief, another army was called from among the *Yürük* population. In the previous year, the order pointed out, 1,000 *Yürük*s had been sent from the Tikveş district,

---

26   Historical Archive of Macedonia, Judicial registers, 210, p. 3/3 (2 Cemaziyülevvel 1238 / 15 January 1823).

27   *Neferat-i merkume ba irade-i seniye tertib ve tanzim olunmuş oldığından gayrı küffar ile fi sebil-i muharebe ve mucahide eylemek bazı belden islamiyeye nisbet ile her ne kadar farz küffaye isede emr-i evla-ı ül-emr padışahanemle matlub olan neferatın sefer gelmeleri farz-ı ayin ve derya muharebesinde olan fezayil-i cihad cümleye malum iken bu babda bidayet ve irad 'uzr ve 'illet edenler olur ise o makuleler yarın ruz-ı cezadan görecekleri 'ukubat-i şedideden başka dünyada dahı mazhar mucazat olacakları bi istibah olmağla.*

28   Historical Archive of Macedonia, Judicial registers, 210, p. 7 (23 Cemaziyülahır 1238 / 7 March 1823).

29   *Bu sene-i mübarekede tedabir-i diniyesi ve mülkiyesi cem'-i ehl-i iman ele alınarak enas üllahurrahman şevkadırların kahr ü tedmirine ikdam olunmak cümleye farz olmuş.*

30   Historical Archive of Macedonia, Judicial registers, 216, p. 81 (25 Zilkade 1241 / 1 July 1826).

but they were not enough; the Porte now required 500 soldiers from the same group, whose main task was to guard and protect the coasts from the rebels.

Immediately after the naval battle of Navarin, the Porte tried to respond with a general recruitment order in the Balkans.[31] In a final attempt to counterattack, the Sultan ordered the gathering of all cavalrymen [*sipahis*] – including children deemed capable of carrying weapons. Particularly urgent were the needs of the Ottoman army for artillery men [*humbaracı*] and diggers [*lağımcı*] and in these troops should be included in the recruitment corps.

At the same time, another decree[32] informs on the movements of the Greek rebels on the outskirts of Salonica. Coming from the south, it was written, they had made their ships caverns of robbery and attacked the Macedonian coasts.[33] For their suppression, the Sultan gives strict orders and calls on the provincial governors to make a general campaign to combat the phenomenon. The Sultan also uses strict expressions in order to mobilise local authorities.[34] The decree does not provide specific information on the particular incidents, which should have been connected to the known pirate raids of the Greeks against the coasts of Halkidiki and Salonica, having their base in Northern Sporades islands.[35] The mobilisation of the authorities continued in early 1828, when the Governor of Salonica demanded that the *kadı* provide him with 30 brave soldiers of between twenty and thirty years of age to join the army from the city of and the *kaza*.[36]

From the aforementioned cases it becomes clear that Salonica was a recruitment and collection centre for Ottoman troops directed to the south of the Greek peninsula. In addition, the existence of a significant Muslim population in the area – provincial cavalrymen or of *Yürük* origin – also played a decisive role in revealing that Salonica was not only a transit point for troops or

31   Historical Archive of Macedonia, Judicial registers, 217, p. 207/1 (III Rebiyülahır 1243 / 11–20 November 1827).

32   Historical Archive of Macedonia, Judicial registers, 217, p. 215/2 (I Cemaziyülevvel 1243 / 20–9 November 1827).

33   *Akdenizde kişi ve güzar eden bir takım eşkıya muktinne menhusları gözleri kesdiği yere sarkındılığa ve isal hasar da'ye-i fasidesinde oldıklarına ve Selanik sevahili eşkıyayı merkume teknelerinin cevelangahı olarak ve sairlerinden ziyade vacib ül-hurras mehallardan idüğine binaen me'azüllahu te'aliya usat-ı eşkıyanın sevahil-i merkumeye bir gün saka-ı kasd ve tesellütleri takdırında.*

34   Cf. the passages: *asker merkumi taht-ı hükumet ve kazalarınızdan nefir-i amm suretle heman tedarik ve ihrac ... and ... babda iğmaz ve bida'et ve imrar-ı vakt misillü vaz'ı ve halet vuku'a gelür ise mutecasir olanlar hakklarında muceb.*

35   Vakalopoulos 1988, pp. 613–14 and p. 616. Cf. another document in Vasdravellis 1950, pp. 313–14.

36   Historical Archive of Macedonia, Judicial registers, 217, p. 229/1 (3 Receb 1243 / 20 January 1828).

munitions to the war front, but also a place of recruitment. The importance of the city for the Ottoman state resulted in the state taking over its defence even when the Halkidiki uprising had been suppressed and several years had since passed. The fact that it was a port city made Salonica even more vulnerable to the extent that the Greek revolutionaries controlled the Aegean Sea for most of the decade-long war. The Ottoman court's image of the revolutionary conjuncture, albeit with gaps, depicts the general climate and provides the key topics that the Ottoman authorities had dealt with at local and regional levels.

Bibliography

Aydın, Hacı Veli 2018, '1821 Yunan İsyanı Sırasında Selanik Sancağı ve İsyana Karşı Alınan Önlemler' ['The province of Salonica during the Greek Revolution of 1821 and the measures taken against the revolution'], *Tarih İncelemeleri Dergisi* 33, 2: 303–34.

Ilıcak, H. Şükrü 2011, *A Radical Rethinking of Empire: Ottoman State and Society during the Greek War of Independence (1821–1826)*, Ph.D. Dissertation, Harvard University.

Sariyannis, Marinos 2013, 'Ruler and State, State and Society in Ottoman Political Thought', *Turkish Historical Review*, 4: 83–117.

Stamboulis, Georgios 2000, *Τα φερμάνια για την Θεσσαλονίκη 1387–1912* [*The Sultanic orders concerning Salonica, 1387–1912*], Thessaloniki: n. ed.

Vacalopoulos, Apostolos S. 1988, *Ιστορία της Μακεδονίας, 1354–1833* [*History of Macedonia, 1354–1833*], Thessaloniki: Βάνιας.

Vasdravellis, Ioannis K. 1950, *Οι Μακεδόνες εις τους υπέρ της ανεξαρτησίας αγώνας, 1796–1832* [The Macedonians in the wars for the Greek independence, 1796–1832], 2nd ed., Thessaloniki: Εταιρεία Μακεδονικών Σπουδών.

Vasdravellis, Ioannis (ed.) 1952, *Ιστορικά αρχεία Μακεδονίας, Α΄ Αρχείον Θεσσαλονίκης 1695–1912* [*Historical Archive of Macedonia. I. Archive of Salonica 1695–1912*], Thessaloniki: Εταιρεία Μακεδονικών Σπουδών.

CHAPTER 3

Post-revolutionary Salonica and Its Environs

Penal Policies, Precautionary Steps and Institutionalised Rewards in the Aftermath of the Revolt

Dimitris Papastamatiou

This chapter aims to discuss in brief the repercussions of the Greek revolt in Halkidiki, near Salonica, during the spring and summer of 1821, and the restitution politics of the Ottoman provincial administration during and mainly after the insurgency. The events per se and the modes in which they were conceived by the local authorities will not be commented on, as they constitute the topic of another chapter in this book. We will investigate the aftereffects of the revolutionary conjuncture as regards the Christian population of Salonica, and examine the punitive, peace-restoration and re-integration policies of the Ottoman provincial administration. In this context, some fundamental principles, axioms and premises of the romantic and national historiographic argumentation will also be examined with a view to testing their range of accuracy. Specifically, a set of commonplace postulates has been endorsed by most romantic historians of Salonica concerning the aftermath of the rebellion: massive massacres of unarmed Salonicans, including women and children; unjustified and cruel executions of the urban notables along with estate confiscation of the estates; extensive and long-term desolation of the countryside in the urban environs and Halkidiki; persecutions and the flight of villagers and urbanites – all of these events resulting in a general decline for the Christian Salonicans, which supposedly lasted for at least two decades. The massacre clichés have already been discarded as unverified by available sources,[1] but the rest of these motifs are yet to be examined, corroborated or refuted on a documentary basis.[2]

The documentation used for this chapter consists exclusively of the archival corpus [*sicillat*] – that is, proceedings and records of the Islamic court of Salon-

---

1 See Sarigiannis 2015.
2 The literature on the Revolution of Halkidiki and its effects is extensive, but there is no need for it to be repeated here once more *in extenso*. For a very good revision of this literature, see Hekimoglou 2008.

ica.[3] It is a type of documentation unique with regard to a delineation of the Ottoman modes of apprehension of a period of internal disruption, general insurrection and state collapse. This archival material may also help us to depict, on the one hand, the conceptual and political viewpoints, policies and manoeuvres of the Ottoman peripheral administration as well as the local powerbrokers, and, on the other hand, the state public order reinstatement policies and re-legitimisation mechanisms. Though a good many documents are copies of edicts and mandates [Ott. Turk. *fermans*] coming from the imperial centre, the archival material offers us an exclusive opportunity to examine the interplay between the central-state priorities and the provincial administration alignment with them, along with the issues and impediments raised at the local level during the peace restoration process.

From the extensive corpus of the Islamic court of Salonica, a few – significant for their content – documents from volumes 205–20, covering the period between the years 1821–30, have been selected for the needs of this chapter. They are mainly copies of imperial edicts [*ferman*] and inventories of assorted items and their amounts [*tevzi defteri*]. Also, a few pertinent reports [*ilam*], mandates of the local governor [*buyuruldu*], verdicts of Muslim judges [*hüccet*], warrants [*berat*] and letters [*mektub*] have also been taken into account. Translations of some of these documents have been published (but not conducted) by local historian Ioannis Vasdravellis, and a few more translations and summaries have been edited (but not published) by Georgios Stamboulis.[4] Still, all the documents used for this chapter have been studied again from the original Ottoman text, since the aforementioned translation endeavours are problematic and dubious – for reasons not to be discussed here. The documents selected are among those which outline in the most pronounced manner the major practises of the regional administration with a view towards re-establishing public order during and after the Greek revolt in Halkidiki, for a period lasting until the end of the decade. These documents also illustrate some seminal hindrances and perplexities, part and parcel of the peace restoration process, and the respective resolutions adopted by local power brokers.

Ottomans reacted immediately after the outbreak of the insurgency. Save the military measures and the operations undertaken by the Ottoman armed forces, a set of parallel, if somewhat non-military in character, steps were adop-

---

3   The documents are kept in Thessaloniki, Greece, at the Historical Archive of Macedonia [Ιστο-ρικό Αρχείο Μακεδονίας, Ιεροδικαστικοί Κώδικες]. This documentary *corpus* is not limited to the period examined but covers the years 1695–912.

4   See Vasdravellis (ed.) 1952; Stamboulis 2000.

ted by the successive governors [*mutasarrıf*] of Salonica. These practices can be classified in three categories on the basis of their objective; first, they comprised punitive measures – that is to say, executions of the protagonists of the tumult and confiscations of their properties; second, penalty practices were mitigated with peace restoration steps – namely, amnesty granted to the insurgent villagers, tax exemptions and favourable credit settlements for those returning to their homeland, and even regional offices to rebel chiefs willing to co-operate with state authorities; finally, prevention measures – above all, seizure of arms held by Ottoman subjects – were adopted by state authorities so that further order-disrupting aspirations might be rendered unfeasible. Of course, these practices were everything but a novelty and had been applied with consistent success every time Ottoman regularities were unsettled by rioters. A balance policy of lure and penalty was meant to reinstate order and law by reminding subjects of their position in the Ottoman cosmos, the rewards they would relish if they remained loyal to it and the calamities they would suffer when they transgressed it. This well-tried course of action was implemented with success in Macedonia but apparently not in southern Rumeli and the Morea.

1   **Punitive Policies of the Ottoman Provincial Administration**

The penal agenda of the Ottoman Empire typically comprised execution or exile of the rebel leaders and confiscation of their properties. In effect, confiscation implied that mobile assets were auctioned at the local market, with proceeds forwarded to the imperial centre; real estate was set under state control and hired out to individuals; any cash confiscated was directed to the state fisc; debts and credit commitments to the convicted were eagerly collected by state officials, while arrears of the deceased were paid out only if the interested parties were persistent enough. State care for the heirs, if there was any, was contingent on the occasion, the local power balance, individual political connections and access to decision making centres as well as, certainly, on the sincerity of their state allegiance.

This particular agenda was implemented to the point during the summer of 1821 in Salonica. Magnates were probably executed on 21 July 1821. Meletios, Bishop of Kitros and procurator of the metropolitan of Salonica, Hristos[5] Bal-

---

5   His real name must have been 'Hristodoulos', but he is invariably recorded as 'Hristos' in Ottoman documents.

anos and Hristos Menexes were the notables who lost their lives during that tumultuous period. Along with them, a few rather obscure Salonicans were also killed – namely grocer [*bakkal*] Anagnostis, furrier Anastasis, cobbler Nanos and perfumers Konstantis and Nakos.[6] The peculiar and distinct case of the confinement and execution of Manolakis Kyriakos Tzanoglou in March of 1822 can also be added to the list.

The estates of the deceased were all confiscated along with those of magnates or wealthy Salonicans, more often than not women, who evaded capture or execution by departing from the city in due time or in secret later on: the three grandsons of the rich entrepreneur Tzitzi Nano Haftantzoglou; the mother-in-law, wife and son-in-law, named Grigori, of the above-mentioned Tzanoglou; one Yakumi; one Skambalis[7] along with his children and his brother; the wife of one Hristos Hatzidimos; one Panayotis Hatzigousios; the wife of Hristos Hatzidiamandis; one Giorgos Peses; and one Dimitris Papas. No other names of executed or self-exiled Salonicans are recorded in the Islamic court archive of the period 1821–30.[8]

The documents are elliptical in regards to the executions. The dead are recorded with the typical bureaucratic motif 'deceased' [*helak olan*][9] or, more rarely, with a brief and vague reference to execution [*idam*].[10] In general, the edicts are careful not to give any hint of emergency conditions. The first decree of confiscation of Balanos's and Menexes's properties claims that the reason for the penalty was their exorbitant riches.[11] Sometimes, a simple and hasty reference

---

6   The documents which mention these persons will be commented upon later. One chief furrier [*kürkçübaşı*], Anastasis, and one chief grocer [*bakkalbaşı*], Thanos, are also mentioned in only one document, but they must have been among the aforementioned Salonicans. See Historical Archives of Macedonia, Judicial Registers, 207, p. 11/2. For biographical information about these Salonicans, see Hekimoglou 2004, pp. 13–303.

7   He had resorted to Egypt before the events of 1821.

8   It is quite intriguing that all killed notables, except for Meletios, and almost all exiles were merchants of Europe – namely merchants of Ottoman citizenship, but of a privileged status. For the merchants of Europe, see Laiou 2014, where the pertinent literature is also cited.

9   For example, see Historical Archives of Macedonia, Judicial Registers, 205, p. 146: *ferman* dated 4 Zilkade 1236 (3 August 1821).

10   For example see, Historical Archive of Macedonia, Judicial registers, 205, p. 167/2: *Selanik mütemekkinlerinden olub Rum milleti beyyinde hudus eden fesade medhal olduğunu binaen idam olunmuş olan Menekseli Hristo'nın erbab, Ferman* dated 29 Safer 1237 (25 November 1821).

11   Historical Archive of Macedonia, Judicial registers, 205, p. 146: *Balano ve Menekşeli Hristo nam tacirlar icab-i servet ve yesar oldukları hayır verildiğini mebni.*

to the Greek Revolution is made in the document, as in the decrees of property confiscation of Menexes[12] and Meletios[13] as well as the report of the execution of Tzanoglou.[14]

The last case is very particular and unique. Tzanoglou was a seminal entrepreneur and banker of Salonica and possibly the most significant member of the Greek community. In a registry of 1823, 46 loans of a declared aggregate value of 706,324 *kuruş* owed to Tzanoglou were recorded.[15] His debtors were 23 villages of the district [*kaza*], 13 Ottoman officials – among whom the renowned fortress Commander [*muhafiz*] of Patras Yusuf Pasha from Serres and the commander of the Ottoman armies in Rumeli Reşid Mehmed Pasha stand out – and 10 Christians, almost all of whom were captains. The involvement of Tzanoglou in the rebellion was only a secondary and complementary offence added to an extensive indictment comprising his illegal double citizenship (he was vice-consul of Denmark), his unwillingness to return to lawfulness, his persistence to hide his outlaw fugitive brother, his attempted bribery of officials and his escape from prison.[16]

The meaning and objectives of these executions can only be surmised. Contact between Balanos and Menexes with Emmanouil Papas, the leader of the rebels in Halkidiki, is not documented, while a planned *intra muros* insurgency, aiming at joining forces with the advancing rebels of Halkidiki, would have been conducted by militarily untrained and inexperienced urban merchants with little or no aid from the local population. On the contrary, Salonica was a significant base for the Ottoman army, with a janissary garrison and thousands of armed Muslims. Even the cohesion and consensus of the Greek community within the city is under discussion, as it can be assumed for the fact that other notables were not persecuted.

It has been suggested that the involvement of the deceased in revolutionary conspiracies was nothing but a fabricated and stereotypical pretense of their persecutors, who were inspired by the uprising in Halkidiki and had little need

---

12 Historical Archive of Macedonia, Judicial registers, 205, p. 167/2: *Selanik mütemekkinlerinden olub Rum milleti beyyinde hudus eden fesade medhal olduğunu binaen idam olunmuş olan Menekseli Hristo'nun erbab, ferman* dated 29 Safer 1237 (25 November 1821).

13 Historical Archive of Macedonia, Judicial registers, 205, p. 147: *fesada mudahale olanlar, ferman* dated 14 Zilkade 1236 (13 August 1821).

14 Historical Archive of Macedonia, Judicial registers, 208, p. 30: *ihtilal-i Rumda medhal olduğunu', Ilam* of the *kadi* of Salonica dated 2 Şevval 1237 (22 June 1822).

15 The real total value was 429,952 *kuruş*. Historical Archive of Macedonia, Judicial registers, 210, p. 15: *defter* dated 10 Şaban 1238 (22 April 1823).

16 Historical Archive of Macedonia, Judicial registers, 207, p. 42: *ferman* dated evasid-i Receb 1237 (7–17 April 1822); and 208, p. 30. For the confiscation of his property see 207, p. 73.

for hard evidence. According to this hypothesis, the economic predominance of the Greek community of the city in the first two decades of the nineteenth century, the wealth of the executed notables and the politically unorthodox initiatives of the two successive governors of the city, Yusuf Pasha and Mehmed Emin Pasha – who were to self-finance their military campaigns in Halkidiki and central Macedonia – may have been the real motive and meaningful cause of these executions. Thus, in essence, the Ottoman officials assassinated the notables only with a view to apprehending their properties and conducting these financially onerous private military campaigns.[17] Yet the plausibility of this hypothesis is tested by the fact that such an autonomous course of action was not an option for the Ottoman officers, as the confiscation process was directed by the Sublime Porte itself and the management of the properties was set under the auspices of the Islamic court – as will be shown in this chapter.

On the contrary, we tend to consider these penal deeds of the provincial Ottoman administration as the local version of the rather panicky reaction of the Sublime Porte to the news of the Greek Revolution. The elimination of the Greek elites in assorted urban centres seems to have been an official political scheme in fear of a universal Greek uprising.[18] Yet this assumption retains a tentative character, at least in the case of Salonica, since its Islamic-court archival corpus does not offer us any hint of intentions and schemes.

2   The Property-Confiscation Process: Adaptations and Drawbacks

The Ottoman provincial administration of the *kaza* of Salonica spent eight years plagued with impediments emanating from the confiscation of the three notables' properties. In August of 1821, the procedure of confiscation, registration and auctioning of the properties and the dispatch of money to the Sublime Porte was assigned to the special agent [*mubaşir*], superintendent of the imperial tax-farms [*mukataa*], and notable [*ayan*] Salih Lutfi, a high official for a case the central government wished to handle with effectiveness and discretion.[19] The respective edict ordering the confiscation of Balanos's and Menexes's properties emphatically urged Salih Lutfi to conduct the process with integrity and

---

17   For example, see Hekimoglou 2008, pp. 25–32.

18   This thesis has been convincingly demonstrated concerning Istanbul by Ilıcak 2011, pp. 179–89.

19   Historical Archives of Macedonia, Judicial Registers, 205, p. 146: *ferman* dated 4 Zilkade 1236 (3 August 1821).

precision while recording all types of seized fortunes.[20] The same rigour was ordered for the record, clearance and auctioning of the bishop's estate.[21]

Despite the ambition of the Ottoman government to handle these issues quickly,[22] a host of reactions was triggered. The drawbacks were mainly the incompetence of the regional authorities to collect the due amounts and the claims of assorted relatives and partners of the deceased to the confiscated fortunes.

The collection of unpaid debts to the deceased was a significant part of the confiscation process and exploitation of the estates, yet, more often than not, its conduct would become exceptionally problematic because of the unwillingness or (real or affected) inability of the debtors to fulfill their financial commitments. Salih Lutfi soon found himself entangled in a similar stalemate. At least three registries of unpaid debts and six imperial edicts commanding the *mubaşir* to hurry the debt collection and the delivery of cash to the imperial capital have been located in the archive, while reports of similar arrears not gathered can also be found in a good many other pertinent documents.

Two examples are indicative of the dead ends faced by the Ottoman administration. Salih Lutfi must have realised the impediments he would come up with even from the end of 1821, when one *mevlevi* Işkinat Ağasızade Osman Dede secured a postponement of pay for the 26,500 *kuruş* he owed to Balanos, and hence to the imperial treasury, by claiming that his estate was ruined and that his peasants had fled.[23] Likewise, in March of 1822, Salih Lutfi was ordered to go to the neighbouring town of Serres and collect 69,072 *kuruş* owed to Balanos. There, a good number of debtors stated that they were broke, leaving Salih Lutfi with a deficit of 3,066 *kuruş*.[24] It goes without saying that the collection

---

20   *kâffeten emval ve eşyalarının mubaşir marifet ile canib-i miriden zabt hususumu irade-i aliyem teallük etmekle … senki mubaşir-i mumaileyhsin senden her vechile sadakat ve istikamet-i memul ile … bilâ-intihab bu hususa mahsus-i mubaşir tayin kılındığının ecilden … helak-i mersumunan Selanik ve sairü'l-havalede üzereden kâfetten emval ve eşya ve nukud ve zimemat ve emlâk ve akar ve çiftlikân ve hayvanat ve hububat ve sair ism-i mal-i itlak olunur.* Ibid.

21   Historical Archives of Macedonia, Judicial Registers, 205, p. 147: *ferman* dated 14 Zilkade 1236 (13 August 1821).

22   For example, see Historical Archive of Macedonia, Judicial registers, 207, p. 11/2: *ferman* dated evasid-i Rebiyülahir 1237 (5–14 January 1822); 207, p. 12/1: *ferman* dated evasid-i Rebiyülahir 1237 (5 January 1822).

23   Historical Archive of Macedonia, Judicial registers, 207, p. 18: *ol-vechile edaya kudreti olmayub … çiftlikâne … reayaları perakende olub külliyen mutezarrir olub, ferman* dated 16 Rebiyülevvel 1237 (11 December 1821).

24   Historical Archive of Macedonia, Judicial registers, 207, p. 33: *kâffeten muhallefat ve zimemat-i marifet-i şer ve hacekân ve divan-i humayunumdan Salih Lutfi zide mecduhu marifetile*

of the aforementioned 706,324 *kuruş* owed to Tzanoglou, of which more than a third came from 23 burnt-down and unpopulated villages, was more than an unfeasible task for the Ottoman official.

Insurmountable problems were also faced by the Ottoman officials by dint of persistent claims to the confiscated estates posed by assorted relatives, heirs, partners, lenders and creditors of the deceased. These demands usually meant a serious reduction in the ultimate sum collected from the liquidation of the properties. For instance, almost six months after the confiscation, an imperial decree ordered Salih Lutfi to take care of Menexes's six minor orphans and to return the due amount after all creditors and lenders had been satisfied. According to the document, 2,500 *kuruş* were subtracted for arrears and the remaining 24,724 *kuruş* were returned to the heirs.[25] In effect, this meant that the seizure of Menexes's fortune proved of no avail for the imperial fisc. We surmise that the edict must have been issued through political contacts and affiliations of Menexes's family. Yet the intriguing interest of the Ottoman authorities in the fate of Menexes's heirs does not comply with the profile of Hristos Menexes as a true conspirator. In fact, although the decree may have been the result of backstage political negotiations, it demonstrates a peculiar, tolerant and flexible practice of the Ottoman authorities aimed at a swift integration of aberrant subjects into their order.

Similarly, in mid-1825 merchant Nikolos Asteris [*sic*] asked for and took from Balanos's property 33,002 *kuruş*,[26] while the enormous fortune of Tzanoglou triggered long-standing lawsuits which are perplexing in their details. For instance, one Jewish partner of his, named Misir, initially demanded 82,000 *kuruş* and later on some extra 37,500 *kuruş* from Tzanoglou's wife, who had fled to France in the meantime.[27] Likewise, one Salonican named Tziortzio Harisis claimed and succeeded in taking 88,292 *kuruş* from Tzanoglou's prop-

---

zabt ve tahrir olanarak mukaddema varid olan defter natik olduğu üzere helak-i mersumun Siroz ehalinden baz kesan zimmetlerinde fayir-i az teslim 69.072 kuruş zimematın [...] *den cem ve tahsil babında ba-hatt-i humayun ... eshabi-i muflis makulesi olub habs olunmuş isede tahsil mümkün olamamış olduğundan'*, *ferman* dated 28 Cemaziyülahir 1237 (22 March 1822).

25   Historical Archive of Macedonia, Judicial registers, 205, p. 167/2: *mersumun zuhur eden emlak ve eşya ve zimemat ve düyununa nazaren muhallefatı cizye ve zimematın ekser ise mumteni ve 6 nefer-i eytami olub sayeşte-i merhamet olunduklarından*, *ferman* dated 29 Safer 1237 (25 November 1821).

26   Historical Archive of Macedonia, Judicial registers, 214, p. 122: *ferman* dated 24 Zilkade 1240 (10 July 1825).

27   Historical Archive of Macedonia, Judicial registers, 210, p. 17/2: *ferman* dated 12 Cemaziyülahir 1238 (24 February 1823); 213, p. 17: *ferman* dated 6 Cemaziyülevvel 1239 (8 January 1824); 214, p. 9: *ferman* dated 6 Rebiyülahir 1240 (28 November 1824).

erty – taking advantage of his Austrian citizenship, for the Austrian ambassador in Istanbul had intervened in his favour.[28] Still, by 1828 Harisis had not taken his money. On the contrary, the Ottoman fisc, being in desperate need of cash, utilised a reciprocity practice and ordered the transfer of the owed amount to Harisis directly from the debts of the villages of Langada and Sidirokapsia.[29] Such delayed payment tactics were adopted again in the case of Spandonis, who turned up in the same year to claim 12,610 *kuruş* from Tzanoglou's property.[30] It is highly likely that neither Salonican ever got their money.

Lastly, it should be noted that the Islamic court took over the managerial control of the real estates. The buildings, all urban constructions, were hired to foreigners affiliated with the consulates, Muslim notables, Jews and Greek Christians. In effect, the court issued a registry every two or three years of all urban edifices held under its managerial administration, recording the sums of the rent and the tenants' names.[31]

The brief presentation of these cases, seemingly indifferent and irrelevant with the revolutionary events, purports to show that the seizure of the properties and the execution of the notables, whatever initial planning may have served, were not of much avail to the central treasury or to local governors Yusuf Pasha and Mehmed Emin Pasha. Local entrepreneurs and relatives impeded the exploitation of the confiscated properties, either subtracting sums from them or refusing to add to them by paying out their debts. The Sublime Porte adopted an ambivalent stance in this bizarre power balance; on the one hand, it pressed the local governors to liquidate the fortunes and dispatch the money to the treasury, and, on the other hand, it ratified the diverse demands of claimants. And above all, the Islamic court proved to be, once more, the cornerstone of the Ottoman order, exerting its control over the fortunes and safeguarding the public character of the confiscation process. Thus, the histori-

---

28 Historical Archive of Macedonia, Judicial registers, 216, p. 5/2: *ferman* dated 14 Safer 1241 (28 September 1825).

29 Historical Archive of Macedonia, Judicial registers, 220, p. 54/2: *ferman* dated 17 Receb 1243 (3 February 1828); 220, p. 116: *ferman* dated 1 Safer 1244 (13 August 1828).

30 Historical Archive of Macedonia, Judicial registers, 222, p. 81/2: *ferman* dated 25 Safer 1244 (6 September 1828).

31 For examples, see Historical Archive of Macedonia, Judicial registers, 214, p. 6: *ferman* dated 6 Rebiyülahir 1240 (28 November 1824); 214, p. 7/2: undated *defter*; 214, p. 8: undated *defter*; 214, p. 34: undated *defter*; 216, p. 35/1: *defter* dated Cemaziyülahir 1241 (11 January–9 February 1826); 220, p. 29/1: *defter* dated 27 Şaban 1243 (14 March 1828); 222, p. 69: *defter* dated 27 Şaban 1244 (4 March 1829).

ographic pattern of the brutal and unrestrained tyranny of the local adminis-
trators and the intolerable oppression of the Christian *reaya* is not exactly what
is reflected in the Ottoman documentation.

3   Violence Control

The most effective measure against any diffusion of violence and armed social,
religious or ethnic unrest among the assorted populations of the Ottoman
territory was the confiscation of weapons. It was a typical and highly form-
alised practice implemented at any occasion deemed potentially perilous for
domestic security. In reality, the collection of weapons was not forced confiscation but compulsory purchase at fixed prices. Then, the weapons were sold
either to any interested party or were transferred to the imperial capital for
further usage. Hence, this practice disarmed dangerous fractions of the population, but did not offend their property feelings, while providing the treasury
with cash and the army with weapons. Yet this course of action was not always
effective enough, particularly with populations highly inclined to rebellion or
stuck to their military traditions, while weapon concealment was an efficient
countermeasure adopted by all interested parties. For instance, the weapon
confiscation imposed on the population of Peloponnese in 1768–9 did not avert
the so-called Orlov rebellion a year later.

No edict imposing this sort of confiscation is saved in the Islamic court
archive. Yet by the end of 1821, the tower of Kelemerye (today known as the
White Tower) is reported to have been packed with confiscated arms. Battle-
fields must also have provided a constant source of weapon supply, whilst a
good number of arms may also have been discarded by retreating rebels.

Weapon gathering proved to be an essential function of the regional administration in the period 1821–6. Three seminal documents – an imperial edict
[*ferman*], a registry of seized arms and a letter written by the Grand Vezir and
addressed to the court of Salonica – depict a rather clear picture of the pertinent actions of the local administration, the expectations of the central state and
the impediments deviating the process. The mandate ordered rather imperat-
ively the delivery of 756 well-functioning guns from those collected by the local
government to the Sublime Porte.[32] The registry records in detail 3,990 rifles

---

32   Historical Archive of Macedonia, Judicial registers, 208, p. 36/1: *ferman* addressed to the
       mutasarrıf of Salonica Mehmed Pasha and the local Muslim judge, dated 15 Zilkade 1237
       (3 August 1822).

of assorted types, 1,291 pistols, 174 knives and 25 swords, collected from a wide range of towns, villages and land estates [çiftliks] within the boundaries of the *sancak* of Salonica.[33] From those arms, only 1,544 rifles, 963 pistols, 145 knives and 12 swords were at the disposal of the Sublime Porte, as the rest had already been snatched by local armed forces to be used in the war with the rebels. The letter also poses the issue of a belated weapon dispatch from local authorities to the imperial centre.[34]

At any rate, all three documents delineate the dearth of discipline of the local authorities, who alienated the loots and confiscated weapons against the expectations of the Sublime Porte. The governor of Salonica was to finance the war effort by his own means and thus was prone to similar ventures not encouraged by the sultanic centre. Furthermore, the emphasis on the need to reuse the confiscated and seized weapons by the imperial army is a common motif of all three documents. Even if the quantity of the expected weapons is limited to the minimal number of 756 items asked for in 1822, the deficiencies and shortages of the Ottoman army are more than evident. These needs were not covered in the following years, with the imperial forces being unsystematically and haphazardly armed and equipped. They used the weapons of the subjects [reaya], which cannot be regarded as fit for an imperial army or of a reliable military type, and many were allegedly in bad condition.

4   Amnesty, Tax Exemptions and Re-settlements

Amnesty, tax exemptions, favourable credit arrangements and the resettlement of deserted villages constituted the consensual and conciliatory steps of Ottoman peace restoration agenda. The measures aimed at the establishment of public order, the reinstatement of regular economic life and the resumption of fiscal influx to the imperial centre.

In the first days of December of 1821, soon after the suppression of the revolt, the Ottoman government granted amnesty to the rebels. In one of the most remarkable decrees contained in the Islamic court of Salonica, the terms and conditions of the amnesty are stipulated. The amnesty covered the sub-districts [nahiyes] of Kelemerye, Pazargâh, Kesenderye, Mantemohoria, Karvounohoria

---

33   Historical Archive of Macedonia, Judicial registers, 210, p. 49: *defter* dated 7 Zilhicce 1238 (15 August 1823).

34   Historical Archive of Macedonia, Judicial registers, 216, p. 93/1: *mektub* dated 11 Zilhicce 1241 (17 July 1826).

and the imperial *has* of Halkidiki.[35] The text, written in a strict tone, sets the objectives for the recovery of the area along two axes – that is to say, along economic reconstruction and the consolidation of public order. It is emphasised, rather rhetorically, that amnesty was granted after a request of the *reaya* themselves,[36] but then the author of the decree addresses the land-estate owners of the area, who were to resettle their villages and provide their cultivators with tools and seed.[37] Furthermore, cultivation of barren lands and their incorporation into the imperial *has* lands was also considered imperative.[38] At the same time, the governor of the city and the commander [*zabit*] of the janissaries were instructed to take rigorous steps against aimlessly roving Albanians and mercenaries [*sekban*]. Specifically, they had to seek all recalcitrant armed people either in the countryside or in the inns where they frequented, oust them from the province and beat or even execute the unruly who refused to evacuate the area. The local authorities were also to declare their unwillingness to hire armed Albanians and their commitment to prohibiting people armed without an official mission from entering the *kaza*.[39] This order, in its explicit details, reflects the complete suppression of the revolt in Halkidiki and the environs of Salonica at the end of the winter of 1821, and it displays a ready and previously well-tried project for the re-integration of the area in the Ottoman economic, fiscal and public order.

In the same vein, the governor of Salonica issued a mandate [*buyuruldu*] granting amnesty to the inhabitants of the significant nearby village of Epanomi.[40] Their participation in the insurgency made the Ottoman official ask for the surrender of all weapons still owned by villagers, the arrival of all notables to his palace in the city and their promise to never deviate from law. Apparently, the magnates had to go through the symbolic ritual of submission [Gk. *Proskynima*] to the governor, a passage rite of the *reaya* from unlawful-

---

35   Historical Archive of Macedonia, Judicial registers, 205, p. 165/2: *ferman* dated 13 Rebiyülevvel 1237 (8 December 1821).

36   *ihtilal avn-i inayet* [*yari*] *ve kuvvet-i kahren ve hazret-i tacdarı ile def ve ref olub maden ve has ve kömürkeşan kurasına matlubları ile* [...] *eman ve buyurdu verilüb.* Ibid.

37   *imar ve reayaya şimdilik tohum vererek iane ve hoş topunlub istirahat ile iskân devirdiline.*

38   Ibid. *ziraat olunmamış mahal kaldır ise emlak-i humayün tarafından zabt ve ziraat olunmuş iktiza eyleyeceği cümleye vesaya ve ilan olunmak.* Ibid.

39   *nefs-i Selânikte başıboş kapusuz Arnavud ve sekban ve askeri makulesini tezkeresiz derun-i şehirde ve kazada doğmayub hanlarda bulanların ve kazada bulanların cümlesi serdar marifetile def ve ref ve itaat etmeyüb* [*hakkımıları*] *oldur ise zarb ve katl ile izaleleri ... şimdilik tarafımıza Arnavud ve sair askerin lazimi olmadığı cümlesi ifade ve ilan ve bu tarafa geçirmeyüb tezkeresiz olanların silahlarını.* Ibid.

40   Historical Archive of Macedonia, Judicial registers, 205, p. 165/1: *buyuruldu* dated 1 Rebiyülahir 1237 (26 December 1821).

ness to reintegration into Ottoman order. The whole process was instigated by a petition [*arzuhal*] on behalf of the villagers by one silk trader named Isaak.[41]

The return of the peasants to their villages was an indispensable precondition for the restoration of the Ottoman order. The measure, as it was imposed in the above mandate, was applied with relative success, though in a slow pace, as can be inferred from a series of registries issued in 1824.[42]

Details of the process and of the drawbacks encountered by the authorities are not available. However, some interesting details are included in a decree concerning the villages of the peninsula of Kesenderye.[43] Since amnesty either was not known or remained unconvincing to the fugitives of the peninsula, its villages remained uninhabited in 1827, with production non-existent, while bandits occupied the region and turned it into their stronghold.[44] Then, one local fugitive named captain Anastasis, returning from the Aegean islands where he had resorted, offered himself to aid the Ottoman provincial authority to take over control of the area.[45] Apparently, Anastasis had decided to change sides and return to the Ottoman camp, and in this respect he took over the task of persuading the peasants to return to their homeland. The Ottoman government accepted his proposal and rewarded him with the title of *kocabaş*, though not trusting a lot this ex-fugitive and renegade of the Greek navy, appointed a Muslim officer as administrator of the peninsula.[46] At any rate, despite the official reservations, this example shows that cooperation with local elites was sometimes necessary for the conformity of villagers to the central state commands and for the success of the peace restoration policy.

Another significant measure for the success of this economic and demographic revitalisation policy was a favourable adjustment of the peasants' fiscal and credit commitments. In practice, this meant provisional tax exemptions, usually from the poll tax [*cizye*] if the peasants were Christians. On the other

---

41   *Selanik sakinlerinden ipekçi Isak bazirgân istidalar ile eman taleb eyledikleriniz.* Ibid.

42   Historical Archive of Macedonia, Judicial registers, 213, p. 113: *Kelemeriye nahiyesinde vaki Vasilika karyesi reayaların fesad-i reaya cihed ile mukaddema garetzede ve muharrik ve reayası muteferrik olmuş ve muehharen bazıları istiman ile karyelerine avdet eylemiş, defter* dated 9 Safer 1240 (3 October 1824); for similar cases, see pp. 11–5, 117–8 and 122.

43   Historical Archive of Macedonia, Judicial registers, 217, p. 204/2: *ferman* dated evahir-i Zilhicce 1242 (16–25 July 1827).

44   *cezire-i mezburde al-haleten hinde harab ve viran olarak aralık zuhur eden eşkiya-i güruhu derunda temekkün ve tehassün etmiş olduklarına mubni.* Ibid.

45   *Kesenderiye ceziresi mütemekkinlerinden iken bidayet-i fesad Bahr-i Sefid adalarına firar etmiş olan Anaştaş nam kapudan.* Ibid.

46   *ceziresinde mezkurenin kocabaşı kendüye ehali ve ehl-i Islam'dan bir munasib kendü her cezire-i mezkureye zabit nasb kılınarak.* Ibid.

hand, the interference of the Ottoman authorities would comprise the compulsory mediation between the peasants and their creditors by forcing the latter to accept a long-term payout of the debts in installments.

Both practices were adopted and applied by the regional administration in Halkidiki. At the end of 1822, a registry was issued by the Islamic court of Salonica recording the pair of oxen [*çifts*] of 73 burnt-down and deserted villages and towns as well as 61 farms [Gk. *metochia*] of the monasteries of Mount Athos and Halkidiki in the *nahiyes* of Kelemerye, Pazargâh, Kesenderye and the Mademohoria.[47] These registries were prepared so that a series of minor expenses would be distributed on the basis of the number of *çifts* and paid by the owners of these villages. Yet the same documents ordered the exemption of the settlements from any other fiscal burdens or payments. These registries provide a telltale picture of the destruction caused by the military operations in the area and show the difficulty of the restoration task. In spite of the short duration of the uprising, both the advance of the rebels and the suppression of the revolt by the Ottomans wrecked havoc in the countryside.

This picture of devastation and slow recovery is also reflected in another registry, demanded by the notables [*ayan*] of the *kaza* and issued by the Islamic court at the end of 1824. The *defter* was the outcome of a perfectly coordinated record of the financial potential of 103 settlements, villages and land estates [*çiftlik*] and 57 farms of Mount Athos.[48] The registry was meant to display the desolation of the *kaza* to the officials of the Sublime Porte who insisted on the dispatchment of 49,000 *kile* of wheat and 18,000 *kile* of barley. The villages had already sent 18,000 *kile* of wheat and 6,000 *kile* of barley, but they declared that this was the utmost they could offer. This intriguing case shows that the ultimate fiscal burdens imposed on the subjects were often the outcome of interplay between the state and the *reaya* themselves. A favourable fiscal settlement was a prerogative offered by the state to the law abiding subjects and, at the same time, a self-righteous and persistent demand of the *reaya* – part of a legitimisation programme of the Ottoman polity accredited by both sides.

The mediation between the peasants returning to their homes and their lenders was another, even more significant state initiative. By intervening in

---

47   Historical Archive of Macedonia, Judicial registers, 207, p. 101: *defter* dated 23 Muharrem 1238 (10 October 1822).

48   Historical Archive of Macedonia, Judicial registers, 213, p. 130: *defter* dated 9 Rebiyülevvel 1240 (2 November 1824). The register records 11 settlements from the *nahiye* of Vardar-i Kebir, four settlements from the *nahiye* of Langada, three settlements from the *nahiye* of Boğdan, 23 settlements from the *nahiye* of Pazargâh, 28 settlements from the *nahiye* of Kelemerye, one separate village, 12 settlements from the *nahiye* of Kesenderye, 12 villages of Mademohoria and nine villages of the imperial *has*.

the field of private economic transactions and balancing credit relations in a way satisfactory for all interested parties, the Ottoman authority aimed at displaying its seminal regulative role as justice dispenser, protector of the social structure and proponent of an ethic of mutual interest. This policy reinforced the legitimising agenda of the state without depriving the imperial treasury of fiscal inflow.

At the end of 1824, the resettlement of the villages Vasilika, Ay-Giannis Loggou, Zumbat [Trilofos], Zagliveri, Galarinos and the salt villages of Langada was impeded by the over-indebtedness of the peasants. With a view to facilitating the arrival of peasants and the restart of the economy, the Ottoman authorities interfered and imposed debt adjustments for all the residents of these villages. The Islamic court archive contains five debt registries of the lenders and the amounts owed as well as an imperial edict exclusive to the salt villages of Langada. The documents adjust the debt problem of the *reaya* in more or less the same mode for all debtors. For instance, in the introductory text of the registry of Vasilika, it is cited that the residents of the village who had been engaged in the Revolution had returned to their looted and burned village. They were too destitute to pay out their debts, and at the same time they were oppressed by thugs and usurers.[49] The Ottoman authorities intervened, forbade the immediate payment of the debts and set annual installments.[50] The same rescue policy was implemented to all other villages.

The following table depicts the indebtedness problem faced by the villages and the solution imposed by the Ottoman authorities. There is no quantitative information in the decree concerning Langada, and, thus, the small town is missing from the table.[51] It should be noted that the adjustment concerned remaining debts and not initial amounts, which are not recorded; apparently, a substantial part of these initial sums had already been paid before the villagers' flight.

---

49   Historical Archive of Macedonia, Judicial registers, 213, p. 113: *Kelemeriye nahiyesinde vaki Vasilika karyesi reayaların fesad-i reaya cihed ile mukaddema garetzede ve muharrik ve reayası muteferrik olmuş ve muehharen bazıları istiman ile karyelerine avdet eylemiş iselerde matlubat devlet-i aliyeyi tediyeye acizleri dergâr ve murabehacı taifesinden zikri cani kimesnelere, defter* dated 9 Safer 1240 (3 October 1824).

50   *malumü'l-mikdar deynlerini dahi tacil ve taksid-i şer ile razı olacakları bedidar olduğundan reaya-i karye-i mezbure düyun-ı keşideye mubtela ve defaten edayı adimü'l-iktidar olmalarile defaten taleb ettirilmeyub taksit ve tacil ile eda-i deyn ettirilmek babında emr-i celil-i alişan varid olmağın.* Ibid.

51   Historical Archive of Macedonia, Judicial registers, 213, p. 114: *ferman* dated 9 Safer 1240 (3 October 1824).

Settlement	Debt	Installment	Number of installments	Interest rate
Vasilika[a]	211,542	21,154	19 annual	–
Ay-Giannis Loggou[b]	163,497	16,349	10 annual	10%
Zumbat[c]	114,483.3	11,440	10 annual	10%
Zagliveri[d]	127,300	12,730	10 annual	10%
Galarinos[e]	20,990	2,099	10 annual	–

a   The real aggregate amount was 207,531 *kuruş* and the installment 20,740 *kuruş*. See Historical Archive of Macedonia, Judicial registers, 213, p. 113.
b   The real aggregate amount was 163,498 *kuruş* and the installment 16,403 *kuruş*. See Historical Archive of Macedonia, Judicial registers, 213, p. 115: *defter* dated 9 Safer 1240 (3 October 1824).
c   The real aggregate amount was 170,421.30 *kuruş* and the installment 11,134 *kuruş*. See Historical Archive of Macedonia, Judicial registers, 213, p. 117: *defter* dated 9 Safer 1240 (3 October 1824).
d   Historical Archive of Macedonia, Judicial registers, 213, p. 118: *defter* dated 9 Safer 1240 (3 October 1824).
e   The real aggregate amount was 24,740 *kuruş*. See Historical Archive of Macedonia, Judicial registers, 213, p. 122: *defter* dated 9 Safer 1240 (3 October 1824).

The table delineates in a most clear way the phenomenon described as the over-indebtedness [*peonage*] of the peasants. The arrears, ranging from significant to exorbitant amounts, are communal; thus, they must have emanated from earlier fiscal impositions and must have been apportioned among the members of the community.

This picture of over-indebtedness can serve tentatively as an analytical tool in an attempted interpretation of the revolutionary initiatives in, at least, Macedonia of 1821. The scholarly literature of the Greek War of Independence has focused, not unjustifiably, on the revolutionary leadership and elites, their political practices, ideological characteristics, economic aspirations and social conceptions as factors urging them to an exodus from Ottoman legality. The revolted armed people remain in the scholarly margin, mainly because of the absence of narratives or other documents written by simple members of the grass roots. Thus, intentions, plans, ambitions, fears, fallacies, ideologies and deeds of the unknown rebel remain in the darkness. Unfortunately, in an early modern world, the documentary traces of the ordinary people are restricted to serial data suitable mainly for quantitative historical approaches. As briefly indicated in the case of the five above-mentioned villages, when economic conjuncture can be quantified, then aspects of reality, otherwise unobserved, can be delved into, and comportments and mentalities may be deciphered.

The over-indebtedness of the villages of Halkidiki and the consequent pro-revolutionary attitudes of its peasants constitute a working hypothesis, only partially documented in this paper – one that, at least with regard to Mace-donia, remains open to debate and further evidential consolidation or refuta-tion.

Conclusively, the Ottoman documentation portrays with clarity the com-plexity and the interactive character of a peace-restoration process. The ulti-mate objective of the Ottoman authority was its re-legitimisation, the consolid-ation of public order and the resumption of the productive processes. It adop-ted the well-tried three-axe agenda of penal measures, like selective executions and confiscations, combined with the general disarmament of the population, and conciliatory steps like tax exemptions, amnesty and re-settlements in the deserted villages. The implementation of these policies was flexible enough and blunted by demands and petitions of *reaya* willing to remain in or re-enter the Ottoman legality. The *reaya* would take advantage of these steps if they considered them beneficial or if they wished to boost their own economic or social status. This was an age-old power game well known and heavily practised by both sides; it seems that it was still popular in Macedonia, and, despite the obstacles and the delays, it contributed to the re-establishment of the Ottoman order.

Bibliography

Hekimoglou, Evangelos 2004, Ἡ ἱστορία τῆς ἐπιχειρηματικότητας στη Θεσσαλονίκη. Οθω-μανική περίοδος' ['Business history in Salonica. The Ottoman period'], in Ἱστορία τῆς ἐπιχειρηματικότητας στη Θεσσαλονίκη [*Business history in Salonica*], edited by Har-alambos Papastathis and Evangelos Hekimoglou, vol. 3, Thessaloniki: Πολιτιστική Εταιρεία Επιχειρηματιών Βορείου Ελλάδος.

Hekimoglou, Evangelos 2008, Τὸ 'Κοινόν τῆς Πολιτείας' καὶ οἱ περιπέτειές του. Ο χριστιανικός πληθυσμός τῆς Θεσσαλονίκης πρὶν, κατά καὶ μετά τὴν ἐπανάσταση τοῦ 1821 [*The 'Commune of the Town' and its adventurues. The Christian population of Salonica before, during and after the revolution of 1821*], Thessaloniki: Εταιρεία Μακεδονικῶν Σπουδῶν.

Ilıcak, H. Şükrü 2011, *A Radical Rethinking of Empire: Ottoman State and Society during the Greek War of Independence (1821–1826)*, Ph.D. Dissertation, Harvard University.

Laiou, Sophia 2014, 'The Ottoman Greek 'Merchants of Europe' at the Beginning of the 19th Century', in *Festschrift in Honor of Ioannis P. Theocharides: Studies in the Ottoman Empire and Turkey*, edited by Evangelia Balta, Georgios Salakides and Theocharis Stavrides, Istanbul: The Isis Press: 313–31.

Sarigiannis, Marinos 2015, 'Μια πλαστή πηγή για τις σφαγές του 1821 στη Θεσσαλονίκη. Ο

Χαϊρουλλάχ Εφέντης του Αβραάμ Ν. Παπάζογλου' ['A fake source for the supposed massacres in Salonica in 1821. Hayrullah Efendi, a creation by A.N. Papazoglou'], *Μνήμων*, 34: 11–36.

Stamboulis, Georgios 2000, *Τα φερμάνια για την Θεσσαλονίκη 1387–1912* [*The Sultanic orders concerning Salonica, 1387–1912*], Thessaloniki: n. ed.

Vasdravellis, Ioannis (ed.) 1952, *Ιστορικά αρχεία Μακεδονίας, Α´ Αρχείον Θεσσαλονίκης 1695–1912* [*Historical Archive of Macedonia. 1. Archive of Salonica 1695–1912*], Thessaloniki: Εταιρεία Μακεδονικών Σπουδών.

PART 2

Times of Transition: Continuity and Rupture

∴

The Developing Idea of Liberation in the Course of the Greek National Movement in the Early Nineteenth Century

The Case of Christophoros Perraivos

Nikos Rotzokos

This chapter focuses on the changes the idea of liberation underwent at the time of the formation of the Greek national movement in the first two decades of the nineteenth century. We shall begin by examining the historical processes through which the idea of liberation was disconnected from the imperial model of an enlightened rule and an enlightened ruler-liberator, becoming instead associated with the nation's self-conciousness and self-determination. We will subsequently analyse the association of the idea of liberation with the new political practices of secret revolutionary societies that were emerging at the time of the Napoleonic Wars. We hope to show that the Friendly Society [Gk. *Philiki Hetaireia*] succeeded in its development as a result of the *interstitial emergence*[1] of revolutionary conspiracy through manifold and intersectional economic, political and ideological networks in which the Greek Orthodox of the time functioned – especially through those networks by which Russian diplomacy operated, which the Friendly Society put at the service of its own liberation project. Christophoros Perraivos's trajectory from Rhigas's revolutionary group to his participation in the Friendly Society is paradigmatic of the way in which this crucial juncture in the history of nascent Greek nationhood came about.

---

1 According to Mann 1986, vol. 1, p. 16, *interstitial emergence* is 'the outcome of the translation of human goals into organisational means. Societies have never been sufficiently institutionalized to prevent interstitial emergence. Human beings do not create unitary societies but a diversity of intersecting networks of social interaction. The most important of these networks form relatively stably around the four power sources [ideological, economic, military and political] in any given social space. But underneath, human beings are tunneling ahead to achieve their goals, forming new networks, extending old ones, and emerging most clearly into our view with rival configurations of one or more of the principal power networks'.

The Greek national movement was a product of the great *European crisis* of the late eighteenth century and of the Age of Revolution.[2] The idea of liberation itself was, for sure, age old. It dated back to the Ottoman conquest of Constantinople, but there are no mentions of it in projects of social and national emancipation prior to the era that concerns us. Founded upon providential and eschatological myths and doctrines around the Day of Judgement, the end of Ottoman rule and the Resurrection of the Orthodox people, liberation was not perceived as a product of human action, but rather as an outcome of divine intervention.[3]

It was among intellectual circles of Greek education of the Greek Orthodox diaspora that this idea of liberation was secularised during the late eighteenth century. It was connected with the Enlightenment's ecumenical, reformative ideal, and it partook of the prospect of a Greek cultural 'regeneration'. Even in its earlier version, however, the idea of liberation did not consist in a project of national action. As a prospect, it aspired more to the imperial paradigm of an enlightened rule and its attendant monarch liberator, represented by Catherine II's Russia and the France of Napoleon and the Revolution. On the one hand, continuous Russian-Ottoman wars inculcated this perception of Russia as a liberating and protective power. Besides that, intellectuals' notions about enlightened Russian absolutism dovetailed with age-old religious myths pervading Christian populations that regarded Russian wars as providential interventions in support of God's chosen people.[4] On the other hand, the French Revolutionary and Napoleonic wars in the East cultivated an affinity for France in intellectual circles, whose members were inspired by radical Enlightenment ideas and, as a consequence, connected Greek liberty to political virtue and a citizen's status.[5] Rhigas's liberation project was inspired by the Napoleonic

---

2   At this time, the sense of a stable, indisputable world order was in crisis. The foundations of the traditional legitimacy of power (Ancient Regime) was undermined and political experience radically altered as the exercise of politics was perceived differently. On the Ancient Regime's crisis, see Venturi 1989; Venturi 1991; Venturi 2014. On the Age of Revolution, see Hobsbawm 1962.

3   On providential eschatological myths, see Argyriou 1982, pp. 17–25, 69–113; Stoianovich 1969, pp. 809–19; Theotokas 2006, pp. 11–57; Rotzokos 2007, pp. 249–86; Hatzopoulos 2011, pp. 95–116.

4   On this connection of liberation with an 'enlightened rule', as embodied by the Russia of Catherine II, see Kitromilides 2013, pp. 200–90; Rotzokos 2007, pp. 219–49. On Russia's role as a protector following the Treaty of Küçük Kaynarca, see Davison 1990, pp. 29–59. On Russian politics in the East, see Ragsdale 1993, pp. 82–102; Arsh 2015, pp. 31–247; Arsh 2011, pp. 179–337; Prousis 1987, pp. 259–80; Tzakis 2003, pp. 115–49.

5   On Greek-Enlightenment radicalism, see Kitromilides 2013, pp. 117–55; Dimaras 1990. On the spread of the French Revolution's ideas in the East, see Kitromilides 2000.

model of ruling the 'Grande Nation': a multi-ethnic state under the name 'Hellenic Republic' in the East, which would replace Ottoman 'despotism' with the French Revolution's republican ideas.[6] In 1792 in Paris, Adamantios Korais envisioned a 'Greco-French democracy' in the East.[7] In 1800, he encouraged his compatriots to wage war on Napoleon's side, insisting that Neo-Greeks and French were 'as a nation, Greek-French'.[8]

As Vassilis Panagiotopoulos has shown, it is in the first decade of the nineteenth century, particularly in the years between 1801 and 1806, that we can trace the beginnings of a transition from hope for an enlightened, liberating ruler of the Greek national movement to the movement's own, entirely national idea of liberation,[9] an idea which the revolutionaries were to strive for 'through a political tool of a novel type',[10] the Friendly Society. The Greek national movement developed at a particularly rough and volatile time of wars, crucial social and political transitions and geopolitical reappointments. Expectations were nourished inasmuch as they were refuted at this time, new political experiences were formed and novel possibilities of political thought and action opened up. Intellectual networks in support of the idea of a foreign, enlightened ruler became radically politicised on account of experiencing at close hand the Russian-Ottoman wars under Catherine II's rein, the French Revolutionary and Napoleonic wars and those of the European Restoration; what they therefore experienced was the nationalisation of the ecumenical *spirit* of Enlightenment thought and the idea of a Revolution.[11] To this notion of a Greek 'regeneration', new political meanings were now attached, paving the way to novel communal, political courses of action. It is not, of course, in one single way that most people envisioned its accomplishments. While it is true that most associated it with the idea of an enlightened ruler, conferring on themselves the role of a social reformer, not all assigned to themselves the role of a revolutionary. Even those favouring a revolution associated it with a foreign liberator who was to occupy a central position in the prospect of liberation.

---

6   According to Tolias 2009, pp. 27–8, Rhigas's radical patriotism was inspired by the French Revolution's notions of nationhood, but he also absorbed those notions as per the traditional imperial terms of a 'Christian people', within, that is, 'the models of Byzantium and the Ottoman Empire'. See also Kitromilides 1998.

7   Korais 1885, vol. 1, p. 298.

8   Korais 1983, p. 11.

9   Panagiotopoulos 1989; Panagiotopoulos 1989, pp. 3–12. See also Dimaras 1990, pp. 42–9; Dimaras 1989, pp. 12, 46–7; Rotzokos 2007, pp. 19–38, 59–75; Rotzokos 2011, pp. 151–70.

10   Panagiotopoulos 1989, p. 9.

11   See Kitromilides 2003; Lekkas 2004, pp. 179–93. See also Lekkas 2005, pp. 161–76; Zanou 2018.

These attitudes toward the foreign liberator began to change, as noted, at the very first years of the nineteenth century. These shifts had very much to do with geopolitics, i.e. the negative experience of the continuous presence and policy of European powers in the East. Successive conquests of the Ionian Islands – the (two) French, the Russian-Ottoman and especially the English conquests – belied the prospect of the foreign liberator. It was, however, due to politics, specifically the new type of politics born out of the Napoleonic and post-Napoleonic era, that the crucial transition from hopes for a foreign liberator to collectively organised revolutionary action occured; a transition that directed this ruler's role in the Greek movement wholly anew. Participation in such a conspiratorial organisation as the Friendly Society presupposed and nurtured a novel attitude toward liberation and its accomplishment. The secret society's prospects lied in the nation's leaders and the foreign liberator, but at the same time treated liberation as a matter of collectively organised individual units striving for collective political goals. It thus turned to those available – regardless of social origins, political position and social status – demanding only their political engagement, or their devotion to the matter of national liberation. In the revolutionary mythology of the Friendly Society, it was a protector of the same religious faith, Russia, that incarnated the role of the foreign liberator; this time, however, Russia became a helpful tool that the revolutionary organisation employed to serve its own political project. The revolutionary organisation, with its presence and conspiratorial action, totally redirected the nation's relation to the foreign liberator: it revived its liberating myth but took up on itself the role of the liberator.[12]

Let us now trace through this lens Christophoros Perraivos's political and ideological trajectory over the course of the Greek national movement in the first two decades of the nineteenth century. Perraivos embodies the romantic, republican paradigm of the patriotic citizen, the revolutionary conspirator and the professional combatant produced by the post-revolutionary French era. He was ideologically formed and acted politically at a time when French revolutionary ideas and political practices spread to the European peripheries and when antagonisms amid the European powers in the Eastern Mediterranean intensified. A modest intellectual with only minimal military training, more a man of action in pursuit of good luck, he at an early age sought a better life in the commercial centres of the Greek diaspora in Europe. Early on, he was enlisted in the cause of the 'Enlightenment' and the enlightened ruler-liberator, and

---

12   On the Friendly Society, see Frangos 1971; Arsh 2011; Panagiotopoulos 2003, vol. 3, pp. 9–32; Tzakis 2018a, pp. 125–48.

he lived a tumultuous life by serving as a national pedagogue enlightener and as a professional revolutionary combatant. He taught, wrote, conspired and fought, affiliated, on the one hand, with circles of the Greek radical enlightenment and those of Russian and French secret diplomacy and, on the other hand, with military men recruited by European armies – expatriated Souliots, fugitive *klepht*s of the Peloponnese, Maniot chiefs, and the *armatoloi* of Roumeli. Perraivos lived *between* these two worlds – that of modernity and that of tradition – at a time of their ever-denser spread within developing networks of the Greek diaspora, favouring the idea of their union under an enlightened government.

The pseudonym 'Perraivos', used by Christophoros (or Christophis, or Chrisafis) Hatzivasilis from an early age, denotes a provenance from the Perraivia of ancient Thessaly, thereby suggesting Hellenicity. We know little about his actual name, the precise year and place of his birth, nor do we possess accurate information about his family's origins. The relevant clues lead us to surmise that he was born in the Thessalian village of Pourles of Olympus between 1773 and 1776. He took care to retain his personal and family life under complete secretiveness until his death in 1861.[13]

Perraivos first came into contact with the Enlightenment's reformative and patriotic ideas in 1793 at Bucharest, where he associated himself with the enlightened intellectual circles of the Phanariots, particularly associating himself with Rhigas and Dimitrios Katartzis.[14] He devoted himself to his nation's

---

13   The most reliable biographical account on Perraivos is Papageorgiou 2019, pp. 21–66. See also Bees 1956, pp. 9–22. As to the year of his birth, he indirectly mentions that he was born in 1776; see Perraivos 2019, p. 91. Another work of his suggests that he was born in 1773; see Perraivos 1860, pp. 16–17. His apology to the police at Corfu in 1805 implies that he was born in 1774; see Theotokis 1925, p. 143; Bees 1956, p. 12. The information available reveals his real name as Christophoros (or Christophis or Chrysaphis) Hatzivasilis (or Vasilis) and comes from the following source: Legrand (ed.) 1892, pp. 66–7, 178. Secondly, it comes from deciphering Perraivos's seal, on which is written the name Christophoros (but also Christophis and Chrysaphis) Hatzivasilis; see Lampros 1904, pp. 646–7; Amantos 1930, pp. 108–9, 120–1; Bees 1956, pp. 13–14. We possess no exact clues regarding his family. During his interrogation by the police at Corfu, he mentioned that his father's name was Constantinos. Stephanos Papageorgiou regards this as proving that Perraivos was his widowed mother's illegitimate child with the priest Hieremias at the Metropolis of Larissa. This information comes from an anonymous libel against Perraivos, which circulated in the early nineteenth century by ecclesiastical circles; see Papageorgiou 2019, pp. 27–31. Extracts from the anonymous libel are published in Kordatos 1931, pp. 47–50.
14   Perraivos 1860, pp. 16–17. On Katartzis and Rhigas, see Kitromilides 2013, pp. 142–54, 200–29.

cause and served it in accordance with the time's revolutionary model, which was enlightenment (education and ideological instruction) and a connection to what formerly was the ruler, who embodied, in Perraivos's mind, the role of a liberator (political and military action). In 1796, Perraivos became embroiled in Vienna in the precarious conspiratorial plots of the circles of Rhigas, his ideological mentor. They were both arrested by the Austrian police in Trieste in December 1797 and charged with 'trespassing intrigues'. According to the charges, they had been planning to propagandise French revolutionary ideas among the Sultan's subjects and to insurrect the Mani, the Peloponnese and Souli in support of the French, with the intention of subsequently igniting a 'general kind of revolution' among the European provinces of the Ottoman Empire.[15] Perraivos was interrogated and then set free due both to the protection granted him by the French ambassador of Trieste and to Rhigas's testimony to bearing no other relation to him other than that of being his 'fellow traveler'.[16]

At the beginning of 1798, Perraivos fled from Trieste and passed to the French-occupied Corfu, continuing, once there, to perform Rhigas's revolutionary work at the service of the French. He enlisted himself in the French army[17] and defended Preveza, Parga and Souli against Tepedelenli Ali Pasha for the next five years. Up until 1804, Perraivos served the Enlightenment and the French as part of conspiratorial patriotic network with French sympathies, which connected Souli, Parga, Ioannina, Zakynthos, Livorn, and Paris.[18] He performed a teacher's role in Parga, where he was accused by ecclesiastical circles of preaching the 'dogma of the freethinking of the French'.[19] He organised and encouraged Parga's residents to oppose Ali Pasha's plots to besiege their town, connecting them to military and diplomatic officers of Greek origins serving the French and the Russians in the region, and he mobilised them to supply those besieged by Ali Pasha, the Souliots, with weaponry and food, thus ignoring the local ecclesiastical hierarchy's threatening orders for submission to Ottoman rules.[20] He further undertook the mission of travelling to Paris

---

15   Legrand (ed.) 1892, pp. 7–13, 71–3; Perraivos 2019, p. 92; Perraivos 1860, p. 26.
16   He presented himself as a French citizen, for he had declared the French-occupied Parga as his homeland. Perraivos 2019, pp. 92–3; Perraivos 1860, pp. 28–9, 31–2; Legrand (ed.) 1892, pp. 66–7; Katsiardi-Hering 1979, pp. 150–74.
17   On the creation and organisation of Greek mercenary units at that time at the service of the French, see Oikonomou 2016.
18   Perraivos 1956, p. 372; Perraivos 2019, p. 116.
19   As an anonymous pamphlet of the ecclesiastical circles of the time informs us; see an extract, in Kordatos 1931, pp. 47–8.
20   See the letter by the metropolitan bishop of Ioannina to the residents of Parga and against

to convey to Napoleon, via Korais, the Souliots' petition to contribute to their struggle against Ali Pasha.[21] Around the same time he penned and published (in 1803, under a pseudonym) a history of the Parga and Souli, with a particular focus on their struggles against Ali Pasha,[22] so as to hail the much-wanted 'Greek renaissance', their free and patriotic morale which rendered them genuine Greeks and worthy of their glorious ancestors. It was in the same year that Korais declared to 'enlightened Europe' the modern Greeks' achievement, the 'enlightenment', which was at the time 'a peoples' steady decision which readily prepares them to become a nation'.[23] He not only extolled his compatriots' accomplishments in economy and cultural education, but further commended the free and unyielding spirit of those mountainous 'rebel communities' of the Mani and Souli.[24] To the age's romantic patriots, such as Korais and Perraivos, the 'unyielding' Souli symbolised Greek freedom. That is, they did not see the Souliots's conflict with Ali Pasha as what it really was – a conflict over local control – but as a struggle for national liberation, a struggle for which they counted on the French military's presence and contribution. Their hopes were dashed by the French, who showed indifference, and by the Suliots themselves, who made a pact with Ali Pasha and left their land. With the prospect of French aid annihilated, several of these French friendly patriots, including Perraivos, properly turn to the Russians.

From 1804, Perraivos was in the service of the Russians of Corfu. It was at this time that the so-called 'Septinsular Republic' was formed, the first Greek

     Perraivos, in Perraivos 1857, vol. 2, p. 93. On Ali Pasha, see Fleming 1999. On Souliots, see Psimouli 1998.

21   See the Souliotes' letter in the newspaper *O Φιλόπατρις*, no. 202, 20 December 1858. See Korais's reply, in Korais 1966, vol. 2, pp. 77–80. See also Perraivos 1857, vol. 2, p. 119; Perraivos 1956, p. 372.

22   The work was first published in 1803 under a pseudonym with the title: *Ιστορία σύντομος του Σουλίου και Πάργας περιέχουσα την χρονολογίαν και τους ηρωικούς αυτών πολέμους, εξαιρέτως τους των Σουλιωτών μετά του Αλή Πασιά, ηγεμόνος της Ελλάδος. Ιστορία του Σουλίου και Πάργας, περιέχουσα την αρχαιότητα αυτών και ηρωικούς μετά των Τούρκων πολέμους, και μάλιστα τους του Σουλίου μετά του Αλή Πασιά κατοίκου των Ιωαννίνων και ηγεμόνος της Γραικίας και Μακεδονίας*, Paris. The second edition (1815) is under a cipher. [Perraivos], *Ιστορία Σουλίου και Πάργας περιέχουσα την χρονολογίαν και τους ηρωικούς αυτών πολέμους, εξαιρέτως τους των Σουλιωτών μετά του Αλή Πασιά, ηγεμόνος της Ελλάδος*, 2 Volumes, Venice. It was published for the third time in 1857 under the title: Χριστόφορος Περραιβός, *Ιστορία του Σουλλίου και Πάργας*, 2 Volumes, Athens. In 1823, it was published in English as *History of Suli and Parga, containing their chronology and their wars, particularly those with Ali Pasha, Prince of Greece*.

23   Korais 1803, p. 44.

24   Korais 1803, p. 45.

state under the Russian emperor's protection.[25] As he announced to the political authorities of Corfu in 1805, Perraivos had decided to live in the city, 'led
by his desire to serve and prove beneficial for a Greek state, like the Septinsular Republic, that had already been liberated and that was in the process of
being shaped'.[26] Availing of his connections to the Russian political-diplomatic
and military network on the Ionian Islands,[27] Perraivos was appointed to teach
the Greek language at the town's public school with the support of the Zakyn-
thian count Giorgio Mocenigo – Russia's ambassador on the island – and the
politically emergent Ioannis Kapodistrias.[28] In 1806, Giorgio Mocenigo enlisted himself as a major in the Russian army of the Ionian islands. He served
under the irregular body formed by warriors from Souli, Epirus, Cheimarra,
the Peloponnese and the Mani in addition to defending, under Kapodistrias's
authority, Hagia Mavra [Santa Maura] against Ali Pasha's army.[29] A while later
(1815), Perraivos wrote of the reasons for which he and his co-combatants enlisted themselves in the Russian army: 'Everyone willingly rushed to serve the
Russians for being co-religionists, and for hope of the Nation's liberty, as well
as for the regard each enjoyed by the Government'.[30] Generally, this was the
Orthodox Greeks' perception of Russia at the time. Russia had them under her

---

25   In March 1799, Corfu was conquered by the Russian-Ottoman fleet. The Ionian Islands
      became an autonomous state, the 'Septinsular Republic', under Ottoman rule and Rus-
      sian protection (1800–7). See Nikiforou (ed.) 2001; Michalaga with Moschona (eds.) 2016.
      See also Saul 1970, pp. 78–104; Zanou 2018, pp. 75–82.
26   See Theotokis 1925, p. 144.
27   Following the shift in the political regime on the Ionian Islands in 1799, Perraivos found
      himself in the adverse position of being characterised as a friend of the French. As he
      mentions a long time later in his memoir, the new Russian-Ottoman government ignited
      'fear and aversion against those with democratic sympathies', although, to his great luck,
      'the Russians proved sympathetic to their co-religionists, the Greeks'. Perraivos 1860, p. 40.
      He therefore luckily came upon the protection of the Russian consul in Corfu, Limberakis
      Benakis (hailing from the Mani), that 'brave and real Greek', as he calls him, regarding him
      as one of the few protectors of Parga against Ali Pasha. See [Perraivos] 1815, vol. 1, p. 144.
      Limberakis Benakis was the scion of one of the most prominent Peloponnesian families
      of notables that had been at the forefront of the Orlov Revolt. On the Benakis family, see
      Papastamatiou 2009. Perraivos also came under the protection of the Kephalonian Geor-
      gios Palatinos, who served as the secretary of the Russian naval officer Theodore Ushakov.
      His brother, Gabriel Palatinos – at the time the Rear Admiral of the Russian Navy as well
      as a noteworthy defender of Parga against Ali Pasha – had led Perraivos to Trieste's French
      ambassador, to ask for his protection, after his arrest by the Austrian authorities. See [Per-
      raivos] 1803, vol. 1, p. 119. On the Palatinos brothers and their relationship with Perraivos,
      see Katsiardi-Hering 1977, pp. 36–68.
28   See Kapodistrias 1976, vol. 1, pp. 242, 252–3, 263, 267, 271, 293.
29   [Perraivos] 1815, vol. 2, p. 77; Perraivos 1956, p. 372.
30   [Perraivos] 1815, vol. 2, p. 75.

wings, supplying them with life resources, offering respect and recognition to them while cultivating their expectation for national liberation.[31]

The Ionian Islands were reconquered in 1807 by the imperial French. As expected, Perraivos and his comrades-in-arms were re-conscripted by the French army. He remained in the army until the middle of 1814. From 1809 onwards, the Ionian Islands began to be captured by the English. With Corfu as the last island conquered by them in 1814, they thereafter proceeded to disintegrate the irregular military units formed by the French and the Russians as well as those units they had created after 1809. Following this shift in the regime in the Ionian Islands, Perraivos and his comrades – formerly at the service of the so-called 'Greek unit' of the Russians and later the French – were left unemployed and under dire financial duress. The unit's officers, including Perraivos, signed a petition to the tsar, who at the time was present at the Congress of Vienna to request his own protection. As part of a veterans' committee, Perraivos, via Kapodistrias, delivered the petition to the tsar – 'Alexander the Great and Father of the Greek people', as the request proclaims him.[32]

For the following eighteen months, Perraivos resided with his family in Barletta.[33] He was a close associate of Kapodistrias. The latter's Russian consular network – consisting of several of his confidants, who were his military and diplomatic officers – subsidised Perraivos. Perraivos was hired by the Ferdinand's army at Naples through the mediation of Kapodistrias, Benakis and Georgio Mocenigo, ambassador of Russia at the Italian town.[34]

In December of 1816, Perraivos travelled to Russia to request Kapodistrias for payments long due, renewed subsidy to the veterans, in addition to asking for himself to be re-hired by the Russian army.[35] Via Alexandru Sturdza,[36] secretary and close friend of Kapodistrias, he voiced to the tsar the services he was able to offer at times of peace and of war between the Russians and the Ottoman Empire. He vowed to organise and maintain military alertness

---

31   On the perception of Russia, see Photakos 1960, pp. 26–8; Xanthos 1845, p. 12. See also Arsh 2011, pp. 179–242; Panagiotopoulos 2003, p. 10.

32   See the letter in Chiotis 1874, vol. 1, pp. 309–11. See also Arsh 2015, pp. 99–102.

33   Perraivos, Σύντομος παράστασις, in Perraivos 1956, p. 373.

34   G. Mocenigo, a former benefactor of Perraivos's, had also mediated in the milieu of the king of the Kingdom of the two Sicilies, so that Ionian veterans would be hired to his service. See Kapodistrias's letter to Benakis, in Kapodistrias 1976, vol. 5, p. 232. See also Arsh 2015, pp. 126–7. In his letter of initiation to the Friendly Society Peraivos states that he had been militarily serving Naples; see Mexas 1937, p. 4.

35   On his departure to Saint Petersburg and communication with Kapodistrias, see Arsh 2015, pp. 120–1.

36   On Sturdza, see Prousis 1992, pp. 309–44; Ghervas 2008.

among Christians and Muslims of the regions of Central Greece, Thessaly, Epirus and the Peloponnese. These services he offered with a look to 'the glory of the Imperial Russian Throne and my Nation's benefit'.[37] He noted that he had pledged himself to similar aims in the past, to the Russians and the French he at times served.[38] All of these projects follow the same model of insurrection: the foreign aid's exercise of influence over local populations – organising their revolutionary availability, maintaining their military alertness and calling them to action in case of war.

As is obvious, Perraivos was a professional warrior. Like many others, at times he served the French and at other times the Russians. Not only that, we have also seen that he was an intellectual of the Enlightenment and a 'Jacobine' patriot. In that period, he was part of networks of Russian diplomacy in eastern Mediterranean. His 'high' patrons, Kapodistrias, Benakis, Mocenigo and Sturdza, provided him with employment and allowed him to support his family. We can nonetheless see that the relationships that were being cultivated among these people were not strictly professional. They also shared political ties. They believed that by serving the Russians they were serving their own nation, the national Enlightenment and expected liberator.[39]

During his stay in Russia, Perraivos often met Nikolaos Galatis, who was a member of the Friendly Society, which was at the time in its early conspiratorial stages. Galatis had been sent to Kapodistrias to offer him the leadership of the secret society, which at the time consisted of a few members. In February 1817, Perraivos and Galatis were arrested and incarcerated. They were released upon Kapodistrias's intervention.[40] The crucial point of Perraivos's political action came a month later, while he was staying in Moscow. It was there that members of the Friendly Society approached him. The society's documents indicate that most of its members had been recruited only a few months prior to Galatis.[41] The merchant Antonis Komizopoulos initiated Perraivos to the society on March 13 1817,[42] and the society itself initiated other veterans during the same period.[43] He thereafter devoted himself to serving the secret brotherhood. As his letter of initiation shows, his plans of insurrection, formerly at

---

37   See Perraivos's plan in Philemon 1859–61, vol. 1, pp. 134–7.
38   Philemon 1859–61, vol. 1, p. 135.
39   Zanou 2018, pp. 94–103.
40   On his contact with Galatis and his arrest and incarceration, see Arsh 2015, pp. 207–16; Arsh 2011, pp. 245–73; Panagiotopoulos 2003, pp. 18–22. On Galatis in general, see Moraitinis-Patriarcheas 2002.
41   Mexas 1937, pp. 2–3.
42   Mexas 1937, p. 4.
43   Mexas 1937, pp. 4–5.

the service, as we have seen, alternately of the Russians and the French, he now put at the organisation's disposal.[44]

At the beginning of 1819, Perraivos travelled to the Mani. His mission there is indicative of the way in which he understood his dual role – at once the Russians' agent and a member of a national revolutionary organisation – as well as of the mechanisms through which this organisation functioned. He is therefore paradigmatic of a crucial point in the development of the Greek national movement, at which its relation to the foreign aid was being entirely redirected while new possibilities of political thought and action were emerging.

We know that Perraivos's mission in the Mani had been approved of by Kapodistrias, with the aim of establishing a school in the area, while it was also supported by the Patriarchate. He was therefore acting under the purview of his 'superiors', his nation's leaders, and with foreign aid. Kapodistrias, in a letter to his friend and associate Alexandru Sturdza, dated 20 February 1820, mentions that it was he who sent Perraivos to the Mani, 'to that last sanctuary of Greek freedom', in the spring of 1819, so that Perraivos would become 'one of the teachers of this new school' which would function under the aegis of the Patriarchate.[45] As the letter informs us, plans for establishing a school at the Mani partook of the wider enlightenment project of the 'Society of the Friends of the Muses', an organisation founded by Kapodistrias himself at the Congress of Vienna in 1814, aiming at nationally educating his compatriots; he also aimed at offsetting the political influence of Britain on the homonymous Society in Athens, where it had been established only a year earlier.[46] Kapodistrias's national enlightenment project was intended to subsidise schools in Greek countries and grant scholarships to the young to pursue studies in Europe. The Society of the Friends of the Muses was collectively led by Kapodistrias, Sturdza, the scholar Anthimos Gazis and the former metropolitan bishop of Hungary-Wallachia, Ignatios, an agent of Russia living in Pisa.[47] They were primarily concerned with concealing that their initiative was coming from Russia, and they had to appear to stem from local communities, appointed by their leaders. The letter informs us that one of the projects of the Society of the Friends of the Muses was to contribute 'indirectly to the creation of a school to be established by Petro Bey, the leader of the Spartans'.[48]

---

44   Mexas 1937, p. 4.
45   See the letter in Kapodistrias 1976, vol. 6, pp. 83–5; Arsh 2015, pp. 343–6. See also relevant commentary in Panagiotopoulos (ed.) 2015, p. 128.
46   See Kapodistrias 1968, pp. 58–9.
47   On the Society of the Friends of the Muses, see Arsh 2015, pp. 160–74.
48   He is referring to Petros Mavromichalis, who had been the Governor [Bey] of the Mani

However, as indicated by two letters addressed to Christodoulos Prinaris, a member of the Friendly Society, by Perraivos from Barletta sometime before his departure to Mani, as well as by his correspondence with the organisation's leadership in the first months of his stay in the area, he did not limit his activities to the responsibilities conferred on him by Kapodistrias, i.e. establishing the school. It is revealed that he had set his eyes on a different prospect. He travelled to Mani as a member of a revolutionary organisation under the conspiratorial mission of organising the local leadership groups around the organisation's project and to direct them to a revolution.[49]

We have seen that it was under the aegis of Kapodistrias and the Patriarchate that Perraivos was sent to Mani to establish a school. We also know that a member of the Friendly Society, a higher official of the Patriarchate, had taken care to have a letter by the Patriarch sent to the Maniots, in which he commended them for their decision to found a school and promised to provide for it financially.[50] The organisation, then, was attempting to make it appear as if the plan for a revolution, on the pretext of forming a school (national enlightenment) was being led by the nation's leaders and the foreign aid, Russia and the Patriarchate, through itself.

We also know that several of Kapodistrias's associates of Greek origin in the networks of Russian secret diplomacy had been initiated into the Friendly Society around that time. In Patras, the consul of Russia Ioannis Vlassopoulos[51] had been initiated, as had his dragoman (interpreter) Ioannis Paparrigopoulos.[52]

---

since 1816, hence Petrobey; see Arsh 2015, p. 345. According to Benakis, the plan had to appear to be the Maniots' own initiative. On the letter to Ignatios, dated 24 January 1816, see Protopsaltis (ed.) 1961, pp. 73–4; as he instructs, 'take care of the project involving the schools, because only through them can "national restoration" follow without being known to others' (p. 74). See also Mavromihalis's letter to Kapodistrias, dated 1 August 1819, in which he writes that 'Mr. Perraivos's arrival here – a great friend of the Muses – with his family was of great emotional relief to me'; Arsh 2015, pp. 335–6.

49   See the letters to Prinaris, in Philemon 1859–61, vol. 1, pp. 383–84. In one of them, Perraivos mentions that he may be distinguished by his 'prudence' in addition to being fully aware of the danger that he is embarking on, but that he does not intend to seem 'petty', refusing to do or to talk about anything, indulging only in 'boasts and flighty fantasies which are the Nation's defects' (p. 384). In his letters to the society's leadership, sometime after his arrival in Mani, Perraivos requests money to prepare for the Revolution, presenting the Mani as unified and ready to revolt. In their response, the organisation's leaders express their satisfaction, but at the same time they stress to him that 'missing this opportunity is harmful but rushing at this moment may be more so' (p. 165).

50   Philemon 1859–61, vol. 1, pp. 157–8. See also the correspondence among members of the Society in Meletopoulos 1967, pp. 51, 53.

51   Philemon 1859–61, vol. 1, p. 389. On Vlassopoulos's action, see Frary 2019, pp. 57–78.

52   Mexas 1937, p. 73.

Prior to Perraivos's departure for Mani, Vlassopoulos and Paparrigopoulos, in close collaboration with the Friendly Society's leaders as well as the equally proselytised Petros Mavromichalis, aided the escape of two members who had assassinated Galatis.[53] Numerous consuls and sub-consuls of Russia on the Ionian Islands and in the Ottoman Empire who were of Greek origin were also members of the secret organisation: Spyridon Destounis, consul of Smyrna;[54] Nikolaos Mylonas, consul of Chios;[55] Gerasimos Svoronos, consul of Samos;[56] Georgios Mostras, a diplomat attaché at the Russian embassy of Constantinople;[57] Gabriel Katakazy, secretary at the Russian embassy at Constantinople.[58] The Russian consular network in the Eastern Mediterranean that had been under Kapodistrias's eye had been put at the service of the Friendly Society. The same applied to Kapodistrias's associates in the Society of the Friends of the Muses, the metropolitan bishop Ignatios[59] and the scholar Gazis, the latter belonging to the leading group of the revolutionary organisation.[60]

As we can see – despite traveling to Mani under the authority of Kapodistrias and the Patriarchate, and far from acting sole upon his role as an agent of the Russians according to Russian protection politics – Perraivos also operated as a member of a Greek revolutionary organisation. He took advantage of the former mission to serve the latter, and his case demonstrates to us that revolutionary conspiracy emerges out of the interstices in the networks via which the Greek national movement operates. As suggested at the beginning of this paper, this is a process of 'interstitial emergence', of consequences unintended by those involved. Regardless, therefore, of precisely what Kapodistrias knew,[61] the revolutionary organisation's conspiratorial web

---

53   Philemon 1859–61, vol. 3, pp. 402–3.

54   Philemon 1859–61, vol. 3, p. 391.

55   Mexas 1937, p. 18.

56   Mexas 1937, p. 59.

57   Mexas 1937, p. 6.

58   Mexas 1937, p. 10. On the consuls of Russia at that time, see Frary 2013, pp. 46–65.

59   See Xanthos 1845, p. 14; Philemon 1859–61, vol. I, p. 394, and vol. 4, pp. 346, 515–16; Mexas 1937, p. 2.

60   Mexas 1937, p. 3.

61   The case of Perraivos's dispatch to Mani relates to the still historiographically debated subject of the Friendly Society's relationship with Kapodistrias and, more generally, with Russia. See a presentation of different historiographical approaches in Arsh 2015, pp. 11–38. See also Woodhouse 1973, pp. 104–34. We saw that Kapodistrias was from early on informed of a Greek conspiracy afoot, ever since the visit paid to him by Galatis. We also must bear in mind Perraivos's implication in this affair. Particularly sound is the question V. Panagiotopoulos's raises as to whether Kapodistrias would possibly believe that Perraivos – widely known for his revolutionary action and with whom he had been collaborat-

was woven within the networks and mechanisms of Russian secret diplomacy and of the Patriarchate, which the organisation used to its own advantage. It recruited such people as Perraivos, who associated liberation with foreign aid, and it put them at the service of its own liberation project. This new, albeit unsteady, factor that entered Kapodistrias's relations with his associated agents in the Eastern Mediterranean – men like Perraivos – became a Greek revolutionary conspiracy organisation. Perraivos's case sheds light on a crucial juncture not only of his history, but also widely of the Greek national movement.

Bibliography

Amantos, Konstantinos 1930, *Ανέκδοτα έγγραφα περί Ρήγα Βελενστινλή* [Unpublished Documents concerning Rhigas Velestinlis], Athens: Βιβλιοπωλείον Ι. Ν. Σιδέρη.

Argyriou, Asterios 1982, *Les exégèses grecques de l'Apokalypse à l'époque turque (1453–1821): esquisse d'une histoire des courants idéologiques au sein du peuple grec asservi*, Thessaloniki: Εταιρεία Μακεδονικών Σπουδών.

Arsh, Gregory 2011, *Η Φιλική Εταιρεία στη Ρωσία* [The Friendly Society in Russia], Athens: Παπασωτηρίου.

Arsh, Gregory 2015, *Ο Ιωάννης Καποδίστριας στη Ρωσία* [John Kapodistrias in Russia], Athens: Ασίνη.

Bees, Nikolaos 1956, 'Εισαγωγικά εις τον Βασίλην Περραιβόν' [Introduction on Vassilis Perraivos], in Christophoros Perraivos, *Άπαντα* [Collected Works], edited by M.M. Papaioannou, Athens: Εκδοτικός οίκος Σεφερλή.

Chiotis, Panagiotis 1874, *Ιστορία του Ιονίου Κράτους από συστάσεως αυτού μέχρις ενώσεως (έτη 1815–1864)* [*History of the Ionian State from 1815 until 1864*], 2 Volumes, Zakynthos: Τυπογραφείον Η Επτάνησος Χρίστου Σ. Χιώτου.

Davison, Roderic H. 1990, *Essays in Ottoman and Turkish History, 1774–1923: the Impact of the West*, Austin: University of Texas Press.

Dimaras, Konstantinos 1989, *Νεοελληνικός Διαφωτισμός* [*Neohellenic Enlightenment*], Athens: Ερμής.

---

ing since 1804 in Corfu – was sent to Mani simply to serve as a teacher at its local school. See Panagiotopoulos (ed.) 2015, p. 131. See also the hypotheses he tests regarding Kapodistrias's relationship with Perraivos, and with the Friendly Society in general, based on Parraivos's being sent to Mani; Panagiotopoulos (ed.) 2015, pp. 128–41. However, Perraivos appears to belong to the category of the Society's leading members, which Panagiotopoulos calls 'the hot-headed ones' and 'the unyielding ones', mentioning that they 'were propagandising and organising the revolution'; see Panagiotopoulos (ed.) 2015, p. 114.

Dimaras, Konstantinos 1990, *Ο Ρωσοαγγλογάλλος. Κριτική έκδοση με επιλεγόμενα* [*Rosoag-glogalos: Critical Edition with intriduction*], Athens: Πορεία.

Fleming, Katherine 1999, *The Muslim Bonaparte: Diplomacy and Orientalism in Ali Pasha's Greece*, Princeton: Princeton Legacy Series.

Frangos, Georgios 1971, *The Philike Etaireia, 1814–1821: a Social and Historical analysis*, PhD Dissertation, Columbia University, New York.

Frary, Lucien 2013, 'Russian consuls and the Greek War of Independence (1821–31)', *Mediterranean Historical Review*, 28, 1: 46–65.

Frary, Lucien 2019, 'The Russian Consulate in the Morea and the Outbreak of the Greek Revolution, 1816–1821', in *Diplomacy and Intelligence in the Nineteenth-Century Mediterranean World*, edited by Mika Suonpää with Owain Wright, New York: Bloomsbury.

Ghervas, Stella 2008, *Réinventer la tradition: Aleksandre Stourdza et l'Europe de la Sainte-Alliance*, Paris: Honoré Champion.

Hatzopoulos, Marios 2011, 'Oracular prophecy and the politics of toppling Ottoman rule in South-East Europe', *The Historical Review/La Revue Historique* 8: 95–116.

Hobsbawm, Eric 1962, *The Age of Revolution, 1789–1848*, New York: World Publishing.

Kapodistrias, Ioannis 1968, *Αυτοβιογραφία Ιωάννου Καποδίστρια* [*Self-biography of Ioannis Kapodistrias*], edited by M. Laskaris, Athens: Εκδόσεις Γαλαξία.

Kapodistrias, Ioannis 1976, *Αρχείον Ιωάννου Καποδίστρια* [*Archive of Ioannis Kapodistrias*], 9 Volumes, Kerkyra: Εταιρεία Κερκυραϊκών Σπουδών.

Katsiardi-Hering, Olga 1977, 'Ελληνικά διαβήματα στον Βοναπάρτη. Η περίπτωση του Γεωργίου Παλατίνου' ['Greek appeals to Bonaparte: the case of Georgios Palatinos'], *Ο Ερανιστής*, 14: 36–68.

Katsiardi-Hering, Olga 1979, 'Ὁ Ρήγας Φεραίος. Νέα στοιχεία από τα Αρχεία της Τεργέστης' ['Rhigas Pheraios: New Evidence from the archives of Trieste'], *Μνήμων*, 7: 150–74.

Kitromilides, Paschalis 1998, *Ρήγας Βελεστινλής. Θεωρία και πράξη* [*Rhigas Velestinlis: theory and action*], Athens: Hellenic Parliament Foundation.

Kitromilides, Paschalis 2000, *Η Γαλλική Επανάσταση και η Νοτιοανατολική Ευρώπη* [*The French Revolution and the Southeastern Europe*], Athens: Πορεία.

Kitromilides, Paschalis 2003, 'Reappraisals of Enlightenment Political Thought', in *From Republican polity to National Community: Reconsiderations of Enlightenment Political Thought*, edited by Paschalis Kitromilides, Oxford: Voltaire Foundation.

Kitromilides, Paschalis 2013, *Enlightenment and Revolution: The Making of Modern Greece*, Cambridge, MA and London: Harvard University Press.

Korais, Adamantios 1803, *Mémoire sur l'état actuel de la civilisation dans la Grèce, lu à la Société des Observateurs de l'Homme*, Paris: Société des observateurs de l'homme.

Korais, Adamantios 1885, *Επιστολαί Αδαμάντιου Κοραή* [*Letters of Adamantios Korais*], 3 Volumes, Athens: Αδελφοί Πετρή.

Korais, Adamantios 1966, *Αλληλογραφία* [*Correspondance*], 6 Volumes, Athens: Βιβλιοπωλείο της Εστίας.

Korais, Adamantios 1983 [1800], *Άσμα Πολεμιστήριον των εν Αιγύπτω περί ελευθερίας μαχομένων Γραικών* [*Battle hymn for the Greeks fighting for liberty in Egypt*], Athens: National Hellenic Research Foundation [1st ed.: εν τη κατ᾽ Αίγυπτον ελληνική τυπογραφία].

Kordatos, Giannis 1931, *Ο Ρήγας Φεραίος και η εποχή του* [*Rhigas Pheraios and his time*], Athens: Κωνσταντινουπόλεως.

Lampros, Spyridos 1904, *Μικταί σελίδες* [*Varia*], Athens: Σακελλαρίου.

Legrand, Émile (ed.) 1892, *Documents inédits concernant Rhigas Vélestinlis et ses compagnons de martyre, tirés des archives de Vienne*, Paris.

Lekkas, Pantelis 2004, 'Από το οικουμενικό πνεύμα του διαφωτισμού στις μερικεύσεις της πολιτικής σκέψης τον 19ο αιώνα' ['From the ecumenical spirit of the Enlightenment to the partial political thinking of the nineteenth century'], *Τα Ιστορικά* 40: 179–93.

Lekkas, Pantelis 2005, 'The Greek War of Independence from the perspective of Historical Sociology', *The Historical Review/La Revue Historique* 2: 161–76.

Mann, Michael 1986, *The Sources of Social Power*, 4 Volumes, New York: Cambridge University Press.

Meletopoulos, Ioannis 1967, *Η Φιλική Εταιρεία. Αρχείον Π. Σέκερη* [The Friendly Society: Archive of P. Sekeris], Athens: n. ed.

Mexas, Valerios 1937, *Οι Φιλικοί* [The members of the Friendly Society], Athens: n. ed.

Michalaga, Despoina with Panagiota Moschona (ed.) 2016, *Επτάνησος Πολιτεία, 1800–1807: Μνήμη Σπύρου Δ. Λουκάτου* [*Septinsular Republic, 1800–1807. In memoriam of Spyros Loukatos*], Athens: Κέντρο Μελετών Ιονίου.

Moraitinis-Patriarcheas, Eleftherios 2002, *Νικόλαος Γαλάτης ο Φιλικός, Ιστορική μονογραφία* [*Nikolaos Galatis, member of the Friendly Society: historical monograph*], Athens: Κέδρος.

Nikiforou, Aliki (ed.) 2001, *Επτάνησος Πολιτεία (1800–1807): τα μείζονα ιστορικά ζητήματα* [*The Septinsular Republic (1800–1807): the major historical issues*], Kerkyra: Γ.Α.Κ. Αρχεία Νομού Κέρκυρας.

Oikonomou, Foivos 2016, *Έλληνες μισθοφόροι στην υπηρεσία της Γαλλίας (1789–1815)* [*Greek mercenaries at the service of France (1789–1815)*], Thessaloniki: University Studio Press.

Panagiotopoulos, Vassilis (ed.) 2015, *Δύο πρίγκιπες στην Ελληνική Επανάσταση. Επιστολές αυτόπτη μάρτυρα και ένα υπόμνημα του πρίγκιπα Γεώργιου Καντακουζηνού* [*Two princes in the Greek Revolution*], Athens: Ασίνη.

Panagiotopoulos, Vassilis 1989, 'Η εμφάνιση της σύγχρονης πολιτικής σκέψης στη νεότερη Ελλάδα' [The emergence of modern political thought in modern Greece], *Τα Ιστορικά* 10: 3–12.

Panagiotopoulos, Vassilis 1994, Ένα σχόλιο στον Ρωσσοαγγλογάλλο [*A comment on the Rossoagglogallos*], Athens: Hellenic National Research Foundation.

Panagiotopoulos, Vassilis 2003, 'Η Φιλική Εταιρεία. Οργανωτικές προϋποθέσεις της εθνικής επανάστασης', *Ιστορία του Νέου Ελληνισμού 1770–2000* [The Friendly Society: organisational preconditions of the national revolution], edited by Vassilis Panagiotopoulos, vol. 3, Athens: Τα Νέα.

Papageorgiou, Stephanos 2019, 'Εισαγωγή' ['Introduction'], in Christophoros Perraivos, *Απομνημονεύματα Πολεμικά* [*War Memoirs*], Athens: Hellenic Parliament Foundation.

Papastamatiou, Dimitrios 2009, *Οικονομικοκοινωνικοί μηχανισμοί και το προυχοντικό φαινόμενο στην οθωμανική Πελοπόννησο του 18ου αιώνα. Η περίπτωση του Παναγιώτη Μπενάκη* [*Economic and social mechanisms and the notables in the Ottoman Morea during the eighteenth century: the case of Panagiotis Benakis*], Ph.D. dissertation, Aristotle University of Thessaloniki.

[Perraivos], Christophoros 1803, *Ιστορία του Σουλίου* [*History of Souli*], Paris.

[Perraivos], Christophoros 1815, *Ιστορία Σουλίου και Πάργας περιέχουσα την χρονολογίαν και τους ηρωικούς αυτών πολέμους, εξαιρέτως τους των Σουλιωτών μετά του Αλή Πασιά, ηγεμόνος της Ελλάδος* [*History of Souli and Parga*], 2 Volumes, Venice: Νικόλαος Γλυκύς.

Perraivos, Christophoros 2019, *Απομνημονεύματα Πολεμικά* [*War Memoirs*], Athens: Hellenic Parliament Foundation.

Perraivos, Christophoros 1857, *Ιστορία του Σουλλίου και Πάργας* [*History of Soulli and Parga*], Athens: Τυπογραφείο Φ. Καραμπίνη – Κ. Βάφα.

Perraivos, Christophoros 1860, *Σύντομος βιογραφία του αοιδίμου Ρήγα Φεραίου του Θετταλού* [*Short biography of the late Rhigas Pheraios from Thessaly*], Athens: I. Αγγελόπουλος.

Perraivos, Christophoros 1956, *Άπαντα* [*Collected Works*], edited by M.M. Papaioannou, Athens: Εκδοτικός οίκος Σεφερλή.

Philimon, Ioannis 1859–61, *Δοκίμιον Ιστορικόν περί της Ελληνικής Επαναστάσεως* [*Essay on the Greek Revolution*], 4 Volumes, Athens: Π. Σούτσας και Α. Κτενάς.

Photakos [Photios Chrysanthopoulos] 1960 [1899], *Απομνημονεύματα περί της ελληνικής επαναστάσεως Memoirs concerning the Greek revolution*], Athens: Φιλολογικά Χρονικά.

Protopsaltis, Emmanouel (ed.) 1961, *Ιγνάτιος Μητροπολίτης Ουγγροβλαχίας (1776–1828). II. Αλληλογραφία., Πολιτικά Υπομνήματα, Λόγοι, Σημειώματα περί Ιγνάτιου* [*Ignatios, Metropolitan of Hungary and Wallachia (1776–1828): Memoranda, Spechees, Notes concerning Ignatios*], Athens: Academy of Athens.

Proussis, Theofilos C. 1987, 'The Greeks of Russia and the Greek Awakening 1777–1821', *Balkan Studies* 28: 259–80.

Proussis, Theophilos 1992, 'Aleksandr S. Sturdza: A Russian Conservative Response to the Greek Revolution', *East European Quarterly*, 26, 3: 309–44.

Psimouli, Vaso 2005, *Σούλι και Σουλιώτες*, Athens: Εστία.

Ragsdale, Hugh 1993, 'Russian Projects of Conquest in the Eighteenth Century', in

Imperial Russian Foreign Policy, edited by H. Ragsdale, Cambridge: Cambridge University Press.

Rotzokos, Nikos 2007, *Εθναφύπνιση και εθνογένεση. Ορλωφικά και ελληνική ιστοριογραφία* [*National awakening and nation building: The Orlov rebellion in Greek historiography*], Athens: Βιβλιόραμα.

Rotzokos, Nikos 2011, 'The Nation as a Political Subject. Comments on the Greek National Movement', in *The Greek Revolution of 1821. A European Event*, edited by Petros Pizanias, Istanbul: The Isis Press.

Saul, Norman E. 1970, *Russia and the Mediterranean, 1797–1807*, Chicago: University of Chicago Press.

Stoianovich, Traian 1969, 'Les structures millénaristes sud-slaves aux XVIIe et XVIIIe siècles', in *Actes du Premier Congrès International des Etudes Balkaniques et Sud-est Européennes*, vol. III, Sofia.

Theotokas, Nikos 2006, 'Η επανάσταση του έθνους και το ορθόδοξο γένος. Σχόλια για τις ιδεολογίες στο. Εικοσιένα' ['The revolution of the nation and the Orthodox community. Comments on the ideologies of 1821'], in *Η οικονομία της βίας. Παραδοσιακές και νεωτερικές εξουσίες στην Ελλάδα του 19ου αιώνα* [*The economy of violence. Traditional and modern powers in nineteenth-century Greece*], edited by Nikos Theotokas and Nikos Kotaridis, Athens: Βιβλιόραμα.

Theotokis, Spyridon 1925, 'Ο Χριστόφορος Περραιβός κατά το 1805' ['Christophoros Perraivos in 1805'], in *Ημερολόγιον της Μεγάλης Ελλάδος*, Athens: Εκδόσεις Ι.Ν. Σιδέρης.

Tolias, Georgios 2009, *Αποχαιρετισμός στο Γένος. Αυτοκρατορία και πατριωτισμός στο χαρτογραφικό έργο του Ρήγα (1796–1797)* [*Farewell to the Community: Empire and patriotism in the chartography of Rhigas (1796–1797)*], Athens: Μένανδρος.

Tzakis, Dionysis 2003, 'Ρωσική Παρουσία στο Αιγαίο: Από τα Ορλωφικά στον Λάμπρο Κατσώνη' ['Russian presence in the Aegean: from the Orlov rebellion to Lambros Katsonis'], in *Ιστορία του Νέου Ελληνισμού 1770–2000* [*History of Modern Hellenism 1770–2000*], edited by Vassilis Panagiotopoulos, vol. 1, Athens: Τα Νέα.

Tzakis, Dionysis 2018, 'Από την Οδησσό στη Βοστίτσα: η πολιτική ενσωμάτωση των τοπικών ηγετικών ομάδων στη Φιλική Εταιρεία' ['From Odessa to Vostitsa: the incorporation of the local notables into the Friendly Society'], in *Οι πόλεις των Φιλικών: οι αστικές διαδρομές ενός επαναστατικού φαινομένου. Πρακτικά Ημερίδας* [*The towns of the Friendly Society: the urban itineraries of a revolutionary phenomenon*], edited by Olga Katsiardi-Hering, Athens: Hellenic Parliament Foundation.

Venturi, Franco 1989, *The End of the Old Regime in Europe, 1768–1776: The First Crisis*, Princeton: Princeton University Press.

Venturi, Franco 1991, *The End of the Old Regime in Europe, 1776–1789, I: The Great States of the West*, Princeton: Princeton University Press.

Venturi, Franco 2014, *The End of the Old Regime in Europe, 1776–1789, II: Republican Patriotism and the Empires of the East*, Princeton: Princeton University Press.

Woodhouse, Christopher M. 1973, 'Kapodistrias and the Philiki Etairia, 1814–21', in *The Struggle for Greek Independence*, edited by Richard Clogg, London and New York: Archon Books.

Xanthos, Emmanouel 1845, *Απομνημονεύματα περί της Φιλικής Εταιρείας* [*Memoirs concerning the Friendly Society*], Athens: Α. Γκαρπολάς.

Zanou, Konstantina 2018, *Transnational Patriotism in the Mediterranean, 1800–1850: Stammering the Nation*, Oxford: Oxford University Press.

CHAPTER 5

The Greek Revolution in the Morea

Economies, Societies, and Cultures

Aliki Fakoura

The history of the Morea, the Peloponnese, from the mid-eighteenth century to 1821 was marked by the so-called Orlov rebellion (1770), the subsequent rule of Albanian mercenaries in the Morea (1770–9), the persecution of the klephts (1805–6), the plan of French General François-Xavier Donzelot in the neighbouring Ionian Islands to submit the Morea to the Napoleonic Empire (1808) and the outbreak of the Greek Revolution in 1821. These were fields of action that shaped the collective memory of the people of the Morea, who lived in an era of great change both in Western Europe[1] and in the Ottoman Empire.[2] Many but not all of the Christian Orthodox notables of the Morea organised or took part in operations against Ottoman rule during these years. Research on their attitudes and decisions can show, at least partially, the underlying mechanisms that made them open, under pressure, to modernity, along with their local and genealogical particularities.

The Moreot notables who participated in the Revolution of 1821 were born from approximately the mid- to the end of the eighteenth century,[3] and their descendants were born after 1795,[4] according to the memoirs and biographical accounts of the revolutionaries whose paternal and family history was tied with the Orlov rebellion. They had experienced the ultimate political sovereignty of their times, and up to 1821 the revolutionary discourse had been accepted and handled in ways directly in keeping with the political rivalries that were typ-

---

1 For the impact of the French Revolution in Southeastern Europe, see Kitromilidis 2000; Apostolopoulos 1989.
2 The Ottoman imperial administration's policy of curtailing the power of the mighty provincial notables culminated in the early nineteenth century, following reforming orders that had been issued for that very purpose during the period 1765–91; see Yaycıoğlu 2016. For a more specific analysis, see Ilıcak 2011; Georgieva 2007, pp. 3–19. See also, Kremmydas 1977, pp. 16–33.
3 For instance, Petro Bey Mavromichalis was born in 1765, Panoutsos Notaras in 1752, Georgios Sisinis in 1769 and Sotiris Haralambis in 1770.
4 For the standard division of generations into twenty-five years and its concomitant problems, see Tomara-Sideri and Sideris 1986.

ical of their authority and of the province of the Morea under Ottoman rule. Struggles to achieve local political power were a constant feature in their efforts to overturn Ottoman rule, both during the Orlov Rebellion (conducted by the previous generation) and during the Donzelot plan.

The Orlov rebellion (1770) was attempted with the assistance of Russia,[5] and was organised by eminent notables, marked by local political lobbying.[6] The failure of the uprising was a turning point for the Morea, as it brought an end to the so-called 'peaceful times' by the notables themselves (1715–70).[7] This was followed by a decade of the Morea being ravaged by armed Albanian groups sent by the Ottoman Pashas from Rumelia to suppress the rebellion. The violence exerted by the Albanian warlords illustrated the military and fiscal disintegration of the Ottoman Empire and was inscribed in the collective memory of Moreots as a consequence or even a part of the rebellion.[8] References to the rebellion of 1770 implicitly included the ensuing disastrous period of Albanian rule, or were even overshadowed by the latter, and perhaps this was a significant reason for the continued hope of most Moreots for the help of the 'fair-haired people', i.e. the Russians, according to popular tradition.

Political balances in the Morea shifted after 1770, as the eminent figures of the rebellion were among the notables; important families were no longer in power and new ones were established. Thereafter, the notables used that failure and the 'Russian threat' as political arguments both against their fellow Orthodox and against the Muslim notables, while factions were engaged in fierce diplomatic rivalry. When Teceli Ahmed Efendi, originating from the town of Tripolitsa [mod. Tripoli], was appointed Deputy Governor [*kaymakam*] of the Morea in 1795, the dragoman of the Morea, Giannakis Palamidis, was beheaded (1796). The documents sent to the Sublime Porte by Palamidis's political opponents, who had devised the plot against him, included claims such as: 'if he stays alive for another six months, the Morea will become a Russian province'.[9] Christians and Muslims collaborated in order to assume or preserve their profits and the prestige ensured by their posts in the Ottoman provincial administration. In

---

5   See Rotzokos 2007.

6   Phrantzis 1839, vol. 1, pp. 6–7, 9; Droulia 1969, p. 63.

7   Deligiannis 2005, vol. 1, p. 9; Papatsonis 1960, p. 28. As the Bishop Germanos of Palaiai Patras wrote, the peace between Russia and the Ottomans left the people of the Peloponnese helpless 'with empty words of amnesty'; see Palaion Patros Germanos 1900, p. 16.

8   The inhabitants of Dimitsana participated in the rebellion, and their small town, which was considered sacred by Christians and Muslims alike, was ravaged extensively during those years. The Greek school of Dimitsana was demolished, and many inhabitants migrated. See Kabouroglou 1916, p. 4.

9   Deligiannis 2005, vol. 1, p. 20.

his treatise on the flaws of the Ottoman administration in the Morea (1785), the Moreot Süleyman Penah Efendi stressed that the established alliance between the *ayans*, *kocabaşıs* and *kadıs* was particularly harmful for both the tax-paying subjects and the Ottoman state.[10]

In the years of the second conquest of the Ionian Islands by the French, Christian and Muslim notables negotiated the submission of the Morea to the Napoleonic Empire. The Ionian Islands were centres of social change for both the Moreots and the Roumeliots and served as pockets of security while favouring the forging of bonds beyond Ottoman rule. The conquest of the adjacent islands by the French played an important role in spreading the ideas of the French Revolution[11] to Christians and Muslims alike, as demonstrated by the Donzelot plan. The conspiracy that came close to developing into a rebellion[12] had been organised by the political opponents of Veli Pasha, governor of the Morea and son of Ali Pasha of Ioannina. The secret arrangements were made with the French Governor of the Ionian Islands, General François-Xavier Donzelot, but the plan fell through when the British gained control over Zante in 1809.[13]

The consequences of the failed Orlov rebellion and the frustrated Donzelot plan had an impact on collective psychology, triggering a series of inhibitions and social fatigue. In February 1817, one year before the Moreot notables started to join the revolutionary Friendly Society [Gk. *Philiki Etairia*],[14] Christoforos Perraivos, a member of the secret society, submitted to the emperor of Russia a revolutionary plan involving Rumelia, for which he counted on 150,000 soldiers, Souli, in Epirus, which they would retake from Ali Pasha, and the Morea. He wrote, 'I find no difficulty in having an organisation set up for the Peloponnese (with the exception of the Spartans); however, my only hesitation at the moment is the lack of familiarisation of the locals with arms and their great inclination for trade, as well as the risk they had experienced in other occasions in the past'.[15]

Given Russia's stance in the Orlov rebellion and after seeking its assistance in vein, the leadership of the Friendly Society did not expect any foreign power to help them in the project of the Greek Revolution. Nevertheless, they spread the idea of independence in line with collective mentality, which considered

---

10   Sarris 1993. See also Laiou and Sarigiannis 2019.
11   Vournas (ed.) 1974.
12   Holland 1815, p. 429.
13   Kolokotronis 1846, pp. 37–8. Deligiannis 2005, pp. 54–5, lists the names of the Christian and Muslim notables. See also Stamatopoulos 1997, pp. 205–6.
14   Tzakis 2015, pp. 104–10.
15   Philimon 1859–61, vol. 1, p. 136.

alliances and redeemers indispensable. The secret operational plan that was implemented persuaded those initiated into the Friendly Society that Russia was behind its secret Supreme Authority, and most people came to believe that Greece would be saved by 'Herculean arms'.[16]

The Moreot notables, unaware of who the Supreme Authority of the revolutionary project was, were very concerned about the position that Russia would adopt. During a meeting in Tripolitsa in May 1820, they expressed fears about the disproportionate confrontation with the Ottoman troops as well as suspicions, as reported by Kanellos Deligiannis, over 'whether what was divulged by the various advocates was a Russian scheme ... for its own purposes ... as it also happened in 1769 and ruined us'. This time, Russia would leave them exposed in the most dangerous times, the times of the Holy Alliance 'of all tyrants on earth'.[17] Being experienced politicians, the notables sent delegates to gather information on the support of the Russian monarchy. Panagiotis Krevvatas (b. 1785) was sent to Pisa to the Metropolitan of Hungary-Wallachia Ignatius, and Ioannis Paparrigopoulos (b. 1780) headed to Russia, where he met with Alexander Hypsilantis.

The Ottoman authorities believed that the province of the Morea could initiate a new rebellion abetted by the Russians. However, in 1821, the Ottoman fortresses were extremely disorganised and the Muslim officials had difficulty accepting that the Greek Revolution was a fact.[18] At that extremely dangerous pre-revolutionary conjuncture, when the Revolution could no longer be postponed and rumours about the upcoming event had reached the ears of the local Aghas, Andreas Londos tried to dispel their suspicions and reassure the latter by putting forward the Orlov rebellion as an argument: 'We are rich and landlords like you are. We remember that our fathers who revolted a few years ago were left bare and starving and we do not wish to suffer the same misfortunes'.[19]

Although the Moreot notables had become more powerful and were the recipients of extensive signs and indications of the changes taking place in Western Europe, they did not at first seem open to civil education or Western-style development in the profitable Morea. The Orthodox Christian notables in other prospering regions in the Balkans were then showing their progressivism

---

16   Spiliadis 2007, vol. 1, pp. 1–2. The so-called prophecies of Agathangelos, who had allegedly foretold the salvation of Greece from the Turks, were very widespread in all Christian-Orthodox populations under the Ottomans. The prophecies of Agathangelos were so well rooted in the populations that local Muslims, too, believed in 1821 that their political power had come to an end. Philimon 1834, vol. 1, pp. 59, 179–80.

17   Deligiannis 2005, vol. 1, p. 115.

18   Laiou and Sarigiannis 2020.

19   Trikoupis 1978, vol. 1, p. 54.

and patriotism by establishing Greek schools and steering their descendants to higher education. Educational administration in the Morea shows specific cultural particularities in the field of reception of the revolutionary ideas, partly due to the dispersion of populations. Towns like Corinth, Nafplio, Mystras, Monemvasia and Coron had a large concentration of Muslims. In Tripolitsa, the seat of the Pasha of the Morea, and Patras, which were the largest towns in the peninsula, the population was divided between Christians and Muslims. Based on these realities, the Christian notables had formed a distinctive parental, residential and communication network that offered them more freedom. Many eminent notables lived in mountainous villages, such as the Zaimis family in Kerpini, district of Kalavryta (altitude ~1,080 m.), the Deligiannis family in Lagkadia, district of Karytaina (~900 m.), and the Notaras family in Trikala in the mountains of Corinth (~1,000 m.).

According to Ioannis Philimon, the Moreot notables did not favour the establishment of schools because they were devoted to politics, nor did they send their children to study in Europe, for fear of atheism. Widespread superstition resulted in having monk teachers 'bursting with piety and partisans of a monotonous system of tedious learning'.[20] Conservative intellectuals of the Greek Orthodox society, very influential up to the Revolution, always proclaimed that the 'root of all evils' was in Europe, contrary to what was believed and pursued by the representatives and recipients of the so-called Neohellenic Enlightenment.[21] In their majority, the old notables barely knew how to write their name, and the high priests had just practical knowledge of their ecclesiastical duties, 'but none of them were educated'.[22]

However, towards the end of the eighteenth century, the situation started to change as eminent notables provided quality education and home tutors for their offspring. Around that time, notables started establishing schools where reading and writing were taught. Kanellos Deligiannis (at that time called Papagiannopoulos) presents the example of his father, Ioannis (b. 1738), who, although 'illiterate', established a Greek school in their hometown, the village

---

20   Philimon 1834, p. 55. See also Hobsbawm 1996, p. 218: 'Frank atheism was still comparatively rare, but among the enlightened scholars, writers and gentlemen who set the intellectual fashions of the later eighteenth century, frank Christianity was even rarer. If there was a flourishing religion among the late eighteenth century elite, it was rationalist, illuminist and anti-clerical Freemasonry'.

21   'They are atheists all those that study in the land of the Franks, and upon their return, they convert others to atheism as well' was the view put forward by Hierotheos Dendrinos, a leading teacher in Smyrna in 1753. See Iliou 2003, p. 11.

22   Kolokotronis 1846, p. 48.

of Lagkadia, district of Karytaina.[23] In the study of Phillipos Iliou regarding the subscribers to books in the early nineteenth century, given that only 5 percent of the 24,617 subscribers lived in areas that were later integrated into the Greek state, the map of the Morea was sparsely dotted with subscriber figures (less than ten individuals) while the largest concentration was recorded in Patras and Argos (101–200 individuals) and in Tripolitsa (51–100 individuals).[24] The beginning of a shift among the notables towards education, which benefited the next generation, can therefore be observed.

The milestone of the new generation of the Revolution can be traced back to the turn of the eighteenth century, with 1795 being the indicative starting point of the births of people who played a decisive role in the Revolution. New beliefs marked their era, at a time when the Ottoman administrative and economic crisis was aggravated and deeply affected all social classes.[25] This adverse conjuncture was a catalyst for the Revolution and finally changed the notables' attitudes and gradually threw their former feudal image into oblivion. These political and social changes had a direct impact on their descendants, whose generation spent their youth amidst the crisis and the Revolution.

In the revolutionary spring of 1821, many rooted social conditions were shaken. Public sentiment turned against the higher clergy and disregarded their orders. The patriarchal excommunication of Hypsilantis and Soutsos, urging the Christian Orthodox to remain loyal to the Ottoman sultan, were signed on the high altar of the Patriarchate of Constantinople, only to arouse a greater sentiment of horror.[26] In sharp contrast to what had happened earlier during the persecution of the klephts in 1806, the menacing documents of the Patriarchate of Constantinople were sent to the provinces but had no effect on Christian Orthodox. Although it had been organised by the Friendly Society in such a way that the Russian support was considered granted, the people did not wait for any Russian military assistance to launch the Revolution in the Morea.

In the meantime, the traditional society was 'violently' exposed into modernity during the Revolution and started to change: the liberals, however, were in general not at the front of change, while the conservatives were more traditional and some of the Great Powers, like Russia, strongly opposed the Greek Revolution. Revolutionary initiative seems to have been identified conceptually with the youth without taking into account the real ages of the social actors.

----

23   Deligiannis 2005, vol. 1, pp. 21, 89. It seems that this particular school was established by the first Deligiannis family, at the end of the seventeenth century. See Liata 1992, p. 18.
24   Iliou 1997, pp. 54–5.
25   Kremmydas 1977; Karageorgiou-Kourtzi 2010.
26   Trikoupis 1978, vol. 1, p. 76.

Looking at the divergences in the official separation of age groups (childhood, youth, middle age and old age) and their terminology, M. Tomara-Sideri and N. Sideris lay down, in their relevant study, the concept of youth in the nineteenth century:

> ... youth existed neither as a biological category nor as a single and constant social or intellectual category ... Inter-generational legitimacy, as well as control of sexual activities before establishing bonds of affinity, dependence on institutions and the role of potential parental substitute: these were fragments of the life of young people defining the status of youth in this society.[27]

During the Revolution, youth emerged as a problematic condition, for some only, and regardless of a person's age. Youth was ascribed recklessness (i.e. rebelliousness) and a way of dealing with misfortunes that lacked composure (i.e. the demand for a better life). When the Greek Revolution broke out, Alexander I, the Russian tsar, expelled Alexandros Hypsilantis from his service and the Russian territory, and he declared that Hypsilantis's movement was the 'outcome of a trendy spirit of disorder and of the inexperience and naivety of his young age'.[28] In a letter dated 14 March 1821 and addressed to Hypsilantis on behalf of the Tsar, Ioannis Kapodistrias wrote: 'The emperor never thought that you could be possibly carried away by that spirit of vertigo that makes people of our century go out of control, seeking to obtain goods by forgetting their utmost duties, where it is not possible to acquire them unless through strict adherence to religious and moral stipulations'.[29]

Ioannis Philimon notes that some people held the belief that the movement of Alexandros Hypsilantis (b. 1792) against Ottoman rule was due to an 'extreme ambition' and to his desire, 'specific to his young spirit', to take vengeance for his grandfather's death and the ensuing ruin of his family estate.[30]

'Skoufas! You are young': this is how Anthimos Gazis responded when he diplomatically turned down Nikolaos Skoufas's proposals for the Friendly Society, saying 'I do not agree with them but neither do I oppose them'.[31] Born in 1779, Skoufas was fifteen years younger than Gazis. Adamantios Korais expressed his scepticism about the early timing of the Greek Revolution, advocating always

---

27   Tomara-Sideri and Sideris 1986, pp. 212–13.
28   Trikoupis 1978, vol. 1, p. 101.
29   See the letter in Spiliadis 2007, vol. 1, pp. 44–6.
30   Philimon 1834, p. 247.
31   Philimon 1834, pp. 155–6.

the issue of education. He believed that the Greek Revolution should take place in the 1850s, when students would be older – thirty to forty years of age or more – and when they would have drawn on the lessons of what was happening in Europe and so have the power to bring down the factions.[32]

The ideological interactions and relations between radicals and liberals shaped the dialectical development of the Greek Revolution. During the Revolution, the notables of the Peloponnese acquired new skills in the emerging political scene, had new ambitions and forged new alliances. At the same time, they remained firm on their long-held beliefs: politicians against military men, demarcated regions and autonomous local systems as opposed to central government. All of these objections had to be overcome in order to achieve the formation of a Greek State, and they were ultimately overcome amid various political conflicts and interests which led to the civil wars (1823–5) during the Revolution.

The intellectual tools used for this transition from tradition to modernism concerned the end of Ottoman rule and the shift of the Greek society toward Western-European standards. During the nineteenth century, the age of Romanticism[33] and nationalism, it was the progressive beliefs that helped shape the diversity of young people, which gave priority to the emergence of the free citizen as a 'sprout' of the ideas of Enlightenment in education[34] and war as an ideal of Freedom. The motto of the Friendly Society, 'Freedom or Death',[35] emphasises the definitive rejection of everything stood for

---

32   Politis 2008, pp. 244–5.

33   Ever since the Industrial and the French revolutions established urbanism in Europe, Romanticism was the ideological and artistic movement that stood against it – the only movement that benefited young people considerably, largely due to the currently so-called *generation gap*. 'There is, of course, nothing universal in this revolt of the young against their elders. It was itself a reflection of the society created by the double revolution' (Hobsbawm 1996, pp. 365–6). When Fernand Braudel referred to the period of economic recession throughout Europe (1817–52), which does not explain *romantic angst* alone, he noted that 'Every generation, at all events, likes to contradict its predecessor; and its successor will do the same and more. So there is likely to be a perpetual swing of the pendulum between classicism and romanticism (or baroque, as Eugenio d'Ors called it), between cool intelligence and warm, troubled emotion – often in striking contrast' (Braudel 2017, p. 81).

34   The Enlightenment persisted in sciences and education during the nineteenth-century Europe. 'If something was lost is the omnipotence of sound discourse, its dominance over the intellectual edifice' (Politis 2009, pp. 11–12).

35   For the conceptualisations of the motto 'Freedom or Death' and its uses in historiography, see Theotokas 1992, pp. 363–5.

under Ottoman rule and the ambition for an end to moral, religious and economic suppression under the sultans. In the new world established through the Revolution, in which the new generation was now playing the leading part, Western lifestyle started spreading to the towns with modern perceptions and agents of the new cultural trends. 'Everything is new', Panagiotis Soutsos (1806–68) wrote when commenting on the unprecedented changes in his novel *Leander*, published in 1834: 'A new generation succeeds the old one; a new world of things, ideas, morals, customs, garments enters slowly from the doors of Greece, and tacitly sits on the ruins of the old world, while Greece is similar to a deer thirsty for lights and modernity'.[36]

Bibliography

Apostolopoulos, Dimitrios G. 1989, *Η Γαλλική Επανάσταση στην τουρκοκρατούμενη ελληνική κοινωνία. Αντιδράσεις στα 1798* [*The French Revolution in the Greek society under Ottoman rule*], Athens: Αθηνά.

Braudel, Fernand 2017, *Γραμματική των πολιτισμών* [*Grammar of Civilisations*], Athens: Μορφωτικό Ίδρυμα Εθνικής Τραπέζης.

Deligiannis, Kanellos 2005 [1957], *Απομνημονεύματα* [*Memoirs*], 3 Volumes, Athens:

Droulia, Loukia 1969, 'Η οικογένεια Ζαΐμη ως τα 1840, Αθησαύριστα κείμενα' ['The Zaimis family until 1840. Uknown sources'], *Επετηρίς των Καλαβρύτων*, 1: 61–76.

Georgieva, Gergana 2007, 'Administrative structure and government of Rumelia in the late eighteenth and early nineteenth centuries: the functions and activities of the *vali* of Rumelia', in *Ottoman rule and the Balkans, 1760–1850: Conflict, Transformation, Adaptation*, edited by Antonis Anastasopoulos and Elias Kolovos, Rethymno: Department of History and Archaeology, University of Crete.

Hobsbawm, Eric 1996 [1962], *The Age of Revolution, 1789–1848*, New York: Vintage Books.

Holland, Henri 1815, *Travels in the Ionian isles, Albania, Thessaly, Macedonia, &c. during the years 1812 and 1813*, London: Longman, Hurst, Rees, Orme, and Brown.

Ilıcak, H. Şükrü 2011, *A Radical Rethinking of Empire: Ottoman State and Society during the Greek War of Independence (1821–1826)*, Ph.D. Dissertation, Harvard University.

Iliou, Philippos 1997, *Ελληνική βιβλιογραφία του 19ου αιώνα. Βιβλία, φυλλάδια* [*Greek bibliography of the nineteenth century. Books and pamphlets*], vol. I: *1801–1818*, Athens: Benaki Museum.

Iliou, Philippos 2003, 'Νεοελληνικός Διαφωτισμός, Η νεωτερική πρόκληση' ['Neohellenic Enlightenment: The challenge of modernity'], in *Ιστορία του Νέου Ελληνισμού 1770–*

---

36 Soutsos 1834, pp. 69–70.

2000 [*History of Modern Hellenism 1770–2002*], vol. 2, edited by Vassilis Panagioto-poulos, Athens: Τα Νέα.

Kabouroglou, Dimitrios 1916, *Μελέτη περί του βίου και της δράσεως του παλαιών Πατρών Γερ-μανού 1771–1826* [*Study of the life and action of Germanos of Palaia Patras 1771–1826*], Athens: Π.Δ. Σακελλαρίου.

Karageorgou-Kourtzi, Olga 2010, *Οικονομικές και κοινωνικές συνθήκες στη βόρεια Πελοπόν-νησο την εικοσαετία 1800–1820 (Με βάση το Αρχείο της Οικογένειας Περούκα του Άργους)* [*Economic and social conditions in the northern Peloponnese between 1800–1820*], Pat-ras: Σύλλογος Αργείων 'Ο Δαναός'.

Kitromilidis, Paschalis 2000, *Η Γαλλική Επανάσταση και η νοτιοανατολική Ευρώπη* [*The French Revolution and Southeastern Europe*], Athens: Πορεία.

Kolokotronis, Theodoros K. 1846, *Διήγησις συμβάντων της ελληνικής φυλής από τα 1770 έως τα 1836* [*Account of events concerning the Greek people from 1770 until 1836*], Athens: Χ. Νικολαΐδης Φιλαδελφεύς.

Kremmydas, Vassilis 1977, 'Η οικονομική κρίση στον ελλαδικό χώρο στις αρχές του 19ου αιώνα και οι επιπτώσεις της στην Επανάσταση του 1821' ['The economic crisis in the Greek lands at the begginings of the nineteenth century and its effects on the revolution of 1821'], *Μνήμων*, 6: 16–33.

Laiou, Sophia and Marinos Sarigiannis 2019, *Οθωμανικές αφηγήσεις για την Ελληνική Επα-νάσταση: από τον Γιουσούφ Μπέη στον Αχμέτ Τζεβντέτ Πασά* [*Ottoman narratives on the Greek Revolution: From Yusuf Bey to Ahmed Cevdet Pasha*], Athens: National Hellenic Research Foundation.

Liata, Eftychia 1992, *Αρχεία οικογένειας Δεληγιάννη, Γενικό ευρετήριο* [*Archive of Deligiannis Family, General Index*], Athens: Εταιρία των Φίλων του Λαού.

Palaion Patron Germanos 1900 [1837], *Απομνημονεύματα* [*Memoirs*], Athens: Τυπογρα-φείο Σπύρου Τσαγγάρη.

Papatsonis, Panagiotis 1960, *Απομνημονεύματα από των χρόνων της Τουρκοκρατίας μέχρι της βασιλείας Γεωργίου Α΄* [*Memoirs from the Tourkokratia until King George 1*], Athens: Εθνικό Τυπογραφείο.

Philimon, Ioannis 1834, *Δοκίμιον ιστορικόν περί της Φιλικής Εταιρίας* [*Historical Essay con-cerning the Friendly Society*], Nafplio: Θ. Κονταξής και Ν. Λουλάκης.

Philimon, Ioannis 1859–61, *Δοκίμιον Ιστορικόν περί της Ελληνικής Επαναστάσεως* [*Historical Essay concerning the Greek revolution*], 4 Volumes, Athens: Π. Σούτσας και Α. Κτε-νάς.

Phrantzis, Amvrosios 1839, *Επιτομή της ιστορίας της αναγεννηθείσης Ελλάδος* [*Compendium of the history of resurrected Greece*], 4 Volumes, Athens: Βιτώρια.

Politis, Alexis 2008, '"Αν ήρχιζε μετά είκοσι χρόνους …". Ο Κοραής, οι κοινωνικές ιδέες του Διαφωτισμού και η Ελληνική Επανάσταση' ['"If only twenty years later …" Korais, the social ideas of the Englihgtenment and the Greek Revolution'], *Ερανιστής*, 26: 241–254.

Politis, Alexis 2009, *Ρομαντικά χρόνια. Ιδεολογίες και Νοοτροπίες στην Ελλάδα του 1830–1880* [*Romantic years. Ideologies and Mentalities in Greece between 1830–1880*], Athens: Εταιρία Μελέτης Νέου Ελληνισμού – Μνήμων.

Rotzokos, Nikos 2007, *Εθναφύπνιση και εθνογένεση. Ορλωφικά και ελληνική ιστοριογραφία* [*National awakening and nation building: The Orlov rebellion in Greek historiography*], Athens: Βιβλιόραμα.

Sarris, Neoklis 1993, *Προεπαναστατική Ελλάδα και οσμανικό κράτος: Από το χειρόγραφο του Σουλεϋμάν Πενάχ εφέντη του Μοραΐτη (1785)* [*Greece before the revolution and the Ottoman state: excerpts from the manuscript of the Moreot Yusuf Efendi (1785)*], Athens: Ηρόδοτος.

Soutsos, Panagiotis 1834, *Λέανδρος* [*Leander*], Nafplio: K. Τόμπρας και K. Ιωαννίδης.

Spiliadis, Nikolaos 2007 [1851–57], *Απομνημονεύματα ήτοι Ιστορία της επαναστάσεως των Ελλήνων* [*Memoirs, or history of the revolution of the Greeks*], 6 Volumes, Athens: Ινστιτούτο Ανάπτυξης Χαρίλαος Τρικούπης.

Stamatopoulos, Dimitrios 1997, 'Κομματικές φατρίες στην προεπαναστατική Πελοπόννησο (1807–1816): Ο ρόλος των 'Τουρκαλβανών' του Λάλα ως παράγοντας πολιτικής διαφοροποίησης' ['Factions in the Peloponnese (1807–1816): The role of the Muslim Albanians of Lala in the political game], *Ίστωρ*, 10: 185–233.

Theotokas, Nikos 1992, 'Παράδοση και νεοτερικότητα: Σχόλια για το 'Εικοσιένα'' ['Tradition and modernity: Comments on the 1821'], *Τα Ιστορικά*, 17: 345–70.

Tomara-Sideri, Matoula and Nikos Sideris 1986, *Συγκρότηση και διαδοχή των γενεών στην Ελλάδα του 19ου αιώνα: Η δημογραφική τύχη της νεότητας* [*Formation and succession of generations in Greece during the nineteenth century: the demographic fate of the youth*], Athens: Ιστορικό Αρχείο Ελληνικής Νεολαίας.

Trikoupis, Spyridon 1978 [1857], *Ιστορία της Ελληνικής Επαναστάσεως* [*History of the Greek Revolution*], 4 Volumes, Athens: Γιοβάνης.

Tzakis, Dionysis 2015, 'Η εφορία της Φιλικής Εταιρείας στην Πελοπόννησο. Σκέψεις για τη συμμετοχή των τοπικών ηγετικών ομάδων στο εθνικό κίνημα' ['The Ephorate of the Friendly Society in the Peloponnese. Thougts on the participation of the local notables in the national movement'], *Ιόνιος Λόγος*, 5: 104–10.

Vournas, Tassos (ed.) 1974, *Ταξίδι του Δήμου και του Νικολό Στεφανόπολι στην Ελλάδα κατά τα χρόνια 1797 και 1798 (Μάνη-Ήπειρος)* [*Itinerary of Dimos and Nicolo Stephanopoli in Greece in 1797 and 1798 (Mani-Epirus)*], Athens: Αφοί Τολίδη.

Yaycıoğlu, Ali 2016, *Partners of the Empire: The Crisis of the Ottoman Order in the Age of Revolutions*, Stanford: Stanford University Press.

CHAPTER 6

Alliances, Factions and Political Practices of the Moreot Notables before and during the Greek Revolution

The Cases of the Families Kanakaris-Roufos, Peroukas and Charalambis

Dimitris Bacharas

The Greek Revolution was an extraordinary event in the years of peace that the Holy Alliance was trying to establish in Europe after Napoleon. Even more surprising was the revolutionaries' final success, managing to implicate the Russian Empire, Great Britain and France in their cause. The involvement of these powers eventually led to the declaration of the Greek Independence in 1830, an outcome indebted to a great number of factors: the pre-revolutionary organisation of the Greeks, i.e. the Friendly Society [Gk. *Philiki Hetaireia*]; the Greek notables; the Phanariots; the Greek Orthodox Church; the chief-captains [*klephts* and *armatoloi*]; the Greek Enlightenment; and last, but not least, the altered power relations between European states and the Ottoman Empire during the 1820s and the search for diplomatic opportunities on a global scale by some of the most important ones. All these factors together contributed somehow to the outbreak of the Greek Revolution as well as to its successful conclusion.

This chapter does not aim to rewrite the history of the Greek War of Independence from its very beginning. It will rather explore the course of a particular group of notables and the important role they played in the Greek Revolution, which has been underestimated and to this day has not received enough scholarly attention. Indeed, the notables of the Peloponnese played a crucial role in shaping the course of the Revolution while also having been accused many times of self-interests and intrigues against those rising in power.[1] In this context, to examine one such group will allow us to better understand their historical role, revealing a much more complicated framework of alliances, bonds and political and social networks pre-dating the Greek Revolution, highlighting

---

1   See, for example, Spiliadis 1851–57; Photakos [Photios Chrysanthopoulos] 1858.

the ways in which such alliances continued to act and transform in the wake of the Revolution and after the emergence of new players and powers.

The group of notables under consideration in this chapter consists of the families Kanakaris-Roufos, Peroukas and Charalambis. Given that family history in Greece – especially well-documented biographies[2] – is an under-researched field,[3] the focus on the above families, documented on an economic and social basis, will allow a better understanding of their action, their alliances and their claims for power, as well as their participation in different administrative and political institutions during the early years of the Revolution. This course not only involved allies but also enemies and enemy alliances, though the alternation of alliances between people and families was not rare at that time.

Before studying the above-mentioned notables as a group, it is important to introduce the main characters of each family. The Kanakaris-Roufos family was represented by Athanasios Kanakaris, notable of Patras [Palaiai Patrai], *vekil* [deputy] of the Peloponnese in Istanbul and Vice President of the Greek Executive elected in the First National Assembly at Epidavros in January 1822. The same family was also represented by Benizelos Roufos, son of Athanasios, notable of Patras, member of the First National Assemblies and Prefect of Elis, Syros and Western Continental Greece during the administration of Ioannis Kapodistrias; later, he became mayor of Patras and, in 1863, Prime Minister of Greece.[4] The family of Peroukas was represented by Ioannis Peroukas, notable of Argos; Charalambos Peroukas, merchant in Patras and notable of Argos; and Dimitrios Peroukas, *vekil* [deputy] in Istanbul.[5] The family of Charalambis was represented by Sotiris Charalambis, notable of Kalavryta, and Spyros Char-

---

2   The lack of valuable works in Greek historiography is more than evident, with the exception of some biographies, such as Dafnis 1970 and, more recently, Theodoridis 2012; Christopoulou 2017; Tricha 2016 and Tricha 2019. On the importance of the biography, see Dimaras 1977. For the return of the biography in historical studies after the '90s, see Dosse 2005; Meister 2017; Margadant 1996, pp. 1045–58.

3   For some examples of family history concerning this period, see Vogli 2005; Karageorgou-Kourtzi 2010.

4   Athanasios Kanakaris was the son of Benizelos Roufos and Angeliki Kanakari. According to the deal between the two families, Athanasios had to preserve the surname Kanakaris along with his father's surname Roufos. Athanasios opted to keep Kanakaris only during the years of the Revolution, as the surname Roufos revealed his Italian roots and a Catholic faith during times when Orthodoxy and Greekness had to be frontally projected. For more detail, see Bacharas 2020.

5   For the Peroukas family, see in detail Karageorgou-Kourtzi 2010.

alambis, member of the Friendly Society with political activity in lower posts during the years of the Revolution.[6]

The history of the alliance among these families began during the 1810s, when the Pasha of the Morea (Peloponnese) was Veli, son of the powerful Ali Pasha of Ioannina. At that time, the two *factions*[7] that dominated the political scene of the Peloponnese were concentrated around two families: the Deligiannis and Londos families.[8] The families of Kanakaris-Roufos and Peroukas participated in the Deligiannis' faction. Although the two factions had collaborated in order to bring Veli as Pasha of the Morea, a deep-seated antagonism existed around the control of economic resources (rent of tax incomes, lands, trade) and appointments in the local Ottoman administration (of Pashas, Dragomans and *Kadı*s). Both factions had their pressure levers locally but mainly in Istanbul. However, up until 1811–2 they had managed to co-exist without further friction between them. The Russo-Ottoman War that had begun in 1806 disturbed this seeming calmness. Veli Pasha was called to help at the front, and, as a result, he started a race of tax collection in order to support his military campaign, which heavily burdened the people of the Peloponnese and their local masters, both Christians and Muslims (notables and Aghas).[9] Thus, the latter formed an unofficial alliance in order to drive away Veli Pasha, devising different ways of action.[10] One of these actions was to address Napoleon for help in establishing an autonomous state in the Peloponnese under his sovereignty.[11] Nevertheless, the eldest and leader of one of the two factions, Sotirios Londos, was an old

---

6   See *Μεγάλη ελληνική εγκυκλοπαίδεια*, 24 Volumes, 1927–34. No research is yet published on the Charalambis family.

7   For the use of the term *factions*, see Petropulos 1968, pp. 62–5.

8   For the antagonism between these two factions, there is extensive but not exhaustive literature. See the major studies by Sakellariou 2012; Hering 2004; Vlachogiannis 1935; Photopoulos 2005; Pylia 2004.

9   Nevertheless, the Muslim *ağa*s of Peloponnese were very dissatisfied with Veli Pasha even before 1811, for since his arrival to Tripoli he openly proclaimed his favour of the Christian notables, conceding them extensive privileges, whereas he expressed contempt for the *ağa*s. See Deligiannis 1957, vol. 1, pp. 47–8; Vlachogiannis 1935, pp. 184–5.

10   For the 'Greek-Turkish company', see Karageorgou-Kourtzi 2010, p. 39. Gritsopoulos dates the negotiations between the *ağa*s and the notables to 1811, when Veli Pasha was abroad for the war, something also suggested by Vlachoyannis; see Gritsopoulos 1976, vol. I, p. 458; Vlachogiannis 1935, pp. 185–6.

11   'The Muslims and the Christians sworn in the Quran and the Gospel and signed an agreement with fearsome oaths that hereafter they will all be considered as brothers etc' (Deligiannis 1957, vol. I, pp. 50–1). The plan was to ask Napoleon for 15,000 troops and seven or eight battleships in order to conquer the fortresses of Peloponnese and drive away Veli Pasha. Then, they would establish a new autonomous state in the Peloponnese and the islands nearby, in which both Christians and Muslims would be equal. The agreement

friend of Veli Pasha and his father Ali. Londos thus opted to betray the secret alliance to Veli Pasha,[12] who imprisoned members of the Deligiannis faction, although he spared the eldest, Ioannis Deligiannis. In the meantime, the Deligiannis faction had already sent the *vekils* Athanassios Kanakaris, Anagnostis Deligiannis and Papalexis Oikonomou to Istanbul to find political support and leverage to drive Veli Pasha away from his post; in this they were helped by several Muslim Aghas, such as Yusuf Tsaparas and Yakub Agha.[13] The *vekils* approached the sister of Sultan Selim III, Beyhan Sultan, with whom they were closely connected,[14] the Grand Vizier and Halet Efendi, the powerful advisor of Sultan Mahmud II.[15] Their attempts were successful, managing to persuade the Sultan to send a special state commissioner to the Peloponnese to investigate possible irregularities in Veli Pasha's administration. As a result, the Moreot Yusuf Agâh Efendi[16] was sent by mid-1812 to Tripolitsa [mod. Tripoli], where he exposed a series of financial transgressions by Veli Pasha, who was finally driven away from the Peloponnese.[17] Seyyid Ahmed Pasha of İç İl [or Sürücü], who came in Veli Pasha's place[18] and was connected to the Deligiannis faction, as an act of repayment for his appointment to the Peloponnese, ordered

---

was finally delivered to Giannis Deligiannis for safekeeping. For an extensive analysis of the episode, see Vernikos 1969–70, pp. 175–86.

12   Kanellos Deligiannis in his memoirs (1957, p. 57) attributes the betrayal to personal disputes between Sotiris Londos and Giannis Deligiaannis. Obviously, the reasons for Londos's betrayal were not only related to his friendship with Ali and Veli Pashas, nor only to personal disputes, but also to his ambition to occupy the dominant place in the area at the expense of the Deligiannis faction.

13   Vlachogiannis 1935, p. 186.

14   The Deligiannis faction was administrating her land properties in the Peloponnese (which were enormous) and, in return, she was their protector and pressure lever inside the court. Commissioners of Beyhan Sultan in the Peloponnese and responsible for the collection of her incomes, as well as for the appointment of caretakers and stewards among others in her lands, were Deligiannis, Papalexis, and Papatsonis. See Deligiannis 1957, vol. I, p. 58. For the land properties of Beyhan Sultan, see Stamatopoulos 2007, p. 155.

15   Mehmet Sait Halet Efendi (1761–1822) was an Ottoman diplomat and politician with enormous power in the Sublime Porte who has often been depicted 'as master puppeteer, pulling the strings of power behind the scenes of the Ottoman court'. From 1803 to 1806, he was ambassador in Napoleonean Paris. During the 1810s he became the Inner Minister of Sultan Mahmud II. His network of political influence extended from members of the imperial bureaucracy, the Bektashi and the Mevlevi dervish orders, to the eminent powers Ali Pasha of Janina and Mehmet Ali Pasha in Egypt. Philliou 2010, pp. 54–5; Aksan 2007, p. 286.

16   Yusuf Agâh Efendi (1744–1824) was the first permanent ambassador of the Ottoman Empire in England during the eighteenth century. See Aracı 2013.

17   Vlachogiannis 1935, p. 186; Şânî-zâde Mehmed 'Atâ'ullah Efendi 2008, pp. 535–6.

18   For his appointment on January 1811, see Şânî-zâde Mehmed 'Atâ'ullah Efendi 2008, p. 434.

the decapitation of Sotirakis Londos, the leader of the Londos-Zaimis alliance. Their rival faction being suppressed, the Deligiannis faction prospered during the following years;[19] evidently, the families of Kanakaris-Roufos, Peroukas and Charalambis were included as well. Also prosperous were the powerful Aghas that collaborated with the faction: Arnavudoğlu, Şeyh Necib, Defter Kethüda, Kâmil Bey and İnce Bey.[20] However, the latter were mainly protecting their own interests and not permanent allies of the Deligiannis faction. As a result, three years later, in 1815, when the circumstances of power and politics had changed, some of them changed sides, collaborating with the Londos faction; through their leverage in the Sublime Porte they managed to drive away Seyyid Ahmed Pasha of İç İl. The change of political power relations in the Sublime Porte during that time played a crucial role to that aim. The appointment of Mehmed Emin Rauf Pasha as new Grand Vizier in 1815 was of high relevance to Deligiannis' influence in the Sublime Porte, as the former was a major rival of Halet Efendi and Beyhan Sultan.[21] In December 1815, Mehmed Emin Rauf replaced his opponents' favourite, Seyyid Ahmed Pasha of İç İl, with his friend Şakir Ahmed as Pasha of the Morea.[22] Şakir Ahmed was inevitably approached by the Muslim Aghas, seeking good relations with the Sublime Porte, as well as by the Londos faction, with whom the Aghas collaborated hereafter. Aiming to clearly show his allegiance, Şakir Ahmed's first act was to decapitate the head of the opposite faction, Giannis Deligiannis, and imprison Athanasios Kanakaris and Nikolaos Peroukas (February 1816).[23]

It seems that Kanakaris was at that time a crucial member of the Deligiannis faction. Not only had he played a major role as *vekil* in order to machinate the removal of Veli Pasha in 1812,[24] but he was also the first of the faction to be imprisoned in 1816. In the meantime, it should be noted that the power of

---

19 As Vlachogiannis commented, 'the Deligiannis faction will joy' (1935, p. 192).
20 In fact, Vlachogiannis seems to support, based on a manuscript from the Petmezas family archive, that it was during these years that the two factions were divided into two distinct camps: one consisting of the families of Londos [Vostiça, mod. Aigeio], Zaimis [Kalavryta], Sisinis [Elia], Papaphotopoulos [Arcadia], Kopanitsas [Mystras], Karamanos [Hagios Petros]; the other consisting of the families of Deligiannis [Karytaina], Kanakaris [Patras], Charalambis [Kalavryta], Papalexis [Andritsaina], Kougias [Tripoliça] and Notaras [Corinth]. See Vlachogiannis 1935.
21 Stamatopoulos 2007, p. 157.
22 Ibid. See also Vlachogiannis 1935, p. 193.
23 For the imprisonment of Nikolaos Peroukas, father of the Peroukas brothers, see the unpublished letters of the *vekil* Dimitrios Peroukas dated 3 March 1816 and 16 June 1816, in the Peroukas Archive in the Historical and Ethnological Society of Greece.
24 In 1812, Spiliadis referred to Kanakaris as the 'vice-president' of the faction, without, however, mentioning what that title meant; this is something that Vlachogiannis, too,

the Peroukas family was also growing, and it is no coincidence that Dimitrios Peroukas was appointed *vekil* in Istanbul alongside Kanakaris.[25] Hence, when Kanakaris escaped from prison, he met with Peroukas along with Meletopoulos in Istanbul to orchestrate one more time the removal of the Pasha from the Peloponnese.

However, this would be the final act of support for the Deligiannis family. Kanakaris and Peroukas spent more than a year (1816–17) gathering the necessary documents and pulling the right strings in the Sublime Porte to remove the accusations against the entire Deligiannis family, spending enormous sums of money in that aim.[26] It seems that this intense effort exhausted them both financially and morally.[27] Thus, from that moment onwards, Kanakaris and Peroukas went on to follow their own paths. Alongside them came Sotiris Charalambis, a most powerful notable of Kalavryta – probably even more so than Zaimis, who has often been considered wrongfully as the only leader in the *kaza*.[28] Charalambis was the first to sign an agreement of unity [Gk. *hyposchet-*

---

troubles with a question mark (?). See Spiliadis 1851–7, vol. 1, pp. 372–3; Vlachogiannis 1935, p. 186.

25   For the appointment of D. Peroukas as *vekil*, see Stamatopoulos 2007, p. 152.

26   It seems that once again they used the powerful Halet Efendi and Beyhan Sultan, who waited for an opportunity to show their power over the rival Grand Vizier Mehmed Emin Rauf Pasha. Since Şakir Ahmed was a personal friend of Mehmed, the machinations to overthrow him could be considered as an act of political significance. The removal of Mehmed from his place in 1818 cannot be considered as irrelevant to the acts of Halet nor to the dismissal of Şakir Ahmed in 1817. The help of Halet Efendi to the *vekil*s during that time is testified to by Vlachogiannis (1935, pp. 287–8), based on information in a manuscript from the Papatsonis family archive.

27   It is more than evident in the correspondence between the Peroukas brothers during that time. In many letters of Dimitrios from Istanbul (Peroukas family archive, Historical and Ethnological Society of Greece), it was mentioned that he and Kanakaris almost starved in order to do the necessary movements. See, for example, letters to Charalambos Peroukas, dated 28 June 1816 and 16 July 1816 The situation worsened after a summer of plague in Istanbul; see Dimitrios to Charalambos Peroukas, 1 September 1816.

28   Until today, Charalambis has been underestimated in the literature. He controlled two of the four regions [Gk. *semtia*, from Ott. Turk *semt*] of the *kaza* of Kalavryta [Katsana and Chassia], whereas Zaimis had only one under his control [Nezera]. At the same time, Charalambis's network extended from Kalavryta to Patras [Kanakaris] to Argos [Peroukas], and of course to the powerful Halet Efendi and Beyhan Sultan in Istanbul through his liaison with Deligiannis and the above-mentioned families. Nevertheless, Zaimis occupied a dominant place in the historiography of the nineteenth century as the leading notable of Kalavryta, alongside Londos of Vostiça, mainly due to the multiple published archival documents (letters, documents, memoirs) in which he is mentioned, as well as to his projection as a leading figure by major nineteenth-century writers such as Spyridon Trikoupis. For the *semtia* that Charalambis and Zaimis controlled, see Chrysanthopoulos [Photakos]

ikon] between the notables in April 1816.[29] Although this agreement has been perceived as a shared understanding of all Greek notables that fighting should stop,[30] in reality it applied only to a specific number of them;[31] it remains unclear whether they acted on their own will, or whether they still represented the older two factions of Deligiannis and Londos. On the one hand, it is difficult to argue persuasively that the older factions had ceased to exist or that the new powers had already formed a new open alliance. One could argue that drago-man Theodosios,[32] Charalambis, Kougias and Peroukas, who signed first, rep-resented the Deligiannis' collapsing faction;[33] the absence of the Deligiannis brothers was due to their persecution by Şakir Ahmed at that time. During this time, Kanakaris and Peroukas where in Istanbul trying to overthrow Şakir.[34] On the other hand, Peroukas and Charalambis had in that very same year founded a commercial company.[35] Charalambos Peroukas had mutual interests with Kanakaris in Patras, where he was active. It is also worth noting that both fam-ilies had managed to infiltrate the Notaras family. Similar arguments could be used for the opposite faction as well. However, Londos's absence from the peace alliance leaves a serious issue open.

In any case, as it has been already argued by some researchers, the Per-oukas family, as well as Charalambis, must have gained power during that timewho signed first the *hyposchetikon*.[36] At the same time, bonds or common interests and understanding that were built around the old Giannis Deligian-nis seem to have collapsed after his execution. His sons did not manage to gain the trust of the two *vekil*s, Peroukas and Kanakaris. Both of them had been

1888, p. 22. For the villages of each *semti*, see Sakellariou 2012, pp. 147–8. For the oversig-nificance that Trikoupis attributes to Zaimis and Deligiannis's consideration of Zaimis's real power, see Rotzokos 1996, p. 60.

29   The original copy of the *hyposchetikon* was found in the Charalambis archive, Library of the Greek Parliament, published after being deciphered by Konomos 1963–8, pp. 193–4. Vlachogiannis had first noticed a copy of the *hyposchetikon* in the newspaper *Aion*, 27 April 1884, which he published in his book *Κλέφτες* (1935, pp. 194, 289).

30   See, for example, Nikolaou 2010, p. 162.

31   As Vlachogiannis wisely remarked, 'it is odd how few were the signatures' (1935, p. 194).

32   For the role of Theodossios alongside Deligiannis, see Pylia 2007, p. 143; Pylia 2004, pp. 360–63; Stamatopoulos 2007, p. 152.

33   Whereas the others would be Andreas Zaimis, Anagnostis Papazoglou and Panagiotakis Zarifopoulos, who signed the agreement as well.

34   Similar arguments could be used for the opposite faction, Londos's absence being stun-ning but possibly explained by the presence of Papazoglou and Zarifopoulos.

35   Karageorgou-Kourtzi 2010, p. 98.

36   John Alexander has suggested that the true winners of the *hyposchetikon* were the Per-oukas and Charalambis families (1974–5, pp. 484–5). The same argument is adopted by Stamatopoulos 2007 and Sarafis 2017, p. 57.

imprisoned or persecuted to protect Deligiannis's interests, spending enormous sums of money, without seeing any reimbursement from Kanellos or his
brother Theodorakis Deligiannnis.[37] In this context, a new alliance emerged
after 1817, at the same time as Şakir Ahmed was driven away by Kanakaris and
Peroukas. The two would then lead their families to gather the profits of their
exhausting fight, leaving the Deligiannis family to its fate.[38]

   This new alliance not only consisted of Kanakaris, Peroukas and Charalambis, but also of a member of the Zaimis family – Dimitris Zaimis, who had
married the sister of the Peroukas brothers, Evdokia, and changed sides in
1817.[39] At the same time, the group of Kanakaris-Peroukas-Charalambis had a
most powerful ally: Kâmil Bey, the Agha rich in properties and political power,
who had close relations with the Peroukas family at least since 1815[40] and was a
sworn enemy of the Deligiannis family.[41] In 1818, Peroukas and Kanakaris along
with Kâmil Bey tried to drive Anagnostis and Nikolakis Deligiannis away from

---

37   It is not by accident that Kanellos Deligiannis tries in his memoirs to lessen the contribu-
     tion of Peroukas and Kanakaris in the reinstatement of his family. On p. 77, he writes that
     Kanakaris, Peroukas and Papalexis did not manage to deal with the problems, devoting
     the next two pages to showing how the outcome was a personal success of his brother
     Nikolaos Deligiannis. On p. 73, he states that the effort did not cost a lot of money [χωρίς
     δαπάνην χρημάτων πολλών]. The above references comes into clear contradiction with the
     content of the letters between Dimitrios and Charalambos Peroukas, mentioned above,
     and the testimonies from Papatsonis's archive that Vlachogiannis uses in his Κλέφτες (1935,
     pp. 287–8), where he clearly states that the vekils had spent 'too much money' [πλείστα όσα
     χρήματα] and that it was with their help that the Deligiannis brothers managed to be free
     of the accusations against them.

38   The rupture was apparent in many aspects since September 1817, when Şakir Ahmed left
     the Peloponnese. Rhigas Palamidis, a relative of the Deligiannis family, was complaining
     in a letter to Deligiannis for the 'meanness' of Peroukas, who had encroached 30 acres of
     his land. See Pylia 2004, p. 200.

39   It should be noted, however, that it was not the marriage that led D. Zaimis to the other
     side, since the marriage had taken place in 1796. It is most probable that his decision was
     related to economic reasons and to an understanding with the Peroukas family during
     those years. Finally, the fact that D. Zaimis was at that time 46 years old, quite a mature
     age, shows that it was a very well-thought decision. The defect of D. Zaimis enraged the
     rest of the family, with Andreas Zaimis referring to him as the 'warm of Kerpini' [ζωύφιον
     της Κερπινής]. See Zaimis to Londos, 27 March 1819, in Londos 1914, vol. 1.

40   The Peroukas family was in close relation to Kâmil Bey during the years before the Revolu-
     tion, as testified in the correspondence of the Peroukas brothers during that time. See the
     Peroukas correspondence between 1810–20 in the Peroukas archive, Historical and Ethno-
     logical Society of Greece. See also Sarafis 2017, p. 57, where he places the Peroukas family
     in the network of Kâmil Bey based on the tax farming system [iltizam].

41   Kanellos Deligiannis in his memoirs presents Kâmil Bey always in the worst possible ways.
     See Deligiannis 1935, passim.

their posts in Istanbul,[42] but their efforts turned against them. The Deligiannis family approached the Vizier Ali Pasha, successfully getting him to write at the Sublime Porte and recall the abdication of the two *vekil*s; they also managed to hold off Kâmil Bey from the capital of the Peloponnese Tripolitsa, enforcing him to move permanently to Corinth, his hometown.[43]

However, the first collision with the older and powerful faction of Zaimis-Londos, which would be the one to make official the existence of the new political power, took place in 1819, with the appointment of a new Dragoman in the Peloponnese, Postelnikos Samourkasis.[44] Dragoman Wallerianos, who had come in the Peloponnese in mid-1817,[45] succeeding Theodosios Michalopoulos, was clearly in collaboration with the rising Kanakaris-Peroukas-Chalarambis group of notables.[46] When he was removed by the Londos-Zaimis faction by the end of May 1819,[47] Kanakaris-Peroukas and Charalambis successfully tried to overthrow Samourkasis, replacing him with a Dragoman who would support their interests. This would be the Phanariot Stavrakis Iovikis, who was finally appointed as Dragoman in September 1819.[48] Making his appointment happen

---

42 Sarafis 2017, p. 58.

43 Deligiannis 1957, pp. 81–2. However, it must be noted that Deligiannis wrote his memoirs to reinstate his family in history, and his effort to project his family as a powerful one is more than evident. The end of the above story reads: 'and thus he [Kâmil Bey] left by the end of May and we came quits with Kâmil Bey [*Ανεχώρησε και ούτος περί τα τέλη του Μαΐου εκείθεν και ήλθομεν ίσια ίσια με τον Κιαμίλμπεην*]' – assuming, of course, that they were even in political power and machinations.

44 Specifically, Stamatopoulos has argued that it was Sotiris Kougias who wanted Postelnikos Samourkasis, since Kougias's son was to marry the daughter of Ioannis Samourkasis, but this perspective lacks the political and economic interests of Londos's faction, which probably was of higher importance. See Stamatopoulos 2007, p. 159.

45 Photopoulos 2005, p. 83.

46 Sotiris Charalambis, Andreas Notaras, Kopanitzas and other notables had asked Walerrianos to come to Peloponnese in January 1817, as Theodosios had resigned his own accord, 'by reason of age and frailty'. See Stamatopoulos 2007, p. 155 (appendix for the letter). This could be considered as another action to hold off from Deligiannis's family, which is not signing the letter, probably because of its close relation to Theodosios (see above footnote 31). For the good relations of Deligiannis and Theodosios even after the outbreak of the Revolution in 1821 see Pylia 2004, p. 363.

47 Photopoulos 2005, p. 83.

48 Ibid. It has been wrongfully suggested that Theodosios Michalopoulos returned as Dragoman for a short period of time in 1820, mainly due to a paper that has often been used by many researchers – i.e., Gritsopoulos 1974, pp. 165–71. In this paper – based on a letter from Sotirios Charalambis and Asimakis Photilas to the *vekil* Dimitrios Peroukas in September 1820 – it is suggested that the Dragoman the letter refers to was Theodosios Michalopoulos, an old friend of the Deligiannis family. However, following the letters of Stavrakis Iovikis to Andreas Londos from March to October 1820, we can affirm that at least until 23 Octo-

was not an easy task for the *vekil*s in Istanbul, A. Kanakaris and D. Peroukas. Their efforts were given away by their opponents to the Ottoman authorities in the summer of 1819. As a result, Peroukas was arrested and Kanakaris was forced to hide for a short period of time,[49] although they both managed to preserve their titles as *vekil*s of the Morea.[50] It is under this capacity that they arrived in Istanbul pressurise for the appointment of two more *vekil*s in their alliance,[51] replacing the one aligned with Londos-Zaimis families, using the need to counterweigh the appointment of Samourkassis as the Dragoman of the Morea as an argument.[52] Once again, they encountered opposition, this time voiced by the Muslim Aghas of the Londos faction.[53] In this context, achieving the appointment of Iovikis as Dragoman led to enormous sums of money being spent and a long stay in Istanbul, during which they had little means to live on.[54]

During the same time, another point of friction between the two factions emerged. Zaimis and Londos turned against Kâmil Bey, plotting his removal but finding themselves against the faction of Kanakaris-Peroukas-Charalambis. The latter informed Kâmil Bey of the plot and managed to convince their allies in the Sublime Porte to publish a *firman* for the persecution of Londos and Zaimis.[55] Indeed, this story is marked by traitors and changes of sides by faction members. Specifically, in March 1819, Ioannis Papadopoulos, a minor notable of Kalavryta who had exploited circumstances to gain his position,[56] betrayed his

ber 1820, Stavrakis Iovikis was the only Dragoman in the Morea; see Londos 1914, vol. 1, p. 118. Photopoulos who does not follow Gritsopoulos's paper, states that Stavrakis Iovikis was the last Dragoman before the outbreak of the Revolution.

49 Letter of the Bey of Patras to Halil Ağa Voyvoda and Andreas Londos, 10 July 1819, in Londos 1914, vol. 1, pp. 58–9. Cf. Photopoulos 2005, p. 68.

50 Letter of Ioannis Peroukas, 23 July 1819, in the Peroukas Archive, Historical and Ethnological Society of Greece, where he mentions that a decree was issued according to which Athanasios Kanakaris and Dimitrios Peroukas would remain at their positions as *vekil*s.

51 These two *vekil*s were Asimakis Photilas and Aggelis Meletopoulos; both inclined to the side of Peroukas-Kanakaris, although they cannot be considered in the close milieu of the faction. See Stamatopoulos 1971, vol. 1, p. 142.

52 Stamatopoulos 1971, vol. 1, p. 142.

53 Letter of Muslim Aghas to Andreas Londos, 19 May 1819, in Londos 1914, vol. 1, pp. 236–7.

54 Correspondence between Peroukas brothers in 1819, where Dimitrios from Istanbul insists on mentioning his penniless and pitiful situation, asking Charalambos to find and send him money. See the Peroukas archive, Historical and Ethnological Society of Greece.

55 Stamatopoulos 1971, vol. 1, pp. 138–41. The incident has been mentioned by Takis Kandyloros as well: συνεπεία ενεργειών του Περρούκα και του Κιαμήλ μπεη της κορίνθου εξεδόθη εν Κων/πόλη φιρμάνι περί καταδιώξεως του Ασημάκη Ζαΐμη και του Ανδρέου Λόντου, οίτινες αμέσως εκρύβησαν εις τα ορεινά χωρία των Καλαβρύτων, Kandiloros 1926, p. 289.

56 He acquired his property from an Albanian friend, Mourtokalemis, who left his spoils to him for safeguarding and who never returned to claim them. See Vlachogiannis 1935, p. 90.

allies (Kanakaris-Peroukas-Charalambis). Turning to the Londos-Zaimis faction, he reported to Zaimis the accusations that the Charalambis family had made to the Ottoman authorities – that Londos had overlooked several issues of the *kaza* of Kalavryta, bringing 'turbulences and confusion' to the population. As Papadopoulos noted: 'Charalambis was full of hatred and despise for your [Andreas Londos] kindness, and he will try worse machinations to bring disorder and confusion to the kaza' [ἔμπλεος μίσους καὶ ἀπεχθείας ἀπὸ τὴν εὐγένιάν σας κυρ ἀντρέα, καὶ ὅτι θέλει ἐπιχειρήσῃ τὰ δολιοπλόκα στρατηγήματά του νὰ ἐπιφέρῃ ταραχήν καὶ σύγχυσιν εἰς τὸν καζά σας].[57] At the same time, though, Theocharopoulos, another minor notable of Kalavryta, also changed sides, turning away from Londos to Charalambis.[58] It is on that basis that Londos and Zaimis tried to orchestrate the removal of Kâmil Bey, close collaborator of the Kanakaris-Peroukas-Charalambis faction. Informed of the plot, Charalambis wrote to Kâmil Bey, informing him of the imminent danger and urging him to write to Mustafa Efendi to issue a decree to persecute Londos and Zaimis.[59] At the same time, Dimitrakis Zaimis started an open war against his brother A. Zaimis, trying to turn the local population and authorities against him.[60] In turn, all three leading the alliance (Kanakaris-Peroukas, Charalambis) tried to orchestrate the return of Kâmil Bey to the capital of Peloponnese, Tripolitsa.[61]

---

57   Letter of Zaimis to Londos, 12 March 1819, in Londos 1914, vol. 1, pp. 35–6. In the same letter, Papadopoulos also mentioned that he was trying to find a way to move out of Kalavryta because of the betrayal

58   Bey of Pyrgos to Londos and Zaimis, 4 June 1819, reporting that he was surprised to know that Theocharopoulos had changed sides, as he'd thought of him as of 'his [Londos's] own' (Londos 1914, vol. 1, pp. 56–7). However, it is uncertain if Theocharopoulos remained on the side of Charalambis's alliance during the following years.

59   Letter of Zaimis to Londos, 27 March 1819, reporting that Charalambis was informed that Londos and Zaimis came in contact with τὸν ἐνδοξότατον πεγ' ἐφένδην καὶ λοιπούς φίλους in order to drive away Kâmil Bey, providing a lot of money [kuruş] to their men of trust ὅπως λάβωσι αὐτά οἱ φυγάδες καὶ ἀπεράσωσιν εἰς βασιλεύουσα ἵνα ἐνεργήσωσιν περί καταδρομῆς τοῦ ἐνδοξοτάτου κιαμήλ πεγ'ἐφένδη. In the same letter, Zaimis informs Londos of Charambis's actions to persecute them. See Londos 1914 vol. 1, p. 42.

60   Letter of Zaimis to Londos, 27 March 1819 in Londos 1914, op. Cit.: τὸ ζωΰφιον τῆς κερπηνῆς [Dimitris Zaimis] μετὰ τοῦ νετζίπι βοιβόνδα βεεκίλι τῶν καλαβρύτων με ἔβαλλαν τὸ κανόνι: ὁ μὲν βοϊβόνδας ἀπέστειλλεν εἰς ὅλα τὰ χωριά ὅπου δανείζομεν σαημένηδες δια ταχσίλι ἀσπρῶν πράγμα ὅπου με σηκώνει τὴν ἡσυχίαν ἀπὸ τοὺς χωριάτες, ἐρεθίζει τὸν κατή ὁ δὲ δημητράκης κινεῖ εἰς τὸ χωριῶν ἐδῶ κάτι μασκαροδουλίας δια νὰ μας δίδῃ αἰτίαν νὰ φανώμεν εἰς τι ἐναντιουμένοι καὶ νὰ μας κάμουν κανένα ἰλάμι καὶ τέλος πάντων πηγαίνουν κεντώντας δια νὰ μας ἀτημάσουν καὶ αὐτὸ θέλει καταντήσει νὰ τυπανίσω τυπανισμὸν ξύλου [...].

61   Letter of S. Charalambis to Ch. Peroukas and A. Kanakaris, 28 August 1819, in Londos 1914, vol. I.

Londos and Zaimis initially sought for help from the powerful notables of Corinth, the Notaras family, and later from the Bey of Pyrgos. However, the Notaras family refused to take their side, noting they should have gone to Tripolitsa to prove their innocence. The Bey responded that he would do his best, however without promising anything.[62] Hence, the effort was extended to other Muslim ağas as well in Phanariots with access in the Sublime Porte.[63] In this way, they managed to persecute Dimitris Peroukas and Athanassios Kanakaris in Istanbul during the summer of 1819.[64] This did not last long, though, as they were both reinstated soon after.[65]

It is evident from the above that in 1819 the alliance of Kanakaris-Peroukas-Charalambis had the upper hand, having on its side powerful allies – Christians and Muslims – establishing a network that extended from Patras-Argos-Kalavryta to Tripolitsa and Istanbul. Their achievements include the appointment of their own Dragoman in the Morea, the reinstatement of Kâmil Bey in Tripolitsa and the persecution of Londos and Zaimis. However, up until the outbreak of the Revolution, the conflict with the opposite faction manifested in different ways and intensities, up to and including assassination attempts. For instance, at separate moments in 1819, Ioannis Peroukas[66] and Charalambis[67]

---

62   Letter of Notaras family to Zaimis and Londos, 28 March 1819, in Londos 1914: *Ημείς ηκού-σαμεν ότι ο αδελφός κυρ Σωτήρης εν ω προσκλήθη δια την Τριπολιτζάν εζήτησε και τον αδελφόν κυρ ανδρέα. Διατί όμως δεν ηκολούθησεν αυτήν την συνοδίαν δεν ημπορούμεν να καταλάβωμεν. Μήπως αν επήγαινε δεν ήθελεν αποδέιξη ψευδείς τας κατά της ευγενίας σας διαβολάς; Διατί εν ω είσθε αθώοι και αμέτοχοι εις όσα λέγουν παρά τοις προύχοσι περί της ευγενίας σας να δώσητε αξίαν να πιστεύωνται οι εναντίοι; Τι να σας γράψωμεν άλλο δεν ιξεύρομεν.* See also Letter of the Bey of Pyrgos to Londos and Zaimis, 4 June 1819, in Londos 1914.

63   Letter of the Bey of Patras to Halil Ağa Voyvoda and Londos, 10 July 1819, in Londos 1914, vol. I, pp. 58–9.

64   See fn. 48 above and Giannikopoulos 2009, p. 211.

65   See fn. 49 above.

66   When he was attacked, I. Peroukas was accompanied by 11 men, two of whom were killed. Karageorgou-Kourtzi, who describes the incident in detail (2010, p. 41), attributes the attempt to Peroukas's revolutionary activity – something that was extremely unlikely to achieve its ends, considering the era and the Peroukas's position towards the outbreak of the Revolution. Giannikopoulos, who, working from the Peroukas archive, also mentions the incident (2009, p. 211), reports that Charalambos Peroukas was so shocked by the attempt against his brother that he urged Ioannis to resign from politics altogether. The same paper mentions that Ioannis Peroukas attributed the attempt against his life to jealousy of the prosperity of his family.

67   Letter of Dimitris to Charalambos Peroukas, 15 September 1819, where Dimitris mentions clearly that the assassination attempt against Sotiris Charalambis was *κίνημα ή ενέργειες των Α. Λόντου και Α. Ζαίμη.* See Peroukas archive, Historical and Ethnological Society of Greece, doc. 45812.

were ambushed but escaped death. There were also assassination attempts against the other faction; indicative is the attempt against Nikolaos Londos in April 1819 and against Grigorios Papaphotopoulos.[68] It is in this context that Sotiris Charalambis received a cryptographic notice in February 1820, warning him to be careful of assassination attempts in Tripolitsa.[69] Similarly, in October 1820 the opponents of Peroukas-Kanakaris convinced the archimandrite Papaphlessas that the faction was plotting against him, leading him to order their assassination.[70] Although the two sides, Papaphlessas and Peroukas-Kanakaris, later met and resolved the misunderstanding, the above incident reveals the magnitude of the conflict, which was not only confined in the Peloponnese but extended to Istanbul and even to the milieu of the Friendly Society.[71]

On the eve of the Greek Revolution, the alliance preserved its integrity, although new difficulties would arise during the course of the conflict. In January 1821, Kanakaris and Peroukas, unaware that he intended to behead them, responded to the call of the Sultan for the *vekil*s to present themselves in the palace. Upon finding out, they escaped death, secretly leaving the Palace and hiding for some time in Üsküdar. However, their ability to act during that time was very limited. Thus, they missed the first gathering of all sides in Vostitsa that took place at the end of January, for they remained in hiding until the beginning of April, when they finally went by boat to Hydra and then to the Peloponnese.[72] It must be noted that – even though different opinions were voiced, and at some points in a tensed manner – the meeting in Vostitsa was the first time that all sides in the power game came to a kind of understanding. It is, thus, crucial to underline this moment as symbolically denoting a ceasefire between all factions.[73] Indeed, the participation of S. Charalambis, S. Theochar-

---

68 Giannikopoulos 2009, p. 211. For the allegiance of Papaphotopoulos, notable of Arkadia [mod. Kyparrisia], to the Londos faction, see Vlachogiannis 1935, p. 192.

69 Letter to S. Charalambis on 18 February 1820, in Konomos 1963–8, pp. 195–8. The machinations of the Zaimis family in Kalavryta are also described in the same letter.

70 Philimon 1868, p. 55. The incident is mentioned again by Philimon in his *Δοκίμιον Ιστορικον περί της Φιλικής Εταιρίας* (1971, p. 197). Philimon suggests this time that Papaphlessas and others decided the assassination of Peroukas and Kanakaris because they were accused for betraying the secret of the Friendly Society.

71 For an analysis of the above incident, see Bacharas 2017, pp. 229–46.

72 Spiliadis 1851–7, vol. 1, p. 96; Deligiannis 1957, p. 132.

73 Contradicting dominant opinion about this assembly (regarding Papaphlessas versus the notables, unresolved disputes and ruptures), Dionysis Tzakis has persuasively argued that the meeting took place in Vostitsa to organise the Revolution, and that, despite the many disputes between different groups, devotion to the cause and the nation were expressed by all parts. See Tzakis 2015, pp. 108–10.

opoulos, A. Photilas, I. Papadopoulos, A. Zaimis, A. Londos, at the same table, was not commonplace, bearing in mind their above-mentioned relations up to that point.

In this sense, the Vostitsa assembly initiated a different type of struggle between the old factions, as old tools for machinations, pressure levers and plotting had changed (for instance, control of Dragomans, officials in the Sublime Porte and Pashas). In this new world, new ways of political intervention had to be found. This would become even more apparent in the assembly of Kaltezai in May 1821 – two months after the outbreak of the Revolution – aiming at founding a governmental institution for the revolutionary Greeks. With the comeback of Kanakaris and Peroukas, the alliance was regenerated. It was also supported by the powerful notable of Mani, Petro Bey Mavromichalis. On the other hand, Londos and Zaimis, who had lost power, were strongly opposed to the formation of the Peloponnesian Senate. According to Zaimis, 'the attitude and the words of mister Athanasios [Kanakaris] made us look unpleasant concerning the establishment of the Senate ... and we plotted to reverse that system'.[74] As a result, they were left out.

The question of the commander in chief of the Greek Struggle for Independence was the next one to reveal the friction between the different sides and the role of Kanakaris-Peroukas-Charalambis alliance. The latter supported Mavromichalis for the post as expected, not only because he was a recent ally but also because they had made a bad start with Dimitrios Hypsilantis upon his arrival to the Morea. Specifically, when they visited his ship, they were not cordially welcomed by Hypsilantis, who refused to get up from his chair to greet them; on the contrary, he later welcomed cheerfully, in their presence, Kolokotronis, Papaphlessas and Anagnostaras. As Spiliades noted, that once they saw that, they were afraid and became negatively predisposed against him despite the fact that shortly before they were ready to support him.[75] Even a year after

74   *Το ύφος και οι λόγοι του κυρίου Αθανασίου έκαμαν ημάς να μην φανώμεν ευχάριστοι εις την συστασιν αυτής της Γερουσίας [...] και αντιπολιτευόμεθα οργανίζοντες ίνα ανατρέψωμεν αυτό το σύστημα,* 'Σημειώσεις δια χειρός Α. Ζαίμη επί της πολιτικής μορφής του αγώνος', in *Πρακτικά Β΄ τοπικού συνεδρίου Αχαϊκών σπουδών,* Athens 1986, p. 368.

75   The full note was: *Οι πρόκριτοι της Πελοποννήσου εισήλθον εις το πλοίον, όπου ο Υψηλάντης, να τον χαιρετήσωσι και τους εδέχθη καθήμενος εις την καθέκλαν επί του καταστρώματος με πολλήν ψυχρότητα, ώστε ο Αθ. Κανακάρης υπάγει προς αυτόν με θράσος, άπτεται της δεξιάς του και τον βιάζει ούτως είπειν να εγερθή τον λέγει το κ α λ ω ς ή λ θ ε και δίδουσι προς αλλήλους τον ασπασμόν· τουτ' αυτό πράττουσι και οι λοιποί προεστώτες μετά τον Κανακάρην. Αλλ' άμα φανέντων του Κολοκοτρώνη του αρχιμαδρίτου Δικαίου του Αναγνωσταρά και άλλων υπάγει εις την υπάντησίν των και τους δέχεται πολύ φιλοφρόνως. Τούτο ιδώντες οι προεστώτες ισκιάζονται άκτοτε και διανοούνται κακά εναντίον του εν ω ήσαν προ ολίγου διατεθειμένοι να τον υποστηρίξωσι [...].* Spiliadis 1851–7, vol. I, p. 206.

this incident, Kanakaris held the worst of opinions about Hypsilantis. Telling are his words to his friend, collaborator and relative Andreas Kostakis (who was married to his sister Paraskevi Kostaki), that 'responsible for the discord of the country is Dimitrios Hypsilantis with Odysseas [Androutsos] and Theodoros Kolokotronis'.[76]

During that time, the alliance of Kanakaris-Peroukas-Charalambis extended its influence to the Aegean islands. In June, Charalambos Peroukas was elected member of the Peloponnesian Senate with the support of the notables of the island of Spetses;[77] in understanding this, one should bear in mind that Spyridon Charalambis met a warm welcome in Spetses upon bringing news from Vostitsa about the forthcoming Revolution.[78]

The strong presence of the alliance was also visible in the First National Assembly in Epidavros, which began in December 1821. In the twelve-member Committee that was formed (consisting of three members from each district), A. Kanakaris was one of the three to represent the Peloponnese. Additionally, in the subsequent formation of the Executive and Legislative bodies, Kanakaris became Vice President of the Executive while Charalambis Vice President of the Legislative. These posts, as well as all the posts assigned in Epidavros, revealed a new balance of power. New forces had also emerged: the Phanariots Mavrokordatos and Negris led the way; members of the Friendly Society were no longer so present; the chief-captains were claiming participation as well. The old alliances had not yet ceased to exist, but they followed another path, gaining new members or following new powers. In this sense, although the group of Kanakaris-Charalambis-Peroukas is separate from that of Hypsilantis, Kolokotronis and the chief-captains, we cannot identify it with other notables such as Londos and Zaimis, since the previous conflict had not ceased to exist. In addition, Kanakaris-Peroukas-Charalambis directly opposed the Mavrokordatos and Negris alliance, trying from the very beginning to undermine their power. This was first evident during the election of the President of the Executive, when Kanakaris strongly supported the candidature of the powerful notable of Hydra, Lazaros Kountouriotis, against Mavrokordatos. When that move failed, he managed to restrain the power of the latter by opposing a five-year-term presidency.[79] As a result, Mavrokordatos was elected for only one

---

76   Letter of Ath. Kanakaris to Andreas Kostakis, October 1822, in the Roufos archive (private
      collection).
77   Sarafis 2017, p. 56.
78   Spiliadis 1851–7, vol. I, p. 18.
79   Spiliadis 1851–7, vol. I, p. 274.

year as President. In this context, one could argue that the vice-presidential position was a position of power for the alliance and was not understood as a mere placement. The Legislative Body, meanwhile, was dominated by Hypsilantis and the chief captains: Hypsilantis occupied the Presidency, while Charalambis assumed the Vice Presidency.

During the following months, the opposition of the alliance between Mavrokordatos and Negris intensified, focused mainly on the issue of obtaining a loan from abroad. Kanakaris objected to both efforts of Mavrokordatos to get a loan from England or Germany. Specifically, when in 1822 the English proposed to Mavrokordatos a loan of 40 million *kuruş*, with 6 percent interest and the 'national lands' for mortgage, members of the Executive and Legislative bodies assembled and agreed with the terms. However, Kanakaris thought otherwise and stopped the procedure, arguing that the Body members were less than the required number to ratify the deal.[80] Later on, when Mavrokordatos and Negris communicated in secret with the Germans to assure a loan of eight million francs and a corps of 6,000 German soldiers to help the Greeks with their cause, Kanakaris once again stopped the negotiations. He was directly opposed to and criticised Mavrokordatos for not informing anyone before sending envoys to Europe, and he at once tried to convince the Germans that a tactical army would not be efficient for warfare against the Ottomans and nor could the Greeks feed such an army.[81]

In this chapter, I have sketched in detail the struggle for power among the notables of the Peloponnese at the period leading up to the Greek Revolution, showing the nuanced and complicated framework of bonds, alliances and political and social networks. Even though it seems that the struggle for power was overcome for the higher ideal of the Revolution, the resulting ceasefire was brief and rather more symbolic than actual. What changed, though, were the constellations of power with new players and groups of interest. The death of Kanakaris in January 1823[82] marked the end of an era for the alliance, as he had occupied a powerful position in leading the opposition to Mavrokordatos. A year later, the alliance found itself in a difficult situation, when Charalambis and Peroukas were accused for fiscal irregularities as members of the Executive

---

80   *Αλλ'ο Κανακάρης δεν το δέχεται, διατεινόμενος ότι δεν ανήκεν ειμή εις την εθνικήν συνέλευσιν ν'απο-φασίση περί αυτού, ότε Κυβέρνησις δεν υπήρχεν ειμή ψιλώ τω ονόματι, και ούτε το νομοτελεστικόν ούτε το βουλευτικόν σώμα ήτο πλήρες.* Spiliadis 1851–7, vol. I, p. 462.

81   Spiliadis 1851–7, vol. I, pp. 462–3.

82   Ibid. Not without reason, Spiliadis suspected that the death of Kanakaris was probably an assassination plotted by Mavrokordatos and Negris.

Body,[83] an incident that the sparked the official beginning of the first civil war of the Greek Revolution.

Bibliography

Aksan, Virginia 2007, *Ottoman Wars 1700–1870: An Empire Besieged*, London: Routledge.

Alexander, John C. 1974–75, 'Some aspects of the strife among the Moreot Christian Notables 1789–1816', *Επετηρίς Εταιρείας Στερεοελλαδικών Μελετών*, 5: 473–504.

Aracı, Emre 2013, *Yusuf Agah Efendi: The First Turkish Ambassador in 18th Century London*, Istanbul: Pera Müzesi Yayınları.

Bacharas, Dimitris 2017, 'Συμμαχίες, αντιμαχίες και τρόποι ένταξης των Πελοποννησίων προκρίτων στη Φιλική Εταιρεία' ['Alliances, sonflicts and ways of incorporation of the Peloponnesian notables into the Friendly Society'], in *Η Φιλική Εταιρεία, επαναστατική δράση και μυστικές εταιρείες στη νεότερη Ευρώπη* [*The Friendly Society, revolutionary action and secret societies in modern Europe*], edited by Anna Mandilara and Georgios Nikolaou, Athens: Ασίνη.

Bacharas, Dimitris 2020, *Αρχοντικές οικογένειες της Πελοποννήσου: η περίπτωση της οικογένειας Κανακάρη-Ρούφου* [*Notable families of the Peloponnese: the case of the Kanaris-Roufos family*], Athens: Εστία.

Christopoulou, Maria 2017, *Δημήτριος Γούναρης* [*Demetrios Gounaris*], Athens: Hellenic Parliament Foundation.

Chrysanthopoulos, Photios [Photakos] 1888, *Βίοι Πελοποννησίων ανδρών* [*Biographies of Peloponnesian men*], Athens: Π.Δ. Σακελλαρίου.

Dafnis, Georgios 1970, *Σοφοκλής Ελευθερίου Βενιζέλος* [*Sofocles Eleftheriou Venizelos*], Athens: Ίκαρος.

Deligiannis, Kanellos 1957, *Απομνημονεύματα* [*Memoirs*], 3 Volumes, Athens: Γ. Τσουκαλάς και Υιός.

Dimaras, Konstantinos 1989, *Νεοελληνικός Διαφωτισμός* [*Neohellenic Enlightenment*], Athens: Ερμής.

Dosse, François 2005, *Le pari biographique: Écrire une vie*, Paris: La Découverte.

Giannikopoulos, E. 2009, 'Ο Χαραλάμπης Περρούκας ως έμπορος στην Πάτρα προεπαναστατικώς' ['Charalambis Perroukas, merchant in Patras before the revolution'], in *Πρακτικά του Έκτακτου Αχαϊκού Πνευματικού Συμποσίου 2006*, Athens: Εταιρεία Πελοποννησιακών Σπουδών.

---

83   Trikoupis 1860, vol. 2, pp. 57–60, National Library of Greece, Manuscripts, General Archive, A10341.

Gritsopoulos, Tasos 1974, 'Διαμάχη των κομμάτων της Πελοποννήσου δια τον δραγομάνον Θεοδόσιον το 1820' ['Conflict between factions in the Peloponnese concerning Dragoman Theodoios in 1820'], Πελοποννησιακά, 10: 165–71.

Gritsopoulos, Tasos 1976, Ιστορία της Τριπολιτσάς [History of Tripolitsa], Athens: Ένωση Τριπολιτών Αττικής.

Hering, Gunnar 2004, Τα πολιτικά κόμματα στην Ελλάδα, 1821–1936 [Political Parties in Greece, 1821–1936], 2 Volumes, Athens: Μορφωτικό Ίδρυμα Εθνικής Τραπέζης.

Kandiloros, Takis 1926, Η Φιλική Εταιρεία: 1814–1821 [The Friendly Society: 1814–1821], Athens: Ν.Δ. Φραντζεσκάκης.

Karageorgou-Kourtzi, Olga 2010, Οικονομικές και κοινωνικές συνθήκες στη βόρεια Πελοπόννησο την εικοσαετία 1800–1820 (Με βάση το Αρχείο της Οικογένειας Περούκα του Άργους) [Economic and social conditions in the northern Peloponnese between 1800–1820], Patras: Σύλλογος Αργείων 'Ο Δαναός'.

Konomos, Ntinos 1963–68, 'Ανέκδοτα κείμενα (1816–1820) (από το αρχείο Σωτήρη Χαραλάμπη)' ['Unpublished Documents (1816–1820) (from the archive of Sotiris Charalambis)'], Πελοποννησιακά, 6: 191–205.

Londos, Andreas 1914, Ιστορικόν αρχείον του στρατηγού Ανδρέου Λόντου (1789–1847) [Historical archive of General Andreas Londos (1789–1847)], Athens: Π.Δ. Σακελλαρίου.

Margadant, Jo Burr 1996, 'Introduction: The New Biography in Historical Practice', French Historical Studies, 19, 4 [Special Issue: Biography]: 1045–58.

Meister, Daniel R. 2017, 'The biographical turn and the case for historical biography', History Compass, 16, 1: e12436.

Nikolaou, Giorgos V. 2010, 'La famille Deliyannis: un exemple de notables chrétiens', in La société grecque sous la domination ottomane, edited by Maria Efthymiou, Athens: Herodotos.

Petropulos, John 1968, Politics and Statecraft in the Kingdom of Greece, 1833–1843, Princeton: Princeton Legacy Library.

Philimon, Ioannis 1868, Σύντομος βιογραφία του Ν. Σπηλιάδου [Short biography of N. Spiliadis], Nafplio: Ο Κάδμος Κ. Ιωαννίδου.

Philimon, Ioannis 1971 [1834], Δοκίμιον ιστορικόν περί της Φιλικής Εταιρίας [Historical Essay concerning the Friendly Society], Athens.

Philliou, Christine M. 2010, Biography of an Empire: Governing Ottomans in an Age of Revolution, Berkeley: University of California Press.

Photakos [Photios Chrysanthopoulos] 1858, Απομνημονεύματα περί της Ελληνικής Επαναστάσεως [Memoirs concerning the Greek Revolution], Athens: Π.Δ. Σακελλαρίου.

Photopoulos, Athanasios 2005, Οι κοτζαμπάσηδες της Πελοποννήσου κατά τη δεύτερη Τουρκοκρατία, 1715–1821 [The notables of the Peloponnese during the second Tourkokratia], Athens: Ηρόδοτος.

Pylia, Martha 2004, Les notables moréotes (XVIIIe–XIXe siècles): fonctions et comportements, PhD dissertation, Université de Lille III.

Pylia, Martha 2007, 'Conflits politiques et comportement des primats chretiens', in *The Ottoman Rule and the Balkans 1760–1850: Conflict, Transformation, Adaptation*, edited by Antonis Anastasopoulos and Elias Kolovos, Rethymno: Departmen of History and Archaeology, University of Crete.

Rotzokos, Nikos 1996, *Πολιτικές και κοινωνικοπολιτισμικές συγκρούσεις στο εικοσιένα: οι πρού-χοντες της Πελοποννήσου* [*Political and socio-cultural conflicts in 1821: the notables of the Peloponnese*], Ph.D. dissertation, Athens.

Sakellariou, Michail 2012 [1939], *Η Πελοπόννησος κατά την δευτέραν Τουρκοκρατίαν (1715–1821)* [*The Peloponnese during the second Tourkokratia (1715–1821)*], Athens: Ηρόδοτος.

Şânî-zâde Mehmed 'Atâ'ullah Efendi 2008, *Şânî-zâde Târîhî 1223–1237/1808–1821* [*History 1808–1821*], edited by Ziya Yılmazer, 2 Volumes, Istanbul: Çamlıca.

Sarafis, Vangelis 2017, '[...] *να νομίζωμεν εμαυτούς απηλπισμένους, χωρίς να βλέπωμεν διόρθω-σιν τινά προς οικονομίαν. Φόβος για την αναπότρεπτη εξέγερση, Φεβρουάριος 1821*' [February 1821, fear before the outbreak of the revolution], in *Φόβοι και ελπίδες στα νεότερα χρόνια*, edited by Katerina Dede, Dimitris Dimitropoulos, Tassos Sakellaropoulos, Athens: National Hellenic Research Foundation.

Spiliadis, Nikolaos 1851–57, *Απομνημονεύματα* [*Memoirs*], 3 Volumes, Athens: Χ. Νικολα-ΐδης Φιλαδελφεύς.

Stamatopoulos, Dimitrios 2007, 'Constantinople in the Peloponnese: the case of the Dragoman of the Morea Georgios Wallerianos and some aspects of the revolutionary process', in *The Ottoman Rule and the Balkans 1760–1850: Conflict, Transformation, Adaptation*, edited by Antonis Anastasopoulos and Elias Kolovos, Rethymno: Departmen of History and Archaeology, University of Crete.

Stamatopoulos, Takis 1972, *Ο εσωτερικός αγώνας πριν και κατά την επανάσταση του 1821* [*The internal struggle before and during the revolution of 1821*], 4 Volumes, Athens: Κάλβος.

Theodoridis, Georgios K. 2012, *Αλέξανδρος Μαυροκορδάτος: Ένας φιλελεύθερος στα χρόνια του Εικοσιένα* [*Alexandros Mavrokordatos: A liberal in 1821*], Athens: National Hellenic Research Foundation.

Tricha, Lydia 2016, *Χαρίλαος Τρικούπης* [*Charilaos Trikoupis*], Athens: Πόλις.

Tricha, Lydia 2019, *Σπυρίδων: ο άλλος Τρικούπης (1788–1873)* [*Spyridon: the other Trikoupis (1788–1873)*], Athens: Πόλις.

Trikoupis, Spyridon 1860, *Ιστορία της Ελληνικής Επαναστάσεως* [*History of the Greek Revolution*], 4 Volumes, London: Taylor and Francis.

Tzakis, Dionysis 2015, 'Η εφορία της Φιλικής Εταιρείας στην Πελοπόννησο. Σκέψεις για τη συμμετοχή των τοπικών ηγετικών ομάδων στο εθνικό κίνημα' ['The Ephorate of the Friendly Society in the Peloponnese. Thougts on the participation of the local notables in the national movement'], *Ιόνιος Λόγος*, 5: 104–10.

Vernikos, Nikolas 1997, *Το σχέδιο αυτονομίας της Πελοποννήσου υπό γαλλική επικυριαρχία* [*The plot for the autonomy of the Peloponnese under French dominion*], Athens: Συλ-λογή.

Vlachogiannis, Giannis 1935, *Κλέφτες του Μοριά* [*Klephts of the Morea*], Athens: [Πολυ-βιοτεχνική].

Vogli, Elpida 2005, *Έργα και ημέραι ελληνικών οικογενειών 1750–1940* [*Works and Days of Greek families 1750–1940*], Athens: Ελληνικό Λογοτεχνικό και Ιστορικό Αρχείο.

Zeppos, Panagiotis 1969–70, 'Δυο προεπαναστατικά σχέδια της Πελοποννήσου' ['Two plots concerning the Peloponnese before the revolution'], *Πελοποννησιακά*, 7: 175–86.

PART 3

The Dynamics of Modernisation

∵

CHAPTER 7

Irregular Warfare in the Greek Revolution of 1821

Klephtic *or* Partisan *Warfare?*

Dionysis Tzakis

Scholarship on the Greek Revolution of 1821, and Modern Greek Studies more generally, employs the term *klephtopolemos* (and the relevant terms *klephtic warfare*, *klephtic military tactics*, etc.)[1] to describe the irregular warfare the Greeks fought, a term thought to relate to traditional types of war[2] which were obsolete in comparison to the regular European armies at the time. In this chapter, I intend to question this established historiographic notion. I shall contend that during the Greek Revolution traditional warfare was reshaped and upgraded in such a way that it developed traits peculiar to a modern political-military action classified by the term *partisan* or *guerilla* warfare. I shall therefore argue that the irregular combatants of the Greek War of Independence belonged to the same historical context as the Spanish guerilas of the Napoleonic era, i.e. to the same genealogy as the armed national liberation movements of the nineteenth and twentieth centuries.

Alexandros Hypsilantis's decision to begin the Greek Revolution in the Danubian Principalities – i.e. the change of plan brought about by the high-ranking executives of the Friendly Society [Gk. *Philiki Etairia*] in Izmail in the beginning of October 1820 – decisively determined the managing of the Greek revolutionary war in Peloponnese as much as in Roumeli.[3] In accordance with the Izmaïl decisions, Hypsilantis had to travel from Russia all the way to Mani (in the southern edge of the Peloponnese) in order to there start the Greek Revolution. Grigorios Dikaios was sent as Hypsilantis's emissary to the Peloponnese as well as to the islands of Hydra and Spetses. Vassilis Panagiotopoulos has shown that the final preparations for the armed Revolution in the Peloponnese were

---

1   See, selectively, Dakin 1973, p. 172; Brewer 2011, p. 81; Campbell 2002, pp. 172, 174; Pappas 2018, p. 181.

2   According to Apostolos Vakalopoulos (1986, vol. 7, p. 264). Likewise, Douglas Dakin refers to 'traditional irregular bands' and 'traditional type of warfare-kleftic' (1973, pp. 70, 72).

3   According to the Treaty of Bucharest (1812), Izmaïl, today in southwestern Ukraine, was annexed to Russia. The Greek term *Roumeli* for Rumelia was used to denote the southern part of the Ottoman province [*eyalet*] of Rumelia [Ott. Turk. *Rumeli*].

conducted as per this plan and that Hypsilantis was not expected until mid-March 1821 – i.e. until the revolutionary proclamation of 24 February and other documents belonging to Hypsilantis arrived in Mani from Iaşi.[4]

In the last ten days of March, almost all of the Peloponnesian provinces revolted under the leadership of their local notables [Ott. Turk. *kocabaşıs*; Gk. *kotzampasides*] and Orthodox church prelates, the majority of whom were members of the secret Friendly Society.[5] Preparations made in the previous two months proved sufficient for the synchronisation of the various local revolutionary nuclei to achieve a concurrent general rising. Nevertheless, no particular preparations were made in relation to crucial issues of military and warfare planning, since these were matters left to be looked after by the leader of the Friendly Society upon his arrival in Mani. These were the instructions conveyed by Dikaios at the end of December 1820, and according to them, the local notables and prelates proceeded to incite their provinces into rebellion, selecting 'choice men with experience in arms, so as to be regularly led by him [Hypsilantis]' as well as by a 'chiliarch' (a captain leading 1.000 men) per province.[6] In other words, it was thanks to the conspiratorial mechanisms of the Friendly Society, which instigated the local revolutionary nuclei, that the revolution in the Peloponnese became possible, encouraging almost simultaneously the islands of the Aegean and, gradually, the provinces of Roumeli. Yet the Greek Revolution started with no particular military preparation, no leader, no structure and no battle plan. These circumstances did most to define who finally got into the battle and how they fought during the first crucial months of the Revolution.

It was mostly the armed groups of *armatoloi* [Ott. Turk. *martoloz*: local bands with police authority] that ventured to shoulder the war's weight, since they had at their disposal combatants highly experienced in small-scale conflicts, particularly on the mountains. Units of *armatoloi* in mountainous regions as well, as the armed forces of the Souliots in Epirus and the residents of the Dervenochoria [Ott. Turk. *derbent* villages, mountain-pass guards] of Attica, constituted a type of irregular, provincial military grouping whose staffing and internal cohesion depended, to a certain degree, on family and local ties. Those who participated in these units were in some way 'professionals' in the handling of arms, meaning that their inclusion in a group of *armatoloi* was their main or seasonal activity to make a living. We can nonetheless detect in those

---

4   Panagiotopoulos 2015, pp. 65–70, 149–71; Panagiotopoulos 2001–2, pp. 449–61. For the Friendly Society, see Panagiotopoulos 2011, pp. 101–26.

5   Frangos 1971, pp. 140–244; Tzakis 2018a, pp. 125–48.

6   The document containing these instructions was published by Philimon 1834, p. 351.

groups several of the traits common to the militia, as an armed force of a particular place of action with close ties to the local community. The *arma-toloi* exercised recognisable authority in their provinces, which they protected against the *klepht*s [bandits]. In this context, the *armatoloi* created horizontal and vertical networks of relations with the local residents. When required by given circumstances, they would augment the number of their units and widen their operational capacities in similar ways. They were able to achieve this through the mobilisation of conscription and support mechanisms (equip-ment, information, care, etc.) which followed the particular social distributions of roles within mountainous or semi-mountainous regions (e.g. *klepht*s, semi-nomadic pastoral communities and monasteries).

Such urgent circumstances had been afoot since the summer of 1820, when the Sublime Porte began its military campaigns against Ali Pasha of Ioannina. Successive translocations of Ottoman military forces, as well as the general upheaval during the long Ottoman siege of Ali Pasha's base in Ioannina over several months, forced the *armatoloi* to continuously keep their units vigil-ant and supplemented. As a result, the onset of the Greek Revolution in the Peloponnese found Roumeli's captains at the ready, meaning that they too could incite their provinces into rebellion and lead the warfare in their regions. These units' organisational and operational autonomy, which fought in their provinces' frontiers or close to them, created several problems insofar as the planning of collective or coordinated campaigns across a wider geographic area was concerned. However, pre-existing networks of cooperations or alliances – usually between province captains and at times strengthened through family ties and intermarriages – that connected bordering districts allowed neigh-bours and allied *armatoloi* to coordinate the war in their particular regions. Battles usually concerned control over nodal and more or less rugged spots across the road network that linked a province to the nearest Ottoman military centres. The allies would furthermore hinder the dispatch via land of Ottoman forces to the insurrected Peloponnese in addition to making attempts to take control of towns and fort sieges that were protected by limited numbers of inadequately equipped Ottoman guards.

In comparison to Roumeli and to the Aegean islands – the latter having equipped commercial ships and experienced crews at their disposal – the cir-cumstances in the Peloponnese were largely different. There, no armed units similar to those of *armatoloi* were available, and, as we saw, no particular milit-ary preparations were made in February and March 1821. The Friendly Society's regional nuclei would incite the population to rebel in some cases through persuasion and in other cases by means of violence. Moreover, the Friendly Society conspirators had created local revolutionary authorities by adjusting

pre-existing communal institutions so that they could meet the needs produced by the war.[7] Nonetheless, with the exception of the province of Mani,
very few were equipped and competent for combat. They were limited to a few
hundred Napoleonic-war veterans on the Ionian islands, former *klephts* and
kapoi [It. *capo*] at the service of local notables who were called upon as more
experienced by the local revolutionary authorities to lead to the battlefield the
units were rapidly formed in each province (or a part of a province).

These units consisted of farmers, stockbreeders, artisans, town residents and
villagers, the vast majority of whom had never fought and didn't own arms.
We should also consider the several men and women of various ages who
had undertaken unprecedented services in the context of supply and support
mechanisms created in each province. For the most part, armed units were
everywhere formed in similar ways. Photakos, one of Theodoros Kolokotronis's
adjutants, graphically presents in his memoirs the armed groups and camps
that were established in central Peloponnese. He points out that, 'At the beginning of the revolution, the Greeks instantly assembled themselves in the camps
of each group, family, village, and province', and he adds that 'each village had
its own leader, and did not cede command to anyone else, nor did its neigh-
bours follow anyone else'.[8]

Revolutionary military units in the Peloponnese resembled the militia more
distinctly than the ones in Roumeli did, since an extensive rupture from traditional distributions of roles within each province accompanied their creation.
Each one of them had its own leader and consisted of several smaller groups
of relatives and fellow villagers/townsmen who were inexperienced and poorly
equipped for war. Each unit followed social bonds, relations of trust, balances
and hierarchies of the particular community and, more widely, of the province
to whom it belonged, for whom it fought and under whose purview it had
set its preservation. Therefore, during the Revolution's first days and weeks,
each province created its own political and military structures and hierarchies.
As far as military planning was concerned, these conditions were maintained
until the end of 1821, since the provisional collective administration created
in May 1821 for the whole of the Peloponnese (called the Senate) undertook
the coordination of provincial revolutionary authorities, as well as the general
planning of military campaigns, but did not make any decisions with regard to
homogenising the military units in the Peloponnese.

---

7   For a discussion of the various adjustments of communitarian structures to local centres of
    revolutionary power – political and military – in Greece, see Tzakis 2018b, pp. 153–74.
8   Photakos [Photios Chrysanthopoulos] 1974, pp. 85, 124.

The military units that were both in Roumeli and the Peloponnese in the first year of the Greek Revolution were being organised per province, they did not pertain to a central military administration and their preservation depended on the tight bonds that the irregular combatants of each unit maintained with the residents of their province. Their success on the battlefield offered a relatively controllable kind of 'dominance' which allowed the local revolutionary authorities to shape themselves politically toward the end of the year (when the First National Assembly was organised) and to create collective administrative institutions. It was in the context of these processes that the issue of military organisation first arose during the Revolution. Relevant initiatives came from Alexandros Mavrokordatos, and they constituted one of the fundamental aspects of his political vision on the creation of a modern nation's structures and institutions.[9] From that time onwards, he was to become the most ardent advocate of a regular army within the revolutionary leadership. Thus, on 9 January 1822, the first military organisation was elected,[10] aiming at refining the national army with uniform organisational characteristics. In April 1822, a law was promulgated on the formulation of a regular army, while over the following weeks the first battalions with European and Philhellenic officers and expatriate Greeks were formed.[11] However, the organisation essentially remained unenforced, since responsibility for the army belonged to the peripheral Senates and not to the national administration, while the newly formed regular unit suffered massive casualties in its first campaign at Epirus, Peta, on 4 July 1822. At the same time, the irregular combatants secured victories crucial to the Revolution's survival, especially in the Peloponnese, and essentially continued to organise themselves and function as they had done so far.

No particular changes were effected within the military organisation in 1823 and 1824, excepting the troops' direct subdue under the national Greek government[12] since the Senates were abolished. But from the spring of 1825 onwards,

---

9   Diamantouros 2002, pp. 221–39.
10   *Αρχεία της Ελληνικής Παλιγγενεσίας*, Athens 1971–2012, vol. 3, pp. 37–8.
11   *Αρχεία της Ελληνικής Παλιγγενεσίας*, Athens 1971–2012, vol. 1, pp. 22, 154–60. See also St Clair 2008, pp. 83–91.
12   Various reactions to a ranging degree of intensity did not deter the Greek national government's increasingly great capacity to authoritatively interfere in military camps and to determine the relations and hierarchies within them. Georgios Karaiskakis's conviction as a traitor by the revolutionary authorities in Missolonghi in the spring of 1824, as well as Odysseas Androutsos's arrest at the beginning of the following year, were crucial events of the state, which ultimately had to do with the national government's ability to mobilise armed units to serve its warfare plans. For more on Androutsos, see Kotaridis 1993, p. 91 ff.

the issue of the army was urgently addressed and intensely occupied over a long period by the revolutionary authorities. This was due to an initial inability to tackle Ibrahim Pasha of Egypt in the Peloponnese, whose army possessed many of the characteristics of a regular army and was being led by European officers. Under these circumstances, Mavrokordatos's ideas predominated in the administration's bodies and a thorough reformation of the irregular troops into a regular army was decided,[13] an enterprise to be achieved in three inter-complementary ways. The first way was through the conscription of 8,000 European and American soldiers,[14] for whose expenses new loans were required.[15] Second, through reorganising and expanding, the small regular unit formed in the summer of 1824 at Nafplio[16] – this task was left in the hands of the French colonel Charles Fabvier,[17] while local resources for its support were sought and internal recruitment was intended for its staffing.[18] Third, and finally, by means of a direct reshaping of the irregular units into a regular army.

Nevertheless, no new loans were concluded. Additionally, since recruitment did not have satisfactory results, the regular army did not significantly grow.[19] Finally, regularising the units was an impossible task under the circumstances of warfare and economic hardship and without the military captains' consent. Intense pressure was essentially exerted only during the second semester of 1825, on the leader of the Peloponnese troops Theodoros Kolokotronis,[20] who, however, insistently refused to put into practice the new military policy.[21] Against these changes were also the captains of the Roumeli military camps. Many of them, such as Georgios Karaiskakis, who became revolutionary Rou-

---

13   E.g. the Executive Body's president, Georgios Kountouriotis, in a letter to Dionysios Romas in April 1825, stated that 'regular troops, we do not have, and, for the time being, we are in no position that enables us to increase our minor regiment'. In his resignation plan written in February 1826, he urges the Legislative Body to 'increase and train the regular army' as one of the three means by which 'the securing of the liberation struggle is achievable'. See Romas 1901, vol. 1, p. 389; Protopsaltis (ed.) 1963–86, vol. 6, pp. 101–2.

14   Αρχεία της Ελληνικής Παλιγγενεσίας, Athens 1971–2012, vol. 7, pp. 235–6, 239, 248.

15   Αρχεία της Ελληνικής Παλιγγενεσίας, Athens 1971–2012, vol. 7, pp. 196, 222–3, 236, 239, 248.

16   Αρχεία της Ελληνικής Παλιγγενεσίας), Athens 1971–2012, vol. 2, pp. 337, 342, 391; vol. 6, p. 188; vol. 7, pp. 239, 461–3; vol. 10, pp. 379, 404, 475–6.

17   Αρχεία της Ελληνικής Παλιγγενεσίας, Athens 1971–2012, vol. 7, pp. 269–70.

18   Αρχεία της Ελληνικής Παλιγγενεσίας, Athens 1971–2012, vol. 7, pp. 272–3, 275.

19   Αρχεία της Ελληνικής Παλιγγενεσίας, Athens 1971–2012, vol. 7, p. 318; Protopsaltis (ed.) 1963–86, vol. 5, p. 405.

20   Protopsaltis (ed.) 1963–86, vol. 5, p. 370 (G. Kountouriotis's instructions to A. Mavrokordatos on regularising the military units of the Peloponnese, 9 October 1825).

21   See, for example, A. Mavrokordatos's letter to F. Karvellas, 27 January 1826. Romas 1901, vol. 2, pp. 32–4.

meli's military leader in 1826–7, retained tight political bonds with Ioannis Kolettis. Kolettis was a member of the executive body, although it seems he has been consistently undermining the new military policy.[22] Nikolaos Spiliadis wrote in his memoirs that at the Legislative Body's meetings of the fall of 1825, 'many disputes between legislators took place', since many 'supporters of Kolettis's beliefs' criticised the military reform, doubting its usefulness as well as stressing the difficulties and deficiencies that prevented its realisation.[23] Georgios Kountouriotis also stressed this clash of convictions surrounding the army at that time in his letter to Mavrokordatos, dated on 27 October 1825, though he attributed to it mercenary, non-political motives: 'these opponents to the government were unable to otherwise serve their own ends than through the dissolution or nullification of this body [the regular army]'.[24] In other words, since the spring of 1825, two different military rationales co-existed, which could be summarised as the quandary between an irregular and a regular army.

According to those supporting the first of these, the irregular provincial units had to be maintained and made to serve a coordinated type of guerrilla warfare. They believed that this tactic would enable them to regain control over mountainous lands in the Peloponnese and Roumeli. They furthermore believed that it would vitiate the enemy by preventing them from solidifying their rule in regions that they had theoretically conquered. Their goal was to continue fighting[25] to retain Europe's interest in the resolution of the Greek affair and to reinstigate the intention of some of the great European powers to take initiatives to terminate the war. On these grounds, Theodoros Kolokotronis redesigned the military enterprises at the Peloponnese after the summer of 1825[26] – i.e. by employing forms of irregular warfare different to those he had hitherto used.[27] Kolokotronis's son, Gennaios, who took on important roles in these enterprises,

---

22 Diamantouros 2002, pp. 236–7.

23 Spiliadis 2007, vol. 3, pp. 282–3, 450–2.

24 Protopsaltis (ed.) 1963–86, vol. 5, p. 408.

25 In this spirit, the Proclamation of the Third National Assembly, of 5 March 1827, deliberately reiterates throughout the entire text, and especially in the first phrases, the declaratory word 'we are fighting' and stresses the following: 'For the sake of this sacred war we have been fighting for seven years we have hopes for the participation of Christians, of all the powerful of the enlightened world ... Nations are just ... Are they going to abandon us? ... We hope that both kings and peoples shall contribute to our war'. See Αρχεία της Ελληνικής Παλιγγενεσίας, Athens 1971–2012, vol. 3, pp. 557–60.

26 At that time, he had also been actively taking part in a written request to George Canning for the protection of insurrected Greeks, which has been historiographically characterised as the 'Act of Submission'.

27 Apostolos Vakalopoulos (1986, vol. 7, p. 266), writes that this is 'the first time in revolutionary Greece that klephtopolemos is systematically being put into practice'.

later wrote that his father 'planned, by imitating the Spanish, to attack the Turks variously, sideways and from behind, as well as by ambush'.[28] Of the same logic was also Georgios Karaiskakis's plan for Roumeli in the winter of 1826–7. The enterprise's impressive results were reversed as rapidly as they were yielded. This was in part due to the pressures exerted on him to leave his campaign in the mountainous Roumeli and to fight for the liberation of Athens instead,[29] but also to the appointment of two British officers at the head of the Greek land and naval forces. Admiral Thomas Cochrane and General Richard Church enforced their own warfare plan by ignoring their army's objections and enterprising potential. As a result, the greatest army to have been formed since the beginning of the Revolution was led to one of the most important and deadliest defeats on the Greeks' part.[30] Clashes within the revolutionary authorities around the question of a regular or an irregular army, as well as the political instabilities of the years 1826–7, eventually enabled the adherents to one or the other of the two military policies to concurrently favour both regular and irregular warfare. On those occasions where the irregular Greek units were called upon to serve an unfamiliar, inflexible and, in their opinion, unsuitable military rationale – as in 1827 in Athens and previously in the Battle of Peta in 1822 – the defeat that ensued was truly disastrous.

According to those endorsing the resort to a regular army, Greek combatants had to be organised as well as fight in a way similar to that of European armies of the time. They thought that the irregular units could achieve only small and impermanent land conquests and that they were unable to lead to a decisive defeat of the Ottomans, particularly when they were confronted with regularly organised forces such as the Egyptian army in the Peloponnese. It was therefore believed that the conditions afoot after 1825 urged resort to a regular army, the latter being the only secure means to the Revolution's endurance and success. This conviction was founded upon the tenets of post-Napoleonic military theory with respect to the enterprising potential of regular and irregular troops. The ideas advocated during the Greek Revolution by Greeks and Philhellenes in favour of a regular army are present in all major military manuals of the nine-

---

28   Kolokotronis 1856, p. 199. The Italian officer of Ibrahim Pasha's army, Guisseppe Romei, secretly recommended this tactic to the revolutionary authorities in April 1826: 'The Greeks ought to fight the Egyptians in skirmishes … They ought to attack the Egyptian units during the latter's march, within narrow passages, on foothills, on steep paths, at uneven and forested spots … to attack their camps at nighttime, to exhaust them, to deprive them of sleep, to impede their transport'. See Romas 1901, vol. 1, p. 367.

29   Tzakis 2015, pp. 339–54.

30   See Thomas Gordon's scathing remark: 'If the plan deserves the severest censure, what shall we say to the pitiful method in which it was executed' (1832, vol. 2, p. 395).

teenth century, whose authors, including Jomini and Clausewitz, drew upon their experiences in the Napoleonic wars.

In order to understand this quandary between a regular and an irregular army which produced such tensions within the revolutionary authorities after 1825, we should approach the various forms of military organisation and handling of warfare present at the time in their own historical context. Carl Schmitt's analysis of the irregular combatant of the modern era is particularly useful in this respect.[31] In his two lectures published under the title *Theorie des Partisanen*, Schmitt argued that what Spain in the era of the Napoleonic Wars ushered in was a new, historically unorthodox type of warfare.[32] He characterised the new combatant as a *modern partisan*,[33] due to a crucial new element added, he suggests, to the irregular combatant's profile, decisively influencing it and modernising it. The three traditional aspects of this profile are unconventional warfare, increased mobility as well as flexibility and a familiarity with place and local residents.[34] The irregular combatant's new/modern aspect is his action's strong political commitment to a modern political ideology's objectives. It is this aspect that defines him anew[35] and leads him to wage unconventional and continuous war of absolute enmity – a war in which the 'modern partisan expects neither justice nor mercy from his enemy'.[36] It is a type of warfare simultaneously political and ideological, waged between a state's army and irregular combatants. The latter usually organise themselves in a fashion peculiar to a militia, maintain tight bonds with their region's locals and employ unconventional ways to fare war so that they attain the objectives

31   See Hooker 2009, pp. 156–94; Hohendahl 2011, pp. 529–44; Gasché 2004, pp. 9–34; Müller 2006, pp. 65–78; Werner 2009, pp. 126–31; Gayetsky 2015.

32   For resistance to the Napoleonic army on the part of Spain, Tyrol, etc., see Esdaile 2004; Esdaile (ed.) 2005.

33   Schmitt 2004, p. 7.

34   'Such criteria are irregularity, increased mobility of the active combat ... and the tellurian character' (Schmitt 2004, pp. 13–14).

35   As he characteristically writes: 'is the intense political commitment which sets the partisan apart from other fighters. The intensely political character of the partisan is crucial ... and it is precisely the political character of his action that brings to the fore again the original sense of the word partisan' (Schmitt 2004, p. 10). The meaning Schmitt attributes to the partisan's political profile to distinguish him from the traditional irregular combatant, as well as Clausewitz classic distinction between 'small war' and 'people's war' (depending on the ideology of patriotism), has not been adequately deployed in the historiography of irregular warfare, in which the latter is presented linearly from antiquity to the modern era. See, among others, Laqueur 2019. For an entirely different approach, see Scheipers 2015. On the term 'people's war' in Clausewitz's work, see Heuser 2010, pp. 387–418; Heuser 2010, pp. 139–62; Davis 2015, pp. 11–18.

36   Schmitt 2004, p. 7.

set by the revolutionary ideology they serve. In the case of the Spanish partisans of the early nineteenth century – the guerrillas – it was upon the ideology of patriotism that strong political commitment was founded, with which all revolutionary movements of the Napoleonic and post-Napoleonic eras evolved in accordance.

The distinction between a traditional and a modern partisan that Schmitt proposed, based on the relation between military action and a revolutionary ideology, transcends the formalism according to which warfare was identified as traditional or modern by classical military theory. It therefore helps to make us aware that during the Greek Revolution, traditional aspects of unorthodox warfare were reshaped into a new political-military action – modern irregular warfare.[37] This occurred in different ways, at different rates and with varying levels of intensity during the revolutionary years through the contact between irregular combatants of the Peloponnese and Roumeli and the modern political ideology of patriotism. This has not so much to do with changes concerning the institutional context of their organisation and operation. They mostly have to do with the extent of their political commitment to the idea, fostered by a national administration of continuous, non-negotiable and by-any-means-enforced warfare of national independence.

Aspects of this reformation are observable in the military enterprises of the period between 1825–7. The siege of Missolonghi, resistence against Ibrahim Pasha's invasion and Georgios Karaiskakis's campaign in Roumeli are instances of radical reforms in the mentalities and ideas of the irregular combatants involved. Indicative of this revolutionary par excellence process, which alters the terms in which historical subjects rationalise and give a meaning to their actions, is an excerpt from Georgios Karaiskakis's letter to his former personal enemy, Giannakis Rhagos. In this letter, he urges Rhagos to continue fighting, because, he writes, only thus can his nation affirm its existence: 'Brother, captain Giannakis, it is now the time for you to prove your patriotic virtues, and those you have so far fostered, and to many it will become apparent whether there is a nation or not after we have returned from Athens, God willing'.[38] The letter was written on the February 18 1827, right after Karaiskakis's important victories at the village of Distomo – i.e. just before his return to Athens, abiding by the authorities' instructions despite disagreeing with the new plan of enterprises he had to follow. Here, as in the case with the wider, radical changes Georgios Karaiskakis underwent after 1824,[39] we can identify the transforma-

---

37   For discussions to that effect, also see Stites 2014; cf. Skiotis 1975, pp. 308–29.
38   Papageorgiou (ed.) 1982, p. 229.
39   Tzakis 2011, pp. 129–49.

tion from the traditional irregular combatant, the *klephts* of Roumeli, and the *armatoloi* to the modern *partisan*.

Schmitt's analysis also helps us approach, in their historical context, the various ideas that were cultivated among the Greek revolutionary authorities regarding the army and warfare. Schmitt stresses that the Spanish guerillas' victories over the French army were discussed across and deemed impressive by European military circles, but they did not alter the minor value attributed by conventional military thought of the post-Napoleonic era and of the entire nineteenth century to irregular units and unorthodox warfare.[40] Today, however, we know that irregular warfare has been proven as an efficient means to wage wars of national liberation – i.e. wars of a stateless society against a state army. But these members of the revolutionary authorities, as well as most Philhellenes, who disdained the irregular army's potential for campaigns, did not support such an attitude simply because creating a regular army was a vital part of their modernising project. Their favour of a regular army was their response to the question, crucial for every revolutionary leadership, of the means by which war could be won. And their response followed the principles of modern European military theory, according to which irregular warfare was condemned to sooner or later fail due to being anachronistic, barbaric and historically obsolete.[41]

Besides that, irregular warfare's anachronism (but not inefficiency) was even acknowledged by such leaders like Theodoros Kolokotronis[42] – leaders who, through their initiatives and actions, embodied this historically modern political-military tactic. As Nikos Theotokas has pointed out,

> ... we should not regret the fact that the historical subject only rarely has experienced the time in which it lived in the ways invented or discovered

---

40   Schmitt 2004, pp. 31–2. See also Werner 1986, pp. 127–33.

41   'Most Europeans failed to realize that the Greek method of fighting was remarkably effective and that it was military sound for a small badly armed force to employ hit-and-run tactics. They simply regarded the Greek methods as obsolete and barbarous; different from the methods used in Europe and therefore inferior' (St Clair 2008, p. 38). Also see Karakatsouli 2016, pp. 19, 193 ff.

42   See the written request by Theodoros Kolokotronis and other Peloponnesian officers to the government on November 26, 1826, at a time when they were being pressured to reshape their units into a regular army. Although their requests essentially annulled the prospect of their units' egularization, the letter nevertheless begins as follows: 'the need for a regular army, which as an ancestral invention of ours has been known to all enlightened and blessed nations and has been adopted by them'. See Kolokotronis 1856, p. 293. See also a letter to the same effect to the 'Committee of Zakynthos', 9 December 1825, in Romas 1901, vol. 1, pp. 769–81.

by a given historiography. People do not experience the discontinuities which academic scholarship will in their absence and retroactively define as the 'watersheds' of their lives. Their evaluative principles remain attached to lived or inherited continuities which transcend the actual juncture.[43]

The fact that both opponents and supporters of irregular warfare agree on its *traditionalism* constitutes a testimony to the way in which the figures of the Greek Revolution experienced and rationalised a series of changes and reforms. As I have attempted to show, these are adjustments and reforms of what has been classified by historiography as *klephtopolemos*, which occurred over the course of revolution and actually pertain to modern, not traditional, warfare.

Bibliography

Brewer, David 2011, *The Greek War of Independence: The Struggle for Freedom from Ottoman Oppression*, New York and London: Thus.

Campbell, John 2002, 'The Sarakatsani and the Klephtic Tradition', in: *Minorities in Greece: Aspects of a Plural Society*, edited by Richard Clogg, London: C. Hurst & Co.

Dakin, Douglas 1973, 'The Formation of Greek State, 1821–1833', in *The Struggle for Greek Independence*, edited by Richard Clogg, London and New York: Archon Books.

Dakin, Douglas 1973, *The Greek Struggle for Independence, 1821–1833*, Berkeley and Los Angeles 1973: University of California Press.

Davis, J. 2015, 'Introduction', in *Clausewitz: on Small War*, Oxford: Oxford University Press.

Diamantouros, Nikiforos 2002, *Οι απαρχές της συγκρότησης του σύγχρονου κράτους στην Ελλάδα, 1821–1828* [*The beginnings of the formation of the modern state in Greece, 1821–1828*], Athens: Μορφωτικό Ίδρυμα Εθνικής Τραπέζης.

Esdaile, Charles (ed.) 2005, *Popular Resistance in the French Wars: Patriots, Partisans and Land Pirates*, Basingstoke: Springer.

Esdaile, Charles 2004, *Fighting Napoleon: Guerillas, Bandits and Adventurers in Spain 1808–1814*, New Haven: Yale University Press.

Frangos, Georgios 1971, *The Philike Etaireia, 1814–1821: a Social and Historical analysis*, PhD dissertation, Columbia University, New York.

Gasché, R. 2004, 'The Partisan and the Philosopher', *The New Centennial Review*, 4, 3: 9–34.

---

43   Theotokas 2006, pp. 47–8.

Gayetsky, M. 2015, 'Partisans in Empire, or, Carl Schmitt as Revolutionary?,' *Theory & Event*, 18, 4. Available at Project MUSE, http://muse.jhu.edu/article/595842.

Gordon, Thomas 1832, *History of the Greek Revolution*, Edinburgh and London: William Blackburn and T. Cadell.

Heuser, Beatrice 2010a, *The Evolution of Strategy: Thinking War from Antiquity to the Present*, Cambridge: Cambridge University Press.

Heuser, Beatrice 2010b, 'Small Wars in the Age of Clausewitz: The Watershed between Partisan War and People's War', *Journal of Strategic Studies*, 33, 1: 139–62.

Hohendahl, P. Uwe 2011, 'Revolutionary War and Absolute Enemy: Rereading Schmitt's *Theory of the Partisan*', *Constellation. An International Journal of Critical and Democratic Theory*, 18, 4: 529–44

Hooker, W. 2009, 'Partisan', in *Carl Schmitt's International Thought: Order and Orientation*, Cambridge: Cambridge University Press.

Karakatsouli, Anna 2016, *'Μαχητές της Ελευθερίας' και 1821* [*'Freedom fighters' in 1821*], Athens: Πεδίο.

Kolokotronis, Gennaios 1856, *Ελληνικά υπομνήματα αφορώντα την Ελληνικήν Επανάστασιν από 1821 έως 1827* [*Greek memoranda concerning the Greek Revolution from 1821 to 1827*], Athens: Χ. Νικολαΐδης-Φιλαδελφεύς.

Kotaridis, Nikos 1993, *Παραδοσιακή Επανάσταση και Εικοσιένα* [*Traditional revolution and 1821*], Athens: Πλέθρον.

Laqueur, Walter 2019, *Guerilla: A Historical and Critical Study*, New York 2019: Routledge.

Müller, J.-W. 2006, 'An 'Irregularity that cannot be regulated': Carl Schmitt and the War on Terror', *Notizie di Politeia: Rivista di Etica e Scelte Pubbliche*, 22, 84: 65–78

Panagiotopoulos, Vassilis (ed.) 2015, *Δύο πρίγκιπες στην Ελληνική Επανάσταση. Επιστολές αυτόπτη μάρτυρα και ένα υπόμνημα του πρίγκιπα Γεώργιου Κανταχουζηνού* [*Two Princes in the Greek Revolution*], Athens: Ασίνη.

Panagiotopoulos, Vassilis 2001–2002, 'Η έναρξη του αγώνα της ανεξαρτησίας στην Πελοπόννησο. Μία ημερολογιακή προσέγγιση' ['The outbreak of the War for Indepedence in the Peloponnese'], in *Πρακτικά του ΣΤ΄ Διεθνούς Συνεδρίου Πελοποννησιακών Σπουδών (Τρίπολις 24–29 Σεπτεμβρίου 2000)*, vol. 3, Athens.

Panagiotopoulos, Vassilis 2011, 'The Filiki Etaireia (Society of Friends). Organizational Preconditions of the National War of Independence', in *The Greek Revolution of 1821. A European Event*, edited by Petros Pizanias, Istanbul: The Isis Press.

Pappas, Nicholas 2018, 'Brigands and Brigadiers: The Problem of Banditry and the Military in Nineteenth Century Greece', *Athens Journal of History*, 4, 3: 175–96.

Philimon, Ioannis 1834, *Δοκίμιον ιστορικόν περί της Φιλικής Εταιρίας* [*Historical Essay concerning the Friendly Society*], Nafplio: Θ. Κοντάξης και Ν. Λουλάκης.

Photakos [Photios Chrysanthopoulos] 1974 [1858], *Απομνημονεύματα περί της Ελληνικής Επανάστασης* [*Memoirs concerning the Greek Revolution*], edited by Tasos Gritsopoulos, Athens.

Protopsaltis, Emmanuel (ed.) 1963–1986, *Ιστορικόν Αρχείον Αλεξάνδρου Μαυροκορδάτου* [*Historical Archive of Alexandros Mavrokordatos*], 6 Volumes, Athens: Academy of Athens.

Papageorgiou, Stefanos (ed.) 1982, *Το Αρχείο Γιαννάκη Ράγκου* [*The Archive of Giannakis Ragos*], Athens: Ιστορική και Εθνολογική Εταιρεία της Ελλάδος.

Romas, Dionysios 1901, *Ιστορικόν Αρχείον Διονύσιου Ρώμα* [*Historical Archive of Dionysios Romas*], edited by Dimitrios Kampouroglou, Athens:

Scheipers, S. 2015, *Unlawful Combatants: A Genealogy of the Irregular Fighter*, Oxford: Oxford University Press.

Schmitt, Carl 2004, *The Theory of the Partisan. A Commentary/Remark on the Concept of the Political*, translated by A.C. Goodson, East Lansing: Michigan State University.

Skiotis, Dennis 1975, 'Mountain Warriors and the Greek Revolution', in *War, Technology and Society in the Middle East*, edited by V.J. Perry and M.E. Yapp, London: School of Oriental & African Studies.

Spiliadis, Nikolaos 2007 [1851–57], *Απομνημονεύματα ήτοι Ιστορία της Επαναστάσεως των Ελλήνων* [*Memoirs, or History of the revolution of the Greeks*], Athens: Ινστιτούτο Ανάπτυξης Χαρίλαος Τρικούπης.

St Clair, William 2008, *That Greece Might Still Be Free*, Cambridge: Open Book Publishers.

Stites, Richard 2014, *The Four Horsemen: Riding to Liberty in Post-Napoleonic Europe*, Oxford: Oxford University Press.

Theotokas, Nikos 2006, 'Η επανάσταση του έθνους και το ορθόδοξο γένος. Σχόλια για τις ιδεολογίες στο. Εικοσιένα' ['The revolution of the nation and the Orthodox community. Comments on the ideologies of 1821'], in *Η οικονομία της βίας. Παραδοσιακές και νεωτερικές εξουσίες στην Ελλάδα του 19ου αιώνα* [*The economy of violence. Traditional and modern powers in nineteenth-century Greece*], edited by Nikos Theotokas and Nikos Kotaridis, Athens: Βιβλιόραμα.

Tzakis, Dionysis 2011, 'From Locality to National State Loyalty: Georgios Karaiskakis during the Greek Revolution', in *The Greek Revolution of 1821. A European Event*, edited by Petros Pizanias, Istanbul: The Isis Press.

Tzakis, Dionysis 2015, 'Η επίδραση του μύθου της Αθήνας στους στρατιωτικούς προσανατολισμούς της ελληνικής επανάστασης', in *Μυθοπλασίες. Χρήση και πρόσληψη των αρχαίων ελληνικών μύθων από την αρχαιότητα μέχρι σήμερα*, edited by S. Efthimiadis and A. Petridis, Athens: Ίων.

Tzakis, Dionysis 2018a, 'Από την Οδησσό στη Βοστίτσα: η πολιτική ενσωμάτωση των τοπικών ηγετικών ομάδων στη Φιλική Εταιρεία', in *Οι πόλεις των Φιλικών: οι αστικές διαδρομές ενός επαναστατικού φαινομένου. Πρακτικά Ημερίδας*, edited by Olga Katsiardi-Hering, Athens: Hellenic Parliament Foundation.

Tzakis, Dionysis 2018b, 'Πόλεμος και σχέσεις εξουσίας στην επανάσταση του 1821', in *Όψεις της Επανάστασης του 1821. Πρακτικά Συνεδρίου*, edited by Dimitris Dimitropoulos, Chris-

tos Loukos and Panagiotis Michailaris, Athens: Εταιρεία Μελέτης Νέου Ελληνισμού –
Μνήμων.

Vakalopoulos, Apostolos 1986, *Ιστορία του Νέου Ελληνισμού*, Thessaloniki: Α. Σταμούλης.

Werner, H. 1986, 'Clausewitz and Guerilla Warfare', *Journal of Strategic Studies*, 9, 2–3:
127–33.

Werner, W. 2009, 'Rereading: Theory of the Partisan', *Amsterdam Law Forum*, 1, 2: 126–31

CHAPTER 8

Disciplining the Armies

Military Medicine during the Greek Revolution (1821–1831)

Athanasios Barlagiannis

Many studies of the Greek Revolution have highlighted the declaration of the National Assembly in Epidaurus for the 'political existence and independence' of the 'Nation'. However, as the Assembly emphasised on 15 January 1822: 'Before we were sure of our *natural* existence, it was impossible to consider our *political* one' [emphasis is mine]. Winning the armed conflicts had the priority over other political initiatives. The army, or, to be more exact, the armies – the different armed bands and troops that fought among themselves and against the armies of the sultan – were a major concern of all political authorities of the period. This is why their organisation, their fighting tactics, their battles, their personnel and their relationships with political structures are subjects much studied. This chapter focuses instead on a less known subject of the military procedures. Using archival information and material published by authors like Aristotelis Kousis and Theodoros Dardavesis,[1] it discusses the development of military medicine. The chapter argues that, even though the ten-year violent conflicts were progressively putting the endurance of bodies to the test, military efficiency and success in conflict were until 1828 only occasionally addressed in medical terms – in contrast to, for example, medical language used during World War I.[2] In fact, it seems that the introduction of medicine to the military followed political efforts to control the armies of the Greek Revolution and transform their fighters into disciplined soldiers.

1 Sufferings

With regards to the subject of hunger, the Revolution must have been disastrous. According to Kostas Kostis, implicated populations did not know ex-

---

1 Kouzis 1946, pp. 9–15; Dardavesis 2013, pp. 10–26. See also Papageorgiou n.d. and Schizas, Kyriakopoulos and Schizas 2009, pp. 103–16.
2 Cooter and Sturdy 1998, p. 15.

treme famine thanks to the complementarity between the various regions.[3] However, the period between 1821–31 must have progressively torn the commercial networks linking regions with cereal deficits to richer ones. In fact, in order to buy bread the inhabitants of the Peloponnese had to walk long distances of 10, 20 and even 30 hours. Except for the north-eastern Peloponnese, where the food sent by the Greek committees was abundant and better priced, the situation was desperate, especially in the mountains and in besieged and densely populated walled cities, to which too many had fled for protection.[4] Such hunger reinforced the expansion of infectious diseases and resulted in low birth rates. It is no coincidence that Wilhelm Körring, inspector of the *chiliarchies* [the semi-irregular military forces set up by Ioannis Kapodistrias in 1828], 'was not at all pleased with the stature of the soldiers and officers'.[5]

Deteriorating hygiene conditions had a significant effect on health. The military camps were 'full of enemy heads. These, as well as the offal of rotting animals ... and other impurities contaminated the air'.[6] Waters in urban concentrations were also contaminated. The tanks in Missolonghi from one point onward had become 'a weird mixture; You could find inside whatever you wanted; minds, offal, blood, heads',[7] while 'after the fall of Tripolitsa, they threw into the wells the bodies of the enemies, who stinted, and were content to cover them with stones, to avoid the trouble of burying them'.[8] In general, 'whoever at that time [1826] was walking around the Peloponnese did not see but the unburied bodies of Turks and Greeks and many dead animals, as well as other various things scattered here and there. Stench and stink unbearable came out of the unlit and rotting corpses ... Many stray dogs ... ran here and there'.[9]

Stray dogs were a real plague, as farmers abandoned them to save themselves. Already in a semi-wild state (otherwise they would have formerly been of no use to the farmers), the dogs must have reached a point of physical ferocity and aggression under extreme hunger, and they were considered by the French Scientific Mission of the Morea to be more dangerous than thieves.[10] In addition to injuries and death, rabies naturally coincided with dog attacks.

Typhus, a camp disease, was the predominant epidemic throughout the period. Already during the siege of 1821, it struck both inside and outside the

---

3   Kostis 1993, p. 103.
4   Vakalopoulos 1991, p. 211.
5   Vakalopoulos 1991, p. 240.
6   Vakalopoulos 1991, p. 57.
7   Smokovitis 1972, p. 4.
8   Vakalopoulos 1991, p. 170.
9   Vakalopoulos 1991, p. 212.
10   Broc 1981, p. 324.

walls of Tripolitsa. According to reports at the time, the typhus epidemic spread throughout the Peloponnese and lasted until 1826 (with varying degrees of flare-ups per season and place), with between five and six thousand victims, including Benjamin Lesvios, Theodoros Negris and Germanos of Palaiai Patras.[11] In Nafplio, typhus seemed to have become endemic.[12] There was also a smallpox epidemic among the Souliots and on Naxos,[13] and finally, in April 1828, the plague spread to the islands and the Peloponnese (Hydra, Spetses, Argolida, Salamina, Achaia, Megarida and Kalavryta), with 1,113 cases and causing 783 deaths.[14]

To sum up, 'in times ... of hunger and poverty, in the midst of extreme impurity and such a great population density [in Nafplio], mortality was great, and not a day passed without 15–20 dead'.[15] George Siambos calculated the life expectancy for those born in the period of 1821–35 to be 25 years for men and 25.5 years for women.[16]

2   The Emergence of Military Medicine

Beyond any ideological projection that can be made about them (heroes, traitors, patriots), the men and women who participated in the armed conflicts of the Greek Revolution – and/or were experiencing its consequences – had material and biological needs. Their bleeding bodies – as was the most commonly used metaphor – demanded protection from the military and the political authorities who claimed leadership. Assuring protection against suffering was a legitimising enterprise as well as a condition for high morals and obedience. Kanellos Deligiannis remembers that 'the chief provided them [his armed men] with ammunition, shoes and rations, gave grain for the upkeep of their families and money to those in need',[17] and the Mavromichalis family had to 'assume the role of the protector to their numerous followers'.[18] In the same vein, the different established administrations until 1827, and Governor Ioannis Kapodistrias after 1828, tried to ensure that their loyal troops were regularly

11   Kyriakopoulos 2001, pp. 25–30.
12   Millingen 1831, p. 262.
13   Vladimiros 2014, p. 52.
14   Stéphanos 1884, p. 511.
15   Aidek [von Heideck] 1900, p. 59.
16   Siampos 1973, p. 29.
17   Koliopoulos and Veremis 2002, p. 14.
18   Tsakouris 1996, p. 149.

supplied with food and payment or the promise that land would be given to them. It is important to note that professional medical care was neither demanded nor offered, at least not on a regular basis.

Within this general picture, we nevertheless have to recognise a distinction, which existed until the advent of Ioannis Kapodistrias, between the regular troops, the warrior bands [*armatoloi*] of the Pindos mountain range and the armed Peloponnesian peasant forces. This distinction is useful in comprehending the progressive emergence of military medicine among the Balkan armed forces before Ioannis Kapodistrias organised a specialised military medical service.

The regular troops steadily had a medical division. The corps of 300 men organised by Dimitrios Hypsilantis had a 'chief medical officer and surgeon', the Athenian Anargyros Petrakis.[19] On 1 April 1822, Alexandros Mavrokordatos established a mountain artillery corps under the French Olivier Voutier, an infantry regiment led by Pietro Tarella from Piedmont and deputy commander Gubernatis (two battalions of five companies each, a total of 200 strong) and a Battalion (Philhellene Battalion) under Karl Friedrich Lebrecht von Normann-Ehrenfels with 120 men.[20] In this force of 560 strong served two German doctors, Heinrich Treiber and Johann Daniel Elster, and a Dane, Elster's assistant Friedrich Johanssen. Based on Elster's testimony, he and Johanssen served in the Philhellene Battalion. Thus, Treiber must have served in the Tarella Regiment.[21] We note also that the Philhellene Battalion established a military hospital in Mesolongi under the supervision of Johanssen.

After the defeat in the battle of Peta, Treiber continued serving in new formations (the Philhellene Legion in 1823, the 600 men of colonel P. Rodios in 1824 and, a year later, the French Charles Fabvier corps of 3,500 strong). Other military doctors were Johann Peter Knoeffel (German Legion) and K.F. Bojons (replacing Treiber in the Philhellene Legion).[22]

In 1826, King Ludwig of Bavaria sent Karl Wilhelm von Heideck, who replaced Fabvier as head of the regular troops at the end of August 1828. Heideck was accompanied by 13 servicemen, one of whom, Sebastian Schreiner, was a military doctor.[23] A clothing commission was also set up for the new standing army and at least five military hospitals (İç Kale of Nafplio, Naupaktos, Methoni, Acrocorinth and Patras), one for the cavalry (Argos) and one naval

---

19   Kyriakopoulos 2001, p. 25.

20   Vakalopoulos 1991, p. 83.

21   Elster 2010.

22   Dardavesis 2013, p. 23.

23   Aidek [von Heideck] 1900, p. 56.

(Poros) were established.[24] The Bavarian physician Friedrich Zuccarini was named chief inspector. Surgeon Aimilios from Lesvos was appointed to the second cavalry battallion and surgeon Chronias Drosinos from Ampelakia to the second infantry battalion and the hospital of Patras.[25] Finally, all doctors and surgeons in the army were equated, in terms of salaries, with 'officers of the highest order', something that, as it will be explained, was not self-evident.[26]

This composition would change once payments started to come from the French government.[27] In April 1829, 40 French lieutenants, commanders and sergeants were transferred to the Greek force, and Heideck was replaced by Major General Camille Alphonse Trézel (who later became French Minister of Military). However, the number of German-speaking medical personnel did not decline. According to Dardavesis, E. Bormann was appointed to the cavalry, Friedrich Huebel worked in the hospital of Nafplio and Adolf Mann was the director of the military pharmacy based in the same city. A Frenchman, Henri Dumont, entered the service in the artillery alongside Stylianos Aimilios, Chronias Drosinos, Stefanos Kritis and Antonios Polylas from Corfu.[28]

The regime change of 1830 in France saw military conditions in Greece deteriorate. Without payment, the army progressively lost its manpower, and the assassination of Ioannis Kapodistrias gave the final blow. Concerning the medical personnel, information is scarce. In the archives, we meet names such as Louvel (probably French), Mann and Kritis.[29] It is very likely that Dumont was also on duty; this is because we do not know that he left between 1830 and 1834, when he reappears in our archives.

In sharp contrast to the existence of a stable medical division in the different regimental troops, armed local bands – *armatoloi* and Peloponnesian fighters – only had medical treatment on rare occasion and in an unstable manner. In this respect, until 1824–5 there existed an initial difference between warrior groups from Continental Greece – those who occasionally used specialised medical personnel – and the armed bands from the Peloponnese who did not. Even if the data is too scattered to homogenise (which underlines exactly the provisional nature of military medicine during the period), it seems that when

---

24   Stefanitzis 1839, p. 78, and Aidek [von Heideck] 1900, p. 124.
25   In 1830, he was the doctor of the Thermes hot baths. See General State Archives of Greece [Γενικά Αρχεία του Κράτους], Vlachogiannis Collection, Δ106, doc. dated 12 June 1829.
26   General State Archives of Greece, Vlachogiannis Collection, Δ106, doc. dated 16 March 1829.
27   Themeli-Katifori 1985, pp. 70–1.
28   Dardavesis 2013.
29   Kritis was in 1831 responsible for the light infantry hospital in Ermioni.

we come across complaints about medical deficiencies or requests for a doctor, they usually came from warlords [Gk. *Hoplarchigoi*] of Continental Greece and Epirus: the Souliots had Loukas Vagias until 1826, when they started complaining about the absence of treatment; Odysseas Androutsos had at least two surgeons, one of whom, the Muslim Hasan Ağa Kurt Ali, served the besieged troops in Acropolis; and Makrygiannis and Ragkos also had one. It seems that the knowledge of the organisation of an *armatoliki* in Continental Greece – i.e. a centralised, though local, administration system – permitted the appearance of a professionalised medical service. It is also possible that the *armatoloi* were acquainted with the use of medical treatment since the rule of Ali Pasha, who became known for establishing hospitals, appointing doctors and erecting lazarettos.[30]

In the Peloponnese, on the other hand, peasants – that is, non-professionals of war – mostly comprised the bands that fought in battle. According to Dr. Elster, there were only 'priests who treated the sick, as well as the dead' during the siege of Patras by Theodoros Kolokotronis. Further along the way, however, references to doctors begin to appear in the records, and there was a change in the Peloponnese that may be attributed to the presence of Philhellene physicians who arrived around that time. In August 1824, the Bavarian Gaugenrieder was appointed to the camp of Patras; medical surgeon [Gk. *Iatrocheirourgos*] Antonios Mavrogiannis in Acrocorinth; physician Agamemnon Avgerinos treated the Andreas Londos troops; and several surgeons (we know of five of them, all of whom were medical empirics: Sp. Michalopoulos, A. Papagiannopoulos from Gortynia, Konstantinos Pelopidas from Ioannina, K. Tsakalis and Nik. Athanasopoulos) and one physician served in the corps of Kolokotronis.[31]

Notwithstanding, the presence of surgeons and doctors among local Balkan fighters did not gain a stable character and it did not concern all armed bands before 1828. A Christian religion favouring fatalism as well as certain cultural inhibitions in the acknowledgement of infirmity and incompetence played a part in the absence of such stable medical treatment.[32] Meanwhile, Theodoros

---

30   Panzac 1985.

31   Tsagkaraki 2019, pp. 72–3. We of course encounter exceptions. For example, on 31 March 1821, P(aule) Doukakis was appointed in Kalamata as a 'caretaker [ἐπιστάτης] of the wounded of the *Genos* [the Nation]'; see Dimakopoulos 1972, p. 250. As we learn from the archives, he was treating the wounded sent by the various camps; see the General State Archives of Greece, Archive of the Struggle of Independence [Αρχείο Αγώνος], Εκτελεστικόν, f. 23, doc. 3205.

32   For the notion of *philotimo*, a cultural equivalent of *machismo*, see Blum and Blum 1965, pp. 20–22, and Foster 1965, pp. 299–300.

Kolokotronis praised the *klephts* for their capacity to 'endure hunger, thirst, difficult times, dirt etc.'.[33] Elster, meanwhile, offered one more explanation: fear of the chieftain's anger 'in case he [Elster refers to Kolokotronis] gets bored with me, which could be done if he owed me money [salary]'. During times when Kolokotronis had low levels of self-restraint, violent conduct against subordinates was very frequent.

A fourth factor that might have been responsible for minimising the presence of medical treatment for the wounded perhaps had to do with battle tactics. Balkan 'irregulars' – as the *armatoloi* were named for their tactics in the battlefield – did not fight when the cause was predicted to be a lost one. Their actions were limited to skirmishes and sudden attacks, which is why they did not have many casualties. The 'ethos' of the 'regulars', on the other hand, as the military historian John Keegan has underlined, was of a different kind.[34] Their discipline, their obedience to orders and the absence of individualistic heroism (all resulting from the drill), combined with face-to-face combat and a notion of self-respect that prevented soldiers from fleeing the battlefield were responsible for significant casualties, as exemplified by those procured at the battle of Peta. Medical treatment was thus necessary to support the military effort and assure the fighting capacity of soldiers. In 1824, probably the first manual on military medicine written in Greek was published in Missolonghi, by the Italian Francesco Bruno, Lord Byron's staff physician.[35] Bruno considered the body of the soldier as a 'machine' whose 'good health' is 'the source of victory'.

3   Medicine and Military Discipline

The application of medicine was not just a result of tactics in battle; it could also be responsible for the kind of tactics adopted. Medicine, as Michel Foucault has pointed out, plays an important role in promoting social discipline – and therefore military discipline.[36] For Max Weber, on the other hand, discipline is a powerful social process linked to the concentration of the means of warfare. Its results are uniform conduct, direct execution of orders, methodical training and bureaucratic organisation. Closer to our point, Weber writes

---

33   Vakalopoulos 1991, p. 35.
34   Keegan 1994, p. 347.
35   F. Bruno, *Περί των μέσων των προσφυεστέρων εις την διατήρησιν της υγείας των στρατιωτών, κατά τα στρατόπεδα και τας φρουράς*, Mesolongi 1824 (a bilingual manual written in Italian and translated in Greek, probably by its author).
36   Foucault 1972.

that: 'Gun powder and all the war techniques associated with it became significant only with the existence of discipline'.[37] Medicine was important in this
respect, as medical historian Mark Harrison notes when asking 'What, then, did
medicine contribute to this "rationalisation" of military management?' Among
other things, Harrison proposes, the regimental medical officer 'was the principal conduit of propaganda in matters of health and morals. Hygienic rituals,
themselves, formed part of the new forms of discipline which began to emerge
in the European armed forces during the eighteenth and early nineteenth centuries'.[38]

  Therefore, another factor that can explain the difference between 'irregulars'
and 'regulars' might be related to the kind of medical practice adopted by each
of them. We have counted approximately three hundred doctors and surgeons
who participated in one way or another to the Greek Revolution (as private
doctors/surgeons, as violent recruits, as volunteers and as salaried personnel).
Half of them had studied and half of them were medical empirics. There was
not any distinction between them concerning their propensity to participate in
the Revolution. On the other hand, however, it seems that doctors with a formal
education preferred regular troops while medical empirics worked with the
irregulars. This difference can be explained by the cultural community between
the empirics and the local armed bands of Ottoman Balkans. Empirical medical exercise was as inconsistent as local battle tactics. The scientific approach
of empirics lacked the theoretical, diagnostic and taxonomic systematisation
of medicine taught in medical schools. However, empirical medicine was not
an approach of pure empiricism, despite the name, and therefore it should
not be considered as totally lacking systematisation. Empirical medicine is just
less systematic than the one studied in faculties. As fighters were inclined to
leave their posts at their guise, so too could empirics, for they equally could
not understand the need for discipline that a military/administrative position
imposed in the exercise of their profession.

  The failure in the organisation of irregular bands in *chiliarchies* in 1822 also
concerned the military health service. Of the three political constitutions promulgated in 1821, only one, that of eastern Continental Greece, provided the
'*proestoi* [i.e. the notables] for the army' with the responsibility 'to take care
of all that is necessary to the Hospital of the Province ... of the assistance
of sick soldiers ... and of the salaries of all doctors'. On 9 January 1822, the
National Assembly of Epidaurus wanted to put into practice this article with

37   Weber 1946, p. 257.
38   Harrison 2004, p. 3.

the organisation of the *chiliarchies*, each of which was to have 'a Doctor [and] a Surgeon'. The effort was not successful, and we know only of one, the *chiliarchia* of G. Sekeris [in the archives the name is written as *Senieris*], which employed the physician Philippe Jerniansky (?). The impossibility of 'regularising' the irregulars was reflected in the poor development of their military medical service.

Things changed by 1828 in a way indicative of the greater disciplining of the military and society more generally. The different mechanisms of the Kapodistrias administration – the proliferation of hospitals, the adoption of the bayonet, the organisation of a standing army, the schooling system etc. – must all be seen as different aspects of the same process. Governor Kapodistrias managed to impose the form of *chiliarchies*, which functioned alongside regular troops. Two years later, he proceeded to a deeper military reform, organising the *chiliarchies* to light infantry battalions. According to Apostolos Vakalopoulos, these battalions, which incorporated a large body of local fighters and warriors, had a stable medical service of 30 officers and riflemen. Thus, the Englishman David Urquhart could support, having in 1830 observed clean camps and white *foustanellas*.[39]

In conclusion, it seems that there is an element of mutuality between the effort of the military and political authorities to create a disciplined armed force as well as the kind and place of medical practice among troops. During the Greek Revolution, the imperatives of treating wounded and diseased fighters by a specialised medical service was not always obvious for local political and military authorities, though it was for French- and German-speaking officers who organised regimental, tactical-force armed corps. On the contrary, the military medical structure became common after the advent of Ioannis Kapodistrias. This chapter explored this chronological and organisational divergence between the regimental troops and the local armed bands. It argued that medicine had more to do with tactics than with the need for military efficiency. Medicine in the army was the result of military discipline and at the same time the mechanism promoting it.

Bibliography

Aidek, Karolos varonos [Karl Wilhelm von Heideck] 1900, 'Τα των Βαυαρών φιλελλήνων εν Ελλάδι κατά τα έτη 1826–1829', *Αρμονία*, 1: 56–60.

---

39   Vakalopoulos 1991, pp. 267–8 and 179.

Blum, Richard and Eva Blum (assisted by Anna Amera and Sophie Kallifatidou) 1965, *Health and healing in rural Greece: A study of three communities*, Stanford, California: Stanford University Press.

Broc, N. 1981, 'Les grandes missions scientifiques françaises au xıxe siècle (Morée, Algérie, Mexique) et leurs travaux géographiques', *Revue d'Histoire des Sciences*, 34, 3–4: 319–58.

Cooter, Roger and Steve Sturdy 1998, 'Of war, medicine and modernity: Introduction', in *War, Medicine and Modernity*, edited by Roger Cooter, Mark Harrison and Steve Sturdy, Stroud: Sutton.

Dardavesis, T.I. 2013, 'Υγειονομική φροντίδα και περίθαλψη των Αγωνιστών του 1821', *Πάπυροι/Papyri*, 2: 10–26.

Dimakopoulos, G. 1972, 'Η επί του Αγώνος υπέρ της δημόσιας υγείας κυβερνητική πολιτική', *Επιστημονική Επετηρίς της Παντείου Ανωτάτης Σχολής Πολιτικών Επιστημών*, 1972.

Elster, Daniel Johann 2010, *Το Τάγμα των Φιλελλήνων. Η ίδρυση, η εκστρατεία και η καταστροφή του*, Athens: Μένανδρος.

Foster, George 1965, 'Peasant society and the image of limited good', *American Antropologist. New Series*, 67, 2: 293–315.

Foucault, Michel 1972 [1963], *Naissance de la Clinique. Une archéologie du regard médical*, Paris: Presses Universitaires De France.

Harrison, Mark 2004, 'Medicine and the management of modern warfare: an introduction', in *Medicine and Modern Warfare*, edited by Roger Cooter, Mark Harrison and Steve Sturdy, 2nd ed., Amsterdam-Atlanta: Rodopi.

Keegan, John 1994, *A History of Warfare*, New York: Vintage.

Koliopoulos, John S. and Thanos M. Veremis 2002, *Greece, the Modern Sequel from 1831 to the Present*, London: Hurst & Company.

Kostis, Kostas 1993, *Αφορία, ακρίβεια, πείνα. Οι κρίσεις διατροφής στην ελληνική χερσόνησο (1650–1830). Προβλήματα προσέγγισης και εμπειρικές ενδείξεις*, Athens: Αλεξάνδρεια.

Kouzis, A.P. 1946, 'Περί της υγειονομικής υπηρεσίας του στρατού κατά τον υπέρ της ανεξαρτησίας Αγώνα', *Πρακτικά Ακαδημίας Αθηνών*, 21, 2: 9–15.

Kyriakopoulos, K.G. 2001, 'Επιδημίες τύφου κατά τη διάρκεια της Επανάστασης βάσει πηγών της εποχής', *Δέλτος*, 21: 25–30.

Millingen, Julius 1831, *Memoirs of the affairs of Greece; containing an account of the military and political events, which occurred in 1823 and following years, with various anecdotes relating to lord Byron and an account of his last illness and death*, London: John Rodwell.

Panzac, Daniel 1985, *La peste dans l'Empire ottoman, 1700–1850*, Leuven: Peeters.

Papageorgiou, I.K. n.d., *Η ιατροφαρμακευτική περίθαλψις των αγωνιστών του 1821*, Herakleio.

Schizas D.N., K. Kyriakopoulos and N.D. Schizas 2009, 'Οι εμπειρικοί ιατροί και η συμβολή τους στην περίθαλψη των αγωνιστών κατά την Επανάσταση του 1821', *Annuaire de la Fondation des Études Néohelléniques*, 14: 103–16.

Siampos, G.S. 1973, *Δημογραφική εξέλιξις της νεωτέρας Ελλάδος (1821–1985)*, Athens: Ανωτάτη Σχολή Οικονομικών και Εμπορικών Επιστημών.

Smokovitis, A. 1972, *Οι συνθήκες υγιεινής στο πολιορκημένο Μεσολόγγι*, Thessaloniki: n.ed.

Stefanitzis, Petros D. 1839, *Απλή και μεμαρτυρημένη έκθεσις των εν Ελλάδι πράξεων και τυχών αυτού απ' αρχής του αγώνος της επαναστάσεως μέχρι σήμερον*, Athens: Κ. Ράλλης.

Stéphanos, Clon 1884, *La Grèce au point de vue naturel, ethnologique, anthropologique, démographique et médical*, Paris: G. Masson.

Themeli-Katifori, Despoina 1985, *Το γαλλικό ενδιαφέρον για την Ελλάδα στην περίοδο του Καποδίστρια, 1828–31*, Athens: Επικαιρότητα.

Tsagkaraki, Anastasia 2009, *Les philhellènes français dans la lutte pour l'indépendance grecque. La contribution des Français à l'organisation de l'armée régulière grecque pendant la période 1821–31*, Athens.

Tsakouris, K. 1996, *Η φιλανθρωπία στην Ελλάδα του 19ου αιώνα : συγκρότηση και λειτουργία. Η περίπτωση της Αθήνας και του Πειραιά*, Ph.D. dissertation, Thessaloniki.

Vakalopoulos, Apostolos E. 1991, *Τα ελληνικά στρατεύματα του 1821. οργάνωση, ηγεσία, τακτική, ήθη, ψυχολογία*, Thessaloniki: Σταμούλης.

Vladimiros, Lazaros E. 2014, *Γιατροί και ιατρική στην Επανάσταση του 1821*, Athens: Μπαλτά.

Weber, Max 1946, 'The Meaning of Discipline', in *From Max Weber: Essays in Sociology*, edited by H.H. Gerth and C. Wright Mills, New York: Oxford University Press.

CHAPTER 9

Economy and Power in the Greek Revolution

Public Revenues, Powerful Entities and State Formation

Simos Bozikis

Although 1821, the starting date of the Greek Revolution, may be referred to as a milestone in the establishment of the modern Greek state, it is generally recognised by historiography that state formation actually only began in 1828. After 1823, the Greek Revolution demonstrated a downward trend; war and internal conflicts (1824) had a disruptive impact and administration on a (revolutionary) national level was not functional. This chapter, based on recent research on the Greek public revenues during the decade between 1822 and 1832, will put the above chronology of state formation in modern Greece into question. My aim is to contribute to a better understanding of aspects of the Greek Revolution that have been overlooked so far by historiography. More specifically, I will suggest that – throughout the revolution – public finance operations were not without importance and, more significantly, were interwoven with the critical issues of political power and the conduct of war during the Revolution. These financial operations developed together with the efforts to form a national political centre and a state authority, which originated already from the first year of the Revolution and also carried on during Ioannis Kapodistrias's administration (1828–31).

1   Public Finance and Power in 1821: An Essential Parameterisation

The formation of the modern Greek state, as a process, was associated with the coordination and availability of resources and instruments for the conduct of war as well as the institutional organisation of freedom and national independence.[1] However, we should not ignore the fact that the Greek Revolution started in several fragmented outbreaks, though they were certainly linked through the actions of the members of the Friendly Society [Gk. *Philiki Etairia*] and

---

1   Tilly 1990, pp. 20, 25–6; Mann 1992, pp. 18–19, 74–6; Elias 2000, pp. 354–5; Kıvanç Karaman and Pamuk 2013, pp. 603–26.

other aspects of the actual situation at that time. It also began without pooled material resources and instruments of oppression, excluding the battle fleet to a certain degree; the revolutionary fleet actually consisted of private merchant vessels that were made available in service of the nation.

Such a start, relying on poor resources, was followed by rearrangements triggered by the Revolution itself, producing multiple political issues. These issues mainly concerned the creation of a supreme national political authority and the jurisdiction of that authority over the financial resources and management of combat operations – namely, issues that were inherent in the establishment of a national political centre and in the process of integrating a territory within it.[2]

A starting point which might prove useful in approaching the aforementioned issues is the association between the Greek Revolutionaries and public revenues, or more specifically, the financial resources that have been acknowledged as public revenues.[3] This approach provides insight into the essential association between the main types of public revenue and various actors on one hand[4] and into different fields and types of action on the other hand: local/national/international, politics/war, land/sea (**Fig. 9.1**).

The main types of public revenue (**Chart 9.1**) came from: tax farming (lease); ransom money (ransoming the Hursid Pasha's *harem*s captured in Tripolitsa, 1822); spoils (Corinth, 1822); plunder loot, particularly between 1825 and 1827; the sale of national properties (former Ottoman *mülk* and *miri* properties) as of 1823; voluntary contributions and mandatory fund-raising in various instances; funds raised and supplies collected abroad, especially during the crucial years 1826–7; and, last but not least, from the two foreign loans that were concluded during the Greek Revolution (1824–5).[5] At this point, I would like to highlight the impact of the main revenue types on the process of establishing a national political centre, associating them with the national administration and, if applicable, with local or international intermediaries, the armed groups and the battle fleet. The significance of these sources of revenue depended on various criteria (amount; distribution or concentration; natural assets or cash;

---

2   Regarding the distinction between permeable frontiers and borders in the nineteenth-century Greek state, see Kotaridis 2006, pp. 121–2; Kostis 2006, p. 56.

3   General State Archives of Greece [Γενικά Αρχεία του Κράτους], Κατάστιχα και Πρωτόκολλα Οικονομίας των περιόδων Αγώνα και Καποδίστρια, fold. 12.

4   Pizanias 2003, pp. 42–50.

5   Bozikis 2018, pp. 464, 537. The sums have been calculated according to the Greek national administration accounting books. Revenues that failed to be recorded were not taken into account. **Map 9.1** includes Hydra, Spetses and Psara as recipients of a part of the tax product issued to cover the Greek battle fleet needs.

FIGURE 9.1   Types of revenue, powerful entities and their significance for the Greek national administration

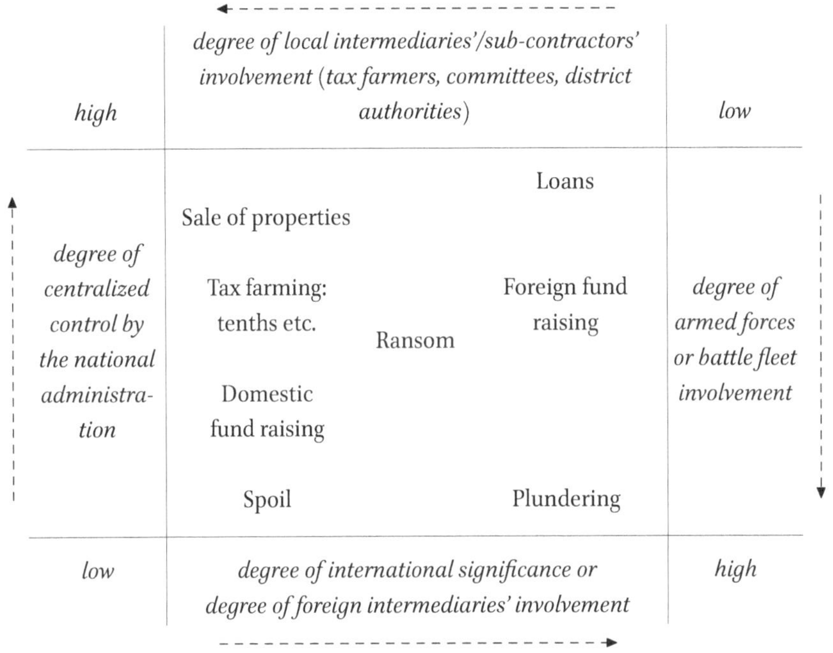

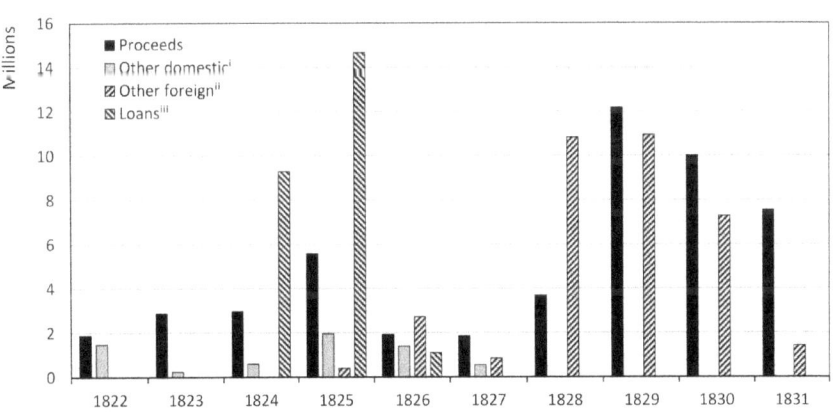

CHART 9.1   Summary of the main types of revenue 1822–31
Note: (i) Plunder-spoil, fund raising, sale of national estates; (ii) fund raising abroad and transfers from foreign governments; (iii) the entire amount paid in cash.
SOURCE: BOZIKIS 2018, PP. 464, 537

duration; and frequency); I will now focus on more significant sources of revenue, namely tax revenue and loans.

Regarding the main ordinary and extraordinary internal revenues (tax revenue, fund raising, sales) it was up to the Greek national administration to
decide and authorise the process and orientation. This process would take
place at local level by various co-operative intermediaries (tax-farmers, district
authorities, armed ranks, quartermasters and fleet vessels),[6] who were linked
to some extent and had representatives in the bodies of the centralised political authorities of the Revolution. The main recipients of the tax revenues were
the armed groups and the battle fleet of the Revolution. A primary feature of
this process, which demonstrated no shortage of conflicts, was its association
with the mutual acceptance of legitimate and illegitimate roles based on the
national administration; it also served as a form of an ordinary system under
clearly exceptional and demanding circumstances.

On the other hand, revenues that were closely intertwined with the war,
namely ransoms, spoils and plunder at sea, formed a special category of multiple direct or indirect importance for the administration. Legalisation provided by the Greek national administration in the issue of plundering did not
only have financial consequences. The fleet and the cruisers were basically of a
regular nature. The Greek fleet activity was based on a political commitment,
to enter the struggle for national independence, which justified its actions.
The battle fleet, as such, presented a form of alignment with the international
maritime law that distinguishes between politically legitimised and recognised
control and operations aimed only at achieving economic gains. This was contrary to the widespread piratical actions (performed almost by all islanders),
because it complied with the conduct of war as provided for by the international maritime law.[7]

Therefore, the revolutionary fleet's activity also involved an alternative path
toward the internationalisation of the issue of the Greek Revolution, to a certain degree through the naval blockades enforced by the Greek Revolutionary
government and the control of the merchant ships. These procedures, in conjunction with other processes, contributed to the achievement of the first steps
towards the recognition of the revolutionaries, beginning with England's recog-

---

6 For a comparison with the Ottoman fiscal system, see Darling 1997, pp. 157–79; Coşgel, Miceli
   and Ahmed 2009, pp. 704–17.

7 Regarding the political significance of the distinction between corsair and pirate, see Schmitt
   2004, pp. 49–50. Regarding the Greek pre-revolutionary experience, see Harlaftis 2013,
   pp. 145–206. About the unintended consequences of the authorised non-state violence, see
   Thomson 1994, pp. 54–9.

nition of Greece as being a nation in a state of war.[8] They were followed by exertion of indirect pressure upon the Great Powers in order to take initiatives towards the diplomatic-settlement end of the war, as the control of their merchant ships – although selective and dependent on their flag[9] – had become a detrimental issue extending beyond the Aegean Sea.

On the other hand, in Continental Greece, ransom paid as a product of negotiations ensured the Revolutionary administration's proximity to the process; however, booty collected from scattered large or small-scale battles was not easy to be controlled, with the exception of a few siege operations.[10] Thus, plundering as well as looting Greek populations,[11] particularly at times when the administration's revenue was limited, enhanced the independence of the Revolutionary armed groups.

It would be interesting to study this by taking into account some ignored impacts of the loans concluded by the Revolutionary Greek national administration in the City of London in 1824 and in 1825. These loans were of major importance internationally as a form of an early official recognition of the Greek issue. At the same time, although the lack of knowledge and failure of the Greek side to completely control the net product of the loans led to considerable losses, it is important to know that the amounts which arrived in Athens were controlled at a local level (**Table 1**), namely in terms of the process, without involving local intermediaries or control by the armed groups or the fleet. This does not mean that Greek national administration officers were not related to armed groups, the fleet, etc., but that the loans implied a fundamental modification to the financial circuit, since they directly provided the national administration with a rather large amount, almost equivalent to the other revenues that were received during the years of the Revolution. As we shall see below, these loans allowed the administration to cater for the enormous needs of the fleet for a period of time and to mobilise armed groups, which in turn recognised the leadership of the political authorities.[12]

---

8   *The Cambridge History of British Foreign Policy 1783–1919*, eds. A.W. Ward – G.P. Gooch, vol. 2, Cambridge 1923, p. 86.

9   General State Archives of Greece, Αρχείο Θαλασσίου Δικαστηρίου, fold. 25, doc. no. 162.

10   General State Archives of Greece, Κατάστιχα και Πρωτόκολλα Οικονομίας των περιόδων Αγώνα και Καποδίστρια, fold. 12.

11   See, for example, *Αρχεία της Ελληνικής Παλιγγενεσίας*, Athens 1971–2012, vol. 6, p. 22.

12   Rotzokos 1997, pp. 38–9 ff.

2   Tax Integration and Territory Development

As expected, in a territory that was changing during a revolution, whose links
with the national administration were yet to take shape, gross agricultural production (any tenth of the value), custom revenues, operation of salt pans, fish
farms, and mines were subject to taxation, in any case using the traditional
Ottoman tax farming system, auctioned off to the highest bidder.[13] In addition
to that, sums were occasionally collected through voluntary or coercive fund-
raising and sale of the so-called national estates,[14] particularly of the former
Ottoman *mülk* properties (mills, houses, warehouses, stores).[15]

This procedure was of course carried out with the support of various local
intermediaries and persons holding official roles (district governors, local officials supervising tax collection, tax farmers, armed groups, the battle fleet, etc.).
In any case, however, it served as a confirmation of the establishment and
implementation of an official fiscal function; it also demonstrated a broader
recognition of the national administration as an entity that legalised anything
to do with ordinary and extraordinary taxation, disposal of national assets and
the channeling of revenues collected from those sources.

If we consider only those more regular revenues (in terms of annual incid-
ence), taking into account two more dimensions, namely time and space, we
may find out how interesting these processes were regarding efforts towards
the formation of a territory integrated in the emergent national political centre.
Thus, we will analyse below the taxation from 1822 to 1832 for the islands of the
Aegean, Continental Greece and the Peloponnese (**Map 9.1**), focusing on the
first critical years of the Revolution.

At first, the integration of the islands of the Aegean Sea, both politically
and in terms of taxation, into the Revolutionary state presented some fluctuations. In some cases, the district authorities that were appointed in April 1822
failed to manage their coexistence with already existing local self-governing
bodies and reinforced or failed to dissolve local disputes – mainly, but not
exclusively, on islands with Catholic residents.[16] Soon, though, this situation
was normalised, obviously also involving local particularities and occasional
fluctuations. This development was facilitated by the activity of the battle fleet,
which was responsible for the collection of tax revenue and other revenues

---

13   Bozikis 2018, pp. 309–10.
14   See Karouzou 2018, p. 173; Nakos 1986, pp. 20–2.
15   Nakos 1986, p. 413 ff.
16   See, for example, *Αρχεία της Ελληνικής Παλιγγενεσίας*, Athens 1971–2012, vol. 7, p. 156.

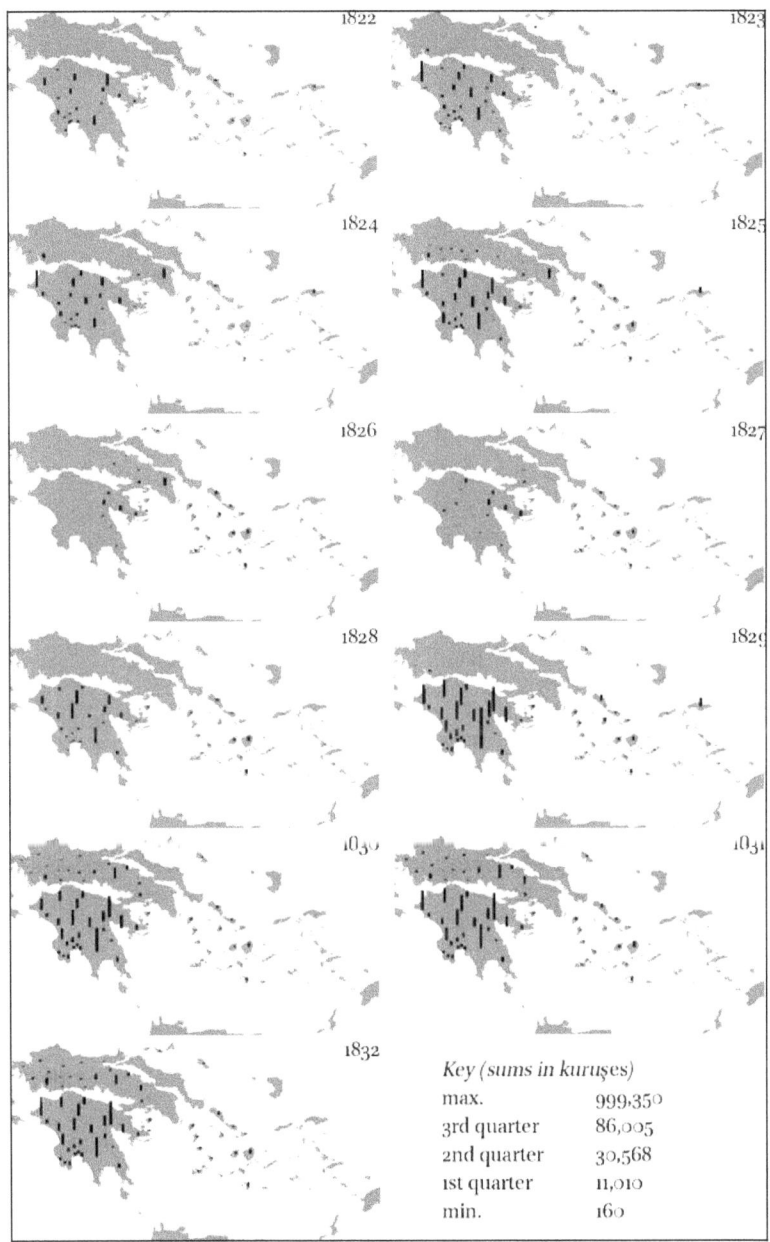

Key (sums in kuruşes)
max.   999,350
3rd quarter   86,005
2nd quarter   30,568
1st quarter   11,010
min.   160

MAP 9.1   Taxation territory 1822–32

from the islands of the Aegean Sea.[17] With its contribution, first with certain flexibility but also with the threat of violence, sovereignty and taxation procedures on the islands were consolidated and revenues increased in 1824–25, even without being significantly reduced in 1826–7, i.e. during the years when continental areas were suffering.

On the other hand, in Continental Greece [*Sterea Ellada* or *Roumeli*] taxation was possible only for a few districts by 1824. This area had been significantly exposed to the Ottoman campaigns.[18] However, the difficulty to impose taxation may have been additionally related to the failure of the Senate in the western part and of the Supreme Court [Areios Pagos] in the eastern part to integrate the *armatoloi* [former Ottoman militia] to a large extent.[19] Tax imposition in the districts of Continental Greece changed only after the civil conflicts among the revolutionaries of 1824 and the arrival of the first loan from London: in other words, after important military leaders from that area represented on the front line, either voluntarily or involuntary, the idea and the institutional status of a *supreme national administration*. Therefore, in 1825, taxes were collected across the area of Continental Greece. The developments that followed did not enable a long-term symmetrical continuation of that situation. This did not last long in the western part, due to the siege of Missolonghi; in the eastern part, it was preserved until the fall of Athens in 1827 (Karaiskakis's operations contributed significantly to that effect). This, however, does not call into question our foregoing suggestions, namely that the national administration was beginning to intervene and legalise the revenue stream in parts of Continental Greece in the same way that it did in the rest of the revolutionary territory.

Finally, the Peloponnese presents particular interest in terms of taxation, as it was the theatre of several internal conflicts during the Revolution.[20] Early in 1822, national administration and the Peloponnesian Senate were disputing each other either directly or indirectly regarding leadership; they cooperated, however, in order to impose taxes on the districts that were controlled by the revolutionaries. In 1823, taxation was further extended geographically. With the eradication of the regional organisations of the first revolutionary years, the existing competitions were transported within the national administration. The two phases of the civil war followed in 1824, a development which was not at all irrelevant with the issue of controlling the tax revenue, on which recruiting ability and, thus, power were dependent. Finally, in 1824, taxation of the

17   *Αρχείον της Κοινότητος Ύδρας*, Piraeus 1921–9, vol. 8, p. 437.
18   Trikoupis 1978, p. 82.
19   Asdrachas 2014, pp. 107–11.
20   Rotzokos 1997.

districts showed a minor decrease, and the year that followed, upon establishment of the national administration, reached its maximum potential since the beginning of the Revolution. In 1826, revolutionary taxation was restricted only to the eastern part of the Peloponnese due to the invasion of Ibrahim Pasha of Egypt, but in 1827 its implementation expanded again across several districts, as it was intertwined with the Greek counteroffensive.

Taxation was consistent in some places but erratic or short-lived elsewhere. This perspective does not mean a lack of particularities; however, it allows us to question the conventional view that a national administration existed only in form during the Revolution, something like an organisation chart in the descriptions of the Constitutions rather than a governance body interwoven with the revolutionary reality. It furthermore allows us to see that it is only after the Naval Battle of Navarino (October 1827) and the assumption of the Governor's office by Ioannis Kapodistrias that we can talk of real state-formation processes. Based on this perspective, as reflected in the upward trend of the tax revenues during the early years of the Revolution and in the downward pressure exerted on it during 1826–7 but not in its elimination (**Chart 9.1**), we can also reconsider the conventional chronology that saw the downward trend of the Greek Revolution after 1823. This chronology was based on the argument that war and internal conflicts played a purely deconstructive part, simplistically equating revolution with wartime events. The argument overlooks the fact that even civil conflicts (1824) caused deconstruction while they also reinforced progress toward the establishment of a national political centre. This argument does not account for the role played by defense against the campaigns of Ibrahim Pasha of Egypt and of Reşid Mehmed Pasha. Processes of reconstruction and partial recapturing and taxation of territories can be located before or after the defeats of the revolutionaries (Missolonghi 1826; Athens 1827). In addition to that, contact with the Philhellenic Committees and delivery of war material and food supplies were under way.[21] These were processes which, in addition to their internal dimension and the fact that they ensured continuity in difficult circumstances, supported Greek positions for a period when it was becoming very clear that a diplomatic solution to the Greek issue was getting on track.

From that time forward, after the Battle of Navarino and in more secured conditions, with the Peloponnese and the Cyclades granted an international protection status, the state-formation processes were further enhanced as previous experiences and new needs were taken into account. Tax revenues and

21   Phrantzis 1841, pp. 61–2.

money sent as financial aid and advance payments of future loans, mainly by France and Russia, were maximised in 1829 (**Chart 9.1**). This development corresponds, on one hand, to the apex of the political hegemony of Ioannis Kapodistrias and his allies until the Fourth National Assembly; on the other hand, it corresponds to the appearance of an organised opposition against – as well as to the withdrawal of French support to – Ioannis Kapodistrias.

3   The Impact of the Loans on the Establishment of a National Political Centre

Both external loans that were concluded by the revolutionary national admin-istration in 1824 and 1825 have been considered from different perspectives in historiography: in terms of the consecutive bankruptcies of Greece, as the origins of foreign interventions and in the context of factionalism patronage and civil conflicts (1824). In short, there is a predominant understanding that the loans affected the external recognition of the Greek Revolution to a cer-tain extent, but also that they had little impact on the war progress and state-formation processes.

The case of the foreign loans has been used by popular historiography in Greece as a case of 'scandal', principally from the perspective of the quality of those involved in their management. It is indeed known that the formation of a national political centre and state authorities created tensions concerning financial resources, offices, etc. It is commonplace to interpret such disputes as personal differences and sufferings, or as unfulfilled expectations claimed by the heroes of the Greek Revolution in their memoirs. We should consider, however, that, in those historical circumstances, choices made were related to the form of the state imagined by social actors. In this respect, it is import-ant to focus on an overlooked aspect of the Greek loans of 1824–5 – that is, the strategeic use of loans aimed at securing concentrated financial resources, which was associated with the organised orientation towards the formation of a national state.

With the establishment of a national administration in January 1822, form-alisation of the three regional senates and multiple messages from the three maritime islands (Hydra, Spetses, Psara) that the war and the excessive costs of the battle fleet were national matters,[22] it was not long before an issue arose

22   Tzakis, forthcoming.

over the question of which body would have governing leadership, the conduct
of war on land and at sea and inevitably the distribution of internal financial
resources. On one hand, the Revolution implied unification processes for the
Greeks; on the other hand, the Revolution constantly gave rise to issues, the
solutions to which required appropriate arrangements to be put into place.
These arrangements were forged through various means: consultations, negotiations, concessions, compromises, disagreements, voluntary and involuntary
coercions.

In this context, marked by the absence of *concentrated* financial resources,
the anticipation of a foreign loan within the national administration progressed rapidly; among other reasons, this was in part because it served as a
strategy associated with the hope that the loans would provide the means to
protect territories captured by the Greek revolutionaries as well as for potential
geographic expansion. A diplomatic recognition of the Greek issue, which was
combined with the establishment of the revolutionary forces, reinforced the
hope that external recognition of the existing sovereignty was close. Finally, the
national political authorities expected to secure the means that would allow
them to hold the actual leadership, integrate the dispersed armed elements,
cover the fleet's costs and thus either deliberately or unintentionally define the
form of power in the country.

At that time, England had become Europe's financial hub, with a relatively
open political system and a public sphere with varied actors, and it was rather
differentiated from the continental countries within the system of European
conferences.[23] In other words, England combined different advantages while
other countries did not. These and other reasons led the Greek mission to
the city of London and the conclusion of two loans, one in February 1824 and
another in February 1825 (**Table 9.1**). Similarly, it is important to also highlight
the channeling of the money that arrived in Greece and that was made available to the national administration.

I will not get into the functional product of the second loan (cash, bills
of exchange, purchases of materials: £304,554). This was primarily associated
with the issue of defense on land and at sea from May 1825 to the end of the
same year. I shall confine myself to mentioning the relevant product of the
first loan (£314,780), which was received by the national administration in six
instalments: four of them in 1824 (two in July, one in September and another in
November) and another two in 1825 (in January and April). Consequently, the

---

23   Tzourmana 2015, pp. 70–1; Neal 1990, pp. 201–18, 223–9; Ball and Sunderland 2001, pp. 338–
      41.

TABLE 9.1   Main funds and utilisation of the first and second Greek loan

Charge		Established amounts
I. Amount received		
Sums and materials for the Greek government (38.7%)		
Liquid capital: Cash (1), bills of exchange		537,599
Purchases: ammunition, clothing, weapons, cannons		81,724
Sums for the establishment of a national battle fleet (19.8%)		
Ships: 'Karteria', 'Hermes', 'Epichirisis', 'Hellas'		279,637
Lord Cochrane's reward		37,000
Operating expenses and losses (2.6%)		
London Committee's expenses		11,662
Management, brokerage and movement costs, purchases		19,674
Losses etc.		11,014
Total (I)	*61.1%*	*978,310*
II. Bond purchases & amortisation		
1st Loan (£280,200)		135,083
2nd Loan (£285,000)		119,025
Total (II)	*15.9%*	*254,108*
III. Interests and loan-issue conclusion expenses		
Interests (17.5%)		280,000
Conclusion expenses, agency commission (5.5%)		89,600
Total (III)	*23.0%*	*369,600*
Grand total (I+II+III)	*100.0%*	*1,602,018*

SOURCE: GENERAL STATE ARCHIVES OF GREECE (ΓΕΝΙΚΆ ΑΡΧΕΊΑ ΤΟΥ ΚΡΆΤΟΥΣ), ARCHIVE OF THE EXECUTIVE BODY, REC. NO. 71, DOC. NO. 58, REC. NO. 137, DOC. NO. 70, REC. NO. 156, DOC. NO. 117, 119, 125–7, REC. 163, DOC. NO. 89, REC. NO. 167, DOC. NO. 170–5; *ΑΡΧΕΊΑ ΤΗΣ ΕΛΛΗΝΙΚΉΣ ΠΑΛΙΓΓΕΝΕΣΊΑΣ*, ATHENS 1971–2012, VOL. 2, 464–6 AND VOL. 4, 194–6; G. SPANIOLAKIS, *ΠΑΡΑΤΗΡΉΣΕΙΣ ΕΠ ΤΗΣ ΑΠΟΛΟΓΊΑΣ Ι. ΟΡΛΆΝΔΟΥ ΚΑΙ ΑΝΔΡ. ΛΟΥΡΙΏΤΟΥ*, ATHENS 1840, 9–11; A.M. ANDREADIS, *ΙΣΤΟΡΊΑ ΤΩΝ ΕΘΝΙΚΏΝ ΔΑΝΕΊΩΝ*, ATHENS 1904, 17.

Draft		Credit	
		I. First Loan	
		Nominal capital: £ 800,000	
		Bond issue price 59%	
		Actual capital	472,000
		Second Loan	
		Nominal capital: £ 2,000,000	
		Bond issue price 55.5%	
		Actual capital	1,110,000
64.9%	1,026,400	*Total (1)*	1,582,000
		II. Profits, interests and funds raised in Calcutta (2)	20,018
11.8%	186,000	*Total (II)*	20,018
23.3%	369,600		
100.0%	1,582,000	*Grand total (I+III)*	1,602,018

initial instalments arrived only after the end of the first stage of the civil war and only the November instalment was received during the second stage of the civil conflict.[24]

What was critical during the spring of 1824 was that Ibrahim Pasha of Egypt was trying to suppress the Revolution in the Peloponnese. Based on more recent evidence, almost 50 percent of the first loan was channeled to the fleet and the defense of the islands of Hydra and Spetses (**Table 9.2**). In other words, it was channeled to military corps that were dispatched in those islands, as after the destruction of Psara by the Ottoman fleet, the Greek Revolutionaries were expecting a similar attack against Hydra and Spetses;[25] if those islands fell to

24   Bozikis 2018, p. 517.
25   Kokkinos 1974, p. 275.

TABLE 9.2   Sums from the first foreign loan to the fleet and for the defense of Hydra and Spetses

Instalment arrival		Number of instalments	I To the fleet	II To camps (Hydra, Spetses)	III (I+II) Total	IV Instalment amount	III: IV
1824	July and Sept.	3	3,063,228	557,756	3,620,984	6,492,033	56%
	November	1	194,672	202,105	396,777	1,974,357	20%
1825	January	1	1,067,332		1,067,332	3,265,580	33%
	April	1	1,800,809		1,800,809	3,066,319	59%
Total		6	6,126,041	759,861	6,885,902	14,798,289	47%

SOURCE: SEE ABOVE, TABLE 9.1

the Ottomans, the Greek fleet, whose role in defending the Revolution was considered vital, would have been seriously jeopardised.[26]

From the middle of 1824 through to October 1825, with the money provided from both loans, the battle fleet was largely supported with direct government payments for the first time. In the second half of 1824, the fleet prevented Ibrahim Pasha's landing in the Peloponnese; Ibrahim Pasha, however, landed in February 1825,[27] at a time when the Greek ships had returned to their base for repairs in the erroneous assumption that the above-mentioned risk had been prevented. Thus, the supply of new sums was necessary within the first semester of 1825 to prepare the ships and their activity.

From the remaining 50 percent of the functional product of the first loan, a small part was channeled to political and administrative costs and directly to the civil conflict; the largest part of that loan was spent in the preparation of the defense, without implying that there were no ineffective actions, personal competitions, etc. Initially, one part was used for the creation of military camps in the western part of the Peloponnese and elsewhere, as there had been rumours about an Ottoman invasion in Patras or Messenia in the Peloponnese.[28] Afterwards, upon the end of the civil conflicts, the preparation of the Greek expedition to capture the fortress of Patras was scheduled to use the sum of the fifth instalment, which arrived in Athens in January 1825.[29] However, upon Ibrahim Pasha's landing, this expedition was cancelled. Thus, the sum, together with the subsequent amounts, was made available for the defense against the Egyptian army – an army that the Greek side underestimated before they recognised its difference from others previously fought.

---

26   Bozikis 2018, p. 522.
27   Sakellariou 2013.
28   *Ελληνικά Χρονικά*, no. 47 (11 June 1824), no. 59 (19 July 1824).
29   *Αρχεία της Ελληνικής Παλιγγενεσίας*, Athens 1971–2012, vol. 5, p. 114.

The occupation of several rural parts of the Peloponnesian territory by Ibrahim Pasha of Egypt was not continuous but rather dependent on the movements and sorties attempted by his troops. In any case, the Peloponnese did not fall completely. The loan sums kept the Revolution going from the summer of 1824 through to the end of 1825. These sums bought the Greeks time, considering also the diplomatic processes that were under way, despite the fact that Missolonghi fell to the Ottomans after a while. At the same time, during the aforementioned period, the loan sums provided the national administration with the means to form and mobilise the armed forces itself. In other words, to set the example to a large extent, not without inconsistencies,[30] of paid armed forces that recognise the leadership of national political authorities and show loyalty to them. Therefore, the establishment of the supreme character of the national administration reinforced the organised orientation of the formation of a national state.

It should be pointed out here that from early enough, and more directly from the end of 1823, the three naval islands (Hydra, Spetses, Psara) played a leading role, along with other politicians and leaders of the Revolution from the Peloponnese and Continental Greece, in acknowledging the actual leadership of the national administration. A critical issue for these islands, which contributed to the above-mentioned development, was the claim regarding reimbursement of the fleet's expenses by the nation. Thus, in a way, Hydra and the other two islands defined what should be considered as national on the basis of their own interests. Serving as the backbone of the national administration for a period of time, they contributed to the political, military and financial unification of the revolutionary territory, but they failed to overcome their boundary – to redefine what should be called national beyond their own world.

Given the developments with the presence of Ibrahim Pasha's army[31] – the unfortunate outcome of the efforts to create a state fleet, the consumption of the loan products, the stock market crisis that worsened access to international credits for the Greeks,[32] the fall of Missolonghi, etc. – Hydra, the key component of political power in revolutionary Greece from the end of 1823 until early 1826, was weakened. However, this development did not preclude that for a period of time the national administration, having a centrally controlled source of revenue at its disposal, established its political leadership and planned the formation of a national state.

---

30   Theotokas 2006, pp. 54–6.
31   Sakellariou 2013.
32   See Craig and Garcia-Iglesias 2010, p. 139; Marriner 1980, pp. 351–66.

In conclusion, taking into account an examination of the public revenues, the relations of individual powerful groups and the deliberate or involuntary consequences of those relations on revolutionary power, we can observe a significant public financial function already from the first years of the Greek Revolution. This function was associated with institutions that represented an emerging national political centre and the integration of the Greek populations within it. At the same time, alongside the war and the creation of modern political institutions, it contributed – more or less effectively and with applicable terms of that time – to the control of a revolutionary territory against an imperial system of domination with significant historical depth.

Bibliography

Asdrachas, Spyros I. 2014, *Υπομνήσεις: Ιστορικότροπα σημειώματα*, Athens: Θεμέλιο.

Ball, Michael and David Sunderland 2001, *An Economic History of London, 1800–1914*, London: Routledge.

Bozikis, Simos 2018, *Δημόσια οικονομικά και συγκρότηση εθνικού κράτους το 1821*, Ph.D. dissertation, Ionian University.

Coşgel, Metin, T. Miceli and R. Ahmed 2009, 'Law, state power, and taxation in Islamic history', *Journal of Economic Behavior & Organization* 71: 704–17.

Craig, L. and C. Garcia-Iglesias 2010, 'Business Cycles', *The Cambridge Economic History of Modern Europe, 1700–1870*, Vol. 1, Cambridge: Cambridge University Press.

Darling, Linda T. 1997, 'Ottoman Fiscal Administration: Decline or Adaptation?', *The Journal of European Economic History* 26/1: 157–79

Elias, Norbert 2000 [1978], *The Civilizing Process*, translated by E. Jephcott, Wiley-Blackwell.

Harlaftis, Gelina 2013, 'Η αρπαγή και οι κίνδυνοι στη θάλασσα: πόλεμοι, κούρσος και πειρατεία στη Μεσόγειο του 18ου αιώνα', in *Η ναυτιλία των Ελλήνων, 1700–1821: Ο αιώνας της ακμής πριν από την Επανάσταση*, edited by G. Harlaftis and K. Papakonstantinou, Athens: Κέδρος.

Karouzou, Evi 2018, *Εθνικές γαίες, εθνικά δάνεια και εθνική κυριαρχία: Βρετανική διπλωματία και γαιοκτησία στο ελληνικό κράτος, 1833–1843*, Athens: Academy of Athens.

Kıvanç Karaman K. and Şevket Pamuk 2013, 'Different Paths to the Modern State in Europe: The Interaction Between Warfare, Economic Structure, and Political Regime', *American Political Science Review* 107/3: 603–26.

Kokkinos, Dionysios 1974 [1936], *Η ελληνική επανάστασις*, Athens: Μέλισσα.

Kostis, Kostas 2006, 'Η συγκρότηση του κράτους στην Ελλάδα, 1830–1914', in *Ελλάδα και Τουρκία: Πολίτης και έθνος-κράτος*, edited by Thaleia Dragonas and Faruk Birtek, Athens: Αλεξάνδρεια.

Kotaridis, Nikos 2006, 'Οι εξεγέρσεις του 1836 στη Στερεά Ελλάδα', in Nikos Theotokas and

Nikos Kotaridis, *Η οικονομία της βίας: Παραδοσιακές και νεωτερικές εξουσίες στην Ελλάδα του 19ου αιώνα*, Athens: Βιβλιόραμα.

Mann, Michael 1992, *States, War and Capitalism*, Cambridge MA: Blackwell.

Marriner, S. 1980, 'English Bankruptcy Records and Statistics before 1850', *Economic History Review* 33/3: 351–66.

Nakos, Georgios 1986, *Εξελικτικές διακυμάνσεις του οθωμανικού γαιοκτητικού συστήματος*, Thessaloniki: University Studio Press.

Neal, Larry, 1990, *The Rise of Financial Capitalism: International Capital Markets in the Age of Reason*, Cambridge: Cambridge University Press.

Phrantzis, Amvrosios 1839, *Επιτομή της ιστορίας της αναγεννηθείσης Ελλάδος* [*Compendium of the history of resurrected Greece*], 4 Volumes, Athens: Βιτώρια.

Pizanias, Petros 2003, 'Επανάσταση και έθνος. Μια ιστορική-κοινωνιολογική προσέγγιση του '21', *Ιστορία του Νέου Ελληνισμού*, edited by Vassilis Panagiotopoulos, vol. 3, Athens: Τα Νέα.

Rotzokos, Nikos 1997, *Επανάσταση και εμφύλιος στο Εικοσιένα*, Athens: Βιβλιόραμα.

Sakellariou, Michael V. 2013, *Η απόβαση του Ιμπραήμ στην Πελοπόννησο καταλύτης για την αποδιοργάνωση της Ελληνικής Επανάστασης*, edited by E. Bechraki, Herakleio: Crete University Press.

Schmitt, Carl 2004, *The Theory of the Partisan. A Commentary/Remark on the Concept of the Political*, translated by A.C. Goodson, East Lansing: Michigan State University.

The Cambridge History of British Foreign Policy 1783–1919, edited by A.W. Ward and G.P. Gooch, vol. 2, Cambridge 1923.

Theotokas, Nikos 2006, 'Η επανάσταση του έθνους και το ορθόδοξο γένος. Σχόλια για τις ιδεολογίες στο. Εικοσιένα' ['The revolution of the nation and the Orthodox community. Comments on the ideologies of 1821'], in *Η οικονομία της βίας. Παραδοσιακές και νεωτερικές εξουσίες στην Ελλάδα του 19ου αιώνα* [*The economy of violence. Traditional and modern powers in nineteenth-century Greece*], edited by Nikos Theotokas and Nikos Kotaridis, Athens: Βιβλιόραμα.

Thomson, Janice E. 1994, *Mercenaries, Pirates, and Sovereigns: State-building and Extraterritorial Violence in Early Modern Europe*, Princeton: Princeton University Press.

Tilly, Charles 1990, *Coercion, Capital, and European States, AD 990–1990*, Cambridge, MA: Blackwell.

Trikoupis, Spyridon 1978 [1857], *Ιστορία της Ελληνικής Επαναστάσεως* [*History of the Greek Revolution*], 4 Volumes, Athens: Γιοβάνης.

Tzakis, Dionysis, forthcoming, 'Η στρατιωτική και πολιτική ενοποίηση των επαναστατημένων Ελλήνων και το ζήτημα του εθνικού στόλου' ['The military and political unification of the revolutionary Greeks and the issue of a national fleet'], in *Ο εμπορικός και πολεμικός στόλος κατά την Ελληνική Επανάσταση (1821–31)*.

Tzourmana, Gianna 2015, *Βρετανοί ριζοσπάστες μεταρρυθμιστές. Φιλικές εταιρείες και κομιτάτα στο Λονδίνο (1790–1823)* [*British radical reformists: Friendly societies and committees in London (1790–1823)*], Athens: Βιβλιοθήκη του Μουσείου Μπενάκη.

CHAPTER 10

Athens and Athenian Politics during the Greek Revolution

Zacharias D. Antonakis

> *We, the people of Athens, after shedding so much of our own precious blood,*
> *and after the absolute triumph of the Laws over oppression; based on our*
> *natural and political rights we already enjoy according to the Law of Epi-*
> *daurus; we have spontaneously gathered to a public and legal Assembly*
> *today, in order to discuss the prosperity and fair harmony of our domestic*
> *affairs.*[1]

During the Greek Revolution, the Commune[2] of Athens, through conflicts and
opposition, gradually integrated into a modern institutional function established by the revolutionary National Government. This integration was facilitated by the rise of new local political forces in the town of Athens, which, gradually, and for various reasons, defeated the former notables; the latter, however,
were also part of the revolutionary process and they were able to retain a part
of their power under the new institutional framework.

Decisions of the Communal Council of the town of Athens, studied between
1821 and 1831, record 191 local 'notables' [Gk. *Proestoi*] and 300 'heads of households' [Gk. *Noikokyraioi*] – 491 Athenians in total who acquired political roles
during the revolutionary years.[3] Judging from their involvement in real estate
during those years, almost one third of them had the necessary capital for buying land. Using the ability to buy land as a marker of social class, my study of
the same sources revealed 619 buyers in Athens who, however, did not hold
political positions during the Revolution. In sum, 1,110 of a total population of

---

1 General State Archives of Greece [*Γενικά Αρχεία του Κράτους*], Vlachogiannis collection, f. 192,
   Αθήναι. Ίσον της των Δημογερόντων εκλογής, 25 March 1825.
2 For the distinction between communities and communes, see Petmezas 2005, pp. 71–116.
3 The 491 name recordings correspond to different individuals, coming from all the Athenian
   Communal councils. In general, for the Communities and the Communal Councils, see
   Asdrachas 1986, pp. 351–445; Pylia 2001, pp. 67–98, and Chadjiosif 2005.

9,040 citizens (including women and children) in Athens in October 1824[4] were involved either in real estate or in the revolutionary politics.[5]

The 'heads of households' in Athens acquired institutional political roles only during the Revolution, entering a field monopolised under Ottoman rule by the traditional notables. By 1825, Ioannis Gkouras, who had been appointed by the Commune in 1822 as the Commander of the garrison in the Acropolis Fort,[6] responded to an expanded Communal Council, including many heads of households. In the important election of the Elders [Gk. *Demogerontes*] on 25 March 1825, almost half of the 131 signatories of the document of the election were heads of households.[7] One month after this election, the Communal Council of Athens, 118 signatories – more than half of them being now heads of households – signed an important memorandum to the revolutionary Provisional Government concerning tax administration in Athens.[8] This expanded composition of the Council attests, according to my interpretation, to a new political balance within the Commune of Athens.[9]

In the beginning of July 1824, the Provisional Government appointed Mikhail Soutsos as the Prefect of Athens, during a period of fear over imminent attack by the Ottoman armies. The local notables did not seem eager to cooperate with him:

---

4   Konstantinidis 1939, p. 899.

5   The presented evidence is based on the author's study of all recorded economic transactions concerning the Province of Athens between 1821 and 1833. The data mainly comes from the notary archives of Athens, found in the General State Archives of Greece. Paul Saint Cassia and Constantina Bada studied the dowry agreements of Athens, based on the same sources; see Saint Cassia and Bada 1992.

6   The official name of the Acropolis for the Provisional Government was the 'Acropolis Fort'; see the General State Archives of Greece, Archive of the Struggle for Independence [Αρχείο Αγώνος], Ministry of Economy [Μινιστέριο της Οικονομίας], f. 47, The Executive to the Ministry of Public Finances, 1 June 1825. In some cases, they also called it the 'Fort of Athens', or even the 'Fort of the Athens' Acropolis'; see the General State Archives of Greece, Archive of the Struggle for Independence, Ministry of Economy, f. 58, The Executive to the Ministry of Public Finances, 11 September 1825.

7   See above, fn. 1.

8   General State Archives of Greece, Vlachogiannis collection, f. 192, The Province of Athens to the Provisional Government, 23 April 1825.

9   The characterisation as 'expanded' refers to a comparison made with the compositions of the Communal Council of Athens before the Revolution. For the pre-revolutionary period of Athens, see Skouzes 1889–92; Philadelpheas 1991 [1902]; Benizelos 1986; Αρχεία της Νεωτέρας Ελληνικής Ιστορίας, ed. I. Vlachogiannis, vol. I: Αθηναϊκόν αρχείον, Athens 1901; Karydis 1981; Kominis 2008.

Since I arrived here, I did not stop asking for the accounts and the records of the national revenues from the Elders [i.e. the notables]. However, I have achieved nothing: one claims that his companion, who kept the books, has left, or, in other cases, he kept no books at all ... I hope that I will gradually install an order ... and stop the embezzlements by the Elders ... and, in this way, fulfill my sacred duty to the Homeland.[10]

The conflict between the appointed Prefect and the Athenian Elders Nikolaos Zacharitzas, Ioannis P. Vlachos, Chatzis Spiros Gigakis, Ioannis Pallis and Ioannis Pantazis was also reflected in the former's report to the Provisional Government for the detrimental financial state of the Province of Athens, dated 7 July 1824.[11] Accused for embezzlement, the Elders of Athens replied to the Prefect in a letter of exactly the same date their personal expenses for the revolutionary cause, specifically for the re-building and restoration of the Acropolis Fort.[12] A week later, on 15 July 1824, the Commune of Athens sent a delegation to the headquarters of the Provisional Government in Nafplio, announcing the inability of the Commune to cater for additional expenses or even meet daily needs.[13]

It was possibly this conflict, which directly affected the revolutionary army, that in 1822 led the Provisional Government to appoint Ioannis Gkouras as the Commander of the Acropolis Fort, perhaps ignoring his involvement in the embezzlements of the Elders as reported by the Prefect. The latter seems to have backed down regarding the issue of the 'national revenues',[14] under the danger of an Ottoman attack, but without forgetting the responsibility of the Elders. He addressed them on 24 July 1824:

---

10   General State Archives of Greece, Vlachogiannis collection, the Prefect of Athens to the
      Ministry of Interior Affairs, 4 July 1824.
11   General State Archives of Greece, Vlachogiannis collection, the Prefect of Athens to the
      Ministry of Interior Affairs, 7 July 1824.
12   General State Archives of Greece, Vlachogiannis collection, the Elders of Athens to the
      Prefect, 7 July 1824.
13   General State Archives of Greece, Archive of the Executive Body [Αρχείο Εκτελεστικού],
      1824, f. 14, The Office of the Prefect of Athens to the Provisional Government, 15 July 1824.
      Not surprisingly, the Prefect Mikhail Soutsos did not sign the memorandum. The emissar-
      ies sent to Nafplio were the elder Ioannis P. Vlachos and the two 'patriots', P. Pantazis and
      Stamos Serafeim – i.e. one notable and one 'head of household'.
14   The 'national revenues' were the revenues of the revolutionary Government from tax
      farming private and public properties. See Loukos 1980–82, pp. 370–8; Petmezas 1999, p. 58.
      The practise of renting the tax revenues also existed before the Revolution and was asso-
      ciated with the taxation system; see S. Asdrachas et al. 1978, pp. 23–63.

The Administration provided for this Province. They left you the national revenues, the olive grove, etc. ... it is time that you, honourable Elders, eventually come to your senses and you, too, confront your debts; similar complaints are not in your favour and the Administration will want to request, in time, an account for all accusations and for all you could have done but neglected.[15]

The Prefect at the same time made an effort to control all auctions of the 'national revenues', applying to orders sent by the revolutionary Ministry of Public Finances.

In the Assembly at Salona on 24 April 1824, the *traditional* notables of Eastern Roumeli had reached an agreement with the administration of Georgios Kountouriotis, abandoning the resolutions of the Assembly of Athens (1822).[16] On 26 April 1824, the Provisional Government, through the Prefect of Athens, accepted the sale of the high revenues from the 'national' olive grove of Athens to Ioannis Mamouris, the lieutenant of Ioannis Gkouras, for the needs of the revolutionary garrison on the Acropolis Fort and the revolutionary army camp of Attica.[17] Until then, the Commune of Athens retained full authority regarding politics and revenues in the Province of Athens. Ioannis Gkouras and Ioannis Mamouris controlled the Acropolis Fort and the 'national' olive grove of Athens; the Elders supervised the customs office and the wealthier Athenians controlled 'national' houses and workshops. The same power structure also existed in the other provinces of Eastern Roumeli, which were under the control of the revolutionary General-in-Chief Odysseas Androutsos. The aim of all communal leadership was to continue to control politically each community by securing the revenue sources.[18] Gradually, however, the revolutionary Provisional Government, through the appointment of Prefects, started to claim control of public revenue. This transition did not necessarily mean that the local elites were completely excluded from access to the public revenues: on the contrary, new social and political alliances appeared with the aim to control

---

15   General State Archives of Greece, Archive of the Executive Body, 1824, f. 15, The Executive to the Elders of Athens, 24 July 1824.

16   Anninos 1996, p. 42, fn. 1.

17   *Αθηναϊκόν Αρχείον*, Athens 1971, pp. 70–1.

18   See for example the case of the Commune of Thebes in General State Archives of Greece, Archive of the Struggle for Independence, Ministry of Finance [Μινιστέριο της Οικονομίας], folder 41, doc. dated 28 February 1825, signed by 29 residents of Thebes concerning tax farming of the Saline in the District of Thebes, hastened by the military needs of General Eumorphopoulos in 1824. The following year, the Saline of Thebes was put up for auction supervised by the Administration.

the local economies. Actually, for some of the Athenians, the revolutionary conjuncture offered a possibility to expand their interests in adjacent provinces – such as, for instance, in the province of Salona [mod. Amfissa]. It is my interpretation that this transitory period led the traditional notables of the Commune of Athens to accept the new political forces of the heads of households in a common perspective under the revolutionary Government: both the notables and heads of households of Athens sought to become 'members of the entirety of the Nation'.[19]

Local authorities continued to exist after the Assembly of Salona (1824), causing conflicts within the Communes. What the administration of Georgios Kountouriotis did was avoid extreme situations by intervening selectively in internal disputes among traditional groups. Besides that, since 1824, the Elders of Athens considered the institutional framework of the Provisional Government particularly favourable for securing their interests against the military chiefs and, more particularly, against Odysseas Androutsos.

Odysseas Androutsos, an *armatolos* under the Ottomans who became the Commander-in-Chief of the revolutionary army in eastern Roumeli, initially confronted the local provisional government [Areopagus; Gk. *Areios Pagos*], then the local notables in Athens and other areas and then, finally, Ioannis Gkouras and the revolutionary Government of Greece itself. The latter was obviously the fiercest conflict and moved beyond a simple political dispute. In contrast to the previous conflicts involving Androutsos, the conflict between him and the revolutionary Government became violent at his expense. It is my interpretation that this conflict between Androutsos and the Provisional Government was a one about the distribution of power in the town of Athens. Androutsos eventually chose to surrender to Ioannis Gkouras on 7 April 1825.[20]

During the first years of the Revolution – until the end of 1824 – the revolutionary Government overlooked each time that Androutsos resorted to the practices of the former *armatolos*,[21] and they tolerated, under conditions, his disobedience to the orders of the Provisional Government, including his deals with the Ottomans. Towards the end of 1824, however, the revolutionary Government claimed from Androutsos an unconditional acceptance of its authority and tried to secure absolute administrative control over all the communities of Eastern Roumeli. It looks like Androutsos had not taken into account the

---

19   General State Archives of Greece, Archive of the Struggle for Independence, Ministry of Finance, f. 41, Dimitrios Leonardopoulos to the Executive Body of the Provisional Government, 18 March 1825.

20   Kasomoulis 1940, p. 50.

21   Stathis 2007, pp. 167–79.

support that his former subordinate, and now Commander of the Fort of the Acropolis of Athens, Ioannis Gkouras would provide to the notables.[22] The Provisional Government sent Georgakis Valtinos to force all the other military chiefs in the Ambliani military camp to move against Odysseas Androutsos and Georgios Karaiskakis, in accordance with the seventh article of the resolution of the Assembly of Salona (April 1824) which stated that 'no military man can establish any official agreements [Gk. *kapakia*, from Ott. Turk. *kapak*]'.[23]

It is obvious that Androutsos at that time called into question the administrative framework of the revolutionary authority as a whole. To the new state institutions, Androutsos's return to traditional practices, using violence as a means to negotiate, constituted a direct threat to the revolutionary Government and had to be suppressed before others could follow his example. On one hand, Androutsos's financial interests had been harmed by the policy of the revolutionary Government to control the local communities – a policy that also affected the interests of the notables. On the other hand, even in the case that Androutsos had the intention to approach the Government, his gradual isolation since the end of 1824 made such an effort impossible. The revolutionary Commander in Chief of 1822 was now a 'traitor to the Nation' and a 'trespasser of the Law'.[24] The resolution of Salona (April 1824) cancelled the decisions of the Assembly of Athens (September 1822).[25] By 1824, the Provisional Government had already selected the 'patriots' as allies and financed them.

On 24 January 1825, the Commune of Athens sent a report to the Provisional Government, informing it that Androutsos had 'acted secretly as a traitor' and requesting measures against him.[26] Deprived of the support of the local cap-

---

22   During the war operations in June and July 1824, Ioannis Gkouras constantly corresponded with the Elders of Athens, confirming that in each case his actions were in accord with the orders given by them and the Provisional Government. The Elders, from their side, ensured the provisioning of Gkouras's soldiers with food and wages. See for example Αρχείον της Κοινότητος Ύδρας, Piraeus 1921–9, vol. 11, pp. 241–2.

23   Stamatopoulos 1972, vol. 11, pp. 175–7. See also Kotaridis 1993, pp. 171–8.

24   General State Archives of Greece, Archive of the Struggle for Independence, Executive Body, f. 72, The Minister of War to the Executive, 14 March 1825.

25   Based on the decisions of the Assembly of Athens, the military chiefs of Eastern Roumeli controlled the local communities politically and economically. However, at the Assembly at Salona the military chiefs of the Eastern Roumeli as well as the General-in-Chief Odysseas Androutsos accepted the institutional framework of the Provisional Government. This essentially meant conformity with the Laws, acceptance of the representatives of the administration and, finally, obedience to Government orders.

26   Αρχεία Ελληνικής Παλιγγενεσίας, Athens 1971–2012, vol. 8, p. 113, The Legislative Body to the Executive, 24 January 1825.

tains of Athens Nikolaos Saris and Meletis Vasileiou, who had been assassinated by the men of Ioannis Gkouras, Androutsos was himself unable to fight against the alliance between Gkouras and the notables and heads of households of Athens. Androutsos had also, without any success, advised the captains Panourgias, Skaltsas and Dyovouniotis to stay loyal to the decisions of the assembly of Athens (1822) and to refuse any negotiation proposed by the Provisional Administration.[27]

In January 1825, it was clear that the revolutionary Administration would not support Androutsos's local interests: 'On 24 January 1825 ... a report by the Notables of Athens was read. They inform that General Odysseas [Androutsos] accepted obeisance to the Turks[28] and he is recruiting from the provinces of Thebes, Levadeia and Euboea, offering generous military wages'.[29] For the revolutionary Government, Androutsos was now an 'enemy of the patriots' [Gk. *Antipatriotis*]. The Administration was influenced in its change of attitude against Androutsos by the notable of Athens Ioannis Gkouras as well as by Ioannis Kolletis, a powerful man both in Euripos [Euboia] and within the Administration itself. The latter would no more accept a possible return of Androutsos to the politics of Eastern Roumeli, and he had exhausted every available influence on the President of the Executive, Georgios Kountouriotis. Androutsos, disappointed and in despair, decided to approach Ömer Pasha of Eğriboz [Gk. Euripos] with the aim of ensuring financial resources to recruit soldiers.[30] Access to such resources would provide him with the opportunity to increase his military power and to overthrow the notables of Athens. Approaching the Ottomans was a return to the traditional mind frame of the Ottoman era.[31] Androutsos, however, only accepted obeisance to the Ottomans as a temporary strategy to allow him to secure influence on Eastern Roumeli. This, however, did not mean that he perceived Ottoman rule as the most appropriate field for the legitimacy of his claim to power. As soon as he ensured the required resources, Androutsos would disengage from his alliance with the Ottoman side. At the end of January 1825, Androutsos was in position to recruit armed villagers from the district of Levadeia 'for 30 *kuruş* for each soldier'.[32] Starting

---

27   *Αρχείο Ιωάννη Κωλέττη*, Athens 2002, vol. 2, pp. 393, 123, Dimos Skaltsas to the Government, 1 December 1824.

28   Ilıcak 2019, pp. 243–59.

29   *Αρχεία Ελληνικής Παλιγγενεσίας*, Athens 1971–2021, vol. 7, p. 105.

30   *Αρχείο Κουντουριώτη*, vol. 4, 1929, pp. 5–6, I. Katzouris to G. Kountouriotis, 3 January 1825.

31   Kotaridis 1993, pp. 171–8.

32   General State Archives of Greece, Vlachogiannis collection, Androutsos Archive (*Αρχείον Ανδρούτσου*), the notables of Athens to Ioannis Gkouras, 20 January 1825.

with one hundred men under his command at the beginning of December 1824, he reached eight hundred men by the beginning of February 1825. The Prefect of Athens, Mikhail Soutsos, in his report to the Executive Body of the Provisional Government, stressed in particular Androutsos's ability to recruit by prepaying wages.[33] The new Prefect of Salona, Ioannis Mamoukas, expressed to the Provisional Government the threat posed by Androutsos to the collection of revenues from the Province of Salona and for the National Treasury itself. According to Mamoukas, the 'devious' Androutsos had 500 equestrians and an infantry of the same size.[34]

The notables and the heads of households in Athens demanded that the Provisional Government intervene and send the revolutionary army against Androutsos. As noted before, Androutsos surrendered and, accused of collaboration with the Ottomans, was placed under arrest in the Frankish tower of the Acropolis of Athens. Ioannis Gkouras, once Androutsos's second in command, ordered his execution on 5 June 1825. Based on these events, we can suggest that the political and military decline of Captain Androutsos was the result of the opposition of both the traditional notables of the Commune of Athens and the notables of Eastern Roumeli. With the extermination of Odysseas Androutsos, the notables and the heads of households of Athens finally conformed to the laws of the Administration; at the same time, however, they were preserving their own proper economic interests by doing this. My research aims to show that it was the identification of the economic interests of the notables and the heads of households in the town of Athens that contributed to the political fate of Odysseas Androutsos. On 22 June 1825, Alexandros Mavrokordatos wrote the following to Ioannis Gkouras: 'Odysseas [Androutsos] had to suffer the consequences of all his previous and later actions, and certainly this [his execution] is a result of divine retribution'.[35]

Bibliography

Anninos, Babis 1996 [1925], *Η απολογία του Οδυσσέως Ανδρούτσου, η δολοφονία του* [*The defense of Odusseas Androutsos, his assassination*], Athens: Δημιουργία.

---

33 General State Archives of Greece, Vlachogiannis collection, Mikhail Soutsos to the Executive, 20 January 1825. See also *Αρχείο Κουντουριώτη*, vol. 4, 1929, pp. 59–61.

34 General State Archives of Greece, Archive of the Struggle for Independence, Ministry of Finance, f. 38, the Prefect of Salona to the Ministry of Public Finance, 15 March 1825.

35 General State Archives of Greece, Archive of the Struggle for Independence, Ministry of Finance, doc. 8991, Alexandros Mavrokordatos to Ioannis Gkouras, 22 June 1825.

Asdrachas, Spyros I. 1978, *Μηχανισμοί της αγροτικής οικονομίας στην Τουρκοκρατία (ΙΕ΄- ΙΣΤ΄ αιώνας)* [*Mechanisms of rural economy during the Tourkokratia (fifteenth-sixteenth c.)*], Athens: Θεμέλιο.

Asdrachas, Spyros I. 1986, 'Φορολογικές και περιοριστικές λειτουργίες των κοινοτήτων στην Τουρκοκρατία' ['Fiscal and regulatory functions of the communes during the Tourkokratia'], *Τα Ιστορικά* 3,5: 45–62.

Asdrachas, Spyros et al. 2003, *Ελληνική οικονομική ιστορία, ΙΕ΄-ΙΘ΄ αιώνας* [*Greek economic history, fifteenth-nineteenth c.*], 2 Volumes, Athens: Πολιτιστικό Ίδρυμα Ομίλου Πειραιώς.

Benizelos, Ioannis 1986, *Ιστορία των Αθηνών* [*History of Athens*], 2 Volumes, Athens: Εκδοτική Αθηνών.

Chadjiosif, Christos 2005, *Συνασός, Ιστορία ενός τόπου χωρίς ιστορία* [*Synasos, history of a place without history*], Herakleio: Crete University Press.

Ilıcak, H. Şükrü 2019, 'Revolutionary Athens through Ottoman eyes (1821–8): new evidence from the Ottoman State Archives', in *Ottoman Athens: Archaeology, Topography, History*, edited by Maria Georgopoulou and Konstantinos Thanasakis, Athens: The Gennadeion Library, American School of Classical Studies.

Kambouroglou, Demetrios 1889–92, *Μνημεία της Ιστορίας των Αθηνών* [*Sources on the history of Athens*], 2 Volumes, Athens: Αλέξανδρος Παπαγεωργίου.

Karydis, Dimitris N. 1981, *Πολεοδομικά των Αθηνών της Τουρκοκρατίας* [*Urban topography of Athens during the Tourkokratia*], Ph.D dissertation, Technical University of Athens.

Kasomoulis, Nikolaos K. 1940, *Ενθυμήματα στρατιωτικά της επαναστάσεως των Ελλήνων, 1821–1833* [*Military memoirs on the revolution of the Greeks, 1821–1833*], introduction and commentary by Giannis Vlachogiannis, 3 Volumes, Athens.

Kominis, Markos 2008, *Η Αθήνα κατά τα τελευταία χρόνια της Οθωμανικής Διοίκησης (18ος–19ος αιώνας). Η πόλη και το διοικητικό καθεστώς* [*Athens during the final years under Ottoman administration (eighteenth–nineteenth century): The town and its administration*], M.A. thesis, Thessaloniki: Aristotle University of Thessaloniki.

Konstantinidis, K. 1939, 'Απογραφή των Αθηνών κατά το 1824' ['Survey of Athens in 1824'], *Νέα Εστία*, 13: 899.

Kotaridis, Nikos 1993, *Παραδοσιακή Επανάσταση και Εικοσιένα* [*Traditional revolution and 1821*], Athens: Πλέθρον.

Loukos, Christos K. 1980–82, 'Η ενοικίαση προσόδων κατά την καποδιστριακή περίοδο: Απόψεις για την πολιτική διάσταση του ζητήματος' ['Tax farming under Kapodistrias' administration: views for the political dimension of the issue of tax farming'], *Μνήμων*, 8: 370–8.

Petmezas, Socrates D. 1999, *Η ελληνική αγροτική οικονομία κατά το 19ο αιώνα. Η περιφερειακή διάσταση* [*Greek rural economy during the nineteenth century*], Herakleio: Crete University Press.

Petmezas, Socrates D. 2005, 'Christian communities in 18th and 19th centuries Ottoman

Greece: their fiscal functions', *Princeton Papers, Interdisciplinary Journal of Middle Eastern Studies*, 11: 71–116.

Philadelpheas, Themistocles N. 1991 [1902], *Ιστορία των Αθηνών επί τουρκοκρατίας, από του 1400 μέχρι του 1800* [*History of Athens during the Tourkokratia, from 1400 until 1800*], Athens: Βιβλιοθήκη Ιστορικών Μελετών.

Pylia, Martha 2001, 'Λειτουργίες και αυτονομία των κοινοτήτων της Πελοποννήσου κατά τη δεύτερη Τουρκοκρατία (1715–1821)' ['Functions and autonomy of the communes in the Peloponnese during the second Tourkokratia (1715–1821)'], *Μνήμων*, 23: 67–98.

Saint Cassia, Paul and Constantina Bada 1992, *The Making of the Modern Greek Family: Marriage and Exchange in nineteenth century Athens*, Cambridge: Cambridge University Press.

Skouzes, Panagis 1948, *Χρονικό της σκλαβωμένης Αθήνας: στα χρόνια της τυραννίας του Χατζαλή γραμμένο στα 1841 από τον αγωνιστή Παναγή Σκουζέ, παληό και το χειρόγραφο επιμελημένο και αποκαταστημένο από τον Γ. Βαλέτα* [*Chronicle of Athens under capture, during the tyrannical rule of Hacı Ali*], Athens: Α. Κολολός.

Stamatopoulos, Takis 1972, *Ο εσωτερικός αγώνας πριν και κατά την επανάσταση του 1821* [*The internal struggle before and during the revolution of 1821*], 4 Volumes, Athens: Κάλβος.

Stathis, Panagiotis 2007, 'From Klephts and Armatoloi to Revolutionaries', in *Ottoman rule and the Balkans, 1760–1850: Conflict, Transformation, Adaptation*, edited by Antonis Anastasopoulos and Elias Kolovos, Rethymno: Department of History and Archaeology, University of Crete.

PART 4

Contested Lands, Shared Sovereignties

∴

CHAPTER 11

The 1821 Greek Revolution in Central Greece

The Catalytic Role of the Military Confrontation between Tepedelenli Ali Pasha and the Sublime Porte

Panagiotis Stathis

Since the fall of the Greek junta in 1974, historiography of the 1821 Greek Revolution has, by and large, attributed the event to the so-called 'Neohellenic Enlightenment' and, concomitantly, to the dissemination and adoption of the national ideas, with varying degrees and terms of perception per social group. In particular, the formation of the Hellenic national ideology emerged from rapid economic growth, primarily of long-distance trade conducted by the Greek-speaking Christians during the eighteenth century; that, in turn, facilitated closer contact and familiarisation with European movements of the Enlightenment and nationalism. According to this approach, the economy was not causally related to the Greek Revolution. It constituted the instigating factor for the emergence of a commercial bourgeoisie – one internally divided and diversified in terms of ideology and culture – that became the key recipient, formulator and mediator of the national ideology in an international context marked by the rise of nationalism. As a result, the Greek Revolution was not directly related to economic discontents, impasses and demands either of the merchants or the remaining social strata that organised and joined the rebellion. Accordingly, and contrary to older Marxist views, Greek historiography after 1974 approached ideology and politics as autonomous from the economy, a view widely held by social scientists across the world over the last decades ('autonomy of the political').

Thomas Gallant has developed a fruitful theoretical framework to analyse the conditions of the emergence of a revolution: 'If a revolution is to be successful, three conditions must be met: there must be an ideological framework which gives aims and a direction to the movement; there must be an organisational structure which can coordinate and lead the movement; and finally there must be adverse material conditions among the populace which make mass support for action possible'.[1] The ideological framework was provided by

---

1   Gallant 2001, p. 13. See, also, Gallant 2015, p. 53.

nationalism, as formulated by the radical wing of the Neohellenic Enlightenment, while the Friendly Society [Gk. *Philiki Hetaireia*] offered the organisational structure. Yet, were there 'adverse material conditions among the populace'? And if so, to what extent?

Some historians have sought the roots of the 1821 Greek Revolution in the
severe economic crisis that broke out during the preceding decade, primarily
after the end of the Napoleonic Wars (1815).[2] However, the relevant documentation is confined to Peloponnese and the three naval islands (Hydra, Spetses
and Psara), while little evidence is available for southern Rumelia (the contemporary Sterea Hellada, Epirus, Thessaly and southern Macedonia) which also
witnessed revolutionary movements. After all, the infiltration of both the ideas
of the Enlightenment and of the Friendly Society seems to have been limited
in southern Rumelia.[3]

The theory of revolutions is a branch of historical sociology that, despite its
growth since the 1960s,[4] had narrow impact on the Greek historiography of the
1821 Revolution.[5] In this theoretical context, Theda Skocpol developed in 1979
a framework to analyse the causes of a revolution which, despite all criticism,
remains fruitful. According to the framework, the prerequisite for a revolution
is the weakening or collapse of the state, which, in turn, gives rise to discontent and tensions among the elites and brings severe economic pressures on
the popular strata, all within a short time span. Thus, a considerable part of the
elites and the popular strata turns to violence, which becomes conducive to
uprisings and revolution.[6]

Revolutions are complex and multifaceted phenomena. Any interpretation
of the 1821 Greek Revolution should consider the developments of at least the
preceding thirty years in the fields of culture and ideology, demography, the
economy and the political, social and intra-religious relations and confrontations. This chapter is confined to the examination of the 1820–1 conjuncture in

---

2   Kremmydas 1977, pp. 1633; Kremmydas 2002, pp. 71–84; Hering 1992, pp. 17–30; Asdrachas, 'Το
    ιστορικό του Αγώνα', newspaper *Αυγή*, 25 March 1980; Diamantouros 1972; Beaton 2019, pp. 72–
    3.
3   On the limited impact of the Neohellenic Enlightenment, see the table of book subscribers
    in Iliou 1997, pp. ν΄–να΄. On the limited infiltration of the Friendly Society, see Frangos 1971,
    particularly pp. 185–90, 195, 309–25, tables 7–10; Perraivos 2019, p. 97; Trikoupis 1853–7, vol. 1,
    p. 197.
4   For critical overviews of the relevant debate, see Lachmann 2013, pp. 31–55; Cucută 2013,
    pp. 1107–16; Voglis 2013, pp. 47–56; Wickham-Crowley 1997, pp. 38–72.
5   For one exception as applied to the Greek case, see Hering 1992.
6   Skocpol 1979, pp. 47–157; Skockpol 2005, pp. 3–24.

the region of central Greece. It argues that the conflict that broke out between the Sublime Porte and Ali Pasha of Ioannina (who ruled over central Greece and southern Albania) had consequences similar to the ones mentioned by Skocpol, urging the local Christian elites and broader Christian-peasant strata to participate in the Greek Revolution.

The conventional *national* historiography of the 1821 Greek Revolution – and a considerable part of the contemporary historiography as well – has related the outbreak of the Greek Revolution to the military confrontation between the Sublime Porte and Tepedelenli Ali Pasha. In particular, it has been perceived as an incident accelerated because: a) Ali Pasha was aware of the existence of the Friendly Society (the secret society that organised the Greek Revolution) and thus there was danger that he could pass this information to the Sublime Porte; and b) this intra-Ottoman conflict tied up considerable troops who could be alternatively employed to suppress the Greek Revolution during its early and thus fragile stages.

On the contrary, John Koliopoulos and Thanos Veremis mention, without further support, that 'the disorderly situation in Epirus and the concomitant concentration of large Turkish troops in the region created a power vacuum in southern Greece. This vacuum facilitated the task of the [Friendly] Society agents who managed to join forces with the military element of the region, namely the Souliots and the captains of the *armatoloi* [Ott. Turk. *martoloz*; local armed bands with police authority] who, due to the crisis, had lost their employment or negotiated with both rival sides'.[7]

Thomas Gallant also argues that the attack of the Porte's troops, led by Hurşid Pasha, had some important consequences. He writes:

> ... the imposition of the war requisition tax on an already destitute and desperate peasantry elevated the level of mass discontent in the region to a new high. Paying the war tax was for many farmers and shepherds a life or death issue. Third, the mobilisation of so many warriors depleted the garrison forces along the Danubian frontier and in the Morea. Ali's war had presented the Friendly Society [Gk. *Philiki Etaireia*] with an opportunity.[8]

---

7   Veremis and Koliopoulos 2006, p. 195.
8   Gallant 2015, p. 65.

1   Administrative Changes and the Disintegration of Political Structures

When the Sublime Porte renounced Ali Pasha and sent troops against him, he and his relatives were deprived of the *pashaliks* [provinces] they'd controlled, and, in several cases, even the new commanders they had recently appointed were replaced. In November 1819, Süleyman Pasha was assigned to the Pashalik of Trikala [Thessaly] in place of Veli Pasha, son of Ali Pasha, and in April 1820 he was also appointed as the supervisor of the mountainous passages [*derbendat nazırı*][9] in place of Ali Pasha himself.[10] In June 1820, Süleyman Pasha was replaced in both of these offices by Dramalı Mahmud Pasha.[11] In February 1821, the latter was succeeded as supervisor of the mountainous passages by Hurşid Pasha.[12] In the spring of 1820, Ismail Paso Bey took over the campaign against Ali Pasha, while Şahin Bey was nominated Deputy Commander to the Pashalik of Ioannina and the *sancak* of Delvino. At the end of 1820, Paso Bey was replaced by Hurşid Pasha in all three of these offices. In spring 1820, Hüseyin Gavanozoğlu was appointed Vali [Governor General] of Rumelia, to be replaced in January 1821 by Hurşid Pasha. In spring 1820, Selim Pasha was appointed Governor of Salonica and was replaced by Seyyid Emin Mehmed Pasha [Ebûlübud] in early 1821. In May–June 1820, Pehlivan Baba Pasha was appointed Pasha of İnebahtı [Gk. Nafpaktos], in place of Veli Pasha, and Karlıeli [Gk. Aitoloakarnania]. After his death in October 1821, Pehlivan Baba Pasha was succeeded by Hasan Pasha. In autumn 1820, Bekir Çukadar was appointed commander of Preveza, while in April 1821 Ahmet Pasha, son of Paso Bey, took over and Bekir Çukadar became his deputy. In the Pashalik of Eğriboz [Gk. Euboea], the recently appointed Hasan Baltacı was replaced in early 1821 by Yusuf Pasha from Serres. Yusuf was eventually sent to Patras to confront the Greek Revolution in the Peloponnese, and he was replaced by Ömer Bey of Kızılhisar [Gk. Karystos]. In May–June 1820, Muhtar Pasha, son of Ali Pasha, was replaced in the Pashalik of Berat by Nureddin, who was suc-

9   This was an important office, in charge of the security forces in Rumelia – i.e. of the Muslim and Christian police forces of *kazas*, which consisted mainly of *derbent* Aghas and *derbendci*s who guarded the narrow mountain passages and *armatoloi*.

10   Panagiotopoulos (ed.) 2007–18, vol. 3, pp. 307, 427; Prevelakis and Kalliataki Mertikopoulou (eds.) 1996, p. 85.

11   Prevelakis and Kalliataki Mertikopoulou (eds.) 1996, vol. 1, p. 130; Vasdravellis (ed.) 1954, pp. 266–7.

12   Vasdravellis (ed.) 1954, pp. 269–70.

ceeded in late 1820 by Ismail Pasha Pliasa, who was also replaced by Ömer Vryoni Pasha in May 1821. Finally, Abaz Bey took over command of Dibër in southern Albania.[13]

These changes were not confined to the higher echelons of administration – namely the Pashas of *sancak*s controlled by Ali Pasha – but extended to all administrative ranks. The new Pashas replaced officials loyal to and controlled by Ali Pasha with officials free of his influence and who, primarily, had experienced his persecution.

As far as the Orthodox Church is concerned, many prelates of central Greece were also replaced. In May 1820, the metropolitan of Larissa and Tyrnavos Kyrillos was replaced by the former metropolitan of Larissa Polykarpos Dardaios, who had been cast out by Ali Pasha in 1818. Polykarpos fell into the disfavour of Dramalı Mahmud Pasha in June 1821, possibly because he failed to suppress the Greek Revolution in Pelio and Agrafa. He was arrested, imprisoned and, in September 1821, beheaded.[14] The metropolitan of eight years of Nafpaktos and Arta, Porphyrios, was deposed by Paso Bey in 1820 and replaced by Anthimos. The bishop of Rogoi Joseph was also replaced.[15] In autumn 1820, the metropolitan of Grevena Bartholomew was deposed and replaced by Anthimos.[16] From the diocese of Stagai [Kalambaka], Anthimos[17] was deposed in 1820.[18] Agathangellos was appointed bishop of Geromero in January 1821.[19] Finally, Paso Bey ordered the removal of the metropolitan of Ioannina, Gabriel Gagas, who was also imprisoned for a short time. However, Gagas's deposition was revoked after magnates from Ioannina and Constantinople intervened in his favour in the Patriarchate, and, eventually, with the arrival of Hurşid Pasha, he was restored to his former office.[20] Although there are indications that prelates were replaced in other regions as well, no reliable evidence is available so far. The changes were not confined to replacements of officials but affected the

---

13 On these changes, see Kokolakis 2003, p. 399; Prevelakis and Kalliataki Mertikopoulou (eds.) 1996, vol. 1, *passim*; Aravantinos 1856, pp. 380–90; Aravantinos 1984, vol. 3, pp. 229–30, 250–3; Arsh 1994, pp. 330, 339, 355; Kyrkini-Koutoula 1996, p. 120.

14 Zegos 1927; Drosos 2006, pp. 145–60.

15 Oikonomos 1862–6, vol. 2, p. 20; Xenopoulos Vyzantios 1884, pp. 118–20; Protopsaltis (ed.) 1963–86, vol. 2, pp. 120–1, 127–9.

16 Tsakopoulos 1956, p. 438; Papadimitriou 2014, p. 11; Sarantis 1987–8, p. 281.

17 The appearance of the same name, Anthimos, in three different cases is coincidental. Actually, it refers to three different people.

18 Aravantinos 1856, vol. 2, p. 161.

19 Evaggelou 2010, pp. 209–12.

20 Melas 1967, pp. 424, 430; Kitsou-Pitouli 1974, pp. 386–8.

administrative structure as well: in 1820, the archdiocese of Fanari and Farsala were integrated into the diocese of Litza and Agrafa.[21]

The new Pashas also replaced the local Ottoman authorities held by Muslims: *voyvodas* and *derbent* Aghas. However, evidence relevant to this is limited, because the Ottoman judicial archives of the regions (with the exception of Salonica and Veroia) were destroyed during their successive annexations to the Greek state and because Greek-speaking sources (i.e. memoirs) appear reluctant to record such information. Since the end of 1819, Süleyman Pasha sought to replace the *derbent* Aghas appointed by Ali Pasha with trusted ones in the regions of Agrafa, Domokos, Lamia, Mendenitsa, Turkochori [Kato Tithorea in Lokris], Livadia, Florina and other *kazas* in western Macedonia. However, it seems that, in several cases, the *derbent* Aghas loyal to and benefiting under Ali Pasha refused to obey Süleyman Pasha and put up armed resistance that resulted in bloodied incidents.[22] In June 1820, the Governor General of Rumelia Hüzeyin Gavanozoğlu appointed Hacı Halil Agha as the general *derbent* Agha of Servia, Chasia, Ptolemaida and Grevena.[23] In 1820, Dramalı Mahmud Pasha appointed Demeli Attoulo as the new *derbent* Agha of Lidoriki and Malandrino; Attoulo was deposed in February 1821.[24] In January 1821, the *voyvoda* and *derbent* Agha of Livadia was also replaced.[25] In April 1820, Süleyman Pasha appointed İbrahim Agha *derbent* Agha of Veroia, Naousa and Edessa.[26] In December 1821, to restore order in the *kaza* of Veroia, the Governor of Salonica Ebûlübud Pasha appointed Emin Agha as supervisor of the region.[27] On 13 February 1822, Hurşid Pasha appointed Süleyman Konto Agha *derbent* Agha of Veroia.[28] In March 1822, Ebûlübud Pasha appointed Hacı Mehmet Agha as the commander of the new garrison of the *kaza* of Veroia.[29]

Several of the Christian *armatoloi* were also replaced. As early as May 1820, Süleyman Pasha deposed Giotas Tzimou, chieftain of the *kol* [Gk. *Koli*] of Domenikos in Elassona.[30] In July 1820, Athanasios Diakos was appointed *arma-*

21   Giannopoulos 1914, pp. 288–9.
22   Panagiotopoulos (ed.) 2007–18, vol. 3, pp. 359–60, 427–8, 445–7; Sarris 1997, pp. 222–3.
23   Loufis 1924, pp. 84–5.
24   Certificate of the officers Triantafyllos Apokoritis and Kostas Boias published in the news-
      paper *Αθηνά*, 25 June 1858.
25   Philimon 1859–61, vol. 3, pp. 76–7.
26   Panagiotopoulos (ed.) 2007–18, vol. 3, pp. 427–8.
27   Vasdravellis 1950, pp. 233–4.
28   Vasdravellis 1950, p. 245.
29   Vasdravellis 1950, pp. 246–7.
30   Panagiotopoulos (ed.) 2007–18, vol. 3, p. 447. Cf. Koutsonikas 1863–4, vol. 1, p. 174, where
      the writer, mistakenly, thinks that Giotas was ousted by Ali Pasha. According to the spirit

tolos in the place of the pro-Ali Pasha Odysseas Androutsos.[31] At the same time, Antonis Kontosopoulos, cousin of Diakos, was appointed *armatolos* in Atalanti.[32] On 25 June 1820, the pro-Ali Pasha Lambros Kosmas Souliotis was replaced in the *armatoliki* of Salona by Komnas Trakas.[33] Trakas was replaced by Panourgias on 26 October 1820.[34] In 1820, the *armatolos* of Malandrino Karastathis was replaced by Kostas Chormovas, who was subsequently deposed in February 1821, and Malandrino returned to the jurisdiction of the *armatolos* of Lidoriki, Dimos Skaltsas.[35] In August 1820, opponent of Ali Pasha Dimitris Makris was appointed *armatolos* of Zygos in Missolonghi.[36]

Further to the north, with Dramalı Mahmud Pasha's decree, the *armatolikia* of Vlochos (Trichonida, Agrinio), Sovolakos and Politochorio in Karpenisi changed hands and were bestowed to members of the Vlachopoulos family: Alexakis Vlachopoulos was bestowed the *armatoliki* of Vlochos, Arapogiannis Sykas (uncle of Alexakis) the *armatoliki* of Sovolakos and Spyros and Giannakis Lambropoulos (cousins of Alexakis) the *armatoliki* of Politochorio.[37] In May 1820, Süleyman Pasha attempted to intervene in the *armatoliki* of Agrafa that was controlled by Giannakis Ragos, affiliated with Ali Pasha, by appointing his chosen *derbent* Agha, only to meet powerful resistance by the Ali Pasha faction.[38]

of the relevant documents contained in the Ali Pasha archive, Süleyman Pasha intended to replace the chieftains of the Olympus, Vermio and Chasia *armatolikia* [the administrative district of an *armatolos*], but we lack reliable evidence that he actually did so.

31   Lappas 1949, p. 53. His appointment, dated 26 October 1820, was decreed by the *derbendat nazırı* Dramalı Mahmud Pasha. However, he must have been appointed earlier, in July 1820, by Pehlivan Baba Pasha, and his appointment was renewed in October.

32   Memoirs of Antonis Kontosopoulos published by N. Papalexandris, 'Ἀθανάσιος Διάκος, ο ήρως της Ἐπαναστάσεως βιογραφούμενος από τον λαόν. Ἔρως – Πατρίς – Μαρτύριον. Ἄγνωστοι δραματικαί λεπτομέρειαι του βίου του Διάκου', newspaper *Ἀθῆναι*, 21 April 1903.

33   Lappas 1980, p. 31.

34   Philimon 1859–61, vol. 3, p. 431, publishing the appointment document.

35   Newspaper *Ἀθηνᾶ*, 25 June 1858. Cf. Tsiamalos 2009, p. 160.

36   Kambouroglou [1913], pp. 49–50; Makris Staikos 1958, pp. 247–9.

37   Kasomoulis 1939, vol. 1, pp. 30, 113; Tsiamalos 2009, p. 147. The Vlachogiannis Collection, located in the General State Archives of Greece, contains the non-dated appointment of Al. Vlachopoulos as *armatolos* of Vlochos decreed by Hurşid Pasha. Given that Hurşid Pasha arrived at Epirus and took over his command in March 1821, the decree must have been issued circa spring 1821. See Tsiamalos 2009, p. 63, note 139.

38   Panagiotopoulos (ed.) 2007–18, vol. 3, p. 445; K[rolomilas] 1933, pp. 49–50; G. Vlachogiannis, note. 4 in Kasomoulis 1939–42, vol. 1, p. 254.

Later that same year, the new sultanic authorities, most probably Pehlivan Baba Pasha, bestowed the *armatoliki* to the Boukouvala family.[39] In 1820 or early 1821, they were assigned the *armatoliki* of Tzoumerka, which was controlled by Mitros Koutelidas to Kostas Poulis, and, probably, the *armatoliki* of Radovitsi, controlled by Gogos Bakolas.[40] It also seems that, during the same time, Giannoulas Ziakas momentarily lost the *armatoliki* of Grevena.[41]

When the Tzavelas family joined the Ali Pasha camp in December 1820, they apparently lost control of the *armatoliki* of Chasia.[42] It is possible that the *armatoliki* was bestowed to the Vlachavas family – old-time enemies of Ali Pasha – who served as *armatoloi* in Chasia in 1821. Despite his attempt to build bridges and grovel before new magnates – the Pashas from the Porte – Vlachothodoros, chieftain of the Elassona *armatoliki* and declared friend of Ali Pasha, was arrested and executed by Paso Bey in 1820.[43] On the contrary, the *armatoloi* Kyriakos Basdekis of Pelio, Mitsos Kontogiannis of Badracık [Gk. Ypati], G. Varnakiotis of Xiromero, Andreas Iskos of Valtos, G. Tsogas of Vonitsa, Giannakis Yioldasis of Karpenisi, N. Stornaris of Aspropotamos, Giannakis Georgiou of Lamari in Preveza and Deligiannis of Metsovo seem to have retained their *armatolikia* after submitting to the Sublime Porte.

Apart from the replacements of the *armatoloi*, by 1820 the new sultanic authorities seem to have brought about some, albeit limited, changes in the spatial distribution of the *armatolikia*. They upgraded the *kolia* of Malandrino[44] and Zygos[45] to *armatolikia*. They also conferred upon Kyriakos Basdekis, who controlled the *armatoliki* of Pilio, 'three more warlordships, namely Pherai [Velestino], Amiro [Armyros] and Thavmakos [Domokos], for his services against Ali Pasha'.[46] As a result, out of the 27 *armatolikia* in central Greece (Sterea Hellada, Epirus and Thessaly; I omit Macedonia for lack of reliable evidence), 14 underwent changes. Despite the fact that some of the evidence pertaining to the aforementioned changes is based on later-recorded recollections – and is thus unreliable – it is reasonable to assume that these changes were more widespread, since the writers of memoirs and historical narratives were more concerned about recording the events of the Greek Revolution than

---

39   Kasomoulis 1939–42, vol. 1, pp. 100–1, 290; Kambouroglou [1913], pp. 49–50; Boukouvalas 1980–1, vol. 2, pp. 98–100, 110–12.
40   Aravantinos 1880, p. 97; Karatzenis 1970, pp. 55–7.
41   Vakalopoulos 1961–88, vol. 6, p. 125; Vakalopoulos 1988, p. 582.
42   Kasomoulis 1939–42, vol. 1, *passim*.
43   Kasomoulis 1939–42, vol. 1, p. 66; Koemtzopoulos 1994, p. 38.
44   Newspaper *Αθηνά*, 25 June 1858.
45   Stasinopoulos 1925, vol. 1, p. 227.
46   Philimon 1859–61, vol. 3, p. 134.

of the previous era. The break in their conceptual universe and, concomitantly, in their perception of events that the Revolution brought about was definitive.

Confrontations, conflicts and replacements also took place in the local Ottoman *kaza* administrations and in the Christian communities. Yet the relevant evidence is, too, limited and obscured by retrospective, national-minded interpretations. In Livadia, the Christian notables were accused of siding with Ali Pasha, while Panagiotis Lidorikis, the notable of Lidoriki, was arrested on the same charges. In this confrontational context, Kara İsmail, the *voyvoda* of Livadia, was replaced by Hasan Agha from Salonica.[47] Similar incidents occurred between the pro-Ali Pasha and the pro-Sultan Muslims from Salona [Gk. Amfissa] in Phokis; these also involved local Christian notables. In this context, Osman Bey, the *voyvoda* of Salona during Ali Pasha rule, was replaced by Izzet Bey,[48] while in Kozani the brothers Ioannis and Georgios Papadimitriou or Papadopoulos, pro-Ali Pasha notables, were replaced as well.[49] The 1820–1 changes in the local and regional administrative positions across the area formerly controlled by Ali Pasha, as well as the broader political context, were described with clarity by Lambros Koutsonikas. When Ali Pasha fell into the disfavour of the sultan in 1820, Koutsonikas wrote:

> To all of the provinces [*pashaliks*], be they small of big, that he [Ali] controlled or had conquered by military means from other governors or had received by the sultan's administration, to all, I say, of these provinces new governors were appointed, and none of them were friends to Ali. These governors, upon their arrival at the seat of their provinces, immediately appointed new notables, by dispelling their predecessors from their posts due to their affiliation with Ali Pasha; those who retained their offices with many sacrifices and financial burdens enjoyed standing opposition from those who had long suffered in their hands, and, thus, the whole region of Sterea [Hellada] was under overall turmoil and agitation. The newly appointed Pashas had received strict orders from the sultan not to lose time in their provinces but to dash to Ioannina to siege Ali Pasha and bring him down, thus they all hurriedly and rapidly moved to that direction. The Pashas were joined by the lords of the new order, for they also had an interest in the annihilation of Ali Pasha and, being close to the Pashas, they would foil the plots of the former lords who had also

47   Philimon 1859–61, vol. 3, pp. 76–7.
48   See, memoir of G. Papaspiliopoulos in Lappas 1973, pp. 37–40, and in Aravantinos 1895, pp. 583–7, 610–11; Goudas 1876, vol. 8, p. 243, 'Πανουριάδες'.
49   Lioufis 1924, p. 77.

moved to Ioannina and tried, by any means available, to redeem themselves and reclaim their offices. Apart from the lords, the *armatoloi* and
chieftains also dashed to Ioannina in order to introduce themselves to the
governors and declare their devotion so as to secure their chieftainships;
the prelates, the abbots of the monasteries and all kinds of officials, be
they political or military, acted similarly, and so, from mid-August of the
year 1820 onward, and from all regions, they all rushed to Ioannina.[50]

Frequent changes in official posts are not rare in Ottoman history. However,
the extensity and intensity of the changes during 1820–1 was unusual, covering a particularly large area that included the totality of the region formerly
controlled by Ali Pasha, whose administration had been stable for at least a decade. They also attempted to restore those removed by Ali Pasha by promising
to return their confiscated or trespassed property. In this way, the Christian
Souliots, who had been exiled to the Ionian Islands in 1803, the Muslim Chams
[Alb. *Çamë*; Gk. *Tsamides*; also exiled in 1807] and the Christian armed populations, who had resorted outside Ali Pasha's region, were restored. Their return,
however, gave rise to new problems, triggering disputes over land: typical in this
respect is the conflict between Souliots and Chams over the control of western Souli. Previously ousted chieftains also reclaimed their former *armatolikia*.
For example, Kostas Poulis apparently managed to restore his chieftainship in
Radovitsi and Tzoumerka.

The new sultanic authorities found it hard to process these problems. Ismail
Paso Bey, Pasha of Ioannina, constantly postponed the return of Souli to the
Souliots due to the pressure of the neighbouring Chams, who claimed part of
the region and were reluctant to share borders with their armed and dangerous
rivals. Thus, the Souliots switched sides and joined Ali Pasha's ranks.[51] The new
sultanic authorities also reclaimed Ali Pasha's *çiftliks* [estates], which either
became public (that is, sultanic property) again or were appropriated by new
Pashas and local Ottoman magnates.[52] As a result, the changes brought about
by the new administration extended to the whole administrative structure and
to aspects of the economy that affected the established social hierarchy.

---

50   Koutsonikas 1863–4, vol. 2, pp. κδ΄–κε΄.
51   On the return of Souliots, see Psimouli 2005, pp. 466–7; Psimouli 2010, pp. 24–5. On the
      return of Tsamides, see Krapsitis 1991, pp. 244–5. For other cases, see Prevelakis and Kalli-
      ataki Mertikopoulou (eds.) 1996, vol. 1, pp. 209, 239–40; Athinagoras 1929, p. 40.
52   See, inter alia, the dispute between the so-called Koniaroi of Thessaly and Ali Pasha, in
      1820, over the *çiftliks* seized in Panagiotopoulos (ed.) 2007–18, vol. 3, *passim*.

The Porte actually sought to dismantle the power structure established by Ali Pasha during his almost thirty-five years of rule, which comprised a considerable number of subordinate, dependent, affiliated or devoted officials that sustained his power: Pashas, *voyvodas*, *mütesellims*, *ayan* and Christian-Orthodox notables, bishops, *derbent* Aghas and *armatoloi*.[53] Ali Pasha was, in essence, a traditional Ottoman governor: the central axis of his rule, which sought to preserve his power and maintain his dominating force, was the immediate – and by means of violence – control of persons or factions and the persecution of those who did not submit to his will.[54] This also betrayed his weakness, as, during the crisis that broke out in 1820, his control system collapsed; Ali Pasha was thus abandoned, at least initially, by the vast majority of the officials and local social elites of his Pashalik. However, some of the *armatoloi*, notables and prelates who were devoted followers of Ali Pasha and who enjoyed his trust, like Odysseas Androutsos, could not join the sultanic army. The cases of Manthos Oikonomou and Spyros Kolovos, secretaries and advisors of Ali Pasha, who were imprisoned and executed,[55] are typical of the way in which the new sultanic authorities dealt with those identified with the Ali Pasha regime. This also allows us to surmise the fear that marked those who fell beneath the category. Many were also displeased either because they were deposed from their offices or because their expectations for restoration were frustrated.

Thus, two factions, whose politics cut across the local Muslim populations, were established, distinguished by their attitude towards the new sultanic authorities and the policies they implemented. In most cases, these factions evolved out of others already in existence during Ali Pasha's rule. In 1820–1, there were two factions in Epirus: as N. Kasomoulis writes, the first comprised of 'those notables and others who were content with Ali Pasha's administration, had flourished ... looked forward to his success and thus joined the rebels' cause'. Kasomoulis makes no reference to the second faction, but as Vlacho-giannis remarks, it obviously consisted of 'those who opposed Ali and were loyal to the Sultan'.[56] However, even those who had joined the 'sultanic fac-

---

53   Kokolakis 2003, pp. 124–5.

54   On Ali Pasha and his endeavour, see Panagiotopoulos's thought-provoking essay in Pana-
      giotopoulos (ed.) 2007–18, vol. 4, pp. 13–126. See, also, Panagiotopoulos 1986, pp. 289–96;
      Politis 2009, pp. 75–89.

55   See, with caution, Oikonomou 1959, pp. 617–29. On Spyros Kolovos, see Kremos 1883–4,
      p. 974.

56   Kasomoulis 1939–42, vol. 1, p. 142. Cf. Loukopoulos 1932, p. 304. For Naoussa, see, inter alia,
      Philippidis 1881, pp. 39–40; Stougiannakis 1924; Kasomoulis 1939–42, vol. 1, pp. 203, 205.
      On Grevena, see Papadimitriou 2014, p. 10.

tion' and received an office could not have been satisfied, as offices were not tenured but contingent upon the frequent changes in the higher administrative ranks. For example, it seems that the posts of the *armatoloi* experienced three waves of change: the first, between spring and summer 1820, by *derbendat nazırı* Süleyman Pasha and Pehlivan Baba Pasha of İnebahtı and Karlıeli; the second, in autumn 1820, by *derbendat nazırı* Dramalı Mahmut Pasha; and the third, in spring 1821, by the new *derbendat nazırı* Hurşid Pasha. These developments intensified competition over the available posts. Indicatively, the *armatoliki* of Agrafa was claimed by six warlords: Giannakis Ragos, Stamoulis Gatsos, Georgios Karaiskakis, Sotiris Stratos, the Boukouvalas family and Kostas Velis.[57] Uncertainty was also intensified by the lack of trust the new authorities, particularly Hurşid Pasha, showed for both the Christian officials and the local Muslim Albanians.[58]

To wind up, during 1820–1, policies implemented at the regional and local administration by the Sublime Porte's representatives triggered discontent, frustration and dissatisfied expectations; spread fear, insecurity and uncertainty; and caused frequent changes in factions and camps. On the whole, it led to the disintegration or even collapse of administrative authorities and political structures and to the emergence of three centres of power, each of which claimed, by various means, legitimacy and sovereignty: the Sublime Porte, Ali Pasha and the aspiring Greek revolutionary authority through delegates of the Friendly Society in southern Roumelia. Still, none could claim uncontested rule. The disputes and conflicts among the lower-rank officials could not be resolved by resorting to a sovereign. Typical in this respect is the fact that to resolve a dispute between the chieftains, Georgios Varnakiotis and Georgios Tsogas, over the borders of the *armatolikia* of Xiromero and Vonitsa, Varnakiotis did not resort to a higher conflict resolution order but to a horizontal alliance with other chieftains (Christians and Muslims) who signed an agreement of support and solidarity.[59] Likewise, the alliance treaty – signed in September 1821 by Muslim-Albanian Aghas, Christian-Orthodox Souliots and chieftains of western Sterea Hellada and Epirus – included two clauses that

---

57 Papageorgiou (ed.) 1982, pp. κδ'-κε'; Tsiamalos 2009, pp. 143–4.
58 On the lack of trust towards Souliots and their removal from the central camp of Ioannina, see Psimouli 2010, p. 25; Perraivos 2019, pp. 101–3; Philimon 1859–61, vol. 2, pp. 239–41. On the removal of *armatoloi* from the siege, see Pouqueville 1824, vol. 2, pp. 150–1. On the lack of trust towards shown by Hurşid Pasha towards Albanians, Christians and Muslims, and their removal from Ioannina, see. Prevelakis and Kalliataki Mertikopoulou (eds.) 1996, vol. 1, pp. 333, 424; Aravantinos 1895, p. 315.
59 Physentzidis 1893, p. 95.

sought to protect the signatories from Ali Pasha's arbitrariness. According to the first, if Ali Pasha, in the case of his survival, attempted to harm any of the signatories or their future allies, all allies would be obliged to resist; according to the second, the towns that Ali Pasha had conquered and turned into *çift-lik*s by force would be freed and would pay the taxes as they did before their seizure.[60]

Consequently, the disintegration of the power structure in southern Rumelia opened a political opportunity to structure and expand the repertoire of action to include armed uprisings. The local Christian elites saw in this the possibility of manoeuvring within rival power structures to improve their social status; in engaging in armed uprising, crowned with foreseeable success, they even saw the possibility of establishing a new political structure with privileged access to its top tiers. This scenario could have included Ali Pasha as an ally or future ruler, albeit with curtailed powers.

The upheaval in southern Rumelia during the Sublime Port-Ali Pasha conflict bears certain resemblances to the catalytic conquests of the Italian and Iberian peninsulas in the French Revolution by Napoleon's troops and later in the Bourbon Restoration. The administrative and political transformations and institutional changes brought about by the conquerors and later during the Restoration triggered ideological and political shifts in social groups and figures, which led to the enhancement of liberal and national movements.[61] Similar ideological and political shifts took place between 1797 and 1815 on the Ionian Islands due to consecutive conquests by France, Russia, France and England.[62]

2   Economic Crisis

The military confrontation between the Sublime Porte and Ali Pasha put the populations of southern Rumelia under severe economic pressure, adding to a preceding economic recession that had marked the pre-revolutionary decade but whose depth is unknown. In any case, the liberalisation of the market after the Napoleonic Wars, and the decrease in the value of products due to the Industrial Revolution, brought the cottage industries of the mountainous areas

---

60   Physentzidis 1893, pp. 93–4; Protopsaltis (ed.) 1963–86, vol. 1, pp. 61–3.
61   Isabella 2009.
62   Arvanitakis 2020.

of central Greece to economic recession.[63] At the same time, the merchant fleet
of Missolonghi also declined.[64]

The living conditions of the population had started to deteriorate even
before the military operations broke out, as Ali Pasha, in view of the siege of
Ioannina, had ordered the confiscation of products from various areas while
he also imposed forced labour to restore the fortification of castles.[65] On top
of this, the advance of the sultanic troops towards Ioannina increased the economic burden, as the organisation of the Ottoman military logistics was rudi-
mentary and the troops survived at the expense of the local populations.

Between 9 July 1820 and 1 February 1821, the financial needs of the *sancak*
of Karlieli for irregular taxes and other military expenses quadrupled, and the
agreed annual flat tax skyrocketed from 60,000 to 271,000 *kuruş*.[66] In addition, the loose discipline that pervaded the Ottoman army allowed soldiers to
engage in arbitrary taxation, thefts and looting. Moreover, the protracted siege
of Ioannina, due to the underestimation of Ali Pasha's resistance, exacerbated
the problem of purveyance, while the upcoming winter deteriorated overall living conditions.[67] This led to increased forced taxation of the surrounding areas
and to the desertion of soldiers from the Ottoman army, who thus resorted to
raids and looting – not only to survive but also to make a profit, as the main
motivator of conscription was not the wage but the expected spoils.[68]

---

63   On the cottage industries of Pelio and the southern edges of Olympus, see Petmezas 1990,
      pp. 593–601; Stamatogiannopoulou 1984, pp. 385–93; Katsiardi-Hering 2003; Nikolopoulos
      1988, pp. 318–60. On the mainland cottage industries of Syrrako and Kalarrytes, see Mag-
      laras 2004, vol. 2, p. 92.

64   Papakonstantinou 2010, pp. 277–97.

65   Prevelakis and Kalliataki Mertikopoulou (eds.) 1996, vol. 1, pp. 98, 103, 110, 133–4; Athin-
      agoras 1929, p. 40; Papakostas (ed.) 1962, p. 23.

66   Konstantinidis 1900, pp. 473–4. On the irregular taxes paid by the *kaza* of Karpenisi in
      spring 1820 that exceeded 2,000 *kuruş*, in the context of Ali Pasha's preparations for the
      upcoming confrontation, see Mavromytis 2006, pp. 111–14. Selitsa [now Eratyra] in Kozani
      was burdened with irregular taxes of 40,000 *kuruş* in 1821 and of 3,500 *kuruş* in 1822; see
      Gioblakis 1968, pp. 79–80.

67   On the heavy winter of 1820, the lack of grain and the concomitant increase in prices, see
      Athinagoras 1929, p. 41; Prevelakis and Kalliataki Mertikopoulou (eds.) 1996, vol. 1, p. 384;
      Prappas 1999, p. 183. For the lack of supplies in the sultanic camp, see Aravantinos 1856,
      vol. 1, p. 333; Pouqueville 1824, vol. 2, p. 124; Kremos 1883–4, p. 68; Prevelakis and Kalliataki
      Mertikopoulou (eds.) 1996, vol. 1, p. 238.

68   Prevelakis and Kalliataki Mertikopoulou (eds.) 1996, vol. 1, pp. 204, 241, 232, 237, 255–6;
      Koutsalexis 1882, pp. 21, 28; Philimon 1834, p. 327; Vasdravellis (ed.) 1954, pp. 267–9; Makry-
      giannis 2011, vol. 1, pp. 31–3; Pouqueville 1824, vol. 2, pp. 53–4, 84–6, 97, 114–16, 560; Kremos
      1883–4, pp. 975–6 and 68; Koutsonikas 1863–4, vol. 1, p. 187; Soulis 1934, p. 112; Aravantinos
      1856, vol. 1, p. 327; Papakostas (ed.) 1962, pp. 38, 47 and *passim*.

The testimony of a person who worked for the sultanic faction is telling. When tempers flared on 29 April 1821, Nikolaos-Anagnostis Laspas, secretary of Hurşid Pasha, wrote to Alexakis Vlachopoulos, *armatolos* of Vlochos, to convince him to bow before the Sublime Porte:

> If you do not surrender, you will suffer a crushing defeat and the blame will be on you. Open your eyes. See how willing the Albanians, along with almost all of the Ottomans, are to enslave children and women and how eager they are to grab the apostates' property. And not for any other reason but these are the times we are living in. Even my master cannot stop them, for they have raised their own banner and willingly engage in disorder to the benefit of the mercenaries with our own belongings, and they are not even satisfied with the wage of 25 piasters they receive, for they earn much more selling women and children for slaves. Thus, take your measures accordingly and think wisely in order to be forever happy and grateful to the king master.[69]

The building of the anti-sultanic alliance between Souliots and Muslim-Albanian Aghas in December 1820 intensified the problem as battles, raids and looting spread. Thus, many of the residents of the broader Ioannina region fled to the mountains for shelter. Several resorted to the neighbouring areas of Ioannina and even further to Thesprotia, Arta, Preveza, Trikala and Aitoloakarnania.[70] The multiple dangers that threatened peasants, their flight from their villages and their conscription to military forces left the fields uncultivated. This in turn resulted in a decrease in agricultural production, a lack of grain and other basic products and a high increase in prices. Warfare paralysed trade in Epirus and held it back in the surrounding areas.[71] In some regions, the advent of epidemics, primarily plague, further deteriorated the overall situation,[72] leading to an economic crisis in Epirus and to a lesser degree in bordering regions. All this largely disturbed the local populations and created great discontent. As N. Kasoumoulis, an acute contemporary observer, wrote in Siatista in May 1821, 'citizens gathered from all around and we did not know

---

69 Kokkinos 1956–60, vol. 2, pp. 303–4.
70 See, for example, Koutsalexis 1882, pp. 21–51; Kougeas (ed.) 1939, pp. 122–3, 234–36, 248; Melas 1967, pp. 422–40; Papakostas (ed.) 1962, p. 26; Aravantinos 1856, vol. 1, pp. 331–2; Soulis 1934, pp. 112–13; Panteliou 1976, pp. 146–7; Xanthos 1845, pp. 98–9; Papageorgiou 1988, pp. 118–19.
71 Prevelakis and Kalliataki Merikopoulou (eds.) 1996, vol. 1, pp. 232, 242.
72 On the appearance of plague in Epirus and Thessaly in 1820, see. Kostis 1995, p. 409; Panteliou 1976, pp. 146–7.

what to do. Troops marched by Ioannina and Kozani on a daily basis, and all citizens got depressed day in, night out and, eventually, fed up'.[73]

Consequently, during the Ali Pasha-Sultan conflict, the living conditions of the population – both of the poor and of the local elites – deteriorated rapidly and severely, while uncertainty about the future constantly intensified. The new Ottoman authorities that succeeded Ali Pasha's regime disappointed the expectations cultivated in the summer 1820, when they had promised to reverse the former ruler's injustices by returning the confiscated property and adopting milder and fairer administrative and tax practices.[74] On the contrary, the practices of brutal and excessive taxation and seizure they either implemented or tolerated deteriorated the situation. As a result, the populations, plagued as they were by the consequences of war, became accustomed to violence and predisposed to acts of mutiny and revolt. The local Christian authorities, notables and *armatoloi* received complaints and protestations. After all, the power and status of the *armatoloi* were contingent upon their ability to preserve peace and safety in their *armatoliki* and to protect it against thefts and plundering. Otherwise, they could be sidelined by rival chieftains if the latter proved more effective in dealing with such problems.[75]

Once more, Kasomoulis's testimony is indicative of the tension and receptivity to acts of disobedience and mutiny. In February 1821, when he reached the Olympus shores, he wrote that 'the zealot chieftains were ready, the population was indignant at the taxes that the Turks had levied on them and, being so predisposed, they got disquieted and eager to attack in order to find revivification'.[76]

Reflecting the leap from disappointment to mutiny is an extract from a letter addressed to Stavros Ioannou, notable of Zagorochoria, from Christian refugees in Dourouti, Ioannina, dated 7 December 1820:

> ... given that Christmas is coming and the situation is ungovernable, we decided, having experienced the grievances of our children and famil-

---

73   Kasomoulis 1939–42, vol. 1, p. 139.

74   See, inter alia, the letter of patriarch Gregorios V to the prelates of Thessaly in Zegos 1927, pp. 77–80, and the letter of Ismail Paso Bey to the residents of Ioannina in Kougeas (ed.) 1939, p. 122. See, also, the letters of Ismail Paso Bey to Souliots in Koutsonikas 1863–4, vol. 2, pp. 123–5; Gousis 1887, pp. 44–5; and Rados 1916, p. 99.

75   See Kotaridis 1993.

76   Kasomoulis 1939–42, vol. 1, pp. 184–5. See, also, the archive of the British consul in Preveza, William Meyer, acute and usually well-informed observer, crawling with references to peoples' discontent and the mounting spirit of mutiny since December 1820. Prevelakis and Kalliataki Mertikopoulou (eds.) 1996, vol. 1, pp. 254–6, 263–4, 267, 319–22, 349.

ies ... and our children barefoot and bareheaded, to walk for three days to Ioannina to find our notable and our bishop and our lords to receive alms, and found nobody, we beg you to act hurriedly before the ignorant lot revolts.[77]

In his report to the High Commissioner of the Ionian Islands, Thomas Maitland, an acute contemporary observer and the British consul in Preveza William Meyer, insightfully wrote on 1/13 December 1820:

> In the meantime the demands for the supplies of the Sultan's army and the public service continue to press most heavily on the people. They consider themselves as being treated with great injustice and unnecessary rigour. Seeing no probability of a termination of this state of things; and fearing, in the event of the Sultan's gaining an absolute ascendancy over their country and their affairs, that their condition will become much worse than it now is, when compared with that of the people in most of the other provinces in the Empire; it is understood that the Albanians and the Greeks are now ready to rise en masse, the moment they can see a favourable opportunity for it, and place themselves under a provisional government of their own formation, until the proper appeals can be made to the Sultan on the subject of those causes which may have compelled them for their own preservation to take such a course.[78]

3   Conclusion

The events did not occur as intensively across southern Rumelia. Obviously, Epirus – the epicentre of the military confrontation – suffered the most the consequences of war. But even the rest of the regions – from southern Albania and western and northern Macedonia to Livadia and Missolonghi – did not remain intact.[79] And yet what mattered most was not the degree to which living conditions deteriorated but the rapidity of the change in combination with the disappointment of the expectations caused by the administration of the Otto-

---

77   Papageorgiou 1988, p. 121.

78   Prevelakis and Kalliataki Mertikopoulou (eds.) 1996, vol. 1, p. 255.

79   For example, it was reported that in July 1820 many residents of Livadia and Missolonghi resorted to Vostitsa [mod. Aigio] in the Peloponnese, seeing the advance of the Ottoman troops led by Pehlivan Pasha; see Prevelakis and Kalliataki Mertikopoulou (eds.) 1996, vol. 1, p. 157.

man authorities that succeeded Ali Pasha's regime. Thus, the local populations in southern Rumelia sensed that their living conditions would not improve, and they saw in the disintegration of the regional Ottoman power, as well as in the challenging of the Sublime Porte by Ali Pasha, a chance to revolt against their rulers.

At this conjuncture, the role of the members and delegates of the Friendly Society proved critical. The network they had established in southern Rumelia, despite being relatively feeble, served an exchange role that (in)formed political action. Coincidingly, at the end of 1820 and in early 1821, Friendly Society delegates spread across southern Rumelia, calling for the overthrowing of Ottoman domination and disseminating rumours about upcoming Russian assistance and about glorious victories in the regions in which the Revolution had already broken out. The frustrated populations received the revolutionary message well, as it offered a risky but hopeful prospect. For example, Kasomoulis reported that, in February 1822, Nikolaos Kanousis – a member of the Friendly Society and envoy of Dimitrios Hypsilantis in Macedonia – addressed people gathered in Naousa:

> Kanousis giving, from the pulpit of the church, a fiery speech about freedom, excited the people who suddenly realised how much they had suffered by the Turks and how much they would enjoy being free. After the orator Kanousis stepped down, Zafeirakis also spoke and the people rushed to the market and killed as many Turks as they found there.[80]

While in some cases rebellion broke out without its intervention, the Friendly Society evidently sparked most of the revolutionary fire. The uprising may have been anti-Ottoman in nature, but it lacked a national orientation, as in case of the Souliots in December 1820[81] and of the so-called 'Greek-Albanian alliance', initially built by Souliots and Muslim-Albanian Aghas and later enriched by Christian chieftains.[82] After all, the various social groups and local populations that joined the Greek Revolution did not share motives, objectives or plans for political organisation.[83] The catalytic role of the Friendly Society is

---

80   Kasomoulis 1939–42, p. 203. Zafeirakis Theodosiou was a powerful notable in Naoussa who had been ousted by Ali Pasha. For the role played by rumours to the outburst of the Revolution, see Vakalopoulos 1950, pp. 209–29. For a typical example of these rumours, see the handwritten *Εφημερίς του Γαλαξιδίου* (27 March 1821) in Koumarianou 1971, vol. 1, p. 5.

81   I follow the analysis of Psimouli 2010, pp. 24–64.

82   Phanourakis 1999, pp. 127–56; Stathis 2006, pp. 84–129.

83   See, inter alia, Theotokas 1992, pp. 345–70; Rotzokos 1997; Diamantouros 2002.

revealed in the fact that, through its network, it unified the scattered uprisings and brought them under a common umbrella. In short, the Society provided the revolting areas and social groups with political and ideological cohesion by bringing them under the aegis of a national movement. This does not mean that the rebels shared a common view on the nation or common ideas about the political organisation of the national community, for even the inner circle of the Friendly Society was riven with differences. These culminated in severe controversies and civil conflicts, which broke out during the Revolution. Yet what brought the rebels together was the enduring drive to overthrow Ottoman rule.

Bibliography

Aravantinos, Panagiotis 1856, *Χρονογραφία της Ηπείρου* [*Chronography of Epirus*], 2 Volumes, Athens: Σ. Κ. Βλαστός.

Aravantinos, Panagiotis 1880, *Συλλογή δημωδών ασμάτων της Ηπείρου* [*Collection of popular songs from Epirus*], Athens: Πέτρος Περρής.

Aravantinos, Panagiotis 1984, *Περιγραφή της Ηπείρου* [*Description of Epirus*], 3 Volumes, Ioannina: Εταιρεία Ηπειρωτικών Μελετών.

Aravantinos, Spyridon P. 1895, *Ιστορία Αλή πασά του Τεπελενή* [*History of Ali Pasha of Tepeleni*], Athens: Τυπογραφείο των Καταστημάτων Σπυρίδωνος Κουσουλίνου.

Arsh, Grigori L. 1994, *Η Αλβανία και η Ήπειρος στα τέλη του ΙΗ´ και στις αρχές του ΙΘ´ αιώνα. Τα Δυτικοβαλκανικά Πασαλίκια της Οθωμανικής Αυτοκρατορίας* [*Albania and Epirus in the end of the eighteenth and the beginning of nineteenth century: the Western Balkan Pashaliks of the Ottoman Empire*], Athens: Gutenberg.

Arvanitakis, Dimitris D. 2020, *Η αγωγή του πολίτη. Η γαλλική παρουσία στο Ιόνιο (1797–1799) και το έθνος των Ελλήνων* [*Citizen's education: The French presence in the Ionian Sea (1797–1799) and the nation of the Greeks*], Herakleio: Crete University Press.

Athinagoras, metropolitan of Paramythia and Parga 1929, 'Νέος Κουβαράς, ήτοι χρονικά σημειώματα αναφερόμενα εις την πόλιν ιδία των Ιωαννίνων, εις μονάς αυτής και τας επαρχίας αυτής' ['Notes concerning the history of the town of Ioannina, its monasteries and dependent provinces'], *Ηπειρωτικά Χρονικά*, 4: 1–54.

Beaton, Roderick 2019, *Greece: Biography of a Modern Nation*, Chicago: University of Chicago Press.

Boukouvalas, Euripides 1980–1981, *Το αρματολίκι των Αγράφων* [*The armatoliki of Agrafa*], 2 Volumes, Athens: Χρήστος Χριστινάκης.

Cucută, Radu-Alexandru 2013, 'Theories of Revolution: The Generational Deadlock', *Challenges of the Knowledge Society*, 3: 1107–16.

Diamantouros, Nikiforos 2002, *Οι απαρχές της συγκρότησης του σύγχρονου κράτους στην*

Ελλάδα, 1821–1828 [*The beginnings of the formation of the modern state in Greece, 1821–1828*], Athens: Μορφωτικό Ίδρυμα Εθνικής Τραπέζης.

Diamantouros, Nikiforos 1972, *Political Modernization, Social Conflict, and Cultural Cleavage in the Formation of the Modern Greek State: 1821–1828*, Ph.D. dissertation, Columbia University.

Drosos, Nektarios 2006, "Έξι υπομνήματα εκλογής μητροπολιτών της Λάρισας (1803–1821)' ['Six memoranda for the election of metropolitans in Larisa (1803–1821)'], *Θεσσαλικό Ημερολόγιο*, 49: 145–60.

Evaggelou, Panagiota 2010, *Αλληλογραφία του Πατριαρχείου Κωνσταντινουπόλεως με τη μονή Γηρομερίου Θεσπρωτίας κατά τη μεταβυζαντινή και νεότερη περίοδο. Συμβολή στη φιλολογική έρευνα της πατριαρχικής γραμματείας* [*Correspondence of the Patriarchate of Constantinople with the monastery of Giromerio in Thesprotia during the post-byzantine and modern period. Contribution to the philological study of the patriarchal chancery*], Ph.D. dissertation, University of Patras.

Frangos, Georgios 1971, *The Philike Etaireia, 1814–1821: a Social and Historical analysis*, PhD Dissertation, Columbia University, New York.

Gallant, Thomas 2001, *Modern Greece*, London: Arnold.

Gallant, Thomas 2015, *The Edinburgh History of the Greeks, 1768 to 1912: The Long Nineteenth Century*, Edinburgh: Edinburgh University Press.

Giannopoulos, Nikolaos I. 1914, 'Επισκοπικοί κατάλογοι Θεσσαλίας' ['Lists of bishops in Thessaly'], *Επετηρίς Φιλολογικού Συλλόγου Παρνασσός*, 10: 252–312.

Gioblakis, A. 1968, 'Οι 'χαλασμοί' της Σελίτσης (Εράτυρας)' ['The destructions of Selitsa (Eratyra)'], *Μακεδονικά*, 8: 75–92.

Goldstone, Jack A. 2016, *Revolution and Rebellion in the Early Modern World: Population Change and State Breakdown in England, France, Turkey, and China, 1600–1850. 25th Anniversary Edition*, New York: Routledge.

Goudas, Anastasios 1876, *Βίοι παράλληλοι των επί της αναγεννήσεως της Ελλάδος διαπρεψάντων ανδρών, Ήρωες της ξηράς* [*Biographies of the protagonists in the Greek resurrection: Heroes of the war in land*], vol. 8, Athens: Τύποις Ελληνικής Ανεξαρτησίας.

Gousis, I[oannis] 1887, 'Ιστορικά Σουλίου' ['On the history of Souli'], *Παρνασσός*, 11: 27–51.

Hering, Gunnar 1992, 'Zum Problem der Ursachen revolutionärer Erhebungen am Anfang des 19. Jahrhunderts', in *Nationalrevolutionäre Bewegungen in Südosteuropa im 19. Jh.*, edited by Christo Choliolchev, Karkheinz Mack and Arnold Suppan, Vienna: R. Oldenbourg.

Iliou, Philippos 1997, *Ελληνική βιβλιογραφία του 19ου αιώνα. Βιβλία, φυλλάδια* [*Greek bibliography of the nineteenth century. Books and pamphlets*], vol. 1: *1801–1818*, Athens: Benaki Museum.

Isabella, Maurizio 2009, *Risorgimento in Exile: Italian Émigrés and the Liberal International in the Post-Napoleonic Era*, New York: Oxford University Press.

Kambouroglou, D[imitrios] [1913], *Αρματωλοί και κλέφτες (1453–1821)* [*Armatoloi and klephts*], Athens: Εκδοτικός οίκος Άγκυρας.

Karatzenis, Dimitrios 1970, *Η μάχη του Σέλτσου. Δραματική αντίστασις των Σουλιωτών* [*The battle of Seltso: the dramatic resistence of the Souliots*], Athens: private edition.

Kasomoulis, Nikolaos K. 1940, *Ενθυμήματα στρατιωτικά της επαναστάσεως των Ελλήνων, 1821–1833* [*Military memoirs on the revolution of the Greeks, 1821–1833*], introduction and commentary by Giannis Vlachogiannis, 3 Volumes, Athens.

Katsiardi-Hering, Olga 2003, *Τεχνίτες και τεχνικές βαφής νημάτων: Από τη Θεσσαλία στην Κεντρική Ευρώπη (18ος–αρχές 19ου αι.)* [*Craftsmen and techniques for thread dyeing: from Thessaly to Central Europe (eighteenth–beginnings of nineteenth c.)*], Athens and Ambelakia: Ηρόδοτος.

Kitsou-Pitouli, Christina 1974, 'Μικρή συμβολή στη μελέτη της ζωής και του έργου του Αλέξη Νούτσου. (Συνοπτική αναφορά στο αρχείο Σταύρου και σε ορισμένες άλλες πηγές)' ['A small contribution to the study of the life and works of Alexis Noutsos'], *Ηπειρωτική Εστία*, 23: 1–21, 158–78, 370–92, 485–502, 589–605.

Koemtzopoulos, Kimon 1994, *Οι Λαζαίοι του Ολύμπου και απόγονοι* [*The Lazaioi of Mount Olympus and their descedants*], Athens and Ioannina: Εκδόσεις "Δωδώνη".

Kokkinos, Dionysios 1956–60, *Η Ελληνική Επανάστασις* [*The Greek Revolution*], 12 Volumes, Athens: Melissa.

Kokolakis, Michalis 2003, *Το ύστερο γιαννιώτικο πασαλίκι* [*The late Ottoman Pashalik of Janina*], Athens: National Hellenic Research Foundation.

Konstantinidis, G. 1900, 'Το Κάρληλι και η φορολογία αυτού' ['The province of Karleli and its taxation'], *Αρμονία*, 1/8: 465–74.

K[oromilas] G.D. 1933, Καραϊσκάκης Γεώργιος [Georgios Karaiskakis], entry in *Μεγάλη Ελληνική Εγκυκλοπαίδεια*, vol. 13, Athens: Πυρσός.

Kostis, Kostas 1995, *Στον καιρό της πανώλης: Εικόνες από τις κοινωνίες της ελληνικής χερσονήσου, 14ος–19ος αιώνας* [*In the times of the plague: Images from the societies of the Greek peninsula, fourteenth–nineteenth c.*], Herakleio: Crete University Press.

Kotaridis, Nikos 1993, *Παραδοσιακή Επανάσταση και Εικοσιένα* [*Traditional revolution and 1821*], Athens: Πλέθρον.

Kougeas, Socrates 1939, 'Το ηπειρωτικόν αρχείον Σταύρου Ιωάννου' ['The Epirot archive of Stavros Ioannou'], *Ηπειρωτικά Χρονικά*, 14: 1–350.

Koumarianou, Aikaterini 1971, *Ο Τύπος στον Αγώνα 1821–1827* [*The Press in the Struggle for Indepedence 1821–1827*], 3 Volumes, Athens: Ερμής.

Koutsalexis, A[lexios] P. 1882, *Διαφέροντα και περίεργα τινά ιστορήματα* [*Some interesting and curious stories*], Athens: Εκ του Τυπογραφείου Ερμού.

Koutsonikas, L. 1863–4, *Γενική ιστορία της ελληνικής επαναστάσεως* [*General history of the Greek revolution*], 2 Volumes, Athens: Τύποις του 'Ευαγγελισμού' Δ. Καρακατζάνη.

Krapsitis, Vassilis 1991, *Η ιστορία της Παραμυθιάς* [*History of Paramythis*], Athens: private edition.

Kremmydas, Vassilis 1977, 'Η οικονομική κρίση στον ελλαδικό χώρο στις αρχές του 19ου αιώνα και οι επιπτώσεις της στην Επανάσταση του 1821' ['The economic crisis in the Greek lands at the begginings of the nineteenth century and its effects on the revolution of 1821'], *Μνήμων*, 6: 16–33.

Kremmydas, Vassilis 2002, 'Προεπαναστατικές πραγματικότητες: η οικονομική κρίση και η πορεία προς το Εικοσιένα' ['Realities before the Greek revolution: the economic crisis and the outbreak of the revolution'], *Μνήμων*, 24: 71–84.

Kremos, Georgios 1883–1884, 'Ιστορικά επανορθώματα: Α΄ Αλή Πασάς' ['Historical corrections: I. Ali Pasha'], *Παρνασσός*, 7: 950–79, and 8: 64–75, 139–54.

Kyrkini-Koutoula, Anastasia 1996, *Η οθωμανική διοίκηση στην Ελλάδα. Η περίπτωση της Πελοποννήσου (1715–1821)* [*Ottoman administration in Greece: the case of the Peloponnese (1715–1821)*], Athens: Αρσενίδης.

Lachmann, Richard 2013, 'Revolutions and Social Movements', in *What is Historical Sociology?*, Cambridge-Malden MA: Polity.

Lappas, Takis 1949, *Θανάσης Διάκος* [*Thanasis Diakos*], Athens: Εκδόσεις Μ. Πεχλιβανίδης.

Lappas, Takis 1973, *Αναγνώστης – Νικόλας Γιαγτζής, Γιωργάκης Παπαηλιόπουλος* [*Anagnostis – Nikolas Giagtsis, Giorgakis Papaeliopoulos*], Amfissa: Έκδοση Δήμου Αμφίσσης.

Lappas, Takis 1980, 'Η χειρόγραφη ιστορία της οικογένειας Τράκα' ['The manuscript history of the Trakas family'], reprint from *Δελτίον της Ιστορικής και Εθνολογικής Εταιρείας της Ελλάδος*, vol. 23.

Lioufis, Panagiotis N. 1924, *Ιστορία της Κοζάνης* [*History of the town of Kozani*], Athens: Τύποις Ιωάν. Βάρτσου.

Loukopoulos, Dimitris 1932, ''Ένα χαρτί παλιό που ήρθε να μας θυμίση το Θανάση Διάκο' ['An old paper was found to remind us of Thanasis Diakos'], *Ημερολόγιον της Μεγάλης Ελλάδος*, 11: 295–310.

Maglaras, Manolis 2004, 'Κοινωνικές και οργανωτικές δομές – Διαστρωμάτωση – Οικονομική Ζωή – Επαγγέλματα – Οι Τρεις Μεγάλοι του Συρράκου' ['Social and organisational structures – social stratification – economic life – professions – the three big men of Syrrako'], in *Συρράκο: Πέτρα – Μνήμη – Φως*, 2 Volumes, Syrrako: Πνευματικό Κέντρο Κοινότητας Συρράκου.

Makris Staikos, S.P. 1958, 'Επιλογή εγγράφων Αρχείου στρατηγού Δ. Μακρή' ['Selection of documents from the Archive of General D. Makris'], *Αρχεία Εταιρείας Αιτωλοακαρνανικών Σπουδών* 1: 245–59.

Makrygiannis, Ioannis 2011, *Στρατηγού Μακρυγιάννη Απομνημονεύματα* [*Memoirs of General Makrygiannis*], 3 volumes, edited by Georgia Papageorgiou and Alexis Politis, Athens: Εστία.

Mavromytis, Anargyros-Ioannis 2006, *Καρπενήσι 1810–1820* [*Karpenisi 1810–1820*], Athens: Πανευρυτανική ένωση.

Melas, Leon I. 1967, *Μια οικογένεια – μια ιστορία* [*One family – one history*], Athens: private edition.

Nikolopoulos, Ilias 1988, *Κοινωνικοοικονομικές δομές και πολιτικοί θεσμοί στην τουρκοκρατία:*

Τα θεσσαλικά Αμπελάκια (1770–1820) [*Socioeconomic structures and political institutions during the Tourkoratia: the Ambelakia in Thessaly (1770–1820)*], Athens: Κάλβος.

Oikonomos, Sophocles (ed.) 1862–1866, *Τα σωζόμενα εκκλησιαστικά συγγράμματα Κωνσταντίνου Πρεσβυτέρου και Οικονόμου του εξ Οικονόμων* [*The surviving ecclesiastical writings of Konstantinos the Elder and Oikonomos from the Oikonomos family*], 3 Volumes, Athens: Φ. Καραμπίνος και Κ. Βάφας.

Oikonomou, Manthos 1959, 'Μάνθος Οικονόμου' ['Manthos Oikonomou'], *Ηπειρωτική Εστία*, 8: 88–9, 617–29.

Panagiotopoulos, Vassilis 1986, 'Ζητήματα της Ηπειρωτικής Ιστορίας στα χρόνια του Αλή Πασά' ['Issues of the history of Epirus under the rule of Ali Pasha], in *Πρακτικά Συνεδρίου: Ήπειρος, Κοινωνία-Οικονομία 15ος–20ός αι.*, Ioannina: Δήμος Ιωαννιτών.

Panagiotopoulos, Vassilis (ed.), in collaboration with D. Dimitropoulos and P. Michailaris 2007–18, *Αρχείο Αλή πασά Συλλογής Ι. Χώτζη Γενναδείου Βιβλιοθήκης της Αμερικανικής Σχολής Αθηνών: Έκδοση – Σχολιασμός – Ευρετήρια* [*Archive of Ali Pasha*], 5 Volumes, Athens: National Hellenic Foundation of Research.

Panteliou, Maria 1976, 'Ο Αθανάσιος Ψαλίδας στην Κέρκυρα (1822–1828)' ['Athanasios Psalidas in Corfu (1822–8)], *Ηπειρωτική Εστία*, 25, 287–8: 145–54.

Papadimitriou, Apostolos 2014, *Σελίδες ιστορίας των Γρεβενών* [*Pages from the history of Grevena*], vol. 2, Grevena: private edition.

Papageorgiou, Giorgos 1988, *Οι συντεχνίες στα Γιάννενα κατά τον 19° και τις αρχές του 20ού αιώνα* [*The guilds in Janina during the nineteenth and the beginnings of the 20th c.*], Ioannina: Ίδρυμα Μελετών Ηπειρωτικού και Αδριατικού Χώρου.

Papageorgiou, Stefanos (ed.) 1982, *Το Αρχείο Γιαννάκη Ράγκου* [*The Archive of Giannakis Ragkos*], Athens: Ιστορική και Εθνολογική Εταιρεία της Ελλάδος.

Papakonstantinou, Katerina 2010, 'The Port of Messolonghi: Spatial Allocation and Maritime Expansion in the Eighteenth Century', *The Historical Review*, 7: 277–97.

Papakostas, A. (ed.) 1962, 'Ιστορία της πολιορκίας των Ιωαννίνων 1820–1822' ['History of the siege of Ioannina 1820–1822'], *Νέος Κουβαράς*, reprint from 2.

Perraivos, Christophoros 2019, *Απομνημονεύματα Πολεμικά* [*War Memoirs*], Athens: Hellenic Parliament Foundation.

Petmezas, Socrates D. 1990, 'Patterns of Protoindustrialization in the Ottoman Empire: The Case of Eastern Thessaly, ca. 1750–1860', *The Journal of European Economic History*, 19, 3: 593–601

Phanourakis, Mamolis 1999, 'Η 'ελληνοαλβανική συμμαχία' του 1821' ['The Greek-Albanian alliance in 1821'], *Δοκιμές*, 8: 127–56.

Philimon, Ioannis 1834, *Δοκίμιον ιστορικόν περί της Φιλικής Εταιρείας* [*Historical Essay concerning the Friendly Society*], Nafplio: Θ. Κονταξής και Ν. Λουλάκης.

Philimon, Ioannis 1859–61, *Δοκίμιον Ιστορικόν περί της Ελληνικής Επαναστάσεως* [*Historical Essay concerning the Greek revolution*], 4 Volumes, Athens: Π. Σούτσας και Α. Κτενάς.

Philippidis, Nikolaos G. 1881, *Η επανάστασις και καταστροφή της Ναούσης* [*The revolution and the destruction of Naousa*], Athens: Τύποις Αδελφών Βαρβαρρήγου.

Physentzidis, Nearchos 1893, *Ανέκδοτοι αυτόγραφοι επιστολαί των επισημοτέρων ελλήνων οπλαρχηγών και διάφορα προς αυτούς έγγραφα της Διοικήσεως* [*Unpublished letters of the prominent Greek revolutionary leaders and correspodece of the administration with them*], Alexandreia: Τυπογραφείο του 'Ταχυδρόμου'.

Politis, Alexis 2009, 'Η εξέγερση του Αλή πασά και η ελληνική επανάσταση. Μια παράλληλη θεώρηση' ['The revolt of Ali Pasha and the Greek revolution: A parallel study'], *Αριάδνη*, 15: 75–89.

Pouqueville, F.C.H. 1824, *Histoire de la Régénération de la Grèce*, 4 Volumes, Paris: Chez Firmin Didot Père et Fils.

Prappas, G.I. 1999, 'Ενθυμήσεις από τα χωριά των Τρικάλων Αγία Κυριακή, Καρυές και Φλαμούλι 1775–1886' ['Chronicles from the villages of Trikala Hagia Kyriaki, Karyes and Flamouli 1775–1886'], *Θεσσαλικό Ημερολόγιο*, 36: 177–92.

Prevelakis, Eleftherios and K. Kalliataki Mertikopoulou (eds.) 1996, *Epirus, Ali Pasha and the Greek Revolution: Consular Reports of William Meyer from Preveza*, vol. 1: *1819–1821*, Athens: Academy of Athens.

Protopsaltis, Emmanuel (ed.) 1963–1986, *Ιστορικόν Αρχείον Αλεξάνδρου Μαυροκορδάτου* [*Historical Archive of Alexandros Mavrokordatos*], 6 Volumes, Athens: Academy of Athens.

Psimouli, Vasso 2005, *Σούλι και Σουλιώτες* [*Souli and Souliots*], Athens: Εστία.

Psimouli, Vasso 2010, *Μάρκος Μπότσαρης* [*Markos Botsaris*], Athens: Τα Νέα.

Rados, Konstantinos N. 1916, *Οι Σουλιώται και οι αρματολοί εν Επτανήσω* [*Souliots and armatoloi in the Seven Islands*], reprint from the *Επετηρίς του Φιλολογικού Συλλόγου Παρνασσός*, Athens: τύποις Π. Δ. Σακελλαρίου.

Rotzokos, Nikos 1997, *Επανάσταση και εμφύλιος στο εικοσιένα* [*Revolution and civil war in 1821*], Athens: Βιβλιόραμα.

Sarantis, Theodoros 1987–8, 'Τα Γρεβενά (Συμβολή στην ιστορία τους)' ['The town of Grevena: contribution to its history'], *Μακεδονικά* 26: 242–307.

Sarris, Neoklis 1997, 'Οργάνωση και λειτουργίες των δερβενίων' ['Organisation and functions of the *derbent* villages], *Προβληματισμοί και επισημάνσεις 1*, edited by Vassilis Philias, Athens: Ι. Σιδέρης.

Skocpol, Theda 1979, *States and Social Revolutions: A Comparative Analysis of France, Russia, and China*, Cambridge: Cambridge University Press.

Skocpol, Theda 2005, 'Explaining Social Revolutions: First and Further Thoughts', in *Social Revolutions in the Modern World*, Cambridge: Cambridge University Press.

Soulis, Christos 1934, 'Επιγραφαί και ενθυμήσεις ηπειρωτικαί' ['Inscriptions and chronicles from Epirus'], *Ηπειρωτικά Χρονικά*, 9: 81–126.

Stamatogiannopoulou, Maria 1984, 'Αγορές της πρώτης ύλης και οικονομικές συμπεριφορές των θεσσαλικών βιοτεχνιών βαφής (1780–1820)' ['The economic behaviours of the dying industries in Thessaly (1780–1820)'], *Θεσσαλικά Χρονικά*, 15: 385–93.

Stasinopoulos, K.A. 1925, *Το Μεσολόγγι* [*Messolongi*], vol. 1, Athens: Θ. Τζαβέλλας.

Stathis, Panagiotis 2006, 'Ο Αλή πασάς και η επανάσταση στη Στερεά' [Tepedelenlii Ali Pasha and the Greek Revolution in Continental Greece], in *Ιστορία των Ελλήνων*, vol. 9: *Η ελληνική επανάσταση 1821*, vol. 9, Athens: Δομή.

Stougiannakis, Efstathios I. 1924, *Ιστορία της πόλεως Ναούσης από της ιδρύσεώς της μέχρι σήμερον κατά ανέκδοτον σχεδίασμα Δ. Πλαταρίδου* [*History of the town of Naousa from its founfation until today, according to an unpublished draft essay by D. Plataridis*], Edessa: Εκδόσεις Γ. & Ε. Στουγιαννάκη.

Theotokas, Nikos 1992, 'Παράδοση και νεοτερικότητα: Σχόλια για το 'Εικοσιένα'' ['Tradition and modernity: Comments on the 1821'], *Τα Ιστορικά*, 17: 345–70.

Trikoupis, Spyridon 1853–7, *Ιστορία της ελληνικής επαναστάσεως* [*History of the Greek revolution*], 4 Volumes, London: Taylor & Francis.

Tsakopoulos, Aimilianos 1956, 'Επισκοπικοί κατάλογοι κατά τους κώδικας των υπομνημάτων του Αρχειοφυλακείου του Οικουμενικού Πατριαρχείου' [*Lists of bishops in the registers of the archive of the Ecumenical Patriarchate of Constantinople*], Ορθοδοξία, 31,1: 417–52.

Tsiamalos, Dimitris 2009, *Οι αρματολοί της Ρούμελης* [*The armatoloi in Continental Greece*], Athens: Παπαζήσης.

Vakalopoulos, Apostolos 1950, 'Φήμες και διαδόσεις κατά την ελληνική επανάσταση του 1821 (Συμβολή στην ψυχολογία των ελληνικών επαναστατικών όχλων)' ['Roumors circulation during the Greek revolution of 1821 (Contribution to the psychology of the Greek revolutionary crowds)'], *Επιστημονική Επετηρίς της Φιλοσοφικής Σχολής Θεσσαλονίκης*, 6: 209–29.

Vakalopoulos, Apostolos 1961–88, *Ιστορία του Νέου Ελληνισμού* [*History of New Hellenism*], 8 Volumes, Thessaloniki: Α. Σταμούλης.

Vakalopoulos, Apostolos 1988, *Ιστορία της Μακεδονίας 1354–1833* [*History of Macedonia 1354–1833*], Thessaloniki: Βάνιας.

Vasdravellis, Ioannis 1950, *Οι Μακεδόνες εις τους υπέρ της ανεξαρτησίας αγώνας, 1796–1832* [*The Macedonians in the struggles for independence, 1796–1832*], 2nd ed., Thessaloniki: Εταιρεία Μακεδονικών Σπουδών.

Vasdravellis, Ioannis (ed.) 1954, *Ιστορικά Αρχεία Μακεδονίας Β΄. Αρχείον Βεροίας – Ναούσης 1598–1886* [*Historical Archve of Macedonia II: archive of Veroia and Naousa 1598–1886*], Thessaloniki: Εταιρεία Μακεδονικών Σπουδών.

Veremis, Thanos and Giannis Koliopoulos 2006, *Ελλάς: Η σύγχρονη συνέχεια από το 1821 μέχρι σήμερα* [*Greece: the modern sequel from 1821 until today*], Athens: Καστανιώτης.

Voglis, Polymeris 2013, ''Talkin' about a Revolution, it Sounds like a Whisper': Theories and Debates on Social Revolutions', *Historein*, 13: 47–56.

Wickham-Crowley, Timothy P. 1997, 'Structural Theories of Revolution', in *Theorizing Revolutions*, edited by John Foran, London and New York: Routledge.

Xanthos, Emmanuel 1845, *Απομνημονεύματα περί της Φιλικής Εταιρείας* [*Memoirs concerning the Friendly Society*], Athens: Εκ του Τυπογραφείου Α. Γκαρπολά.

Xenopoulos Vyzantios, Serapheim, 1884, *Δοκίμιον ιστορικής τινός περιλήψεως της ποτέ αρχαίας και εγκρίτου Ηπειρωτικής Πόλεως Άρτης και της ωσαύτως νεωτέρας πόλεως Πρεβέζης* [*Concise historical essay concerning the ancient and prominent town of Art and the modern town of Preveza in Epirus*], Athens: Τυπογραφείον Κάλλους.

Zegos, Spyros 1927, *Βιογραφία Πολυκάρπου του Δαρδαίου* [*Biography of Polykarpos the Dardaios*], Athens: I. Βάρτσος.

CHAPTER 12

The Catholics of Syros between Empire and Nation (1821–1832)

Dimitris Kousouris

> *A precarious, restricted, and threatened life, such was the lot of the islands, their domestic life at any rate. But their external life, the role they have played in the forefront of history far exceeds what might be expected from such poor territories. The events of history often lead to the islands. Perhaps it would be more accurate to say that they make use of them.*[1]

Although the archives of Syros are some of the best organised in Greece, and the history of the island is among the most researched in contemporary Greek historiography, the story of the local Catholic population, for whom revolution and inclusion in the nation-state literally meant the end of an era and of a world in which they had lived for centuries, it has generally been treated with secondary importance. Scholarly research has hitherto mainly focused on the making of a new town by Orthodox settlers. The story of Hermoupolis, the town of the merchant God Hermes, has often been told as one of the triumph of modernity and industrialisation over tradition and backwardness; in such accounts, the island's indigenous Catholic population appears, if at all, in the background, as a traditional community that withdraws into its citadel. But did the four to five thousand Catholics only so withdraw passively, watching from afar the coming of a new era and the integration of their island into the emerging Greek state? Were they not also forced in various ways to meet the new challenges? After all, how did the secular and religious leaders, as well as the common people, deal with the challenge of the Greek Revolution? In order to investigate such questions, I have conducted archival research on the 1820s in the archives of the community of Ano Syros, the Catholic diocese of Syros, the Catholic archdiocese of Naxos-Tinos, the Sacra Congregatio de Propaganda Fide and the Vatican Apostolic Archives in Rome as well as in the French and Austrian diplomatic archives. Based on this work, as well as published second-

---

1 Braudel 1972, vol. I, p. 154.

ary sources, I present here, within the limits of space available, a sketch of my findings and questions for further research.

After introducing Syros as an advanced outpost of the Latine culture within the territories of the Ottoman-dominated Orthodox East, I follow how the island was caught up in the whirlwind of the Greek insurrection. Looking from Syros outwards, the indigenous Catholic community itself seems to have been fractured, split by the tensions between the introversion of the land, the cyclical time of agricultural societies and the opening to the sea, full of the ordinary upheavals of trade and piracy. The port under the town of Syra offered a neutral territory, somewhat a safehaven on the roads of the Eastern Mediterranean, where trade of all sorts could go on unhindered. Like other island towns, the new city that emerged within a few years during the Greek Revolution might seem somewhat isolated, facing seawards and having little to do with the rest of the island,[2] but remained linked to – and finally transformed – not only the local land-property regime but the whole economy of the nation. Given that the boundaries between the religious communities were still quite porous, religious denomination alone, however important, would not suffice to elucidate the conflicts that took place after the outbreak of the Revolution. Approaching the island as part of the dispersed city of the archipelago, as an open and closed world at the same time, in order to explore the dialectic of isolation and connectivity,[3] one can trace how the local structures (and the local elites) were overwhelmed by the swift integration of their territory into the emerging nation-state.[4] The intense activity and the division of labour between secular and religious authorities of the community during the 1820s indicates a concerted effort to maintain extraterritorial autonomy. Hence, the conflicts about and property and taxation between Latins and Greeks came down to a pre-national/extraterritorial conception of state sovereignty versus a national one. Syros thus entered general history through the initiatives of a Greek revolutionary government, petitions of the local catholic clergy and the direct involvement of Vatican and Paris. After all, within a decade, the erstwhile 'Latins' of Syros and the other islands were rechristened 'Greeks of the Western Church' and integrated as citizens within the new nation-state. Seen in the magnetic field of the struggle between revolution and counter-revolution in Europe, the transformation of this small island dominion – both oriental and occidental, a

2   Braudel 1972, vol. I, p. 151.
3   On the archipelago as a dispersed city, see Asdrachas 1999, pp. 235–48. For an overview of the recent literature on insularity in the Ottoman context, see Kolovos 2018, pp. 9–28. For some case studies in this perspective, see Liata 1987; Zei 2017; Dimitropolous 1997.
4   Theotokas 1992, pp. 345–70; Kotaridis 1993.

crossroad and hub of interaction between different cultures[5] – into a long nine-teenth century frontier between West and East, also reflects the emergence of a new sense of history, whereby the future, emancipated from divine provid-ence, remains open and available to the social, political and economic action of humans.

1   Catholics in the Ottoman Empire and the 'Pope's Island'

Since the Ottoman conquest in the late sixteenth century, Catholics lived as ethno-religious minorities in Ottoman cities or on the islands of the Archipela-go and other enclaves of the empire.[6] During the first period after the conquest, the Greek-Orthodox church exploited its high status within the Ottoman power system, thus regaining influence on the islands. However, the Catholic church and hierarchy was soon to be recognised by the Sublime Porte, and the status of the Catholic population would evolve, taking advantage of the capitula-tions between Western sovereignties (particularly the French) and the Sultan. Throughout the seventeenth century, protection from Western-Christian sov-ereigns gradually expanded to include the consuls/members of the local olig-archies and their translators (dragomans); this drastically reduced the active role and actual presence of the Ottomans on the Cyclades, thus strengthening their autonomy.[7]

The specificity of Syros was its overwhelmingly Catholic majority. As part of the Latin communities of the Archipelago, the island became a stronghold of the Catholic faith, the 'most Catholic of all islands,' or the 'island of the Pope'. For the majority of the population, use of the Greek language remained mainly oral, and teaching in the schools of the Capuchins (since 1622) and the Jesuits (since 1733) was mainly in Italian. Meanwhile, the intense cultural and political presence of and protection by France – often managed directly by the French Ambassador in Istanbul in collaboration with the local Bishop and vice-consul – had de facto created a situation of shared sovereignty and mixed loyalties to the Sultan and the *Rex Christianissimus*.[8]

---

5   Cf. the remarks of Zei 2017, pp. 34–5.
6   Frazee 2006.
7   Slot 1982.
8   Drakakis 1948, pp. 245–7; Printezi-Kabeli 2012; Roussos Milidonis 1993. Of the most character-istic attributes of the cultural hybridity of those island communities were the Greek religious catechisms printed in Latin script throughout the eighteenth century; see Foskolos 2012.

2   The Outbreak of the Greek Revolution and the Reaction of the
European Powers

For the Christian sovereigns of Europe, the Greek Revolution was one in a wave
of revolts that disquieted Restoration Europe, together with the anti-Bourbon
liberal insurrections in Naples and Spain. Although the Greek case, a revolt of
Christian subjects against a Muslim sovereign, presented important discrep-
ancies from the other two, the spirit of Vienna still prevailed in the Congress
of Laybach (1821), and the Tsar denounced the revolt. Meanwhile France and
the United Kingdom acknowledged the Greek insurrection as an internal issue
of the Ottoman Empire and declared their neutrality, as did the Holy See; the
latter, since 1815 under the guidance of Cardinal Ercole Consalvi, had held a
line of neutrality towards all European conflicts.[9] The following year, in their
consecutive petitions towards the European sovereigns in Verona, the representatives of the Greek government recognised the authority of the Pope as the
'head of Christianism [*Capo del Cristianesimo / chef de la Réligion Chretienne*]',
'Supreme Pontiff [*Sommo Pontefice*]' and 'Protector of the Church [*Protettore
della Chiesa*]'. Unlike petitions to the Tsar, which made explicit references to
the Orthodox faith, references to Christianity remained deliberately blurred in
the petitions towards the Pope through the intermediary of Cardinal E. Consalvi, depicting Roman Catholics of the islands – implicitly or explicitly – *as
members of the Greek nation.*[10]

3   The Revolution and the Island's Catholics: First Contacts and
Negotiations

The main force of the revolutionary Greek fleet came from islands that lie on
the western tip of the Peloponnese, Hydra and Spetses, and Psara, next to Chios
on the North of the Archipelago, Following the policies of France and the Holy
See, the Catholics of Syra declared their neutrality in the conflict between the
insurgents and the Ottoman Empire. This attitude, like the reticence of many
Orthodox notables to join the Revolution,[11] was based on the anticipation of

---

9   See Thomson 1990, pp. 107–38; Schütz 1975; Heraclides and Diala 2015, pp. 105–33.
10   Hoffmann 1952, pp. 81–2, 131–5; cf. the discussion by Manikas 2001, pp. 142–64. Cf. Asimakis
2007.
11   Most significant was the case of Santorini, where local Orthodox and Catholic notrables
alike organised themselves against the Greek authorities; see *Αρχείον της Κοινότητος Ύδρας*,
Piraeus 1921–9, vol. 8, p. 608; vol. 9, pp. 290, 302 and 433–4; see also Manikas 2001, pp. 101–3.

an imminent Ottoman counter-offensive that would prevent the insurrection from producing any permanent political outcome – or anything at all beyond Peloponnese. From early on, this prospect led the various representatives of the archipelago Catholics to the adopt a realistic wait-and-see approach in an attempt to maintain their semi-autonomous tributary and extraterritorial legal status. In practice, this meant that by the summer of 1821 already, in order to avoid taxation or conscription, bishops and notables, including local vice-consuls, appealed to the French for protection, occasionally raising the French flag at their churches.

Those reactions, together with some acts of liberation of Ottoman prisoners, irritated the insurgents, triggering tensions between Latins [Λατίνοι] and Romans [Pωμ[α]ιοί: Greek Orthodox] on islands where the two communities coexisted (Tinos, Naxos, and Santorini). However, as the relationship with the Catholics of Syra directly influenced their communication with the Vatican and the European Powers, the Greek revolutionary government sought a rapprochement from the outset. The first appeals to the 'Western Christians' to join the insurgency offered them guarantees of civic equity and freedom of worship. Despite the local tensions, the first constitutional texts established freedom of worship and citizenship for all 'inhabitants of Greece who believe in Jesus Christ', and addressed the Latins repeatedly as compatriots, 'children of the same mother' and 'Greeks [Έλληνες: Hellenes] of the Western Church'.[12] Attributing a confessional but not a political or ethnic status to the Catholics, the insurgents solicited first the collaboration of the Archbishop of Naxos. Fearing possible Ottoman reprisals, the latter tried to buy some time to receive instructions from the French Ambassador in Constantinople.[13]

4   Administrative Division of the Greek Territories and the Exemption of Syros

Not surprisingly, what was concretely at stake in a conflict between a national/territorial and an imperial/extraterritorial conception of state sovereignty was

---

12   The commissioners were instructed to 'conciliate as much as possible the tensions between the Greeks of the Eastern and those of the Western Church' and to 'appoint if possible some of the Western Church, the worthiest and wisest, to public offices'; see *Αρχεία Ελληνικής Παλιγγεννεσίας*, Athens 1971–2012, vol. 1, p. 330.

13   See the two letters of Andrea Veggetti to La Tour-Maubourg, dated 20 May and 5 July 1822: Sacra Congregatio de Propaganda Fide, SC Arcipelago, vol. 35, f. 140–9, where he admitted he was only buying time while waiting for protection from the French.

taxation, especially of church property. After the refusal of the Catholics to pay tax and send representatives to the national assembly, the first systematic attempt to control the entire national territory came in April 1822 with the 'Organisation of the Greek Provinces'. That very first administrative division of the Greek state was actually implemented with the appointment of prefects charged with establishing an elementary fiscal and administrative apparatus in several east Aegean islands and the Cyclades, excluding Syros. The reticence of the Greek revolutionary government concerning the only island entirely under the jurisdiction of a Catholic community attests to their awareness of the complications entailed by its neutrality and of the distinct identity of the Syriots.[14]

5   The Making of a New Town: Refugees, Traders, Pirates and Smugglers

The declared neutrality and effective allegiance to the Sublime Porte, as expressed in the continuing payment of the yearly tribute to the Kapudan Pasha,[15] raised more suspicions and antipathies among the fighters of the Greek cause towards the Syros Catholics. Meanwhile, the existence of a neutral territory where merchants of all nations, including Greeks and Turks, could trade untroubled by the turbulences of war was soon to transform the shore of the island into a commercial hub. Within the first year of the war, some rich merchants from Chios and Asia Minor sought to acquire a foot on the island, as did refugees who came to the island with increasing pace after the Chios massacres in April 1822, seeking a safehaven after the first wave of Ottoman reprisals. Although the Syriot representatives did not miss the opportunity to protest over raids, thefts and trespassing on private or church property by Orthodox refugees, the lucrative opportunities offered by the de facto transformation of Syros into a free port for Orthodox and Catholics alike kept the tensions between the two communities under control until the end of 1822, when the Greek government began to claim its share in political power and capital accumulation. Likewise, the sea trade had thus far remained relatively safe. However, the end of the military operations and the internal strife among

---

14   Drakakis 1979, vol. 1, pp. 36–43; see also Αρχείον της Κοινότητος Ύδρας, Piraeus 1921–9, vol. 8, pp. 266–7.

15   Drakakis 1979, pp. 43–8. For the expense of the annual tribute, see the balance sheet of the 1822 Community in the Archive of the Community of Ano Syros, f. 173.

Greeks on the mainland pushed many ship owners and captains to seek profit in privateering for the government and in piracy raids.[16]

From that point on, the port of Syros very quickly became a hub for all sorts of lucrative activities, including legal trade of wheat and cereal as well as of luxury products such as wine, textile, perfumes, spices and condiments – but also for all sorts of illegal traffic, including pirate booties, counterfeit coins and slaves.[17] Although slave trade was formally forbidden by the fresh Greek constitution, Ottoman captives were exchanged for Greeks, redeemed (mainly by the Catholics) or traded in plain sight at the port of Syros until the late 1820s.[18] The regularity of such unlawful transactions, together with the supply of Ottoman fortresses in Euboea and Peloponnese, corroborate that the main purpose of the Orthodox businessmen in Syros was profit-making rather than patriotism.[19] Be that as it may, that primitive accumulation of capital attracted a great number of refugees, who provided the workforce for the further development of sea trade as well as the shipbuilding industry. Until 1826, the settlement of 30,000 refugees in the port of the island completely reversed the demographic equilibrium and power balance between the two communities.

6   First Attempts of Incorporation: Nestor Faziolis's Incursions and Taxation

On Christmas Eve 1822, a military corps under the command of Cephalonian ship-captain Nestor Faziolis and his brothers attempted to invade the citadel of Syra, but the attack was called off after the intervention of a French warship. Faziolis soon reorganised his force on the nearby island of Tinos with the support of the Greek Prefect [*Eparchos*] and attempted a second invasion in February 1823. Once more, the attack was nipped in the bud after the French

---

16   Themeli-Katifori 1987, pp. 239–54; Mylonakis 2018, pp. 74–94; Dimitropoulos 2016, pp. 29–40; and Dimitropoulos 2007, pp. 115–34.

17   See Delis 2016, pp. 41–54; Drakakis 1979.

18   'Εἰς τὴν ἑλληνικὴν ἐπικράτειαν οὔτε ἀγοράζεται οὔτε πωλεῖται ἄνθρωπος. Ἀργυρωνήτος πάσης θρησκείας καὶ γένους, ἅμα πατήσῃ τὸ ἑλληνικόν ἔδαφος εἶναι ἐλεύθερος καὶ ἀπό τὸν δεσπότην αὐτοῦ ἀκαταζήτητος.' Mamoukas 1839, vol. 2, p. 129. Redemptions of Muslim prisoners by Catholics were not rare in the Cyclades during the first years of the war. Concerning the visibility of slave labour, cf. for example, the account of the American Waddington, p. 37: 'Every constitutional Greek will tell you, that the sale of prisoners is forbidden by the Law of Epidaurus. Every day I pass a cottage, occupied by four or five Turkish slaves, so notoriously for sale, that the prices of each have been communicated to me. All are females'.

19   Cf. Delis 2016, p. 47.

navy intervened, after which Faziolis was provisionally taken into custody by Captain P. Hargous. This was not long before it became clear that Faziolis had acted in collusion with the Greek government of Nafplio in the Peloponnese. Shortly after his incursions, a Hydriot flotilla entered the island's port, forcing the payment of an extraordinary levy of 40,000 *piasters*. After the new administrative division issued by the government in May formally incorporated Syra into its territories,[20] Faziolis was officially appointed as Chief of the police of Syros under the command of the Prefect Alexandros Axiotis. His arrival on the island provoked the immediate reaction of De Rigny, who arrived on the spot on his frigate 'La Médée', arrested Faziolis, dismantled his military unit and issued a sharp warning to the Greek government for appointing a bandit [*forban*] as chief of police.[21] Nevertheless, by the end of 1823 the Prefect had carried out a first census of the people living in the port under the Catholic citadel and had established a police force (whose jurisdiction, however, was still called into question by the French consul and the leaders of the Catholic community). Moreover, in his correspondence with the Greek authorities, De Rigny had to circumscribe the limits of French protection in the equality of treatment before the law, without distinction of religious denomination, and in the free exercise of religious rites.

7   Conflicts and Cleavages among Catholics

Some of the most common misconceptions in the discussion of religious rivalries in the late Ottoman Empire are due to the false impression of stability and homogeneity within the different groups and denominations. During the three decades after the French Revolution, the rapid expansion of Greek shipping and trade in Eastern Mediterranean led to the rise of local entrepreneurial elites and deepened social inequalities within the communities of the Greek Archipelago.[22] Where Orthodox and Catholic communities shared the island, in the power vacuum created by the revolutionary events, conflicts between leading factions would take on religious connotations.[23] Symptomatically, it was not unusual for individual members of one community to side with the

---

20   Dimakopoulos 1966, pp. 154–7.
21   See *Αρχείον της Κοινότητος Ύδρας*, Pireaus 1921–9, vol. 9, p. 260; cf. the report of the events by the French consul in Smyrna P. David: *AMAE*, CCC, Smyrne, 39 (juillet–décembre 1823), pp. 28–9.
22   Dimitropoulos 2008, pp. 55–75.
23   Cf. Mazower 2008, pp. 69–88.

other: such was the case, among several others, of the local Latin peasant [*paesano*] Giorgio Xantaki, collector of the tithe [*decimatore*] in Syros for the Greek government in 1826, who was straightforwardly threatened with excommunication by the Apostolic Administrator Luigi Maria Blancis.[24] The antagonisms between villagers and notables, and also between rival factions of the local elite, came to the surface with a peasant revolt in 1814, which temporarily deposed the *Epitropos* [Governor; It. *Governatore*] N. Capella and substituted him with G. Salacha before the latter was eventually arrested and jailed in Constantinople by the Ottoman authorities.[25]

It is unclear whether this revolt had any direct or indirect connection with the period in office of the Catholic Bishop G.B. Russin, who, facing charges of factionalism, was recalled in spring 1821 from the Holy See to Rome, where he remained until his death in 1829.[26] From 1822 to 1825, L.M. Cardelli, Archbishop of Smyrna, ensured, as Apostolic Visitor, the connection with the Holy See through a series of reports to the Propaganda Fide on the situation at Syros.[27] In autumn 1825, L.M. Blancis da Cirè, a Franciscan who was until then at the service of the Apostolic Vicariate of Istanbul, became titular Bishop of Canatha and Apostolic Administrator of the Syros bishopric.[28]

8   L.M. Blancis and the Adjustment into the New Reality

It may well be argued that, in the larger context, the designation of Blancis was an expression of a broader policy of the Holy See since the Napoleonic Wars to fill the most mission-critical positions of the hierarchy with priests from Rome or Italy, rather than with members of the local clergy, in order to have a direct insight into the social and ideological cleavages within each community. Thus, we can start discerning the story of the small, insular community through the prism of the Braudelian dialectics of isolation and connectivity. The Catholics of Syros did not all nor only retreat to their citadel on the hill;

24   Sacra Congregatio de Propaganda Fide, SC Arcipelago, vol. 36, f. 441–2.
25   Drakakis 1948, pp. 75–7.
26   According to Blancis, his 'party' would still exist at the end of the decade. See his report to the SCPF, dated 2 September 1829, in Sacra Congregatio de Propaganda Fide, SC Arcipelago, vol. 37, f. 230–2.
27   Sacra Congregatio de Propaganda Fide, SC Arcipelago, vol. 35, f. 288–97, 306–17, 320–6, 640–3, 923–6, and vol. 36, f. 33–5, 49–50. See discussion on the activity and conterarguments in SC Arcipelago, vol. 35, f. 716–19 and 746–7.
28   He officially became Bishop after the death of his predecessor. See *Sacra Congregatio de Propaganda Fide*, SC Arcipelago, vol. 36, f. 179, 197.

rather, once it became clear that the situation would be different than expected, they also gradually sought to enhance their connection to their traditional patrons (i.e. France and the Vatican) and to the Sublime Porte. The election of Giovanni Marinelli, member of a prominent family of the Syriot diaspora in Istanbul,[29] as Governor [Gk. *Epitropos*] in 1824 was certainly a move in that direction. During his period in office, Marinelli repeatedly solicited support and protection from the French diplomats and the Catholic hierarchy in Istanbul and Smyrna.[30] Blancis himself was quite prolific at the time in his correspondence both within and without Syros – with Rome, Istanbul and Smyrna. Internally, he tried to ease inter-community tensions by limiting points of contact or friction between fractions, using measures such as the strict prohibition of mixed marriages.[31] In his response to the pressures of the embryonic Greek state, after convening for several months with the local clergy and the Bishops of the Archipelago and receiving the approval of the Propaganda Fide, Blancis upheld and endorsed the line of maintaining the tax immunity of Catholic Church property.[32]

9   Future's Past: About the New Legal and Political Status of the Island

If the Catholics of Syros nursed the belief that the wounds inflicted on them by the war would be short lived, two events in late 1827 and early 1828 definitively buried the prospect of a return to the status quo ante and demonstrated that those upheavals rather heralded a transition to unmapped territories. The first was the complete destruction of the Ottoman fleet in Navarino in October 1827. A series of alarming reports coming to the Vatican in the aftermath of the naval battle revealed widespread panic over possible reprisals among the Levantine communities of Istanbul and Smyrna after the mobilisation of Tatar troops by the Sultan.[33] But the end of the illusion was to be sealed shortly afterwards, in the spring of 1828, after the definitive failure of an ill-prepared expedition for the reconquest of Chios, the former inhabitants of which represented half of

---

29   Karachristos 2004, pp. 161–71; Schmitt 2005.

30   Sacra Congregatio de Propaganda Fide, SC Arcipelago, vol. 35, f. 698, and vol. 36, f. 77, 153–4, 189–90, 308.

31   Sacra Congregatio de Propaganda Fide, SC Arcipelago, vol. 37, f. 15–16.

32   Sacra Congregatio de Propaganda Fide, SC Arcipelago, vol. 36, f. 437–8.

33   The account of V. Coressi also mentions a wave of migration towards safer havens far from the centre of Ottoman power. See, indicatively, Sacra Congregatio de Propaganda Fide, SC, Romania C/poli, vol. 26, 1185–6, and SC Arcipelago, vol. 36, f. 599–600.

the Orthodox community of the new town.[34] The question thus, then, turned to the status of the archipelago Catholics within the new situation that was taking shape.

Reviewing the various plans devised and promoted by the different representatives of the Catholic hierarchy during that period is perhaps the best way to grasp the transition as an 'Arendtian gap' – i.e. between what is not anymore and what is not yet.[35] People tend to make projections into the future according to their field of experience. This becomes all the more evident in the way Syros first became a parameter of the Holy See's foreign policy in 1822–3, when, following instructions of the Secretary of State Cardinal Consalvi, the French philhellene Captain J. Jourdain, as representative of the Greek government, entered negotiations with the Order of the Knights Hospitaller for an alliance against the Sultan. This would be sealed with the concession of Syros to the Order and the transformation of the island into a 'new Gibraltar'.[36] In early 1826, after Blancis had taken office, he wrote a detailed report on Syros in which he supported its transformation into a free port [It. *porto franco*], tributary to the Greek state. '[B]ut to reach this point', he wrote, 'it would be enough to make the allies understand that these small colonies that are begging for protection ... are not Hellenes, but European Latines, as demonstrated by the family name of each Grimaldi, Giustiniani, Vitali, Rossi, Freri, Privilegio'.[37]

Protection and recognition of the distinct identity of local Catholics remained an indispensable parameter for the different scenarios promoted by the Catholic Church all through the 1820s. During the negotiations on the borders of Greece, the newspaper *Courier de Smyrne* published a petition from the clergy and notables of Syros to the Holy See in which they expressed the wish *not* to become part of the new state.[38] Although the authenticity of this document was denied by the Syriots, it nevertheless corresponds to the scenarios promoted by the Catholic bishops to the representatives of France in the region. In a later report, dated 17 September 1827, Blancis enumerated for an umpteenth time the crimes committed by Orthodox settlers against the Catholics and proposed that Syros obtain a status similar to that of the Republic of San Marino, autonomous and directly connected to the Holy See.[39] Almost a year later, in August 1828, Blancis recounted to the Prefect of the SCPF Mauro

34 Drakakis 1979, vol. II, pp. 175–85.

35 Arendt 1961, p. 9.

36 Daskalakis 1967, pp. 298–351; Jourdain 1828, pp. 215–17, 230, 276, 285.

37 Hofmann 1937, p. 152.

38 *Le Courier de Smyrne*, no. 57, 22 March 1829.

39 Sacra Congregatio de Propaganda Fide, SC Arcipelago, vol. 36, f. 579–80.

Cappellari (who would soon become Pope Gregory XVI) the initiatives he had jointly taken with the Bishop of Tinos, G. Gabinelli, to promote a special status for the Catholic Church and encourage the gathering of all Catholics of the Greek archipelago on one of those islands.[40]

Nevertheless, all of this remained only a paper exercise, as the position and status of the Catholics in the new Greek kingdom was finally decided with the Treaty of London of 1832 and with the coronation of King Otto, a Catholic and the second-born of the Bavarian monarch Ludwig I. Another report on the situation and on the prospects of the island, written by three members of the communal Council in April 1833, just after the arrival of the new king, demonstrates that the secular authorities were at that point compelled to deal with the urgent demands of adapting to the new circumstances.[41] Within a decade, the ethno-religious identity of the Latins had given way to that of the 'Greeks of the Western Church', demonstrating how changes in context and in points of reference on the map led to a conceptual shift. Thus, the phrase *'Sira nostra patria'*, which often appears in the petitions of local priests against the invasion of the 'foreigners' [It. *forestieri*], corresponds to a pre-national conception of 'homeland'. At the same time, the emergence of the notion of nation-state sovereignty on a Catholic territory – a meeting point for merchants, pirates, diplomatic agents, warriors and adventurers of all kinds right in the middle of the archipelago – allows us to follow the formation of a new border between Europe, or the West, and the Ottoman East within the magnetic field of revolution and counterrevolution.

Bibliography

Arendt, Hannah 1961, *Between Past and Future. Six Exercices in Political Thought*, New York: Viking Press.

Asdrachas, Spyros 1999, 'Το ελληνικό αρχιπέλαγος: μια διάσπαρτη πόλη' ['The Greek Archipelago: A dispersed city'], in *Χάρτες και Χαρτογράφοι του Αιγαίου Πελάγους* [*Maps and Chartographers of the Aegean Sea*], edited by Vassilis Sfyroeras, Spyros Asdrachas, Anna Avramea (eds.), Athens: Ολκός.

Asimakis, I. 2007, Η *πορεία των σχέσεων Ελλάδας και Αγίας έδρας (1820–1980), από την γαλλική προστασία έως τη σύναψη διπλωματικών σχέσεων* [*The course of relations between*

---

40   Sacra Congregatio de Propaganda Fide, SC Arcipelago, vol. 37, f. 88–9.

41   Archive of the Community of Ano Syros, Documents ['Εγγραφα], f. 13. The main chapters of this report concern the fiscal immunity of commercial transactions, the new port, the lazaretto, the customs office, the warehouses and the taxation of exports.

Greece and the Holy Sea (1820–1980), from French protection to the establishment of diplomatic relations], Thessaloniki: Αποστολικό Βικαριάτο Θεσσαλονίκης.

Braudel, Fernand 1972, *The Mediterranean and the Mediterranean World in the Age Of Philip III*, Berkeley: University of California Press.

Daskalakis, Apostolos 1967, *Κείμενα, πηγαί της ιστορίας της Ελληνικής* Επαναστάσεως [*Texts and sources concerning the Greek revolution*], Athens: Αφοι Κλεισιούνη.

Delis, Apostolos 2016, 'A hub of piracy in the Aegean: Syros during the Greek war of independence', in *Corsairs and pirates in the Eastern Mediterranean. Fifteenth–nineteenth centuries*, edited by G. Harlaftis, D. Dimitropoulos and D. Starkey, Athens: Sylvia Ioannou Foundation.

Dimakopoulos, G. 1966 *Η διοικητική οργάνωσις κατά την Ελληνικήν Επανάστασιν 1821–1827* [*The administrative ogranisation during the Greek revolution 1821–1827*], Ph.D. dissertation, Athens: Panteion University.

Dimitropoulos, Dimitris 1997, *Η Μύκονος τον 17ο αιώνα: γαιοκτητικές σχέσεις και οικονομικές συναλλαγές* [*The island of Mykonos during the seventeenth century: landowing relations and economic transcactions*], Athens: National Hellenic Research Foundation.

Dimitropoulos, Dimitris 2007, 'Η πειρατεία στο Αιγαίο. Όψεις και αντιφάσεις των στερεοτύπων' ['Piracy in the Aegean Sea: aspects and contradictions of the common stereotypes'], in *Επιστημονικό Συμπόσιο: Μύθοι και ιδεολογήματα στη σύγχρονη Ελλάδα (23–4 Νοεμβρίου 2005)*, Athens: Ίδρυμα Μωραΐτη.

Dimitropoulos, Dimitris 2008, ''Ένα συριανό κτηματολόγιο του 19ου αιώνα' ['A cadastre of Syros in the nineteenth c.'], in *Σύρος και Ερμούπολη: συμβολή στην ιστορία του νησιού, 15ος–20ός αι.* [*Syros and Hermoupolis: contribution to the history of the island, fifteenth–twentieth c.*], edited by Christina Agriantoni and Dimitris Dimitropoulos, Athens: National Hellenic Research Foundation.

Dimitropoulos, Dimitris 2016, 'Pirates during a revolution: the many faces of piracy and the reaction of local communities', in *Corsairs and pirates in the Eastern Mediterranean. Fifteenth–nineteenth centuries*, edited by G. Harlaftis, D. Dimitropoulos and D. Starkey, Athens: Sylvia Ioannou Foundation.

Drakakis, Andreas 1948, *Η Σύρος επί τουρκοκρατίας* [*Syros during the Tourkokratia*], 2 Volumes, Syros: Εκδόσεις Ερμούπολη.

Drakakis, Andreas 1979, *Ιστορία του οικισμού της Ερμουπόλεως (Σύρας)* [*History of the town of Hermoupolis (Syra)*], 2 Volumes, Athens: n. ed.

Foskolos, Markos 2012, *Τα 'φραγκοχιώτικα' βιβλία. Ένα κεφάλαιο από την ιστορία της καθολικής ευσέβειας στον ελληνικό χώρο* [*The 'Fragkochiotika' books: A chapter from the history of Catholic piety in the Greek lands*], Thessaloniki: Αποστολικό Βικαριάτο Θεσσαλονίκης.

Frazee, Charles 2009, *Catholics and Sultans: The Church and the Ottoman Empire 1453–1923*, Cambridge: Cambridge University Press.

Heraclides, Alexis and Anta Dialla 2015, *Humanitarian Intervention in the Long Nineteenth Century. Setting the Precedent*, Manchester: Manchester University Press.

Hofmann, Giorgio 1937, *Vescovadi Cattolici della Grecia, III. Syros*, Rome: Pont. Institutum Orientalium Studiorum.

Hoffmann, Giorgio 1952, *Das Papsttum und der griechische Freiheitskampf (1821–1829)*, Rome: Pont. Institutum Orientalium Studiorum.

Jourdain, J. 1828, *Mémoires historiques et militaires sur les événements de la Grèce depuis 1822 jusqu'au combat de Navarin*, Paris: Brissot-Thivars.

Karachristos, Ioannis 2004, 'Μετανάστευση Συριανών στην Κωνσταντινούπολη (1759–1818)' ['Migration of the islanders of Syra in Constantinople (1759–1818)'], in *Η Ελλάδα των νησιών από την Φραγκοκρατία ως σήμερα* [*The Greece of the islands from Frankish rule until today*], edited by A. Asteriou, Athens: Ελληνικά Γράμματα.

Kolovos, Elias 2018, *Across the Aegean: Islands, Monasteries and Rural Societies in the Ottoman Greek Lands*, Istanbul: The Isis Press.

Kotaridis, Nikos 1993, *Παραδοσιακή Επανάσταση και Εικοσιένα* [*Traditional revolution and 1821*], Athens: Πλέθρον.

Liata, Eftychia 1987, *Η Σέριφος κατά την Τουρκοκρατία (17ος–19ος αιωνας)* [*The island of Seriphos during the Tourkokratia (seventeenth–nineteenth c.)*], Athens: Εμπορική Τράπεζα Ελλάδος.

Mamoukas, A. 1839, *Τα κατά την Αναγέννησιν της Ελλάδος, ήτοι Συλλογή των κατά των εν τη αναγεννωμενη Ελλάδα συνταχθεντων νόμων, πολιτευμάτων και άλλων επισήμων πράξεων* [*Collection of laws, constitutions and other official acts issued during the Greek ressurection*], Piraeus.

Manikas, K. 2001, *Σχέσεις ορθοδοξίας και ρωμαιοκαθολικισμού κατά τη διάρκεια της Επαναστάσεως (1821–1827)* [*Relations between Orthodoc Christianity and Roman Catholicism during the revolution (1821–1827)*], Ph.D. dissertation, Athens: National and Kapodistrian University of Athens.

Mazower, Marc 2008, 'Villagers, notables and imperial collapse: the Virgin Mary on Tinos in the 1820s', in *Networks of Power in Modern Greece: essays in honor of John Campbell*, edited by Mark Mazower, New York: Hurst & Company.

Mylonakis, L. 2018, *Transnational Piracy in the Eastern Mediterranean, 1821–1897*, Ph.D. Dissertation, University of California San Diego.

Printezi-Kabeli, E. 2012, *Η ιστορία της εκπαίδευσης στην Άνω Σύρο (17ος–19ος αι.)* [*History of education in Ano Syros (seventeenth–nineteenth c.)*], PhD dissertation, Athens: National and Kapodistrian University of Athens.

Roussos Milidonis, Markos 1993, *Syra Sacra, Θρησκευτική Ιστορία της Σύρου* [*Syra Sacra: Religious history of the island of Syros*], Athens: Κίνηση Καθολικών Επιστημονών και Διανοουμένων Ελλάδος.

Schmitt, O.J. 2005, *Levantiner. Lebenswelten und Identitäten einer ethnokonfessionellen Gruppe im Osmanischen Reich im 'langen 19. Jahrhundert'*, Munich: R. Oldenbourg Verlag.

Schütz, E. 1975, *Die europäische Allianzpolitik un der griechische Unabhägingkeitskampf 1820–1830*, Wiesbaden: O. Harrassowitz.

Slot, Benjamin 1982, *Archipelagus turbatus: les Cyclades entre colonisation latine et occupation ottomane c. 1500–1718*, Istanbul: Nederlands Historisch-Archaeologisch Instituut te Istanbul.

Stewart, Charles 2008, 'Dreaming of buried icons in the kingdom of Greece' in *Networks of Power in Modern Greece: essays in honor of John Campbell*, edited by Mark Mazower, New York: Hurst & Company.

Themeli-Katifori, Despoina 1987, 'Καταδρομή και πειρατεία κατά την Επανάσταση του 1821. Φαινόμενα οικονομικών και κοινωνικών μετασχηματισμών' [Piracy during the revolution of 1821: phenomena of economic and social transformations], *Παρουσία*, 5: 239–54.

Theotokas, Nikos 1992, 'Παράδοση και νεοτερικότητα: Σχόλια για το 'Εικοσιένα'' ['Tradition and modernity: Comments on the 1821'], *Τα Ιστορικά*, 17: 345–70.

Thomson, David 1990, *Europe Since Napoleon*, London: Penguin Books.

Waddington, George, *A visit to Greece in 1824 and 1824*, London: John Murray.

Zei, Eleftheria 2017, *Visages et visions d'insularité: l'île de Paros dans l'archipel grec pendant la première moitié du XVIIIe siècle*, Istanbul: The Isis Press.

CHAPTER 13

New Perspectives in Local Politics before and during the Greek Revolution

Consular Institutions in the Greek Archipelago (Late Eighteenth–Early Nineteenth Century)

Eleftheria Zei

Recent studies, adopting newly developed *problematiques* concerning confessional identities, local-national collectivities and extra-territorial political networking, have focused again on consuls and consulates as commercial, political or administrative agencies of different state powers in the early modern Mediterranean. In the first part of this chapter, I will give a short survey of the main trends in earlier and contemporary research. In the second part, I will trace the principal consular institutions in the eighteenth- and nineteenth-century Greek Archipelago, which will allow me to introduce, in the third part, some preliminary observations concerning the roles of indigenous consuls and vice-consuls in the political developments before and during the Greek Revolution.

1 Past and Present Historical and Historiographical Context[1]

Consular institutions in the Ottoman Empire were closely related to a *country-trade* system, which consisted of a network of ports or harbours to be found in one or two days' distance from a large commercial centre, along the coast, equipped with docks, storehouses and customs' installations with scales, weights and measures, as well as with lodgings for captains and merchants. Thus, harbours served as port stations where the ships stopped over to exchange merchandise and to take passengers.[2] The Greek Archipelago constituted such a network of small ports, which were connected to important commercial crossroads of the Empire, such as Istanbul, Smyrna and Salon-

---

1   Cf. the concise historiographical survey in Grenet 2016, pp. 24–34; see also Ülbert 2006, pp. 9–20.
2   On the history of station ports in the Orient more specifically, see Ahrweiler 1974, pp. 161–78; Faroqhi 1979, pp. 32–80; Harlaftis and Laiou 2008, pp. 1–44; Asdrachas et al. 2015, p. 491.

ica. This system principally functioned on a commission economy: the foreign merchant sent merchandise to his assignors at the ports; the assignors sold wholesale to the country's merchants and received the articles of the local production. Moreover, these transactions were arranged through local agents – Armenians, Ragusans, Greeks or Jews – called *censaux* and assignees,[3] the only persons to get in direct contact with the assignor of the port. The *censaux* elected all commercial agents that were to be found in urban centres or dispersed in the greater peripheries of the Ottoman trade. As the eighteenth century moved on, the distribution of functions seems to have followed the development of the establishment and organisation as well as the developing economic importance of local ethnicities, notably those of the Greeks: the local assignee ended, therefore, by electing the particular agent who would receive, buy and expedite the commissioned merchandise, while the *censal* assumed control of the transactions.

Earlier historiography tended to regard the seventeenth- and eighteenth-century consular officers in the Eastern Mediterranean and the Ottoman Empire principally as commercial and economic agents of different European states that had missioned them overseas [*missi*], or as representatives of different ethno-religious communities of the Empire who elected them [*electi*] to protect and support their proper, often-conflicting commercial interests.[4] The former, placed under a protected sign since the seventeenth century, were not generally allowed to involve themselves in mercantile activities, receiving fixed retribution from the appointing state for their offices; the latter received no retribution at all and drew their revenues from their proper commercial enterprises.[5] Representatives thus elected could also hold various local administration offices and revenues, as quite often was the case with early modern insular elites.[6] However, both *missi* and *electi* agents, as I will show below, drew a considerable amount of money from consular rights imposed upon merchandised items and transactions, thus clearly forming an economic elite in the Levant.

---

3   Rich literature has treated the subject in the context of the history of different mercantile *diasporas* in the Ottoman Empire. See, selectively, Rozen (ed.) 2008; Vlami 2015, with a useful, relevant bibliography. On the general organisation of Greek commerce in the Ottoman Empire and the European-Atlantic networks, see Asdrachas et al. 2015, pp. 448–72.
4   Oikonomou 1990. Cf. an early modern example in Corfou, Pangratis 2000, pp. 22–45.
5   Bartolomei 2018.
6   Cf. for instance, the case of the merchants of Mykonos at the end of the eighteenth century, in Kremmydas 1993; or the case of the merchants of Paros in the first half of the eighteenth century, in Zei 2017a, pp. 289–305 and 349–61.

The political-diplomatic aspect of eighteenth- and nineteenth-century consular institutions has been emphasised in recent studies,[7] which have turned
attention to the role of European consuls in the Levant as political and cultural mediators participating in different national-confessional networks of
power.[8] These new perspectives in the history of consular institutions offer a
very useful framework for the study of the role of consular officers in the Greek
Archipelago in the development of local elites and political milieus before and
during the Greek Revolution.

2   Consular Institutions of the Archipelago before and during the Greek Revolution

The establishment of local consular officers in the Greek Archipelago in the
eighteenth century certainly indicates the flourishing of local commerce and
the enrichment of local mercantile elites, but it also reflects the transformation
of the consular system, toward the end of the century, from a thick mesh of
promiscuous functions into organised national networks, with varying spread
and distribution. As Mathieu Grenet points out, the above transformation was
accompanied by a progressive stabilisation of nomenclature under the effect
of an international homogenisation of grades and professionalisation of personnel.[9] Around the same period, legislative texts appeared, regulating the
capacities and rights of European commercial agencies in the Mediterranean
and stressing the necessity and importance of their existence and function. The
first of such work to appear was *Lex Mercatoria Rediviva* (1754).[10] Consular institutions in the Levant were based upon a capital distinction of offices – that of
consuls and vice consuls. Consuls were generally – but not always, as we will see
below – foreign *missi*, established in important commercial centres and ports
of the Ottoman Empire, operating under the title of *general* or *principal consuls*.
Vice consuls, meanwhile, were elected among the local mercantile elites, and

---

7   Goey 2016, pp. 61–75; Ulbert and Le Bouëdec (eds.) 2010.
8   Marzagalli (ed.) 2015.
9   Grenet 2018, pp. 9–18.
10   On eighteenth- and nineteenth-century literature regulating consulate offices and activ-
      ities, by authors such as the German Wilhelm de Steck (1730–97), the Russian Franz
      Frantsevich Borel (1775–1832) or the American David Bailie Warden (1772–1845), cf. de
      Goey, 'Les consuls et les relations internationales', p. 1; von Miltitz 1839. It is only Dimitrios
      Paschalis who has examined the subject of conflicting interests and relations of power
      among local consuls and vice consuls; see Paschalis 1931, pp. 437–56.

nominated by the general consul or the ambassador in Istanbul, and they were established in ports of secondary importance, lying in a limited zone around the *general consulate* of the region.

Contemporary travel or diplomatic literature assumes that consuls in the Mediterranean were typically of European origin; however, according to the local archives, it seems that appointment of indigenous consuls and sub-consuls had already become the norm in the Greek Archipelago at the end of the seventeenth century. Their national distribution varied during the eighteenth century and the beginning of the nineteenth century. Therefore, exploiting the notary archives of the period and the rare Greek records on the subject,[11] I have tried to reconstitute the distribution of local consuls and vice consuls in the Archipelago since the end of seventeenth century, focusing on the period between the end of the eighteenth century and 1821. It is useful to note that consulate officers are defined by a variety of terms in the archives [Gk. *Κονσό-λος, πρόξενος, βαρατάριος, καρικάτος*, and *ατζέντης*]. The richness of nomenclature as well as the confusion between the terms *consul* and *ambassador* is often emphasised by recent literature, attributed precisely to the confusion regarding their economic and political capacities and roles in the Eastern Mediterranean.

3   Consular Institutions of the Venetian State[12]

During the eighteenth century and the beginning of the nineteenth century, the Venetian state maintained its local agents on the Aegean islands of Andros, Kea, Naxos, Paros and Syros, among which Naxos held a vice consulate that also served the islands of Paros, Antiparos and Santorini, while Andros had a consul of Latin origin. It is quite curious that although they had remained under Venetian influence until the beginning of the eighteenth century, the islands of Mykonos and Tinos do not appear to have any Venetian agents during this period. It is true that at the beginning of the eighteenth century, Venice seems to have reconsidered the profitability of consular establishments on the islands compared to that of consulates on the coast (Peloponnese, Smyrna

---

11   Greek historiography has generally integrated consulates and their officers among the 'privileged' categories of the population of the Ottoman Empire. See Kontogiannis 1917, pp. 1–160. Cf. Rey 1899.

12   Upon consular institutions of the Italian States in the Levant in general, see the more recent project of research and site, *Consoli. Consuls et services consulaires italiens XVIII–XXe siècles.*

and Dyrrachium), since the cost of their personnel and services surpassed that of their commercial profit, even on the islands with which the Venetian state maintained important commercial relations. Extending the economic argument, historiography of the twentieth century attributed the retreat of Venetian consulates exclusively to the retreat of Venetian commerce in the Levant,[13] particularly after the Ottoman-Venetian War of 1714–18, alongside the expansion of British and French Mediterranean commerce. However, by putting forward the role of local elites and of individual networks, conflicts and aspirations of power, the publication of the correspondence of the eighteenth-century consular officers of Nicosia appointed by Venice[14] has come to largely modify this conventional picture of the Venetian economic retreat in the Levant.

4   Consular Institutions of the French State

A first survey of the Cyclades islands in the archival material reveals the fact that French consular institutions had been established in almost every island (with the exception of Serifos and Sifnos?) since the seventeenth century, but mostly during the eighteenth century, to be maintained after the Greek Revolution, as important colonisation factors in the Eastern Mediterranean.[15] The islands of Tinos, Andros, Ios, Kea and Naxos certainly held a general consulate, as possibly did Paros, while Mykonos was supposed to have a vice consul from the general consulate of Tinos or the French ambassador in Istanbul. It is also interesting that consular capacities could be extended to other islands, as in the case of the consul of Tinos in the seventeenth century, whose capacities were extended to Syros.

---

13   Twentieth-century Greek historiography generally tended to regard Venetian consulates of the Levant in the years before the Greek Revolution as parts of a maritime territory bearing Greek-Latin characteristics, or as parts of the history of Greek commerce under Venetian rule. See Lambros 1914, pp. 312–27; Ploumidis 1990; Oikonomou 1991, pp. 434–81; Vetsios 2007.

14   Karapidakis (ed.) 2013. Cf. the book review by Zei 2017b, pp. 247–50. Upon the internal organisation of consulate institutions and personnel, and the limits of their networking, see also Pangratis 2019, pp. 167–82.

15   Massé 2019. On the organisation of French consular institutions, see also Bartolomei, Grenet, Jesné and Ulbert 2016; Mézin 1997; cf. also Tournefort 1717, vol. 1, *passim*, and p. 508, on the constitution of offices' corps for the embassy and the French consulates of the Orient.

The above distribution and persistance of French consular institutions in the Archipelago seems to contradict the contemporary literature upon the subject, which testified to, regretted or advised for the retirement of indigenous vice consuls of France, a system implemented under the reign of Louis XIV and in the context of Colbert's mercantilistic policy.[16] According to the testimony of C.S. Sonnini, sent over by Louis XV to explore the possibilities of French commercial expansion in the East, the commission economy and the ports' system of the Ottoman Empire hindered enormously the thriving of French commerce. Sonnini saw that, as a complex system of intermediaries and taxes, the commission system resulted in a loss of profit for the merchant and for French commerce at the almost exclusive advantage of the assignee, especially of the merchant of the Orient. In the eighteenth century, the commission percentage for wheat was 2 percent on the commerce capital and 2 percent for the captain; if the merchant was in charge of the cargo himself, the assignee kept 4 percent of the commission, and in a past-due case, the *censaux* rights, that were 1–2 percent for each transaction depending on the article, plus 1 percent that they collected from the vendor and the debtor respectively; this way, the assignee could draw a profit of 6–9 percent upon the price of the merchandise, which was also influenced by the commercial capital deposited to the captain, the freight cost, the interest or the insurance, the cargo's transportation expenses, the ports' storehouses' expenses, the demurrage expenses – a frequent case in this system – plus the special taxes upon the products that appeared in the end of the eighteenth century (exportation tax, transit tax etc.) and the particularly elevated customs' taxes.[17] Nevertheless, Sonnini regretted the 1756 retirement of French-appointed vice consuls,[18] notably those of Mytilini, from where Marseilles imported large shipments of olive oil.[19] Being Greek in their majority, Sonnini approximated, the vice consuls were considered useless, even

---

16   Zei 2006, pp. 61–71; M. Grenet, 'Consuls et 'nations étrangères', p. 6 and bibliography.

17   Svoronos 1996, pp. 117–18, 127–8. Cf. Kremmydas 1993, pp. 106, 131–8; Zei 2017a, pp. 289–305 and 316–33.

18   According to Kontogiannis, the king of France recalled the consuls and vice consuls of the islands in 1755, a decision he soon revised; from then on, the majority of the appointed consuls were French, but still some were indigenous Catholics and some Orthodox; see Kontogiannis 1917, pp. 42–4. According to P. Zerlentis, this occurrence took place a little earlier; see Zerlentis 1918, pp. 133–36. During the eighteenth century, the majority of consuls in the Ottoman Empire were French; see Rey 1899, p. 450. Under Napoleon I, there were around two or three thousand French consuls in the Orient, the protection of which resorted all those representing States conquered by Napoleon, as well as those of England in Smyrna; see Hobhouse 1813, vol. 2, pp. 618, 826–8; Rey 1899, p. 158.

19   Boulanger 1991, vol. 1, pp. 273–98.

dangerous, and they were retired from almost all islands except Scio, Stan-
cho and Rhodes[20] as well as from the great neighbouring ports where business
with merchants from Marseilles was made. Experts in markets and commercial
affairs as well as in the waters of the Archipelago, and experienced in maritime
commerce, these indigenous agents were indispensable, Sonnini confirmed,
in the speculation of commercial affairs in the Orient, while French consuls,
reduced to simple diplomats, were useless in countries where diplomacy 'is
absolutely unknown'.[21]

5   Consulates of the United Kingdom[22]

Commercial agencies of the United Kingdom had been established on the
islands of Kea – where the office was constituted of a consul, a vice consul
and a commercial secretary – as well as on Mykonos, Naxos and Syros. Vice
consulates have been established on the islands of Tinos, Andros, Milos and
Mykonos, where the vice consul extended his capacities to Paros and other
islands, serving also as vice consul of Austria in 1821.

6   Consular Institutions of the Russian Empire

Russian agencies seem to have been established from the end of the eighteenth
century until the beginning of the nineteenth century – that is, after the end of
the Russian-Ottoman War of 1768–74 and the short-lived Russian principality in
the Archipelago. Russian consular institutions seem to have been established
on the islands of Tinos (where the consul extended his capacities to Mykonos),
Andros, Ios (where the consul Loues Staes also officed as consul of the Kingdom
of Two Sicilies), Mykonos and Naxos (where Russian interests were served by a
vice consul).

---

20   It should be noted that the French consuls of Chios, Naxos and Milos received their assign-
       ment letters [*lettres-patentes*] from the king of France, while those of Rhodes, Santorin,
       Ios, Sifnos, Syros, Skopelos, Mytilini, Samos, Kos and Euboia were assigned by the ambas-
       sador of Constantinople. See Rey 1899, p. 245.
21   On the contrary, William Turner, secretary of the English embassy of Constantinople,
       regreted the placement of Greek consuls in English consulates of the Orient; see Turner
       1820, vol. 1, pp. 222–3, 355. Hobhouse proposed to place agents recruited from the com-
       mercial institutions of Malta; see Turner 1820, vol. 2, p. 604.
22   On the English consular institutions in the Levant since the seventeenth century, see Bar-
       bano 2018, pp. 253–63.

Finally, between the seventeenth and nineteenth centuries, there were also a few independent establishments of Danish,[23] Austrian,[24] Dutch[25] and Spanish[26] consular institutions.

7   Individual Itineraries and Political Networking during the Greek Revolution

Viewing consular institutions mainly as an extension of different state or ethnic economic strategies in the Mediterranean, the above bipolar approach also presupposed a view of local ethno-confessional communities as homogeneous corpuses developing collective interests and strategies [corps de nations]. Nevertheless, a systematic study of the relevant archival material – that is, of the correspondence between consuls and the appointing authorities, the correspondence between various commercial agents or documents edited by local administration (or insular communes) – shows that far from being homogeneous, local confessional or ethnic communities were enmeshed in a rich and varied spectrum of political, social and cultural claims and strategies. Thus, conflicts were quite often generated or nourished after the intervention of foreign consuls in local affairs – economic as well as political or social – which a former historical literature considered either as commercial competition or as outbursts of national or confessional emotionalism;[27] instead, they should be studied as strategic oppositions or coalitions of power. Consequently, the variety of national spread and distribution of consular institutions in the Archipelago should not be connected only with European commercial expan-

---

23   Youroukou 2010.
24   Ulbert 2006, pp. 317–32.
25   Slot 1978, pp. 157–267; Slot 1983, pp. 59–80.
26   Bertrand and Priotti (eds.) 2011.
27   Cf. for instance, Volney, who at the end of the eigtheenth century noted that hatred and jealousy seethed in every harbour among its main orders, consuls, merchants and interpreters; he nevertheless did not fail to observe the lack of unity inside the corps de nations themselves: 'chaque échelle [du Levant] est une coterie où règnent les dissensions, les jalousies, les haines d'autant plus vives qu'elles y sont sans distraction. Dans chaque échelle on peut compter trois factions habituellement en guerre par la mauvaise répartition des pouvoirs entre les trois ordres qui les composent, et qui sont le consul, les négociants et les interprètes ... on l'a vu ... essuyer des tracasseries incroyables de la part de ses compatriotes, et n'être pas admis dans ce qu'ils appelaient le corps de la nation, titre fastueux qui paraîtra extrêmement ridicule, quand l'on saura que ce corps de nation était composé de cinq à six facteurs' (Volney 1843, p. 766). Cf. Sonnini 1801, p. 280.

sion, but also with the ways in which local political claims and European policies in the Levant interweaved.

Therefore, the systematic study of local notary archives, commercial correspondence and archives of the Greek Revolution[28] has permitted the study of European consular institutions on the islands not only as economic and commercial agencies in the Levant, but also as institutionalised political, social and ideological localities of action, often independent of the broader political crises in that part of the world. These institutions did not only constitute the vital space of Mediterranean commerce but also the vital space of Mediterranean politics during the eighteenth and nineteenth centuries, which strongly influenced politics during the Greek Revolution. Thus, consular offices of the islands appear as a total political space in which commercial contracts and treaties among different states translated the turbulent negotiations between different – often parallel or conflicting – networks of influence during the Greek Revolution: European states, consular officers, merchants and captains of various nationalities, Ottoman provincial authorities and local administration elites. In this enlarged political space, the very decision to establish a European consulate or vice consulate became a high-stake action.

On the other hand, consular institutions in the Levant constituted a thick, less visible mesh of social, political and cultural relations. Therefore, personal relations, marriage alliances or local interconnections among different confessional communities[29] offer a rich field of research, as they participated directly or indirectly in even more complex but less conspicuous political aspects of the islands during the years of the Revolution.

In order to decipher and understand the above aspects of consular institutions in the Archipelago at the beginning of the nineteenth century, it is necessary to explore individual and family itineraries of indigenous consular officers during the pre-revolutionary and revolutionary period.

Through initial research in the archival material, it is obvious that:

a.   It seems that indigenous consular officers were first selected among the well known local notability – that is, religious or secular members of communal councils – also involved in the Ottoman administrative and

---

28   Research has been completed in the Library of the Greek Parliament, *Αρχεία της Ελληνικής Παλιγγενεσίας*. This chapter is also based on the research in the General State Archives of Greece: Αρχεία Εκτελεστικού (1822–6); Διοικητικής Επιτροπής (1822–7); Γραμματείας των Ναυτικών (1821–8); Γραμματείας Θαλασσίου Δικαστηρίου (1824–7); Γραμματείας της Θρησκείας και Παιδείας (1821–7); Αντικυβερνητικής επιτροπής (1825–7); Κατάλογος Α' Συλλογής Γιάννη Βλαχογιάννη (1588–902); υποσειρά 1, *Αρχείον Αγώνος*, 1793, 1821–8, 1866, f. 4–19.

29   Cf. the anthropological view on networks of influence in Boissevain 1974.

tax-collecting system [*Voyvodas*: tax farmers or/and drogmans]. However, this remains to be verified, since the late-seventeenth century local consuls and vice consuls were possibly elected from elites spread all over the Archipelago, having developed a mercantile and entrepreunerial profile. This is suggested by the transfer of consular capacities from families such as that of Coronello of Naxos to that of Frangopoulos,[30] or by the attachment to consular capacities of the Kokkos family, converted Orthodox in seventeenth century Naxos,[31] or of Anastasios Cornelios in the eighteenth century, doted with the capacity of vice consul of Venice, who moreover served Venice's interests in all the central islands of the Cyclades' complex. Families such as the Kampani, the Kondyli and the Mavrogeni,[32] branching out all over the Archipelago, still hold onto the above offices in the Cyclades at least until the outburst of the Revolution. It is interesting to note that quite a few families were reported to have been converted Catholics – such as the Baos family, who until the Greek Revolution held the offices of consuls and vice consuls of the United Kingdom in Sifnos and of France in the island of Ios.[33]

b.   In the case of involvement of the local notability in the consular system, transmissions of consular offices among members of the same family were not rare, nor were appointments of sons, brothers, cousins, etc. as highly ranked consular personnel (e.g. as secretaries). Such was the case of the Gizis family on Mykonos, members of which served as consuls and vice consuls of France through the eighteenth century and after the Greek Revolution. Such was also the case of the Mavrogenis family, branches of which were established all over the Cyclades since the eighteenth century; since the pre-revolutionary period, the Mavrogenis branch of Mykonos held consular offices of both Austria and the United Kingdom (Petros and Dimitrios Mavrogenis), while the Paros branch held the office of consul of Venice. In 1821 Dimitris Kampanis,[34] born in the Mavrogenis

---

30   On the Frangopoulos family of Naxos, of Phanariot origin and having also served in high Ottoman posts (as drogmans, for instance), see Slot 2017.
31   On the Kokkos family and their involvement in Venice, see also Kasdagli 1999, pp. 187–8.
32   On the Mavrogenis, the Kambanis and the Kondylis families of Paros, see also Zei 2017a, *passim*. On the Mavrogenis family in particular, cf. Blancard 1909.
33   On the Baos family during the Greek Revolution, see also Symeonidis 2013, pp. 5–33 and *passim*; Petropoulos 1956, p. 86.
34   According to information given by Dimitrios Paschalis, Georgios Kambanakis, who had served as vice consul of the United Kingdom in Andros [Messaria] for a very long period before and after the Revolution (1812–41), could have belonged to a branch of the same family. See Paschalis 1931, p. 447.

family, was appointed consul of Russia in Mykonos, where he had also the capacity of notable [*kocabaşı*].[35] Finally, Nikolaos Frangopoulos, consul of the United Kingdom in Naxos, had his son serving as secretary.

Parental transmission of consul and vice consul capacities also seem to have been observed by the commercial elite of the islands: the case of the Pangalos family of Kea[36] before the Greek Revolution possibly belongs to the same category. Nikolaos Pangalos was appointed as consul of France, and his brother, who was the *voyvoda* of the island, obtained the office of 'baratario' (?) of Naples. Furthermore, their cousin, Joseph Pangalos, was appointed as consul of the United Kingdom; Nikolaos's son in law was appointed as consul of Venice; another Pangalos was consul of Dane-mark; and, finally, another member of the family was appointed as vice consul of the United Kingdom in 1818, while a commercial agent of the United States served as his secretary.

c.   It was mentioned above that, since the late seventeenth century, con-suls of the Archipelago were often elected among mercantile elites of the islands and were therefore involved in commercial affairs. A particular network of influence seems to have been developed between the con-sulate personnel and the ship pilots of the islands,[37] who constituted a distinct professional and social milieu of the Archipelago, such as the case of the Stais family of Milo, whose members had taken over both capacit-ies.[38] This field of research needs to be further explored.

d.   During the period between 1821 and 1824, the same individuals are often found to have participated in several revolutionary institutions. They were proposed or/and elected as members of different revolutionary comittees: Ioannis Pangalos appeared in the Charity Society (1822)[39] while another member of the family participated in a revolutionary com-mittee against pharmaceutical abuses (1822),[40] and Ioannis Mavrogenis participated in the Committee for the Regular Collection of National Income.[41] Each were elected deputees of their provinces in the revolu-tionary Assemblies: Logothetis Pangalos was elected deputee of his prov-

35   Upon the role of *kocabaşı*s in the insular space in the revolutionary period, see Tansuğ 2014, pp. 223–44.
36   General State Archives of Greece, K 131α (1766–1834), K 142α και 142β.
37   On the ship pilots of the Cyclades and their capacities, rights, fees and obligations, as well their relations with consuls, see B.J. Slot 1983; Pagonis 1989, pp. 159–230.
38   Pagonis 1989, p. 167.
39   Αρχεία της Ελληνικής Παλιγγενεσίας, Athens 1971–2012, vol. 2, p. 385.
40   Αρχεία της Ελληνικής Παλιγγενεσίας, Athens 1971–2012, vol. 2, p. 383.
41   Αρχεία της Ελληνικής Παλιγγενεσίας, Athens 1971–2012, vol. 2, p. 258.

ince in 1823;[42] Dimitris Kambanis appeared as deputy of Andros in the Fourth Assembly;[43] Georgios Mavrogenis along with Ioannis Paximadis, consul of Denmark in Tinos, appeared in the same Assembly as deputies of the province of Tinos;[44] Nikolaos Frangopoulos participated as deputy in the Fourth Assembly;[45] Louis Stais, notable and consul of Ios, participated in the Assembly of 1823 as deputy of Ios, Sikinos, Amorgos and Pholegandros;[46] and a certain Vitalis,[47] having served in 1821 as consul of the United Kingdom in Syros, possibly appeared as deputy of the province of Athens in 1826.[48] Some were also appointed as Prefects [Gk. *Eparchoi*] of the Cyclades: in 1822, Ioannis Mavrogenis was proposed for the office of Prefect of Patmos, Leros, Kalymnos and Icaria,[49] while Michael Pangalos was appointed Prefect of Androussa in the Peloponnese.[50] Finally, some also seem to have been appointed Superintendents [Gk. *Ephoroi*] of the islands, such as Frangopoulos of Naxos, who was appointed Superintendent of Chios in 1822.[51] Although the precise distribution of the above offices among the ancient notability and modern political milieus of the islands still remains to be confirmed, this general picture suggests the active participation of both in the political developments during the Revolution.

8   Preliminary Conclusions

Social and political transformations that consular offices and officers of the Archipelago underwent during the pre-revolutionary period seem to have largely contributed to the development of an indigenous political elite in the Cyclades. This in turn seems to have played a role in forming the administrative and political milieux of the Revolution. This elite combined the profile of

---

42   *Αρχεία της Ελληνικής Παλιγγενεσίας*, Athens 1971–2012, vol. 3, p. 286.
43   *Αρχεία της Ελληνικής Παλιγγενεσίας*, Athens 1971–2012, vol. 4, p. 75.
44   Ibid.
45   *Αρχεία της Ελληνικής Παλιγγενεσίας*, Athens 1971–2012, vol. 4, p. 609A.
46   *Αρχεία της Ελληνικής Παλιγγενεσίας*, Athens 1971–2012, vol. 1, p. 511; vol. 2, pp. 332, 377, 387, 420.
47   The connection with Cesare Vitali, consul of Athens during the period 1821–4, whose journal is included in the Vlachogiannis Collection of the General State Archives of Greece, is to be explored in the future.
48   *Αρχεία της Ελληνικής Παλιγγενεσίας*, Athens 1971–2012, vol. 20, p. 81.
49   *Αρχεία της Ελληνικής Παλιγγενεσίας*, Athens 1971–2012, vol. 2, p. 128.
50   *Αρχεία της Ελληνικής Παλιγγενεσίας*, Athens 1971–2012, vol. 2, pp. 340–2, 357.
51   *Αρχεία της Ελληνικής Παλιγγενεσίας*, Athens 1971–2012, vol. 1, p. 543.

older notability – holders of various local communal offices, secular as well as ecclesiastical – with that of actors with a wider geographical range of entre-preunerial and political activities. The Latin origin or confession of the former, and the Orthodox confession of the latter, as emphasised in recent literature, remains to be further explored in relation to consuls and vice consuls of the Archipelago along with their in intricate foreign dependencies and local net-working during the revolutionary period.

Conflicts among consuls and vice consuls of different national mandates often reflected larger as well as less conspicuous social or political claims and transformations since the early seventeenth century: this could be the case of the violent opposition between the Kokkos and Coronello families – who respectively held the consular capacities of Venice and France in seventeenth-century Naxos – an opposition which historiography has integrated into the long series of modern *rural revolts* on the island.[52] Religious confessions were largely instrumentalised in local conflicts up until the Revolution. For this reason, it would be interesting to follow the involvement of indigenous consuls and vice consuls of the Cyclades in local political oppositions during 1821–3 – and in particular against the authorities of Prefects and their officers – such as, for instance, in the case of the families of Matsas and Baos, holders of consular offices who seem to have held crucial roles in the violent attacks against the Prefect of Sifnos; or in the case of Louis Stais, who in 1824 was in conflict with the secretary of the Prefecture of Ios.[53] While European consuls were instruc-ted to observe and implement policies of neutrality and non-intervention towards the revolted populations of the Ottoman empire,[54] indigenous consu-late officers and personnel appear to have been deeply enmeshed in multiple local and interlocal circuits of political influence and conflict. Therefore, their influence on the installation of revolutionary institutions in the Cyclades mer-its further exploration.

Bibliography

Ahrweiler, H. 1974, 'L'Escale dans le monde byzantin', *Recueils de la Société Jean Bodin*, 32: 161–78.

Asdrachas, Spyros, et al. 2015, *Greek Economic History 15th–19th C.*, Athens: Πολιτιστικό Ίδρυμα Ομίλου Πειραιώς.

---

52   On the subject, see Zei 2021.

53   *Αρχεία της Ελληνικής Παλιγγενεσίας*, Athens 1971–2012, vol. 6, p. 265.

54   Massé 2019. See also Heraklides and Dialla 2015, pp. 105–33.

Barbano, M. 2018, '*A lucrative, dangerous business*: le consulat anglais à Alger, Tunis et Tripoli dans la deuxième moitié du XVII siècle', in *De l'utilité commerciale des consuls. L'institution consulaire et les marchands dans le monde méditerranéen (XVIIe–XXe siècles)*, edited by A. Bartolomei, G. Calafat, M. Grenet and J. Ulbert, Rome and Madrid: Publications de l'École française de Rome.

Bartolomei, A. 2018, 'Entre l'État, les intérêts marchands et l'intérêt personnel: l'*agency* des consuls', in *De l'utilité commerciale des consuls. L'institution consulaire et les marchands dans le monde méditerranéen (XVIIe–XXe siècles)*, edited by A. Bartolomei, G. Calafat, M. Grenet and J. Ulbert, Rome-Madrid: Publications de l'École française de Rome.

Bartolomei, A., M. Grenet, F. Jesné and J. Ulbert 2016, *La chancellerie consulaire française, XVIe–XXe siècle: attributions, organisation, agents, usagers*, Rome: École française de Rome.

Bertrand M. and J.-P. Priotti (eds.) 2011, *Circulations maritimes: l'Espagne et son empire (XVIe–XVIIIe siècle)*, Rennes: Presses universitaires de Rennes.

Blancard, T. 1909, *Les Mavroyéni: histoire d'Orient de 1700 à nos jours*, Paris: Leroux.

Boissevain, J. 1974, *Friends of Friends: Networks, Manipulators and Coalitions*, Oxford: Oxford University Press.

Boulanger, P. 1991, 'L'île de Mytilène et le négoce français au XVIIIe siècle', in *Les villes dans l'Empire Ottoman: activités et sociétés*, edited by Daniel Panzac, Paris: CNRS.

Faroqhi, Suraiya 1979, 'Sixteenth Century Periodic Markets in Various Sancaks: Icel Hamid, Karahisar-i Sahib, Kütahya, Aydin and Mentese', *Journal of the Economic and Social History of the Orient* 22, 1: 32–80.

Goey, F. de 2016, 'Les consuls et les relations internationales au XIXe siècle', *Cahiers de la Méditerranée*, 93: 61–75

Grenet, Matthieu 2016, 'Consuls et 'nations' étrangères: états de lieux et perspectives de recherche', *Cahiers de la Méditerranée*, 93: 24–34.

Grenet, Matthieu 2018, 'L'institution consulaire en Mediterrannée, des stratégies commerciales différenciées. Introduction', in *De l'utilité commerciale des consuls. L'institution consulaire et les marchands dans le monde méditerranéen (XVIIe–XXe siècles)*, edited by A. Bartolomei, G. Calafat, M. Grenet and J. Ulbert, Rome-Madrid: Publications de l'École française de Rome.

Harlaftis, Gelina and Sophia Laiou 2008, 'Ottoman State Policy in Mediterranean Trade and Shipping c. 1780–1820: the Rise of the Greek owned Ottoman Merchant Fleet', in *Networks of Power in Modern Greece: essays in honor of John Campbell*, edited by Mark Mazower, New York: Hurst & Company.

Heraclides, Alexis and Anta Dialla 2015, *Humanitarian Intervention in the Long Nineteenth Century. Setting the Precedent*, Manchester: Manchester University Press.

Hobhouse, J.C. 1913, *A Journey through Albania and other Provinces of Turkey in Europe and Asia to Constantinople during the years 1809 and 1810*, London: James Cawthorn.

Karapidakis, Nikos (ed.) 2013, *Le Consulat de Venise à Chypre. Documents inédits 1719–1749*, Nicosia: Cyprus Research Centre.

Kasdagli, Aglaia 1999, *Land and Marriage Settlements in the Aegean: A Case Study of Seventeenth-century Naxos*, Venice: Hellenic Institute of Byzantine and Post-Byzantine Studies & Vikelea Municipal Library of Iraklion.

Kontogiannis, P.M. 1917, 'Οι προστατευόμενοι' ['The *Beratlis*'], *Αθηνά*, 29: 1–160.

Kremmydas, Vassilis 1993, *Εμπορικές πρακτικές στο τέλος της Τουρκοκρατίας: Μυκονιάτες έμποροι και πλοιοκτήτες* [*Commercial practices at the end of the Tourkokratia: merchants and shipowners from the island of Mykonos*], Athens: Ναυτικό Μουσείο Αιγαίου.

Lambros, Spyridon 1914, 'Τα βενετικά προξενεία εν Ανατολή τω 1718' ['The Venetian consulates in the Levant in 1718'], *Νέος Ελληνομνήμων*, 11: 312–27

Marzagalli, Sylvia (ed.), with the collaboration of M. Ghazali and C. Windler 2015, *Les Consuls en Méditerranée, agents d'information, XVIe–XXe siècle*, Paris: Garnier.

Massé, Alexandre 2019, *Un empire informel en Méditerrannée: Les consuls de France en Grèce et dans l'Empire Ottoman: images, ingérences, colonisation (1815–1856)*, Paris: Garnier.

Mézin, A. 1997, *Les consuls de France au siècle des Lumières (1715–1792)*, Paris: Peter Lang.

Miltitz, Alex von 1839, *Manuel de Consuls*, 2 Volumes, London: A. Asher.

Oikonomou, M. 1990, *Ο θεσμός του προξένου των Ελλήνων εμπόρων κατά την περίοδο της Τουρκοκρατίας. Το εμπόριο του Αρχιπελάγους και το ελληνικό προξενείο της Βενετίας* [*The institution of the consul for the Greek merchants during the Tourkokratia: the commerce of the Archipelago and the Greek consulate in Venice*], Ph.D. dissertation, Athens.

Oikonomou, M. 1991, 'Το προξενείο του αρχιπελάγους στο βενετοκρατούμενο Ναύπλιο' ['The consulate of the Archipelago in the town of Nafplio under Venetian rule'], *Παρουσία*, 7: 434–81.

Pagonis, G.C. 1989, 'Ο Μηλιός πιλότος Μιχελάκης Νικολάκη Τζούλιας' ['The pilot Michelakis Nikolakis Tzoulias from the island of Melos'], *Μηλιακά*, 3: 159–230.

Pangratis, Gerassimos 2000, 'Το κονσουλάτον των Μυτιληναίων στην Κέρκυρα (1548–1549)' ['The consulate of the merchants from Mytilene in Corfu (1548–1549)'], *Εώα και Εσπέρια* 4: 22–45.

Pangratis, Gerassimos 2019, 'Το προξενείο της Επτανήσου Πολιτείας (1800–1807) στα Δαρδανέλια' ['The consulate of the Septinsular Republic (1800–1807) in the Derdanelles'], *Περί Ιστορίας*, 9: 167–82.

Paschalis, Dimitrios 1931, 'Πρόξενοι και προξενεία εις τας νήσους κατά την Τουρκοκρατίαν' ['Consuls and consulates on the islands during the Tourkokratia'], *Ημερολόγιον Μεγάλης Ελλάδος*, pp. 437–56.

Petropoulos, G. 1956, *Νομικά έγγραφα Σίφνου της συλλογής Γ. Μαριδάκη 1684–1835, μετά συμβολών εις την έρευναν του Μεταβυζαντινού Δικαίου* [*Legal documents from the G. Maridakis collection concerning the island of Siphnos 1684–1835, with contributions to the research on post-byzantine law*], Athens: Academy of Athens.

Ploumidis, G. 1990, *Το Μεσολόγγι και η περιοχή του (17ος–18ος αιώνας)* [*The town of Messolongi and its area (seventeenth–eighteenth c.*), Ioannina: University of Ioannina, Department of History and Archaeology.

Rey, F. 1899, *La protection diplomatique et consulaire dans les échelles du Levant et de Barbarie*, Paris: L. Larose & Forcel.

Rozen, Mina (ed.) 2008, *Homelands and Diasporas: Greeks, Jews and their migration*, London: I.B. Tauris.

Slot, Ben J. 1978, 'Ολλανδοί πρόξενοι Μήλου-Κιμώλου' ['Dutch consuls on the islands of Melos and Kimolos'], *Κιμωλιακά*, 8: 157–267.

Slot, Ben J. 1983, 'Οι πρόξενοι των Κάτω Χωρών στη Μήλο και οι πιλότοι' ['The consuls from the Low Counties on the island of Melos and the pilots'], *Μηλιακά*, 1: 59–80.

Slot, Ben J. 2017, 'Η Νάξος στα Γενικά Αρχεία της Ολλανδίας 1798–1821 Α' ['The island of Naxos in the General Archives of Netherlands 1789–1821'], *Ορεινός Αξώτης*, 10 February.

Sonnini, C.S. 1801, *Voyage en Grèce et en Turquie, fait par ordre de Louis XVI, et avec l'autorisation de la cour ottomane*, Paris: F. Buisson.

Svoronos, Nicolas 1996, *Το εμπόριο της Θεσσαλονίκης τον 18ο αιώνα* [*The commerce of Salonica in the eighteenth c.*], Athens: Θεμέλιο.

Symeonidis, S. 2013, 'Η οικογένεια Μπάου της Σίφνου' ['The Baos family on the island of Siphnos'], *Σιφνιακά*, 21: 5–33.

Tansuğ, F. 2014, 'The kocabaşıs as Intermediaries? The Local and Central Administration in Imvros/Imroz and Lemnos in the early 19th century', *Belleten*, 281: 223–44.

Tournefort, J.P. de 1717, *Relation d'un voyage du Levant*, Paris: Imprimerie Royale.

Turner, William 1820, *Journal of a Tour in the Levant*, 3 Volumes, London: John Murray.

Ulbert, J. 'Les services consulaires prussiens au XVIIIe siècle', in *La fonction consulaire aux temps modernes*, edited by J. Ülbert and G. Le Bouëdec, Rennes: Presses universitaires de Rennes.

Ülbert, J. 2006, 'Introduction. La fonction consulaire à l'époque moderne: définition, état de connaissances et perspectives de recherche', in *La fonction consulaire aux temps modernes*, edited by J. Ülbert and G. Le Bouëdec, Rennes: Presses universitaires de Rennes.

Ulbert, J. and L. Prijac (eds.) 2010, *Consuls et services consulaires au XIXe siècle / Consulship in the 19th Century / Die Welt der Konsulate im 19. Jahrhundert*, Hambourg: DobuVerlag.

Vetsios, Eleftherios 2007, *Η διπλωματική και οικονομική παρουσία των Βενετών στην περιοχή της Άρτας (18ος αιώνας)* [*The diplomatic and economic presence of the Venetians in the area of the town of Arta (eighteenth c.)*], Athens.

Vlami, Despoina 2015, *Trading with the Ottomans: The Levant Company in the Middle East*, London: I.B. Tauris.

Volney, C.F. 1843, 'Considérations sur la guerre des Turks, en 1788', *Œuvres complètes de Volney*, Paris.

Youroukou, M. 2010, *Έκθεση γεγονότων και πολιτισμικές πτυχές του καθημερινού βίου της Νάξου (1822–1827): το ανέκδοτο γαλλικό ημερολόγιο του υποπροξενείου της Δανίας* [*Events and cultural aspects of everyday life on the island of Naxos (1822–1827): the unpublished diary of the Danish sub-consulate*], Ph.D. dissertation, Athens: National and Kapodistrian University of Athens.

Zei, Eleftheria 2006, 'The Proposition of the Traveller Ch. Sonnini on the Organization of French Commerce in the Greek Archipelago (Voyage in Greece and Turkey, Paris 1801): A First Theory of Economic Insularity', in *Following the Nereids: Sea Routes and Maritime Business, 16th–20th centuries*, edited by M.-C. Chatziioannou and G. Harlaftis, Athens: Κέρκυρα.

Zei, Eleftheria 2017a, *Paros et l'Archipel grec, XVII–XVIIIe siècle: visages et visions d'insularité*, Istanbul: The Isis Press.

Zei, Eleftheria 2017b, 'Για τα βενετικά προξενεία της Μεσογείου τον 18° αιώνα' ['On the Venetian consulates in the Mediterranean during the eighteenth c.'], *Τα Ιστορικά*, 65: 247–50.

Zei, Eleftheria, 2021, 'Αγροτικές εξεγέρσεις και κοινωνικοί μετασχηματισμοί στη Νάξο, 17ος–18ος αι.: παλαιότερες προσεγγίσεις και νέες ερευνητικές προοπτικές' ['Peasant revolts and social transformations on the island of Naxos, seventh-eighteenth c.: earlier approaches and new research agendas'], in *Πρακτικά Στ´ Επιστημονικού Συνεδρίου, Η Νάξος διά μέσου των αιώνων*, edited by V. Fragkoulopoulos, Naxos.

Zerlentis, Pericles 1918, 'Ανασύστασις των Γαλλικών Προξενείων εν ταις Κυκλάσιν εν έτει 1724' ['Reestablishment of the French consulates on the Cyclades islands in 1774'], *Νησιωτική Επετηρίς*, 1: 133–6.

Index